THE
COMPACT HISTORY
OF THE
REVOLUTIONARY WAR

Colonel R. Ernest Dupuy, U.S.A., Ret.

★

Colonel Trevor N. Dupuy, U.S.A., Ret.

THE

COMPACT HISTORY

OF THE

REVOLUTIONARY

WAR

HAWTHORN BOOKS, INC.
Publishers

NEW YORK

First Edition, October, 1963

H-1273

Preface

THE BIRTH-PANGS OF OUR NATION deserve the serious scrutiny of all Americans. It is unfortunate that this proud and patriotic retrospection should be hindered today by the inadequacies of most of the existing general and standard historical works upon the American Revolutionary War. The deficiencies range from inaccuracy and incompleteness on the one hand, to imbalance and unsound analyses of the military operations on the other. The gamut runs from gross distortion of the Minuteman legend to derogation of the military qualities of the Father of his Country—General George Washington. These faults are as prevalent in books concentrating on the military side of the Revolution as they are in more general works. Worse, this criticism applies almost as much to scholarly publications as it does to frankly popular books.

It has long been our feeling, therefore, that there is a crying need for an accurate, reliable history of the Revolutionary War, sufficiently short and entertaining to appeal to the general reader; yet so complete, reliable and analytical as to warrant the respect of both civilian and military scholars. This book is the result of our efforts to satisfy those requirements, within the natural limits of human frailty.

At the request of our publisher, we have not attempted to document our text with a formidable array of footnotes. We hope that most scholars will recognize that such notes tend to repel the general readers for whom this book is primarily intended. The absence of notes is at least partly offset, we believe, by a bibliography which includes only those primary and secondary works which we have actually consulted in the preparation of this book (save for some "popular" books omitted as not warranting such distinction). We also draw the attention of the scholar to our appendices—which we trust will also interest some general readers who wish to delve more deeply into some of these topics.

American independence was achieved, of course, by force of arms. In portraying how this occurred, we have written a book that is essentially a military history. As military historians, however, we feel very strongly that military operations cannot be properly presented—or understood—save in a perspective which gives due prominence to all pertinent non-military factors and considerations.

Thus we have endeavored to show the political and economic causes of the Revolution, international as well as domestic. In particular we have endeavored to make clear that the American Revolution was only a part—though the most important part—of a worldwide conflict. We have felt it necessary not only to show the disappointments and hardships suffered by the American patriots, but also the handicaps and frustrations endured by the British, fighting a desperate defensive war around the globe, as well as the problems faced by our French allies in their gallant attempt to wrest command of the seas from Britain. We hope, too, that we have demonstrated that the Revolutionary War was won not by a united people, but by a belligerent minority of the inhabitants of the Thirteen Colonies, who overcame all obstacles to freedom only because they responded—albeit sometimes reluctantly—to the commanding genius of the one man who dominated the war from start to finish: George Washington.

We wish to acknowledge our great debt to three people: Laura Nevitt Dupuy, who painstakingly and carefully reviewed two manuscript drafts, and whose many major and minor suggestions have done so much to clarify the text, to prevent errors, and to assure completeness and balance; Jean Dengler Brennan, who patiently typed the drafts and the final manuscript, and who helped us to correct or to avoid the numerous minor inconsistencies which so stubbornly plague authors of a work such as this; Dyno Lowenstein, of Pictograph Corporation, who produced the excellent maps and diagrams which clarify the operations we have attempted to describe. If this book does, in fact, accomplish our objectives, these three must share in the achievement; if we have failed, it is despite their loyal, intensive and intelligent efforts to help us.

R. ERNEST DUPUY
TREVOR N. DUPUY

Arlington and McLean, Va.

Contents

List of Maps

Map Credits

THE AUTHORS AND THE CARTOGRAPHER wish to acknowledge their indebtedness to Elroy M. Avery's *History of the United States and its People* (Burrows Brothers, Cleveland), which includes what we believe to be the best and most comprehensive map coverage of the Revolutionary War, up to this time. Many maps in most subsequent histories of that war are based directly or indirectly on those in Avery. In particular, we have referred to these maps in our own preparation of maps numbers 5, 15, 26, 28, 30, 31, 34, 35, and 38 in this text. We also wish to express our appreciation to the individuals and organizations which have kindly given us permission to use the maps indicated below; in most instances we have substantially modified the basic maps: numbers 9 and 37 from Christopher Ward, *The Delaware Continentals,* by the Historical Society of Delaware; number 10 from Henry P. Johnston's *Battle of Harlem Heights,* by the Columbia University Press; numbers 11, 23 and 32 from Christopher Ward's *The War of the Revolution,* by the Executor of the Estate of Christopher Ward; numbers 22 and 24 from John R. Alden's *The American Revolution,* Harper & Row; numbers 25 and 29 from R. E. and T. N. Dupuy's *Brave Men and Great Captains,* by Harper & Row; number 27 from Samuel E. Morison's *John Paul Jones,* by Mr. Irwin Raisz; number 40 by the *Encyclopaedia Britannica.*

To Laura and Christine

THE
COMPACT HISTORY
OF THE
REVOLUTIONARY WAR

★ **1** ★ ★ ★ ★ ★

Careering to Collision

In 1764, ELEVEN YEARS BEFORE THE WAR of the American Revolution began, England's king, statesmen and Parliament initiated the first of a series of blunders which progressively uprooted the loyalties of the Thirteen Colonies and stirred the ferment of armed rebellion in a fashion which could not have been bettered had it been carefully planned by some subversive Machiavelli.

For a good half-century—and more in some instances—the colonies had been blessed with local self-government. Although nominally dominated by governors appointed by the Crown, the machinery of self-government, supported by provincial taxes which paid the governors' salaries as well, was carried on through provincial assemblies and provincial courts.

Up to this time there had been no direct taxation by the Crown, though insofar as foreign intercourse was concerned, the Thirteen Colonies were indeed suffering from the Mercantile Theory of trade: colonies as mere instruments for increasing the wealth and power of European mother countries. So restrictions on colonial commerce were galling—in legal theory at least. Actually, many of them were more honored in the breach than in the observance, for customs officers were few and usually complacent, while smugglers were legion.

One year earlier—October 1763—the British government had, however, provided the colonists in general, and frontiersmen in particular, with a common grievance against Royal interference in their affairs. This was the Proclamation of 1763, which established the vast regions between the Appalachian Mountains and the Mississippi

River as a widespread Indian reservation into which settlers were forbidden to move without specific Crown approval. This was intended to prevent renewal of the friction between white colonists and redmen which had been so costly in the recent Seven Years—or French and Indian—War. The proclamation was generally ineffectual, however, since it was ignored. Colonists continued to swarm westward over the mountains, while grumbling loudly at the law they were flouting.

Predominantly Anglo-Saxon in origin, the population of these colonies also contained other strains; Rhinelanders from the Palatinate, Germans, Hollanders, Swedes and French Huguenots. Most of these people had come over voluntarily, seeking a freedom they could not find in Europe. Others had been dumped involuntarily in America— unfortunate law-breakers whose sin, for the most part, was that they had espoused the wrong cause in England's stormy seventeenth-century civil wars.

Thrown on their own resources, the colonists had developed a spirit of individualism, tinctured with a certain scorn for the more orderly conventions and limitations imposed upon the people of their homeland. Intermixed with this was an inferiority complex, too, which bitterly resented the up-turned noses of British aristocracy and politicians towards all "colonial" manners and *mores*.

Already, certain divisions existed in colonial life. The New Englanders looked askance upon Virginians and Marylanders, who were suspect—without too much foundation in fact—of Cavalier and Papist tendencies. Uppity Virginians, living in a plantation atmosphere markedly different from that of more northerly climes, derided the so-called "levelling influence" of Yankee democracy and its strait-laced Puritanical traders. Up north in the New Hampshire Grants internecine warfare between New York and Vermont was under way. Pennsylvania and Connecticut were battling for possession of the Wyoming Valley. The Hudson patroons held their tenant-farmers in virtual serfdom. And out on the fringes—the Carolinas, Georgia and Kentucky—the hard-fighting, hard-drinking, roistering frontiersmen cared little for any of their more domesticated Eastern neighbors.

One common hatred all shared: standing armies. The King of England might be their rightful ruler, but the King's livery stood for all that most colonists had gladly left behind: oppression, repression and the whims of autocratic rulers. The better-educated among the colonists also visualized the threat of military despotism subverting civilian control. Back in 1638, Governor John Winthrop of the Massachusetts Bay Colony set the precedent when young bloods of Boston proposed the formation of what would become the first volunteer militia unit in America—the Ancient and Honorable Artillery Company:

"Divers Gentlemen and others being joined in military Company desire to be made a corporation," declaimed the governor; "but the Council considering from the example of the Pretorian band among the Romans and Templars in Europe how dangerous it might be to erect a standing authority of military men which might easily in time overthrow the civil power, thought fit to stop it betimes; yet they are allowed to be a Company but subordinate to all authority."

So, by 1764 the Thirteen Colonies, thin-spread along the eastern littoral of North America, were an agglomeration of free populations living under the aegis of the British constitution. Each was interested primarily in its own affairs, often sharply divergent from the interests of its neighbors. Within each colony the fires of practical politics burned parochially. There were Tories; there were Whigs. And of the Whigs there was a small, hard-core radical element, mainly clustered in the larger communities. In Boston, in particular, this radical element had developed into a system of ward politics and rough-and-tumble tactics—prototype, in fact, of political America today.

The Boston radicals rallied about one Samuel Adams, arch-rebel by nature, whose Caucus Club—the first of America's "smoke-filled rooms"—harbored within itself those seeds of revolt which stupid men in England would carefully, ineptly nurture into flower.

Boston wasn't alone in this regard. Radicals flourished in New York under Alexander McDougall, in Philadelphia under Charles Thompson, in Williamsburg under Patrick Henry, and in Charleston under Christopher Gadsden, and the Rutledges—John and Edward. But by force of circumstances Boston—thanks to Samuel Adams and King George—would become the focal point of freedom.

An interesting man, this Adams (cousin of John Adams, Boston's foremost lawyer); a rabble-rousing firebrand with a keen sense of public relations and propaganda values; possessing a Harvard M.A., he was as much at home in Beacon Hill parlor as in waterfront taproom, and was a past master at manipulating the strings of political puppet-shows. As we shall see, it is no injustice to other devoted patriots of the period to suggest that without Samuel Adams there might have been no Revolution. That his influence would later wane is beside the point; after the war began, the man had served his purpose. The spirit of freedom would then be served by sounder men.

In 1764, England's pride in the victorious close of the Seven Years War was tempered by the fact that she was staggering under a national debt of £136,000,000, with consequent heavy taxation at home. Worse, she faced the prospect of additional heavy expense to provide for the defense of her new-won empire, for in Europe, in Canada and in the colonies a standing army was essential. In North America alone, it had been decided to keep a force of regulars 6,000 strong.

So, unmindful of the fact that—as Benjamin Franklin would later tell an indifferent Parliament—the colonies had already loyally and potently contributed in men, money and material to the winning of the French and Indian War, England turned to the colonies to help foot the bill. The Sugar Act, passed April 5, became the first direct taxation imposed by the Crown: threepence per gallon on every drop of molasses imported to America from the foreign West Indies. In addition, the Act rudely tightened the colonial customs service, and prohibited further issue of legal tender money by the colonies.

Colonial opposition was immediate and vociferous, for the program threatened ruin to the varied economies of the provinces. And loudest was the roar from Boston, where James Otis' cry—"Taxation without representation is tyranny"—was deftly seized upon by Adams as the keynote of opposition.

The point was well taken. The House of Commons, representing the people, was responsible for tax legislation in England. But the colonies had no representatives in Parliament. Massachusetts' answer to the Sugar Act was "nonimportation" (the word "boycott" had not yet been invented) of British goods, while a Committee of Correspondence—instigated by Adams—contacted patriots in the other colonies and proposed united opposition.

While this pot simmered, more fuel was thrown on the fire. General Thomas Gage, commanding all British forces in America, in 1765 obtained from Parliament a Quartering Act of two-year duration, during which time colonial civil authorities should supply barracks and supplies for the troops, and billets in inns, alehouses and unoccupied buildings. And there was more to come.

On March 22, 1765, Parliament passed the Stamp Act. Ubiquitous in application—it seemed that even the very act of breathing might be illegal without a revenue stamp—this measure overrode colonial sectionalism and broadened the base of opposition. The fact that violators of the Act could be tried in Crown-appointed courts of vice-admiralty and without a jury seemed to many as a direct threat to English constitutional government.

This time Virginia led the protest, as Patrick Henry laid before its House of Burgesses his "Virginia Resolutions," with its fiery peroration:

"Caesar," thundered the red-head, "had his Brutus, Charles the First his Cromwell, and George the Third—" he paused to the rumbled cries of "treason!"—"may profit by their example. If *this* be treason, make the most of it!"

Mob violence now first raised its head. The "Sons of Liberty," a secret organization created by Samuel Adams, went into action. Violence and threats of violence in the larger towns forced stamp agents to resign and importers to cancel orders for British merchandise. In Boston, on August 26, the records of the vice-admiralty court were burned and the homes of officials, including that of Chief Justice Thomas Hutchinson, looted.

Delegates from nine colonies, meeting in New York in October as a "Stamp Act Congress," on Massachusetts' invitation, demanded repeal in protests addressed to King George, the Lords and the Commons. Leading citizens and merchants of New York, Philadelphia and Boston agreed to ban purchase of European goods until the act should be annulled.

When the act became effective—November 1—practically all business in the colonies was suspended. This, of course, could not last. So, in open violation of the obnoxious ordinance, provincial business resumed as usual—minus stamps. Meanwhile legitimate foreign trade froze as nonimportation persisted and smuggling flourished. By the end of 1765, British imports had dropped by £300,000 from £2,249,710 in 1764. Loud was the outcry in England. British firms were going bankrupt, and British workers whose livelihood was threatened faced starvation.

After two months of heated debate in Parliament, with the Chancellor of the Exchequer calling for enforcement by use of troops, and William Pitt (later Earl of Chatham) commending the Americans for their disobedience, the Stamp Act was repealed on March 18, 1766. The affair was, it seemed, ended, and the colonies rejoiced. Nonimportation ceased. In New York, statues were voted to honor both the King and Mr. Pitt. And few heeded that the Parliament, after repealing the Stamp Act, had also enacted into law its authority to bind the colonies by law "in all cases whatsoever."

The year ended on two sour notes: Parliament's proviso that all colonial imports to northern Europe must be cleared through British ports, and the proroguing of the New York Assembly for refusing to subsist British troops quartered there. In New York, too, the erection of a liberty pole brought a brief clash between soldiers and Sons of Liberty.

More taxation came in 1767: the Townshend Acts. These comprised an attempt to offset a £500,000 reduction in English tax income by putting import duties on glass, lead, paints, paper and tea sold in the colonies.

Again Samuel Adams aroused colonial furor. His circular letter, soliciting united action against the Townshend Acts, was supported in Massachusetts, Rhode Island, New Hampshire, New Jersey and Virginia, despite British official denunciation. Customs officials in Boston were harried and the people called to arms, on the pretext that a war with France was imminent. Convocation of an informal Massachusetts Provincial Assembly, with delegates from 96 towns, dared the governor's ire; as a result two regiments of British infantry, with artillery, came into Boston for police duty.

In 1769, George Washington's "Resolves and Association," approved by the Virginia House of Burgesses despite Governor Norborne Berkely Botetourt's injunction, insisted upon Virginia's exclusive right of self-taxation and spread the doctrine of nonimportation. Early next year the "Battle of Golden Hill" in New York—a minor clash between Sons of Liberty and soldiery—and the more serious "Boston Massacre" further stirred colonial resentment. Six Americans died in Boston—March 5, 1770—when a redcoat guard detail, harried by rioters, opened fire. A general uprising was avoided when

Hutchinson, now governor, complied with Samuel Adams' demand and withdrew the troops from the city to harbor islands.

Meanwhile the British Board of Trade gasped at a further drop in trade with the colonies. John Bull's pocketbook had been nicked, in 1769, to the tune of £821,000, as British imports slumped from £2,157,218 in the previous year to a low of £1,336,122. Hastily, Lord Frederick North, the premier, proposed withdrawal of all Townshend taxes except that on tea, and the Quartering Act was permitted to expire without renewal. For the moment, despite continuing non-importation of British tea, moderate men breathed easier; but only for a moment.

Burning of the British customs schooner *Gaspée,* June 9, 1772, as she lay grounded near Providence, Rhode Island, brought swift but futile official reaction. A reward offer of £200 for identification of the attackers drew a blank, for it had also been announced that anyone so identified would be whisked to England for trial. This flouting of self-government, plus announcement by Governor Hutchinson of Massachusetts that henceforth all judges would be paid by the Crown—thus freeing them from colonial ties—startled even the more moderate element in New England. For Samuel Adams it was a golden opportunity.

On his recommendation, a Boston town meeting appointed a 21-member standing Committee of Correspondence, to publish Boston's position not only to the other provincial towns, but also "to the world." Like wildfire, radical elements in other provinces took up the scheme. It led to the establishment of a loose-leaf interchange of information linking most of the colonies; in effect an indispensable clearing-house for intercolonial public relations.

As the *Massachusetts Gazette* would later * well put it from the Tory point of view, Adams had indeed "hatched the foulest, subtilest and most venemous serpent ever issued from the egg of sedition."

Meanwhile, in London, on May 10, 1773, the House of Commons dropped another spark in the powder-keg. The British East India Company, as a result of the American boycott on tea, was slowly going bankrupt, while 17 million pounds of tea went begging in its English warehouses. Only one chest of English tea, for instance,

---

* January 2, 1775.

had entered Philadelphia in five years, although an ample supply was smuggled in from other sources, particularly from Holland. Should the Company crack, England's prosperous Indian empire might crumble with it, for "John Company" ran India for England.

So Parliament rushed to the rescue by remitting duties on the export of Company tea from England, though the import tax in the colonies still stood. The remission of export duties brought down the price of Company tea so that it could undercut all competition—smuggled or legitimate—while, despite the import tax, the thrifty Americans should be only too happy to buy cheaper tea. Happy days, thought London, had come again, and on this rosy prospect a round half-million pounds of tea sailed joyfully to hand-picked consignees in Boston, New York, Philadelphia and Charleston.

The news preceded the laden tea-clippers to America and flowed through correspondence committee channels. An astounding resurgence of radical opposition—screams of "bribery," and of "endangered liberty"—transformed a six-year-old apathy into riotous resistance. Possibly, too, the tea smugglers and their agents, who saw their livelihood threatened, took some part in stirring the flames. In any event, all four ports boiled with riotous indignation meetings, before which most of the consignees quailed.

The tea ships for New York and Philadelphia, unable to land their cargoes, sailed back to England. At Charleston, no consignees appeared to pay duty, so the customs authorities seized the tea-ship cargo and stored it (three years later it would be sold at auction to raise revolutionary government funds).

But in Boston Governor Hutchinson and his Tory consignees defied the town meetings of protest. On December 16 Sam Adams' bully-boys—among them a number of prominent citizens—went whooping to the wharf disguised as Indians, and stormed aboard the ships. They then gleefully dumped £15,000 worth of tea—342 chests—into the harbor water.

That did it. King George, who had insisted on the retention of the tea tax as a concrete example of the royal right to tax, demanded punishment. An irate Commons obliged him, despite the efforts of Chatham and Edmund Burke. Through March to May, 1774, it passed the so-called Coercive Acts.

The Boston Port Bill, effective June 1, 1774, closed the port of

Boston to all traffic until such time as the East India Company and the customs had been reimbursed for the losses caused by the Boston Tea Party. Exceptions were made only for military stores and for such shipments of food and fuel as might receive the blessing of customs officials.

The Administration of Justice Act protected Crown officials in Massachusetts from hostile provincial courts. Anyone indicted for a capital offense committed in quelling riot or enforcing revenue laws could be removed to England or to another colony for trial.

The Massachusetts Government Act practically annulled the colonial charter. Officials would be appointed only by the King, the governor, or the governor's appointees, and town meetings were virtually abolished.

A new Quartering Act, which applied to all the colonies, legalized the quartering of troops not only in taverns and deserted buildings, but also in occupied dwellings.

Unconnected in fact with the Coercive Acts, but also accepted in theory by many of the colonists as "intolerable," was the Quebec Act, extending Canada's boundaries to the Ohio River and providing a centralized Crown-appointed government there. This nullified claims of various colonies to lands west of the Alleghenies and reaffirmed the royal authority asserted in the Proclamation of 1763. It was rightly interpreted as a measure to strengthen Crown control in America at the expense of the colonies.

On May 13, 1774, General Gage arrived in Boston from New York, to supplant Hutchinson as governor of Massachusetts province and to enforce the King's will. An amiable man was Gage, inclined, through years of service in America, to sympathize with colonial aspirations. Doubtless the opinions of his American wife had some influence there, too. But he was also a soldier of the King, a disciplinarian, and he took his orders seriously.

Three days before Gage's arrival, first word of the new British coercion reached Boston by fast ship from London, and the galloping couriers of correspondence committees began spreading the word southward. By the end of May Boston's plight was known to practically every town and village in the Thirteen Colonies.

Sure enough, on June 1, Boston, busiest seaport in North America, stopped on dead center. Gage had taken his orders literally and enforced them vigorously. British warships sealed the sea gate, while within the harbor all water traffic ceased, even to the Bay islands on which Boston's cattle grazed and its produce grew. Gage did not block its one access route to the mainland, via Boston Neck and Dorchester. Otherwise the city was quarantined from the world on which its people depended for livelihood and sustenance.

Throughout the rest of the colonies the fires of resentment burned bright, as protests flared and retaliations were recommended. A more practical and immediate response to the threat of starvation began moving almost at once, over that Dorchester road, not only from other Massachusetts towns but also from other colonies. Sheep came from Connecticut, cattle and other foodstuff from the rest of New England; rice and money arrived from the Carolinas; more money came from Delaware, with promises to continue the alms. From Quebec in Canada, of all places, arrived more than a thousand bushels of wheat. Some of this provender came by land, some was sea-borne to Marblehead, which had now become a port of entry and had offered free wharfage and warehousing to Boston. So Bostonians would live, although belts were tightened.

Now, hastily gathered colonial conventions discussed Boston's plight. As might be imagined, the tone was heated, even among the more deliberative and calm citizens. Typical, perhaps, of the trend things were taking was the speech of one wealthy, conservative and normally dispassionate Virginian in the House of Burgesses:

"I'll raise a thousand men, subsist them at my own expense, and march myself at their head for the relief of Boston." Thus, according to John Adams, spoke George Washington.

The consensus of all these gatherings was that common measures must be taken to assist Massachusetts and Boston. And out of that grew a new entity—the First Continental Congress.

Gathered in Philadelphia by September 5 were delegates—the ubiquitous Samuel Adams among them—from twelve colonies (Georgia would come in later). These men were not yet rebels. With few exceptions, they regarded themselves as loyal subjects of King George —a rightful ruler misled by politicians. Their divided opinion and diverse objectives had but one common base—the restoration of the rights of free men as provided in the British Constitution. As Patrick

Henry put it to them, in his opening address, "All distinctions are thrown down. All America is one mass."

Such was this body, without either legislative or executive powers, which nevertheless would become the catalyst of freedom.

The Congress' first stumbling deliberations were tensed by a flaming canard that Gage had bombarded and burned Boston. The truth of the matter was that Gage had sent a detachment of troops to seize provincial-owned cannon and powder in Charlestown and Cambridge; the countryside had been aroused, but no clash had occurred. Congressional equilibrium had been but briefly restored when, on September 16, Paul Revere came clattering into Philadelphia. In his saddlebags reposed Massachusetts' Magna Carta—the so-called Suffolk Resolves, issued by Boston patriots forbidden to meet in their own city. The resolutions, written by Dr. Joseph Warren, listed the "infractions of those rights to which we are justly entitled by the laws of nature, the British constitution and the charter of this province." They denounced the Coercive Acts as unconstitutional and therefore not to be obeyed; urged that Massachusetts form a government to collect taxes and withhold them from the Crown until the Coercive Acts should be repealed; advised the people to arm and form their own militia; and recommended economic sanctions against England.

This was indeed strong meat. Within and without the Congress the lines began to be drawn between conservative, moderate and radical; between Whig and Tory. After long argument the Suffolk Resolves were approved October 14 and their principles embodied in a new Declaration and Resolves. Four days later the Congress went further, adopting the Continental Association, pledging the provinces to cease all importation from Britain, to discontinue the slave trade, to effect nonconsumption of British products, and to embargo all exports to England, Ireland and the British West Indies.

How were these brave words to be implemented?

By committee. Article XI of the Association reads:

"That a committee be chosen in every county, city or town . . . whose business it shall be attentively to observe the conduct of all persons touching this association; and when it shall be made to appear that any person within the limits of their appointment has violated this association, that [those committees] do forthwith cause the truth of the case to be published in the gazette; to the end, that all such foes to the rights of British-America may be publicly known, and universally condemned as the enemies of American liberty; and henceforth we respectively will break off all dealings with him or her."

Thus was born the instrumentality which, as it turned out, would muster the colonial resources for war: the Committee of Safety, at times a lawless and fearsome thing in whose name opprobrium, and not infrequently tar and feathers and home-burning, would be meted out to the unfortunate loyalist. Haphazard, clumsy and brutal in its methods, the Committee of Safety would nevertheless prove effective.

More to the point, let us remember that each Committee of Safety represented in effect the will of the majority in its own local community only. This was no organized Terror, plunging the colonies into a blood-bath. Here is the basic difference between the American Revolution and the horrors of the subsequent French Revolution and of the Bolshevik upheaval in Russia.

Having thus paved the way, the First Continental Congress concocted addresses to the King, and to the American and British peoples, then adjourned, on October 26, resolving to meet again on May 10, 1775, if by that time American grievances had not been redressed.

While the colonies' protests sailed slowly to London, much happened in New England. Massachusetts by this time meant business and the Congress had pointed the way to action. Thirty militia regiments existed in the colony, with principal command in Tory hands. The Massachusetts House of Representatives, meeting in defiance of Gage, constituted itself a Provincial Congress. John Hancock, one of Boston's leading merchants and foremost citizens, was appointed to head a Committee of Safety empowered to call out the militia. An order went out that all militia officers must resign. The patriots did so willingly; the Tories, intimidated by Committees of Safety, followed suit. New officers were elected—staunch radicals all. The Provincial Congress then directed that each company of militia would enlist one-fourth of its men "to act on a minute's notice"—the origin of the "Minutemen." Artemas Ward, colorless veteran of the French and Indian War, was selected as commanding general of Massachusetts troops.

Collection of arms and ammunition had already begun, as we have noted. Under Hancock's committee the work progressed. They even stole cannon from some of the outlying British fortifications. The Provincial Congress appropriated £15,627 for the purchase of cannon, small arms, and ammunition, to be stored at Concord and Worcester. Rhode Island followed suit, stripping the cannon at Fort Island from the post. Raiders forced a British detachment commander at New Castle to release powder belonging to the province, at the same time seizing muskets and cannon.

By mid-December, militia companies were drilling on village commons throughout New England. Connecticut, Rhode Island and New Hampshire were considering Hancock's request that they share in the composition of an army of 20,000 men. Gage's proclamation that the activities of the Provincial Congress were treasonable was a mere gesture of frustration.

In London, King and Parliament rocked with rage as 1775—the year of decision—rolled in. Chatham, in the Lords, pleading for reconciliation, was quickly voted down. Both houses declared Massachusetts to be in rebellion. Lord North's peace offering—a policy of "forbearance" if the colonies would tax themselves for the common defense—passed the Commons February 27. But that same day they began consideration of the Fisheries Act, which would bar New Englanders from the Newfoundland fishing banks, and forbid them to trade abroad except with Great Britain and the British West Indies. Despite Burke's eloquent opposition, the bill went through—a death-knell to the colonial economy. British merchants, who stood to lose millions of pounds if the colonies could not meet their obligations, pleaded without avail for "healing remedies."

Meanwhile, on February 1, the Second Massachusetts Provincial Congress met at Cambridge. Under the leadership of John Hancock and Dr. Warren it took steps to further prepare the colony for war. Two more generals were appointed under Ward—John Thomas and William Heath. A commissary was established, to supervise the collection of matériel and provisions, and a military code—the "Articles of War"—was adopted. Enlistment of the Stockbridge Indians was solicited. Chosen delegates started conferences with the other New England colonies and, of course, the information couriers spread the news southward.

On February 26 Gage sent a detachment of British troops to Salem, to seize provincial cannon. Landing at Marblehead, they marched through an arousing countryside to their destination. The cannon had been hidden. A bit of *opera bouffe* followed. Colonel Alexander Leslie, the British commander, was permitted to follow the letter of his orders, and to inspect the spot where the guns should have been. Having found nothing, he consented to withdraw.

Down south, on March 23, Patrick Henry's impassioned "Give me liberty or give me death!" electrified the Virginia Provincial Convention.

And on April 14 General Gage received instructions from Lord Dartmouth, Secretary of State for the Colonies, to strike at once, if necessary, to prevent the rebels from completing their organization. King and colonist were careering to headlong collision.

2 ★ ★ ★ ★ ★ ★

Hornets in Homespun

FOR ELEVEN MONTHS, General Gage's finger had lain constantly on the throbbing pulse of rebellion. His intelligence file was almost a transcript of the proceedings of the Massachusetts Committee of Safety. It should have been, for someone high in that committee fed him information regularly. Historians point the finger at Dr. Benjamin Church, Jr., Boston physician long highly respected in patriot circles and later—for a few months—surgeon general of the Continental Army. But whoever he—or they—might have been, Gage's informers served him well. Carefully inventoried by amount and location were the cannon, muskets, ammunition, provisions and other stores so carefully garnered by the radical colonists. The bulk of these munitions lay at Concord. Documented, too, were the Massachusetts militia records: the principal officers, the number and location of units, including the "minute companies," and the general scheme of mobilization and planned resistance.

As a result, when Gage, on April 14, 1775, received his instructions from London to nip revolt before it could go further, he knew what to do and where to go. But he also knew, from past experience and the estimates of resistance to be expected, that his available force was entirely inadequate for any formal campaign. In fact, he had already asked for considerable reinforcement.

Something must now be done immediately. Only the surprise of a lightning stroke would succeed. So, with efficient rapidity Gage acted. Paunchy Lieutenant Colonel Francis Smith, 10th Foot—the Lincolnshire Regiment—would proceed "with the utmost secrecy

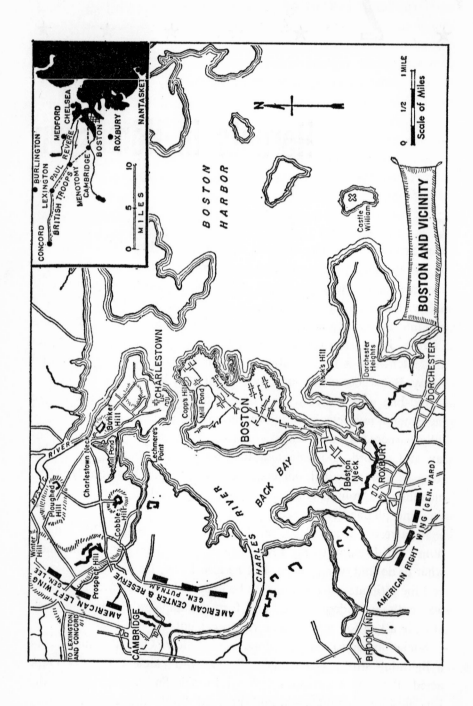

and expedition" to Concord, seize and destroy the rebel stores and then return "as soon as possible." His 700 troops consisted of the élite of the Boston garrison; the grenadier and light infantry * companies of all the regiments there. They would be transported across the bay under cover of darkness by the assembled boats of all the British warships and transports in the harbor, thus avoiding the disclosure and alarm which a march across Boston Neck and through Roxbury would entail. Second in command to Smith was dependable, forceful Royal Marine Major John Pitcairn. The orders were explicit and detailed; the hiding places of the stores were plotted on a sketch map accompanying. Also—and this is important—Gage stressed that Smith "take care that the soldiers do not plunder the Inhabitants, or hurt private property." The point of departure was the Back Bay, the time 10:00 P.M. April 18.

Unfortunately for Gage's plan, he and his redcoats were living in a goldfish bowl. Boston, now a city of arrested movement and of unemployment, contained literally thousands of men and women who had nothing better to do than to stare at, speculate upon, and gossip about the slightest move of the hated garrison. In particular, there was Paul Revere's own private intelligence corps—some thirty individuals whose sole duty it was to funnel every scrap of information to Dr. Warren, Boston's liaison man with the Committee of Safety at Concord.

Sharp eyes had noted the sudden clustering of ships' boats in the water about the ships in the harbor. Sharp ears learned that the flank companies of the British regiments had been relieved of all normal garrison duties. Scurrying batmen (officers' servants), preparing their officers' gear for field service, dropped unguarded hints in billets. Something big was up.

When further word came of British officers, thinly disguised, wandering on the highways and byways of the neighboring counties, suspicion grew to certainty. Gage must be going to grab the munitions at Concord. His redcoats would probably go by boat across the Charles River, and then march west through Cambridge and Lexington, instead of via the roundabout Boston Neck-Roxbury road. An alert went out to the Concord people, and Dr. Warren summoned

---

* See Appendix I for analysis and discussion of British military arms, ammunition, and tactical formations.

to his home two hard-riding, experienced couriers—William Dawes and Paul Revere.

Before the troops had left their barracks that night Dawes was on the way to Lexington, via Boston Neck; his mission to warn John Hancock and Samuel Adams, who were lodging there, and then to go on to Concord. Before the troops had clumped over the cobbles to their assembly point on the Common, Revere had been quietly rowed to Charlestown to await a pre-arranged signal. He, too, would go to Concord, arousing the various communities on the way.

As embarkment began at the Back Bay, two lanterns twinkled from the steeple of Old North Church—the signal that the British were taking boats across the Charles. Watching, Revere swung into the saddle of the horse provided him, and started on his famous ride. It was about midnight when Colonel Smith's command splashed ashore from their boats at Lechmere's Point and fumbled into column on the lonely dirt back road to Cambridge. They were wet, muddy and thoroughly chilled—for at the very onset they had to ford a brook. And they didn't know, as they slogged their way to a rendezvous with destiny, that they were poking into a nest of hornets aroused by galloping couriers.

Revere had already pounded through Medford and Menotomy (now Arlington), and sleepy minutemen were bestirring themselves where he had passed. Once he had had to dodge a British patrol. He reached Lexington, warning Hancock and Adams. Joined there by Dawes, who had met with no interruption on the longer route, he galloped off for Concord. On the way, young Dr. Samuel Prescott, returning from a courtship visit, met and joined them. A short distance on, a British officers' patrol barred the road. Dawes turned back to Lexington; the others attempted evasion. Prescott, putting his mount to a stone wall, got clear. As it turned out, he would reach Concord. But Revere was bagged. So too were three scouting minutemen from Lexington. The patrol seized their mounts and turned the men loose. Revere, walking back to Lexington, found Hancock and Adams about to leave. The trio—in a chaise—drove on to safety at Burlington. And that was the end of the ride of Paul Revere.

Meanwhile the silent British column hiked cautiously through darkened Cambridge, Somerville and Menotomy and then, with six light companies as advanced guard, plodded on to Lexington. Behind them and in front of them communities buzzed and men fanned out to alarm the countryside. To Colonel Smith's ears came recurrent clamor of church bells and occasional shots. As a matter of precaution he sent back word to Gage, suggesting reinforcement. Gage himself had already thought of that. The 1st Brigade—the 4th, 23rd and 47th Foot and a battalion of Marines, with two 6-pounder guns—was to move out at four o'clock in the morning, under Brigadier General Earl Hugh Percy. The idea was excellent; its execution was some· thing else again.

Day was dawning when Smith's advance guard, under Major Pitcairn, arrived at Lexington Common, to find two ragged lines of local militia drawn up on the green: Captain John Parker's minute company, some seventy strong. The British deployed into line.

Pitcairn, riding out in front, called on the "damned rebels" to disperse. Parker's men wavered, started to comply. But someone—no one will ever know if it was redcoat or minuteman—jerked an itchy trigger-finger.

A British platoon volley responded, and then another one, despite Pitcairn's order to cease fire. From the clump of Americans came scattered shots. Then the British, out of hand, came on with the bayonet. The minutemen scampered away, followed by more British musket balls. With them they took ten wounded men. Pitcairn reformed his excited soldiers on the green, where eight American dead lay sprawled. Huzzas and one last volley proclaimed cheap victory. One redcoat had been wounded and Pitcairn's mount creased by a bullet.

The British main body came up, the column reformed, and with rolling drums and squeaking fifes—no further need for stealth now—moved on for Concord, four miles away. It was about six o'clock.

Much of the munitions stored in Concord had already been removed the day before. The remainder began to melt under willing hands as soon as Prescott brought the alarm. For three hours the local minutemen had manhandled light cannon and muskets into furrows quickly ploughed in the nearby fields; stored musket balls, flints and cartridges into attics, under layers of feathers; rolled powder kegs into the woods.

Meanwhile the countryside resembled a disturbed ant-hill. All roads in Massachusetts, it seemed, led to Concord that morning. When the head of the British column came in sight—a brave show of red coats and twinkling bayonets—hundreds of minutemen stood watching from the outskirts of the village, but offered no opposition. Colonel James Barrett, militia leader of the area, shepherded them to the north, beyond the village and west of the Concord River, on the crest of Punkasset Hill.

In the village the British halted. The light companies fanned out —six of them going to the North Bridge, one to the South Bridge. Thus covered, the grenadiers began a methodical search, house by house. They didn't find much; some gun-carriages, which were burned; some barrels of flour, rolled into the millpond; some entrenching tools and other odds and ends, which were set on fire. In the doing, the courthouse and blacksmith shop also began to burn, but the soldiers put these blazes out.

Meanwhile, under the silent stare of the militia on the hill, the light infantry at the North Bridge spread out. Three companies pushed across and up to the Barrett farm, suspected of being the main weapons repository. The other three halted to protect the bridge.

Up on the hill, the mob of militia was whipping itself into fury at sight of the burning and looting. Almost spontaneously, as it seemed to the bridge guards, the Americans, loading their muskets, edged towards them. Then the Acton company, Captain Isaac Davis at its head, with two fifers shrilling "The White Cockade," boldly marched towards the bridge, followed in ragged column by other outfits.

Badly outnumbered, the bridge guard fell back to the eastern side and opened fire. The minutemen blazed back. The smoke drifted away, revealing four Americans down (two were dead, including Captain Davis) and the militia crowding across the bridge. Three British soldiers were dead and nine others—four of them officers— wounded. The regulars fell back on the village in disorder. The undisciplined Americans started pursuit, then hesitated. About half of them turned back. The others lined themselves along a stone wall to the east—out of musket range—and waited for a counterattack which never came.

In the village, Colonel Smith gathered two companies of grenadiers to cover the retreating bridge guard, but did not press further. The companies up at the Barrett farm now hurried back, unmolested— no thanks to over-cautious Smith—by the grim watchers along the stone wall. About noon, Smith, after some more hesitation, decided his work had been accomplished. The British formed into column at noon and started back towards Lexington, taking their wounded with them in two commandeered chaises. As seen through British eyes, Smith's actions thus far had not been impressive. But to Samuel Adams that morning of April 19 had already been a "glorious" one.

The British moved slowly down the Lexington road. The hot sun beat on men who had been up most of the preceding night, had marched more than twenty miles in full kit, and had engaged in two skirmishes. To most of his command, probably, Smith's actions had been inexplicable. Dull anger burned in men who felt that their commander had let them be pushed around by a rabble. They itched to come to grips with this fluid, motley aggregation of armed civilians who even now were scurrying and bobbing along through the fields beside them, keeping up but remaining out of musket range.

For a mile the British moved unhindered, wary of the heavy clusters of militia, with advance and rear guards and flanking detachments out on both sides of the road. Then, at Meriam's Corner, the flankers on the left, alarmed by sight of a new group of minutemen approaching up the Bradford road, suddenly blazed away at them. Almost immediately a trickle of answering fire puffed, increasing in volume, from wall and hedge and tree-trunk, enveloping the column from front to rear, from side to side.

From Meriam's Corner to Lexington the redcoat column writhed, like a whale attacked by sharks, leaving behind it a fringe of red foam—the bodies of its dead. From time to time the light infantry flankers took toll of assailants surprised while firing, but the flankers were tiring fast, and more and more Americans were crowding in now. It seemed, as one Briton later put it, "as if men came down from the clouds." In dazed bafflement the British moved, surrounded by a haze of powder smoke from which musket balls showered on men stifled in their high-stocked regimentals, and half-crazed by thirst and fatigue.

By the time they reached Lexington, British discipline was unravelling, despite the officers' efforts. Smith tried to make a stand there, but the mob closed in on his rear guard. Ammunition was running low, too; they had come out with thirty-six rounds per man, not much for an all-day running fight. Smith himself was wounded in the leg. Pitcairn's horse, maddened by another graze, tossed his rider and galloped into the enemy ring. At a dog-trot now, the British jumbled through the village, past the common where they had fired their first shots that morning, to run headlong into safety—Lord Percy's serried line drawn up across the road. Curtained by the fresh troops, Smith's men flung themselves—as contemporary British historian Charles Stedman put it—"for rest on the ground, their tongues hanging out of their mouths like those of dogs after a chase," with the welcome sound of disciplined musketry and cannon fire ringing in their ears. It was half past two.

Percy, whose previous opinion of Americans as "cowards" and "timid creatures" was to change rapidly, had not gotten away from Boston until nine o'clock after a series of ludicrous blunders wrecked his plan for a four o'clock departure. Once on the road, however, his force of 1,000 men swung smartly over Boston Neck and took the Roxbury-Brookline road to Cambridge, all sparkling brass and steel and pipe-clay, bobbing behind "Yankee Doodle" on the fifes and drums. At Cambridge the bridge over the Charles—partly dismantled by patriots—had to be repaired. He hurried through Menotomy, where his lagging two-wagon baggage train was captured by local militia. He was half-way to Lexington when a wounded British officer, being carried back from the Concord fight, brought news of Smith's plight. The pace increased. Lexington was a mile away when, at the sound of firing ahead, Percy deployed his column into line astride the road and advanced cautiously until the tide of Smith's retreat bulged out of the village and into his lines.

Percy opened fire with his two 6-pounders, clearing the Americans from the southern end of the village, which was then looted. He now prepared to return to Boston. The American fire had subsided temporarily, while the colonists milled and scurried about, uncertain just how to tackle this formidable reinforcement.

At half past three, with Smith's original detachment herded in front, Percy moved out, his strong rear guard and flanking detachments dominating the situation momentarily. But by the time Menotomy was reached the militia pack, still increasing in number, grew bolder. They wouldn't listen to the attempts of Brigadier General William Heath to organize them, but once more swarmed along the

walled fields and even into the houses along the road. The British
flankers had to fight from house to house.

At Menotomy, additional increments of minutemen arrived. Fresh
men took up the task of wall- and hedge-hopping from those whose
ammunition pouches were empty. Here and there individual British
soldiers were dragged down as they straggled for loot; the flankers
were pressed closer to the road. By the time the column reached
Cambridge, Percy realized that it was touch and go. His cannon,
several times unlimbered and put into action, had no targets.

"Many of [the Americans]," as he later reported to Gage, "concealed
themselves in houses & advanced within 10 yds. to fire at me and other
officers, tho' they were mortally certain of being put to death themselves
in an instant. . . ."

Delay at the Charles bridge in Cambridge might be fatal. So Percy
turned sharply northeast and made for Charlestown Neck. He crossed
it at half past six and halted his harried men on Bunker's Hill, above
it. The Americans, filled though they were with the valor of ignorance,
realized that to try to force that narrow Neck would be mass suicide.
The firing died away.

The day of Lexington and Concord was over. Some 1,800 British
regulars had met about 4,000 disorganized Americans, and had been
driven home. The Americans had lost forty-nine dead and forty-six
more wounded or missing. Sixty-five British soldiers were dead, 173
more were wounded and twenty-six were missing. Gage and his officers
could ponder further, too, on the fact that fifteen British officers had
gone down that day; one dead, the others wounded. To the British,
whose mass volley-fire was unaimed, it seemed incredible that the
damnable rebels actually aimed their firelocks at intended targets.
And as Gage, heavy-hearted, issued orders for the evacuation next
day of Percy's command from Charlestown, campfires began to glim-
mer from Dorchester around to Chelsea, and through the night hoofs
clattered southward to spread the news.

Reaction was immediate. Responding almost on the run came the
minutemen of Massachusetts, New Hampshire, Rhode Island and Connecticut, all fired with momentary valor. They ringed Boston and then,
undisciplined, they began to melt away again. Alive to the danger

of temporary ardor, the Massachusetts Provincial Congress on April 23 voted the recruitment, until the year's end, of an army 30,000 strong, of whom 13,600 were to be from Massachusetts, the remainder "requested" from the other New England colonies. So, in the following weeks, a new surge of militia manpower came tramping into the field, ringing Boston in a great semicircle.

The dragon's teeth so wantonly sown by King George had begun to sprout.

3

★ ★ ★ ★ ★ ★

An Army in the Making

WHAT? TEN THOUSAND PEASANTS keep five thousand of the King's troops shut up? Well, let us get in, and we'll soon find elbowroom!"

The speaker was Major General John Burgoyne, just arrived in Boston with Major Generals William Howe and Henry Clinton to reinforce Gage's command. The date was May 25, 1775.

The situation was, in fact, even worse than Burgoyne thought. By this time not only did the uncouth, undisciplined horde of "peasants" have the British troops in Boston penned, but they had also seized Fort Ticonderoga on Lake Champlain, the traditional gateway between Canada and the Colonies. On the seacoast, in Machias Bay, a group of Maine lumbermen had captured the British armed cutter *Margaretta*. Down in Philadelphia, the Second Continental Congress, convening May 10, the very day Ticonderoga fell, was deliberating concerted colonial military action. And overseas a very astute politician and confirmed enemy of England—Charles Gravier de Vergennes, the Foreign Minister of France's King Louis XVI—was studying ways and means to make use of this American ferment.

The little military operations were far more important in psychological than in tactical value. The Ticonderoga affair was pure *opera bouffe*. Dapper, pugnacious Captain Benedict Arnold, who with his company of New Haven militiamen had been among the early arrivals before Boston, suggested it, as the solution of the patriots' need for heavy ordnance.

The Massachusetts Committee of Safety, accepting the recommendation, made Arnold a temporary colonel, and authorized him to recruit "not exceeding 400 men," and to go up and take the place. Meanwhile a Connecticut group had asked Ethan Allen, stormy petrel of the New Hampshire Grants (later called Vermont), to join them with his Green Mountain Boys and capture the fort. They rallied at Bennington, and Allen was elected to command. Arnold, arriving, informed them that by Massachusetts order he was to command the expedition. The Vermonters would have none of that, so after much wrangling Allen led the way with some 200 men, Arnold simply tagging along.

Ticonderoga, an imposing Vauban-type fortress built by the French in 1755, had fallen into decay after the French and Indian War. At the moment it contained a garrison of but two officers and forty-eight men, most of them invalids, together with twenty-four women and children.

At dawn, May 10, the dilapidated fortress fell—without firing a single shot—to Allen's rush and his reputed demand for surrender "In the name of the Continental Congress and the Great Jehovah!"

While most of the Green Mountain Boys enjoyed themselves in looting the place, Allen's second in command, Lieutenant Colonel Seth Warner, gathered a detachment and moved north to Crown Point, capturing the British post there, with its round dozen of soldier guards. Arnold, chafing at his own anomalous position, was delighted when an additional fifty patriots arrived in a schooner captured at Skenesboro (now Whitehall). With them he sailed to St. Johns, a British post on the Richelieu River, a short distance north of Lake Champlain. There he bagged the garrison—a sergeant and fourteen men—together with an armed sloop and its crew. Since British forces were known to be nearby, Arnold prudently returned to Crown Point, with the most precious of the captured munitions.

On the way back Arnold's little flotilla passed a north-bound expedition: Ethan Allen, with ninety men in four bateaux, bent on the harebrained scheme of capturing all Canada. Allen got as far as St. Johns, but the arrival of Canadian militia sent the Green Mountain Boys scampering back home.

The Machias Bay incident—first naval action of the war—brought bloodshed. On June 12, 1775, Jeremiah O'Brien, with a score of other local lumbermen in a commandeered sloop, chased the cutter *Margaretta,* which they boarded and captured in a flurry of pistol fire, pitchforks and axes which cost the lives of several men on both sides.

As for the uproar in the Lake Champlain area, it may not have amounted to much militarily, but it gave heart to the Continental Congress at Philadelphia. After the Congress first decided that Ticonderoga and Crown Point should be abandoned, the protests of New York and New England prevailed. A Congressional resolution on May 31 requested Connecticut to garrison the forts, and New York to furnish supplies. Colonel Benjamin Hinman with 1,400 Connecticut men moved north. Arnold, to his chagrin, found himself unwanted, despite his recommendation that he be permitted to invade Canada with this force. In high dudgeon, Arnold resigned, returning to the Boston area. Ticonderoga's heavy guns, cannon balls, tons of musket bullets and other equipment badly needed by the besiegers of Boston, remained in place. There was no way to transport them.

While the patriot forces milled around Boston—hornets in homespun whose stings would foil any sortie which Gage might make—the Congress in Philadelphia was slowly arriving at historic decisions. Recognizing that a "Continental Army" was in the field, the Congress on June 15 authorized the raising of ten companies of riflemen to join the Boston forces. Thus the United States Army was born.

That same day, too, Congress designated Colonel George Washington, a delegate from Virginia, to overall command of this newly established army.

It is interesting to note the political considerations which influenced the appointment of a Virginian to command what at the moment was an army of New England Yankees. John Hancock hoped for the appointment, but Hancock was a New Englander and astute John Adams knew well the need for obtaining the support of the southern colonies. Washington was wealthy, was an aristocrat, was moderate in his views. These attributes, added to one of the most solid military reputations in the colonies, were overwhelming from a political viewpoint.

Washington, learning that his admirers and their hard-headed political supporters intended to nominate him for the command, was greatly troubled. He was well aware how limited his military experience had been, and he seriously doubted his capabilities as a general-in-chief. He was more than willing to command the Virginia contingent of a national army—but responsibility for the strategy and leadership of the entire army was another matter. He refused to attend Congress on June 14 and 15, apparently in the hope that his absence would lead to the selection of someone else. Nevertheless, to Hancock's personal chagrin, Washington was nominated by Adams, and selected by unanimous consent, "to command all the continental forces, raised or to be raised, for the defense of American liberty."

The Commander-in-Chief-designate spent a sleepless night, debating with himself whether or not to accept the honor and responsibility. Finally, reminded by his friends that there was no one else better qualified, and recognizing the political considerations involved, he decided to accept, on the one condition that he serve without pay. On these terms, sincerely and humbly repeating his personal doubts as to his capabilities, next day the tall, imposing figure, dressed in the buff and blue uniform of the 1st Virginia Regiment, accepted "the high Honour [and] Approbation" of his fellow-delegates.

But before Washington could take command of the patriot forces gathering outside Boston, red war had blossomed there.

4

★　★　★　★　★　★

A Hill by Any Name

EVENTS HAD MOVED RAPIDLY in the Boston area that June. On the 12th Gage made one last effort to bring peace, but his florid proclamation—probably written by Burgoyne—aroused only derision and resentment. Proclaiming martial law throughout the province—an idle threat under the circumstances—Gage declared all Americans in arms and those assisting them to be rebels and traitors. Then he offered "the infatuated multitude" full pardon if they would lay down their arms, excepting always Samuel Adams and John Hancock, whose offenses were "of too flagitous a nature to admit [other than] condign punishment."

By now Gage had been reinforced to a strength of about 6,500 British regulars. He prepared to seize and fortify Dorchester Heights south of Boston Harbor on the Charles River, a commanding point which neither side had as yet occupied. The move was to be made June 18. Someone's tongue clacked too loudly and word of the move came to the Committee of Safety. As result, General Ward was ordered on June 15 to occupy and defend "Bunker's Hill in Charlestown," and also "some one hill or hills on Dorchester Neck." Bunker's Hill was to be secured at once; Dorchester later.

Artemas Ward, whose military experience consisted of participation in Abercromby's disastrous campaign against the French at Ticonderoga in 1758, commanded only the Massachusetts troops. His authority over the Connecticut, Rhode Island and New Hampshire forces was nebulous. As John Adams would later note: "These four Armies met at Cambridge and imprisoned the British Army in Boston.

45

But who was the Sovereign of this united or rather congregated Army and who was its commander-in-chief? It had none. Only Ward was subject to the orders of the Massachusetts Provincial Congress . . ."

Ward not unnaturally took a pessimistic view of any offensive action by this undisciplined conglomeration, short as it was of ammunition and equipment. But he was overruled in the council of war he immediately called, with Brigadier General Israel Putnam of Connecticut the most vocal advocate of action. So a task force under Colonel William Prescott, 62-year-old farmer from Pepperell, Mass., was ordered out to accomplish the Committee's directive to fortify Bunker's Hill (so they called it then) by "a strong redoubt . . . with cannon planted there, to annoy the enemy coming out of Charlestown, also to annoy them going by water to Medford."

The troops consisted of Prescott's own regiment—some 300 strong, from Groton, Pepperell and Acton—and two other Massachusetts regiments of Colonels James Frye and Ebenezer Bridge. With them went a fatigue party of 200 men from Putnam's Connecticut regiment under Captain Thomas Knowlton, and Captain Samuel Gridley's Massachusetts artillery company—49 men, most of whom had never had even the most rudimentary training on their two field pieces.

The task force, approximately 1,200 strong, paraded on Cambridge Common at 6:00 P.M. on the evening of June 16. After a prayer by the Reverend Samuel Langdon, president of Harvard College, it moved out for Charlestown Heights with "all the entrenching tools in camp."

No one but Prescott and Putnam—who joined the column at Charlestown Neck—yet knew the objective and mission of the force. The mile-long, pear-shaped Charlestown peninsula jutted from the low 30-foot-wide Neck. A narrow causeway, separating a mill pond from the Charles River, also carried a road parallel to that across the Neck. Broadening, to the southeast of these defiles, the peninsula rose immediately into three hills ranging southeast in successive downward steps to the confluence of the Mystic and Charles rivers.

Bunker's Hill, the northernmost, and the objective for fortification, rose to a 110-foot crown beyond range from Boston of any but the most powerful ordnance of the day. A ridge ran from Bunker's to Breed's Hill, 600 yards to the south and slightly lower. Charlestown village lay at the western waterfront below it, a half-mile from Boston across the Charles. Breed's Hill was within fair cannon-range from the harbor. At the eastern tip of the peninsula was the flattish bottom step; Moulton's—or Morton's—Hill. The ground, mostly pasture land, was unmown.

On arrival at the Neck, Prescott detached one company to occupy deserted Charlestown village. With some protection thus assured to his right flank, he moved the force up and over Bunker's Hill, behind the bobbing lanterns of two guides. Halting there, Prescott disclosed their job.

At once argument arose. A general officer—unnamed in the records—urged that Breed's Hill, not Bunker's, was the vital point. This was evidently Putnam, who, though having no command status, was the only general officer present. For precious minutes the debate went on, until old Colonel Richard Gridley, engineer officer of the Massachusetts Army, charged with laying out the proposed fortification, warned them sharply to make up their minds lest dawn find them exposed to the enemy.

Breed's Hill was chosen, and pick and shovel began to swing under Gridley's direction. This was in direct violation of the Committee's directive. Worse yet, the violation changed what had been intended to be a precautionary measure into a threat the enemy could not tolerate, since artillery on Breed's Hill could reach British vessels anchored in the harbor.

By dawn a respectable redoubt 130 feet square and six feet high squatted brown on the green hillside, plain to the view of the warships below. A sharp-eyed member of the watch on board the sloop *Lively*, 20, spotted it first. Swinging the vessel smartly by a spring on her cable * to bring her broadside to bear, her captain opened fire and Boston town awoke.

Hastily, Gage huddled in council of war with his three generals: Howe, Burgoyne and Clinton. This threat could not be ignored, for if the shipping were endangered Boston would become untenable. Clinton sagely pointed out that the rebels had really outsmarted themselves. A small force, landed behind them on Charlestown Neck under

---

* See Appendix II for explanations of nautical terms, weapons and tactics.

cover of the heavy naval gunfire available, could cut their communications and starve the hill fort out in a day or so, without loss of British life.

Gage, however, on Howe's recommendation, overruled him. He ordered a full-strength assault at once, with Howe commanding it. So, while drums rolled and fifes shrilled, the élite of the British garrison assembled. Over all, the incessant fire of the British ships thundered, for Vice Admiral Sir Samuel Graves had opened with all his ships present. A heavy British battery on Copp's Hill in Boston joined the cannonade.

The British plan was simple and—for the conditions of the moment as plainly visible from Boston—sound. The assault force, with full

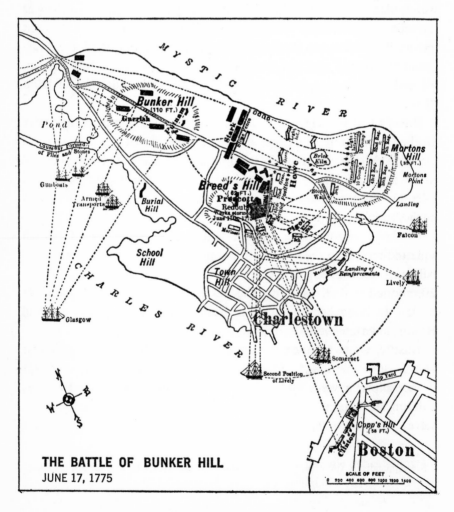

THE BATTLE OF BUNKER HILL
JUNE 17, 1775

kit, blankets and cooked rations for three days, moving by boat to Charlestown, would land on the southeast end of the bulbous peninsula, march up around Moulton's and Breed's Hills on the Mystic River side, out of musket range of the redoubt, and attack it from the rear.

But the water off the landing point was shallow. Not until near high tide, about 2:00 P.M., could the boats approach. So the embarkation did not begin until noon—a waste of six precious hours, during which the American situation changed appreciably.

When daylight came, Prescott, on Breed's Hill, had realized his dangerous situation. While his right flank had some slight protection from his company behind Charlestown village's houses and hedges, his left was naked to British attack. So, while occasional cannon balls bounded in his vicinity, Prescott pushed his workers into increased activity to construct a breastwork running northeastward from the redoubt for some 300 feet. And he sent urgent word back to Ward at Cambridge for supplies (which as it turned out never arrived) and for reinforcements.

The Americans, who had been digging since midnight, were tired, hot, hungry and thirsty. Above all, they were scared. Few of these men had ever before been under fire, and though most of the ships' guns were outranged, occasional round shot came hurtling by. Already one man had been killed, and their two hogsheads of water were smashed by another ball. A trickle of deserters seeped away. But Prescott, his hat and wig doffed, his bald head gleaming with sweat in that blazing sun, kept driving his men.

Behind the delving workers, the ubiquitous Putnam, the only mounted man on the field, raced back and forth between Cambridge and the peninsula, urging Ward to take action. Refusing at first to further deplete his strength, Ward finally—at the order of the Committee of Safety—turned out the two New Hampshire regiments in camp: Stark's and Reed's. They had no ammunition, so flints, powder and sheet lead were doled out and the soldiers set about melting and pounding out bullets and making up paper cartridges—fifteen rounds apiece. It would be noon before they were ready to move. By noon, too, the British began embarking.

Twenty-eight rowing barges, in two long files, at last crept across the bay towards Charlestown, oars flashing in the sun. They were crammed with red-coated soldiers, whose glinting brass and shining bayonets flickered in a thousand points of light as the Americans on Breed's Hill watched. In the two leading craft the snouts of several six-pounder brass field pieces gleamed. Behind them the warships thundered. The *Lively* and her sister sloop *Falcon,* 18, swept the low ground to clear landing space. Over opposite the Neck the frigate *Glasgow,* 24, plus an armed transport and two gunboats moored in the Charles, pounded the causeway and the Neck to cut communications, while HMS *Somerset,* 64, added her thundering broadsides to the fire of the heavy guns on Copp's Hill, trying—without much success—to concentrate on Prescott's redoubt.

By this time Putnam had brought some of his own Connecticut men up to Bunker's Hill, and asked Prescott to send back entrenching tools. Prescott, whose tired, terrified force was continually dwindling, at first refused; he doubted that the men would return. "They shall," swore Putnam, "Every man!" So Prescott yielded. Eager volunteers vied with one another to carry back picks and shovels but—as Prescott had feared—they never returned. Nor did any breastworks rise on Bunker's Hill. The tool-carriers apparently did not stop till they were safely across the Neck.

It was now after one o'clock. By this time the leading British boats had touched land at the point east of Moulton's Hill, Howe with them. His trained eye at once saw that the original redoubt was now extended part way down towards the Mystic by Prescott's new breastwork. On Bunker's Hill, beyond, clumps of men were assembled on the sky line, and even as Howe scanned the scene a column emerged (the New Hampshire regiments), marching down towards the redoubt. In the British general's mind there was no doubt the Americans were being heavily reinforced. His proposed flanking move might find itself caught between two fires.

Howe pushed forward two covering detachments: a battalion under his second in command, Brigadier General Sir George Pigot, westward towards Charlestown; and four companies directly to the front over Moulton's Hill. Howe let the rest of the men break ranks and eat while he waited for the remainder of his force to arrive. Pigot's detachment drew immediate fire from the American company in Charlestown, and he requested naval gunfire support. Admiral Graves, who had come ashore in person to see how best the Navy could assist the assault, almost immediately directed a shower of hot shot into the village; Charlestown went up in sheets of flame.

Up above, Prescott—whose force had now dwindled to his own 300, on whom he could rely, plus Knowlton's 200 stout Connecticut men—could plainly see that the British would strike his left. Cannily he hurried Knowlton's men to a fence—part rail, part stone—about 600 feet in rear of and to the northeast of the breastwork, reaching towards the Mystic. Between these two lines, two or three small V-shaped entrenchments—*flèches*—were also hurriedly dug, as connecting links.

Meanwhile, between the Neck and Cambridge, dust-clouds over the roads and lanes rose on flurries of misdirected activity. Ward belatedly had ordered several Massachusetts regiments to the scene, and these milled about aimlessly—for the most part refusing to dare the British naval fire now sweeping the causeway.

Through this rabble, who were only too glad to let him pass, battle-wise John Stark—second in command of famed Rogers' Rangers in the French and Indian War—had come swinging, at the head of the New Hampshiremen, their bullet-making finished. Refusing to quicken the pace across the fire-swept Neck—"one fresh man in action is worth ten fatigued men," he told a subordinate—he got to the top of Bunker's Hill in time to see Howe's troops slowly forming below. To his eye, too, that left flank was the danger point, and he led his men at the double down towards Knowlton's rail fence. His was the column Howe had seen debouching over the sky line. He did more. Arriving there, he discovered that the fence ended on a bluff several feet above the water-line, with a passable stretch of beach below. At once Stark blocked this with stones torn from adjacent walls, posted there his most reliable men, and spread the rest, with Reed's men, along the fence reinforcing Knowlton.

As matters stood when Howe had finally gathered his forces, the American position consisted of three independent and absolutely un-coordinated groupings. They were, from right to left, the original Charlestown detachment, scattered now behind a barn and a road-way back of the blazing village; Prescott's force manning the redoubt and its extending breastwork; and Stark's and Knowlton's men, eche-loned behind it along the rail fence and the beach barricade. One of the two field guns originally brought up was emplaced at the rail

fence, the other was probably at the redoubt; their positions of no
real moment, since the artillerymen had promptly deserted them.

The American strength can only be approximated. Certainly no
more than 500 of Prescott's original 1,200-man task force remained
at the redoubt position long enough to trade shots with the British.
Adding to them Stark's and Reed's New Hampshiremen and the
handful of brave souls like Dr. Joseph Warren and old General Seth
Pomeroy who joined the force as individual volunteers, and some
others who took part in the last stage of the battle, an educated guess
would be somewhat less than 1,500 men in all.

Against these positions Howe now deployed some 2,000 men. The
main effort, under his personal command, was drawn up on Moulton's
Hill in three lines: eleven companies of light infantry in the first,
eleven of grenadiers in the second, and the 5th and 52nd regiments
of Foot in the third line. Pigot, who would command a secondary
effort on his left, had three companies each of light infantry and
grenadiers, the 38th, 43rd and 47th Foot, and the 1st (Pitcairn's)
Royal Marine battalion.

Howe now apparently briefly considered sending an assault force
to land behind the American positions, but this idea was abandoned
because of the ebbing tide. His revised plan was to send the light
infantry along the river bank to deliver a bayonet attack. It would
turn the rebel left and roll it back into the arms of the main body's
frontal attack. His guns—six or eight in number; the records differ—
on his own left, would support the movement up the hill. So the light
infantry filed off to their right, advancing in column, hugging the
shoreline. The other two lines, the grenadiers leading, burdened by
their packs in the blazing sun, moved slowly up towards the rail fence
through the tall grass, dressing their ranks as they came on unsuspected
obstacles—two swampish ponds, the ruins of a brick kiln, grass-
shielded rocks and pot-holes.

The British guns barked viciously several times, then stopped. Some
idiot, it seemed, had sent twelve-pound shot for six-pounder guns. So
much for that, until more ammunition could be furnished from Boston. The redcoats sifted through the meadow, looming larger every
step to the waiting men at the fence. Over to the left, Pigot's men
were also pressing upward, towards the redoubt.

Somehow, Stark at the rail fence, Prescott in the earthworks, and

Putnam—the omnipresent Putnam—managed to keep the trigger-happy farmers in restraint. Someone—Putnam gets the credit—coined the slogan: "Don't fire till you see the whites of their eyes!"

Even when the British got within musket-range the American line was quiet. Once and then again the grenadiers and the line regiments halted to fire, their bullets splattering harmlessly on or below the earthworks. Still the Americans held fire.

Then came the blast of a fusillade down by the Mystic. The light infantry had closed with Stark's stone barricade. At less than fifty yards range the New Hampshire muskets flamed, tearing apart the leading company in the column. The next, and then the next, pushing through, melted, as historian Christopher Ward puts it, "like a wax candle against a hot plate," as Stark's men kept up their fire. The surviving British turned and ran.

The frontal attack pushed on. And then the rail fence, too, blazed. The Grenadiers staggered, halted; the second line, barging through them, met another blast. Milling in confusion for a few moments, the British lines fell back beyond musket range. Behind them, redcoats strewed the tall grass; every officer on Howe's personal staff was down; either killed or wounded. They were no riflemen, these New Englanders; the rifle was unknown in that region. But they had been brought up from childhood with firearms, taught to make every shot of musket and fowling piece count. At less than 30 yards they couldn't miss.

Over on the British left, Pigot, probing the redoubt, got the same answer. His men, too, recoiled down the hill out of range. The first round was over. But Howe and Pigot rallied their men, re-formed their lines and again moved up the slope, while Prescott, whose redoubt and breastwork defenders had shrunk now to about 150 men, praised the remainder and exhorted them to stand. Putnam, galloping back to Bunker's Hill, vainly urged the crowd of idlers on the crest to reinforce the line.

This time the British converged on the redoubt and its breastwork, while the light infantry merely demonstrated in front of Stark's deadly rail fence and stone barricade.

Once more the American fire, held until the redcoated assault came close, poured point-blank destruction on it. Sweating Putnam, cursing and raving at the skulkers still melting from the defense, manhandled an abandoned cannon himself, spooning powder into its muzzle because the cartridges were too large.

For the second time the British attack went reeling down the hill beyond musket range. Howe, ignoring the deadly fire in a remarkable personal demonstration of leadership and discipline, gathered his survivors once again. They had lost almost 50 per cent casualties. In some companies but a half-dozen men remained of the 30-odd each who had entered the fight. But the survivors shuffled once more into ranks, dropped packs on order, and fixed bayonet.

Bolstered by 400 additional troops rushed over by Gage—the 63rd Foot, another battalion of Marines and a dismounted detachment of the 17th Light Dragoons—Howe made his final bid. He led his own force against the breastwork, while Pigot made for the western corner of the redoubt. General Clinton, who came over without orders to join the fight as a volunteer, accompanied Pigot. It would be cold steel this time, and in column instead of line.

For the third time the American fire shivered the leading files. But the columns kept coming, while the British artillery—once again in action—raked the breastwork. With Pigot leading, the left column reached the redoubt ditch, crossed it, and climbed the parapet. The marines took the major loss this time; Pitcairn, of Lexington fame, being among the fallen. As the red tide lapped the wall, the American fire died away. Their powder horns empty, the defenders clubbed their muskets or threw stones.

It was the end. Some thirty Americans went down under British bayonets. Prescott, fighting in the midst, ordered a retreat, and the survivors crowded through the rear gateway while the British, coming around the fort now on both sides, held fire in the melée lest they hit one another.

From redoubt and breastwork the fugitives flowed in a mob across the ridge and over Bunker's Hill, while the idlers fled in front of them. There was some sporadic hedge-fighting as the Charlestown flanking group and a few fresh fragments coaxed from the Bunker's Hill spectators exchanged fire with the exhausted victors. The rail fence garrison —Knowlton's and Stark's men—who had permitted the British to skirt their position, withdrew in good order, carrying their wounded, dragging their one field gun with them.

There was no pursuit. Howe was well content to hold and establish a strong point on Bunker's Hill, while the Americans, once safe on the heights beyond the Neck, began to dig in, under Putnam's energetic direction.

American casualties were approximately 140 killed—including Dr. Warren—270 wounded, and 30 taken prisoner. No accurate accounting exists. Most of the losses had been incurred during the retreat. But the British had lost 226 killed and 828 wounded—a shocking total of 1,054 men out of some 2,400 men engaged. Of these, 89 were officers (19 killed and 70 wounded), shining marks in their white cross-belts, gold lace and glittering gorgets. This, as Burgoyne later remarked, was a loss "uncommon among the officers, considering the number engaged."

In cold analysis, the Bunker Hill battle consisted of the stand of a few devoted marksmen behind improvised fieldworks until their ammunition was exhausted. There was no over-all leadership and co-ordination on the American side. Prescott, Stark and Knowlton emerge as efficient, great-hearted leaders of small units fighting independently of one another. Ward, at Cambridge, influenced the combat in no way other than by a half-hearted reinforcement which he either would not or could not control. Pugnacious Putnam was a doughty whipper-in, but his frenzied efforts were of no avail over an undisciplined mob paralyzed by the impact of battle and governed only by the instinct of self-preservation. The real mystery is that so much was accomplished by so few.

On the British side, the decision to assault was wrong; Clinton's recommendation to cut off Charlestown Neck and isolate the force on Breed's Hill would have been both better and more economical in life. But once committed on the field, the leadership displayed by Howe and his junior officers, and the response of the disciplined soldiers they led, were both magnificent.

Tactically a British victory, this two-hour span of desperate conflict—forever to be incorrectly labelled the Battle of Bunker Hill—decided nothing strategically. When it was over the British were still besieged in Boston, the Americans still incapable of driving them out.

But psychologically, this battle—fought at the wrong time and in the wrong place—was a spark igniting American will to win throughout the Thirteen Colonies. American farmers, a rabble in arms, had held and thrown back more than their own number of the best regular infantry in the world. A legend had been created: through some miraculous gift of the Almighty the American amateur soldier was superior to the British regular; patriotic valor or ignorance outbalanced discipline and training. No need here to expatiate upon the cost to the United States of this fallacious reasoning throughout our later national existence. The vital thing then, as both sides licked their wounds, was that a tremendous fillip had been given the patriot cause; a psychological kick. A flame had been kindled. And up from Philadelphia was coming a peerless leader who, as it turned out, would nurture that flicker through long, weary years until it blossomed into freedom's torch.

5 ★ ★ ★ ★ ★ ★

Rebellion Becomes War

THE CAPTURE OF FORT TICONDEROGA, the Battle of Bunker Hill, and the transformation of the rebel forces ringing Boston into a Continental Army, crystallized the situation in America along military lines. At least for the moment, it no longer mattered whether, as the liberals among the rebels argued, this was a conflict to redress violations of the rights of free Englishmen; or if, as the extremists demanded, it was a struggle for complete independence. The Thirteen Colonies were at war with the mother country, and the conflict could only be composed by force of arms.

But between the adversaries stretched the broad Atlantic.

On the face of it, all the odds favored England. A compact nation of about 8,000,000 people, her small but efficient professional army was supported by the most powerful navy in the world—and her centralized government opposed an aggregation of colonial settlements whose 2,000,000 people were scattered along a littoral of more than 1,000 miles, lacking a navy, boasting but a rabble of disorganized militiamen, and incapable—except through mutual good will—of exercising any united cooperative effort.

Analysis of the respective military problems posed would show something else again. That of the Colonies was one of defense; hopefully to maintain themselves until England gave up the struggle. The British problem was one of offense. As a matter of fact, England in 1775 faced a situation comparable in principle to that which the United States itself would later face in 1861: the rebellion could be put down and governmental rule restored only by the occupation of hostile territory and the destruction of hostile forces. This necessitated overseas operations of considerable magnitude.

The Colonies comprised a thinly populated coastal belt stretching from Nova Scotia and Quebec's St. Lawrence estuary all the way to the border of British Florida.* Its western boundary brushed the Appalachian highlands. Roads being few and almost rudimentary, water-borne communications were essential between the various colonies. The Eastern seaboard was dotted with coastal ports, the largest being Boston, New York, Philadelphia, Charleston, S.C., and Savannah, Ga. British possession of Boston had already sealed that water gate.

Inland, of course, were rich agricultural areas relatively inaccessible from the sea; the most important lying in the Hudson, Delaware and Susquehanna valleys of New York, New Jersey, Pennsylvania and Maryland, and the extensive farmlands of Virginia. This agricultural spread was capable of sustaining most of the needs of both the civilian population and its fighting forces.

West of the Appalachians and east of the Mississippi, from the Great Lakes down again to Florida, lay a broad, debatable land, much of it nominally—following the controversial Quebec Act of 1774— part of the Province of Quebec, but mostly claimed by the several American colonies.

As for land communications, the one main artery ran from Portland, Me. to St. Augustine, Fla., a tenuous coastal chain of public and post roads linking the seaboard communities. Another post road of sorts linked Montreal with New York, through the Champlain-Hudson valley; and in populous New England, a New Haven-Springfield-Boston interior loop existed. Lateral roads were few and poor; the rivers carried the bulk of the east-west traffic.

The Thirteen Colonies, then, presented to England an accessible eastern seaboard cordon, whose northern flank from the Great Lakes to the St. Lawrence also was vulnerable to invasion from Canada.

Sea power, then, would be the decisive factor in the struggle; that abundant sea power of England. It would enable the transportation and maintenance of armies in the coastal belt, and their transfer

---

* The former Spanish possession of Florida had been ceded to Britain under the Treaty of 1763 ending the Seven Years War. It was to revert to Spain under the Treaty of 1783 ending the Revolution.

north or south as dictated by the situation. Its influence reached beyond that, for so long as England held the seas she was free also to establish bases up the St. Lawrence—500 miles and more from the open sea—for operations on the flank and rear of the rebellious colonies. Exercise of British sea power bade fair also to stop or at least impede American intercourse with Europe and with the West Indies; intercourse vital to the logistical necessities of the rebels.

It would be the irony of fate, as we shall later see, that when this British power to control the Atlantic was interrupted for but one transitory period, England lost the war.

Two factors hampered England's prosecution of the conflict. In the first place, the war was not popular at home. The stupid actions of the King and his cabinet, and of the Parliament, cut across British commercial interests whose livelihood had been seriously impaired by the breakdown of trade with the Colonies. Politically, the Whigs —with Pitt (Earl of Chatham), Edmund Burke and Charles James Fox in the forefront—made clear their sympathy with the colonists as Englishmen entitled to all the rights of British subjects.

In the second place, the direction of the war lay with two individuals most unsuited to the task. The Prime Minister, Lord Frederick North, Earl of Guilford, while a brilliant man, was completely dominated by the stubborn king. And Lord George Germain, Secretary of State for the Colonies in North's cabinet, pampered pet of the king, who to all intents and purposes directed the military operations, was a shocking misfit. Germain, as Lord George Sackville, had been cashiered from the British Army for his disobedience and craven refusal to charge with his cavalry at the Battle of Minden in 1758; adjudged by court martial to be "unfit to serve his Majesty in any military capacity whatever." Restored to favor by the erratic George III, Germain was despised by the majority of British professional military men.

What of the colonies' power to make war? It must be remembered that despite the innate American hatred of standing armies, the colonists had found themselves from the very beginnings of settlement forced to take up arms; first against the Indians, and later against the French and the Spanish.

It was only natural that the colonists would adopt the English militia system: the train band and its militia successors—part-time warriors all. In each English county all able-bodied men were enrolled for home defense, coming under the control of the lord lieutenant of the county. In emergency, these train bands could be mustered for service within the national territory. In America the same system was followed, except that there was no "national territory"; just a group of separate colonies.

The first recorded American train band was that of the Pilgrims, who in 1620 hired Captain Myles Standish, professional soldier, "to organize a train band" for defense. By 1636 a number of Massachusetts train bands were incorporated in the North Regiment, later the Regiment of Middlesex. By 1662 a second regiment, the Hampshire, came into existence.

Down in Virginia the first grouping of the county train bands came in 1652, when the Charles City-Henrico Counties Regiment of Militia came into existence. By 1672 Connecticut produced the Regiments of Hartford and of New Haven Counties.

They went to war when they had to, these farmers, woodsmen and tradesmen; frequently grudgingly, or at best in the spirit of accomplishing an unwelcome chore and then going back home to work. When militia levies of several colonies were gathered for a momentary military undertaking, bickering about command status was common. Not only did individuals resist being put under command of officers from colonies other than their own, but the respective colonial governments, jealous of their rights, sided actively with the malcontents.

Successive generations of colonists had learned about war the hard way—through experience. But, after each crisis was over, the martial spirit would fade; the colonial levies were disbanded, and their veterans were scattered and submerged in the conglomeration of separate militias whose continued existence was sketchy, whose discipline was non-existent, and whose training for the most part consisted of an annual muster—a one-day combination of barbecue roast and whiskey-guzzling.

This, then, was the raw material from which came the troops now ringing Boston—individualistic amateurs hurriedly enlisted for short periods of time (most enlistments expiring on December 31, 1775) to replace the long-departed minutemen who had started the conflict. They numbered 16,770 men when Washington assumed command on Cambridge Common on July 3. But the returns of the first muster

—which took a week to compile—also showed that 1,592 of them were absent (which meant they had gone home), and 1,598 others were sick. To this force the Congress would soon add the first purely Continental troops—ten companies of expert riflemen, six from Pennsylvania, and two each from Maryland and Virginia. These frontiersmen sharp-shooters, enlisted for one year's service, thus became the nucleus of the Continental Army.

The Congress appointed a committee of its members to compose regulations for this army; by June 30 articles of war had been drawn up and approved—rules and regulations sorely needed.

"I found a mixed multitude of People here, under very little discipline [or] order of government. . . . Confusion and disorder reigned in every Department."

Such was Washington's comment after his initial inspection. As he put it, the soldiers "regarded their officers no more than broomsticks."

Why should they? "The natural liberty of man," Samuel Adams had told them in his rabble-rousing oratory, "is to be free from any superior power on earth, and not to be under the will or legislative authority of man, but only to a law of nature for his rule." Later, when Washington was struggling with the problems of discipline and of re-enlistment of these short-term volunteers his pungent remark sheds further light:

"Such a dirty, mercenary spirit pervades the whole, that I should not be surprised at any disaster that may happen."

But there was a leaven of sorts latent in this uneasy mass, too. There were such men as Henry Knox, Boston bookseller who had learned about artillery in that city's militia and in voracious reading of his own books. As we have seen, John Stark had learned about war in Rogers' Rangers. There were five former British regular officers: Charles Lee, respected veteran of Seven Years War campaigns both in America and in Portugal; Horatio Gates, who had been in the Braddock campaign and later a major in the Royal American Regiment; William Alexander (better known as Lord Stirling) *;

---

* A native of New York City, he had gone to England in 1760 to claim succession to the Scottish earldom of Stirling. Although his claim was disallowed by the House of Lords, he was generally considered in America as a nobleman.

and Richard Montgomery, who had been on the second Louisbourg expedition. Pre-eminent among those with militia combat experience was Daniel Morgan, backwoods rifleman, another Braddock veteran. There was Israel Putnam, battle-wise militia fighter from two conflicts —the French and Indian War and Pontiac's Insurrection. There were also such natural leaders as "Mad Anthony" Wayne, Benedict Arnold, and "Light Horse Harry" Lee; men whose sole aim in battle was to close with and destroy the enemy. And there was Nathanael Greene, the volunteer militiaman from Rhode Island, who had learned about war from books and, as it turned out, would prove himself an apt student. Others, too, with military background would turn up as the war went on.

So, when the "embattled farmers" began swarming like angry bees about English-held Boston, there was available in the colonies a certain proportion of men with military experience. Of the thirteen general officers the Continental Congress appointed, all but two had seen war service, and eight of them in the grade of lieutenant colonel or higher. Taken as a whole, however, the available personnel lacked organization, discipline and training, and above all lacked experienced company officers and non-commissioned officers.

Two things most of these men did share: a military concept stemming from a civilian matrix as English as John Bull himself, and a basic obstinacy capable of martial development through extraordinary leadership.

This leadership was furnished by George Washington. It was a leadership all the more remarkable in that it was exercised over a militant minority; for the population of the Thirteen Colonies was divided three ways: more than a third of them vehemently supported the cause of liberty, almost another third was loyal to King George; the remainder consisted of trimmers—those whose one objective was to be safely on the winning side.

It would be hard to better the words of Henry Belcher, British historian, concerning Washington:

"One of those men whom one may without irreverence call divine, the instrument of a divine purpose chosen to lay stronger and better foundations than he knew."

From the economic standpoint, the war needs of the colonies were entirely inadequate. Cannon available were left-overs from the colonial wars, and what had been captured or stolen from English posts (including the guns at Ticonderoga, as yet untransportable). There was no iron industry as such in the colonies, although a number of small foundries existed in the ore-fields sprinkled through the mountains of Pennsylvania and New York. Nor was the small-arms situation much better. Although, as might be expected, the supply was sufficient for peacetime use—and gunmaking was not an uncommon profession—muskets, flints, gunpowder and lead were badly needed. As for manufactured goods, they were already insufficient for normal peacetime needs.

As we have seen, these shortages had engaged the attention of the Massachusetts provincial legislature, the Continental Congress and the various Committees of Safety. Local resources were surveyed and stimulated. But the crying need could be satisfied in only one way: by importation. Already, smart operators in the well-established and organized smuggling trade were exploring what would turn into a thriving traffic between the West Indies and America, and their agents abroad were sounding out adventurous merchants in France and Holland. On July 15 the Congress authorized American vessels to carry munitions, "the non-exportation agreement notwithstanding," thus permitting free resumption of trade. And, having neither money nor power to tax, it proposed the issuance of bills of credit upon a penniless institution—the United Colonies of America—a pretty shaky financial foundation.

Meanwhile a curious web of Franco-Spanish intrigue was slowly spinning overseas. Both nations, nominally at peace with England, were licking the wounds inflicted on them by the Seven Years War. France was hoping for redress for the loss of her North American empire. Spain, though fearful lest this commotion in the British colonies might jeopardize her possessions, had never forgotten her own ulcer—that English-held stronghold of Gibraltar on the tip of the Iberian Peninsula.

French diplomacy started it. As early as 1768 one Johann Kalb, a German officer in French service—we would know him later over here as Baron de Kalb, a doughty leader in the Continental Army— had been sent to America by France's Minister of Foreign Affairs, Étienne François, Duc de Choiseul, as a secret agent to inquire into the feelings of the colonists towards England.

Kalb's report, particularly upon the American militia system, was perhaps too optimistic, but in any event it convinced Choiseul that should a break come, England would be hard put to maintain herself in America; ergo, France might do well to assist in fomenting revolt. Choiseul's successor, Comte de Vergennes, bore this in mind when he assumed office in 1774. Next year, one Pierre Augustin Caron de Beaumarchais, brilliant French dramatist and—*sub rosa*—secret agent of Louis XVI, entered the scene. Beaumarchais, in London, after hobnobbing with Arthur Lee of Massachusetts, one of the two American agents then abroad (Benjamin Franklin of Pennsylvania was the other), hurried back to Paris in September, 1775, to urge on the King, through Vergennes, the importance to France of establishing an understanding with the rebellious colonists. The American crisis, he reported, might well overthrow the North ministry and even bring civil war to England.

Beaumarchais returned to London, equipped with plenty of secret service money, to explore the matter more thoroughly. Meanwhile Vergennes had sent another shadowy individual, one Archard de Bonvouloir, to America with oral instructions to assure the colonial leaders of France's warm feeling for them. Incidentally, Bonvouloir was also to impress on them that France had no desire to regain her Canadian empire. All this he was to do without any formal commitment of the French ministry. Bonvouloir arrived in Philadelphia in September. His report—which did not reach Paris until February, 1776—informed the French government that the colonists would fight for independence, and told of the hopes he had aroused in their leaders to expect shelter for their trade in French ports. It was about this same time that Beaumarchais, again back in Paris, was urging a somewhat reluctant Louis XVI to assist the Americans with munitions and money, but secretly, so as not to compromise France officially.

It is significant that on November 29, 1775, two months after Bonvouloir's arrival in America, the Congress established a secret committee "for the sole purpose of corresponding with our friends in Great Britain, Ireland and other parts of the world." On it originally were Benjamin Franklin (now returned to America) and John Dickinson of Pennsylvania; John Jay of New York, and Thomas Johnson of Delaware. This Committee on Secret Correspondence—forerunner of a State Department—began operations on December 12, by directing Arthur Lee in London to reconnoiter the dispositions of foreign powers towards the colonies. Franklin, at the same time, wrote an old friend at the Hague, one Charles William Frederick Dumas, to sound out the "disposition of the several [European] courts with respect to assistance or alliance." The brew of diplomatic intrigue was fermenting. It would, as it turned out, taste well to American palates.

Before further exploration of the diplomatic front, however, we must return to New England, and the launching of an amazing but ill-starred campaign for the possession of Canada.

6

★ ★ ★ ★ ★ ★

On to Quebec!

CANADA DANGLED FROM THE VERY BEGINNING before the eyes of the insurgent colonist leaders; a most attractive lure. A Canadian alliance to the Thirteen Colonies, either by sympathetic union or through conquest, would solve the military problem presented by that menacing northern flank, would remove the threat of hostile Indian depredations, and would check the spread of Catholic Church influence reestablished by the Quebec Act of 1774. This last motivation was important. The First Continental Congress, in its appeal to England of October 21, 1774, had cited as one of its grievances the reestablishment in Canada of "a religion fraught with sanguinary and impious tenets . . . a religion that has deluged your island in blood and dispersed impiety, bigotry, persecution, murder and rebellion through every part of the world."

Overtures to the "oppressed inhabitants of Canada" were made in May, 1775, by the Second Continental Congress. They might have had some effect, for at the moment Canada was churning in unrest, split into three parties, mutually incompatible. The French *seigneurs* —the landed proprietors—despised the hard-working *habitant* tenant farmers who were strongly influenced by the Catholic clergy. The "Old Subjects"—of British origin, mostly fur-traders in Montreal, and a most unruly class—quarrelled with both the others. The cleavages were deep, but the French-Catholic *habitants* formed the great majority of the population. Thus the anti-clerical fulminations of the First Continental Congress nullified the later overtures of the Second.

However, the two men who had attempted the first invasion after taking Ticonderoga—Benedict Arnold and Ethan Allen—were still of the opinion that Canada could be conquered if not coaxed, and their recommendations went far. The Congress, on June 27, 1775, directed Major General Philip Schuyler to proceed to Ticonderoga and Crown Point and, if he found it practicable "and . . . not disagreeable to the Canadians . . . immediately take possession of St. Johns, Montreal and any other parts of the country."

Schuyler, a Hudson Valley patrician with a smattering of past military experience in the French and Indian War, had been detailed by General Washington to command the New York Department, consisting mainly of the Champlain region posts: Ticonderoga with 600 men, Crown Point with 400 and Fort George with 300 more. The forts were dilapidated, their wretched garrisons undisciplined, and ill-fed. Colonel Benjamin Hinman's Connecticut regiment, which had taken over Ticonderoga after its capture, made up the majority, with a few additional Massachusetts and New York troops, and a sprinkling of Allen's original Green Mountain Boys. Hinman was inefficient, his troops insubordinate. Schuyler indeed had a job on his hands.

Schuyler did three things: he began building a fleet of bateaux on Lake Champlain; he kept up incessant appeals for reinforcements; and—perhaps most important—he sent a small reconnaissance party north. Its leader, one Major John Brown, scout and gentleman adventurer, brought back glowing news. The Canadians would not oppose an American advance; there were few British troops. "Now, sir, is the time to carry Canada."

But Schuyler was not ready; supplies came in driblets, reinforcements in handfuls—from New York and from Connecticut—all bickering among themselves for preference in command and position. Schuyler went to Albany to attend a conference and council fire of Indian chiefs, leaving his second-in-command, Brigadier General Richard Montgomery, in control at Ticonderoga.

Irish-born Montgomery, 39 years old, and seasoned soldier with sixteen years of campaigning in the British Army behind him, was a man of action. He had left the army in 1772, settled in New York, married a New York girl and then threw himself into the cause of freedom. Now he received word from that indefatigable scout Brown that British strength was mobilizing at St. Johns, including two almost completed twelve-gun sloops capable of sweeping the lake. Informing

Schuyler of his intention, Montgomery moved down the lake with some 1,200 men in a flotilla consisting of a schooner, a sloop and an assortment of gondolas, row-galleys and bateaux. His objective was to block British entry from St. Johns into Lake Champlain at Ile aux Noix, and to prepare for the capture of St. Johns. Schuyler hurried back to join him.

British Lieutenant General Sir Guy Carleton, Governor-General of Canada, was not only a far-sighted, just and kindly administrator but also a capable and determined military leader. But he had only two regiments of regular infantry: the 7th (Royal Fusiliers) and 26th (Cameronians) Foot. These, with a detachment of artillerymen, totalled approximately 700 men. In addition, he had a small force of provincials: Colonel Allan Maclean's Royal Highland Emigrants (a company-strength provincial aggregation of Scottish ex-regulars settled in Canada), plus about 100 additional Canadian volunteers. So far, most of his efforts to enlist Canadians for defense had been unavailing.

After the first American threat of invasion, Carleton had to decide whether to abandon the frontier and concentrate in defense of Montreal—which the Canadians and the Indians would interpret as an admission of weakness and fear—or to dispute further invasion by an offensive-defensive stand based on the most favorable point; in this case, St. Johns.

His decision was to do the latter. So the post of St. Johns had been strengthened into a tidy little complex of redoubts ringed by an outer barricade consisting of a moated stockade on the three land sides. The river itself moated the fourth flank. Cannon mounted on the redoubts covered the approaches. Carleton put in a garrison of 500 of his regulars and 200-odd provincials under a Major Preston, and gathered outside of it a screening force of Indian warriors under Tory leadership. His two armed schooners and several bateaux, also mounting light artillery, constituted an additional amphibious threat.

A tentative American effort to land north of the fort ended after a brush with the Indians and an exaggerated report of British strength caused Schuyler to call a council of war. It was decided to fall back on Ile aux Noix without further ado! This timorous move, hailed at Montreal as a British victory, effectively squelched any mass Canadian interest in joining Schuyler, who settled himself down on Ile aux

Noix, threw a boom across the river, and began to erect fortifications to resist British assault. However, when the ordered reinforcements arrived from Ticonderoga—300 Connecticut and 400 New York troops—Schuyler made two successive attempts to bypass the fort and cut its communications with Montreal. Both failed; the Americans each time panicked in the darkness.

Schuyler, seriously ill, was evacuated September 16. That same day, too, additional reinforcements came into the sulky, insubordinate encampment. These were men of sterner stuff: Seth Warner and the Green Mountain Boys, now a battalion "in the service of the United States"; John Lamb's Independent Company of New York Artillery; and some New Hampshiremen—400 in all. Montgomery, who had re-assumed command, now had a good 2,000 men. Slowly the investment of St. Johns began, despite bickering and insubordination in the American camp.

Capture of a British supply train brought joy to the besiegers. Detachments probed towards Montreal. One of these was commanded by Ethan Allen, whose status at the time is worth noting. He and Warner had successfully petitioned Congress to enroll the Green Mountain Boys as a Continental unit, but the men then elected Warner as their leader instead of Allen. So the rambunctious Ethan had turned up in Schuyler's command as an individual volunteer, accepted after making "a solemn promise . . . to demean himself properly."

Allen's detachment fell in with another party under John Brown. The two hotheads, whose combined forces totalled less than 300 men, decided to rush defenseless Montreal in a surprise coup, Allen approaching from below, Brown from above the town. On the night of October 24 Allen got a portion of his men across the St. Lawrence and waited vainly for a signal from Brown. Brown never got there, and at dawn a Canadian volunteer force bagged Allen and his 40 men, a rather serious blow to American prestige.

Meanwhile the siege of St. Johns went on in a nightmare atmosphere of intercolonial jealousy and worsening climatic conditions. Then three separate incidents decided the affair.

Montgomery got two armed bateaux past the fort in an audacious night run-by. He then attacked a Canadian post at Chambly, down river, capturing its garrison of 88 officers and men of the Royal Fusiliers, plus a wonderful windfall of provisions, cannon, muskets and powder. St. Johns was now cut off from Montreal. Next, American gunfire blasted the two Canadian gunboats at St. Johns and sank them. Finally, a British rescue force of 800 men, led by Allan Maclean, found the Green Mountain Boys and the 2nd New York waiting for them as they tried to cross the St. Lawrence from Montreal to Longueuil. Repulse of the relief force was a death-knell to St. Johns. On November 2, with only three days rations left, Preston capitulated after a siege of 55 days. Among the officers of the Royal Fusiliers paroled that day was one Captain John André.

Montreal now lay defenseless. Carleton had left little more than one company of regulars and some inefficient militia. Montgomery, putting both pressure and cajolery on his Connecticut troops, whose time was nearly up and who wanted no more of war, got his column under way on November 5. By the 11th, in snow, rain and mud, they reached the St. Lawrence. Crossing, they drew up in front of Montreal's paper-thin walls. Carleton, with his tiny force and some military stores, dropped down river by boat under American gunfire. Montreal was delivered up by its citizens two days later.

But Carleton's ordeal was not yet over. Adverse winds checked his little flotilla at Sorel. The ubiquitous John Brown boarded, demanded and received surrender. Carleton, wrapped in a cloak disguising his uniform, slipped away in a small boat, Quebec-bound, leaving all his remaining forces in American hands.

Richard Montgomery had done well. While his soldiers relaxed in warm quarters, revelling in good food and new uniforms—courtesy of His Majesty's 7th and 26th Regiments of Foot, whose winter stocks had been bagged—Montgomery turned his eyes towards Quebec.

There something remarkable had just happened, as a nineteen-year-old courier, disguised in the soutaine of a Catholic priest, informed Montgomery. The messenger's name was Aaron Burr, and he came from Colonel Benedict Arnold, who was just now on the Plains of Abraham, confronting the stronghold of Quebec.

Arnold had reached Quebec after one of the great military marches in history, deserving rank beside Xenophon's Anabasis and Hannibal's Alpine crossing. As Britain's General Clinton later remarked, the exploit, "for the boldness of the undertaking and the fortitude and perseverance with which the hardships and great difficulties of it were surmounted, will ever rank high among military exploits."

The plan, as Washington wrote to Schuyler on August 20, 1775, was a hazardous move through the Maine wilderness; up the Kennebec River and adjacent waterways to the watershed, then down the Chaudière River to the St. Lawrence, opposite Quebec. Traditionally, this was an Indian route of long usage, had been considered as a possible invasion route during the French and Indian War, and even been mapped, with shocking disregard for fact—as Arnold and his men would find out the hard way.

Benedict Arnold—still ardently bent on invading Canada, and then in Cambridge to settle his affairs with the Massachusetts Provincial Congress after throwing up his command and commission at Ticonderoga—was the logical man to command such an expedition. Washington commissioned him a colonel in the Continental forces, and turned over to him a force supposedly handpicked for the task. There were two battalions of five companies each, volunteers from New England troops—"active Woodsmen . . . well-acquainted with batteaus." And there were three companies—picked by lot—of Continental riflemen: Daniel Morgan's from Virginia and Matthew Smith's and William Hendricks' of the Pennsylvania contingent.

They were an obstreperous, quarrelsome bunch, these riflemen, particularly Morgan's Virginians, who had kept the American camp in turmoil ever since their arrival. They had come north to fight, but after the first few days, when the British had learned to take cover from their amazing ability to pick off redcoats at twice the range of the military musket, they had had little to do. So they worked off their surplus energy by drinking New England rum, flirting with New England girls and quarreling with New England men. One presumes that Washington was only too glad to get some of them off his hands on detached service.

On September 6, Arnold's force paraded on Cambridge Common. The New England battalions were commanded by Lieutenant Colonels Roger Enos of Connecticut and Christopher Greene of Rhode Island; the rifle corps by Captain Morgan. Including a handful of unattached volunteers, they mustered 1,051 officers and men. Among the volunteers was Aaron Burr.

There was a bit of a boggle at the muster, for the New Englanders refused to march until they got a month's pay. That apparently was adjusted, for on September 13, they moved out by sea for Newbury-

port, whither the rifle corps had preceeded them by 48 hours. A fleet
of eleven sloops and schooners brought them to the Kennebec, and by
the 22nd they disembarked at Gardinerstown (now Pittston).

There, one Reuben Colburn, Kennebec boatbuilder, who had been
given a rush contract to build 200 light, flat-bottomed Kennebec
bateaux, turned over the flotilla. Part of Colburn's agreement was
to reconnoiter the route, arrange for supplies, and accompany the
expedition with 20 "Artificers, Carpenters and Guides," but he appears to have been somewhat vague about conditions along the way.
Many Indians in British pay had been reported and British scouts
had been noted, but the way was marked by blazed trees, and the
portages were "pretty passible."

On September 24, Arnold's command moved into the wilderness
from Fort Western (site of Augusta). Two reconnaissance patrols of
seven men each in canoes led the way. Then came the rifle corps,
moving by bateaux and along the banks, to clear the route. The main
force followed, in three more divisions. Provisions for 45 days—
Arnold's estimate of the time it would take to reach Quebec—were
packed in the boats. Arnold himself, in a fast canoe, shepherded the
procession, incessantly moving between head and tail.

What followed was a nightmare of frustration and privation; a
struggle of man against primitive forces. The advance was baffled by
a succession of rapids and falls, through or around which boats had
to be dragged or carried—"portaging" was the term. The boats, hastily
constructed of green wood, soon began to leak as they scraped over
rocks and bumped into obstacles.

Each portage—and they were innumerable—brought further damage. What was a comparatively easy task with a featherweight birch-
bark canoe proved to be something quite different with a 400-pound
wooden boat. Yet all of these had to be manhandled, as did every
ounce of the 65 tons of provisions, ammunition and other supplies
with which they started. The whirling, tumultuous Kennebec was
bucked at Skowhegan Falls—a fearsome chute through which the
boats had to be dragged, for the rocky banks prohibited landing and
portaging.

By October 6 the expedition had penetrated only to Norridgewock
Falls, where three days were consumed in refitting. Much of the provisions had now been spoiled by water; the troops went on a ration

of salt pork and flour. On October 11, the head of the column reached the first really tremendous portage—the so-called Great Carrying Place, where boats and supplies went on men's shoulders over a long trail between the Kennebec and the Dead Rivers; through bogs and over rocky ledges, while the first snow squalls of the year screamed down from Mount Bigelow's scarps.

Here the food problem became really serious. A driving storm brought the swift-flowing Dead River to flood stage, drowning out campsites and sweeping away the last of their precious pork-barrels. A log hut, hurriedly erected back at the Great Carrying Place, soon filled up with sick and worn-out men. But Arnold, shuttling incessantly from head to tail of the march, had so far whipped most officers and men into unwavering determination.

But now, it seemed, the end was coming. Arnold, with a small detachment, hurried on into the Chaudière Valley, hoping to obtain food from the Canadian settlements there. Behind him, Enos and his officers voted on October 25 to abandon the expedition, and despite the protests of the other commanders, he and his battalion started back, leaving behind them a mere two barrels of flour.*

Morgan's riflemen and Greene's battalion stumbled on. They crossed the watershed, plodding through snow; they wandered along deceptive streams, searching for Lake Megantic; and they chewed raw hide when the last of the pork and flour failed. "No one," later wrote one participant, "can imagine, who has not experienced it, the sweetness of a roasted shot-pouch to the famished appetite."

They got to Lake Megantic and the swift-running Chaudière, where the last of the bateaux were smashed in a treacherous rapid. It was now November 2. The reeling column stretched back for 20 miles along the Chaudière. Then its leading files caught sight of movement ahead; movement which developed, miraculously, it seemed, into a small herd of cattle, driven by Canadians. Arnold had found *habitants* both hospitable and amenable to the specie he carried with him. Up the river behind them came more Canadians in canoes, with mutton, potatoes, meal and tobacco. Starving soldiers gorged on hurriedly slaughtered beef, then spurred themselves to cover the remaining 60 miles.

---

* Court martialed after his safe return to Cambridge, Enos was acquitted of desertion, but soon left the Army under a cloud of popular contempt.

It was snowing; it was cold; but they cared not, now. On November 9 they reached the St. Lawrence at Point Levis, opposite Quebec. It seemed, at first, that their travail had gone for nothing, for Carleton had swept the right bank clean of boats, and in the broad river, below the frowning cliffs of Quebec, lay a frigate and a sloop of war, whose boats kept up constant patrol.

But hustling American search parties gathered up canoes, scouring the country for 25 miles around during the next four days. Thirty or more craft—birch-bark and dug-out—were obtained. In this ram-shackle flotilla Arnold ferried more than half his men across during darkness, after a squall of wind and rain had blown itself out. By morning of November 14, they were safely ensconced on the Plains of Abraham, where the remainder of the force joined them next night. Barely 600 emaciated scarecrows had survived the 350-mile trek through the wilderness.

Carleton had of course discovered the American move, and his patrol boats had exchanged shots with the invaders. But his dependable force was so small—less than 70 British regulars and some 300 marines and bluejackets—that he feared to make a sortie. Arnold, for his part, had no cannon, more than 100 of his small arms were unserviceable, and there were but five rounds of ammunition apiece for the remainder. So his now well-fed and comfortably housed scarecrows faced the walled city in stalemate, receiving occasional artillery fire with derisive huzzas. Carleton contemptuously responded with a roundshot to a white flag and demand for surrender.

But rumors of an impending Canadian sortie, and a threatening shift of the warships in the river, caused Arnold to draw back twenty miles up-river to Pointe aux Trèmbles (now Neuville) and wait for Montgomery, who on December 2 joined him from Montreal. It was a welcome arrival, for Montgomery's Command of nearly 500 men —the 1st New York Continentals and Lamb's artillery company— brought with them field guns and a supply of clothing. Montgomery assumed command of the combined forces. By December 5—with the Canadian winter snows and sub-zero temperature setting in—the Americans were again in front of Quebec, many of Arnold's men now clad in British winter uniform—thanks again to HM's 7th and 26th Foot, whose stores Montgomery had captured at St. Johns and Montreal. Arnold's corps lay on the northern side of the city, Montgomery's force on the Plains of Abraham. American batteries began to pound the walls, but without much effect; they were dominated by the heavier British fortress guns.

Montgomery's problem was a nice one. He had no siege artillery; the winter weather prohibited any formal investment with earthworks; the enlistments of a great proportion of his troops would expire at the end of the year. Yet back home both Congress and Washington himself expected and even demanded early victory. The only solution was to stake all on audacity: take the place by storm.

Two other high-hearted soldiers agreed: Arnold and Morgan. Most subordinate commanders were not so bold; some less than lukewarm. As for the rank and file, "everyone wanted to see the town taken," comments Christopher Ward, "but not everybody wanted to take it."

Quebec perched on a promontory topping the left bank of the St. Lawrence at its confluence with the St. Charles River. The sheer cliff of Cape Diamond, 300 feet high, faced the St. Lawrence, with below it a narrow belt of bottom land widening around to the St. Charles side. Here, around the promontory nose, lay the so-called Lower Town, defended on the south by a blockhouse and a double row of palisades. A timber barricade on the St. Charles—northern—side blocked the opening to the Sault au Matelot, a crooked, narrow street leading to a steep, ladder-like passage into the Upper Town above. The citadel, on Cape Diamond, at the southern edge, topped all. The land, or western side, abutting on the Plains of Abraham, was defended by a 30-foot wall stretching three quarters of a mile from river to river. Heavy cannon were mounted in its six bastions and three gates gave access. Built-up suburbs—at this time partly destroyed—had already overlapped the walls to some extent.

Carleton, considering the means at his disposal, had done his best to garrison the place. His élite corps was composed of the remaining company of the 7th Foot, the marines, and Maclean's dependable Royal Highland Emigrants—some 425 men in all—under Maclean's command. Beside these there were 330 militiamen of British birth and 543 French-Canadian militiamen, raised through the effort of Hector Cramahé, nominal governor of the city. There were also 570 British sailors and artificers from the warships. Available, then, were about 1,800 men.

Against this fortress Montgomery was going to throw some 800

men in a two-pronged assault. The Lower Town was the first objective. Arnold's corps, with a detachment of Lamb's New York Artillery, would assault the northern end, to gain the Sault au Matelot;
Montgomery, leading the 1st New York, would strike through the
southern end. Converging, the combined forces would then drive up
the steep passageway into the Upper Town.

Carefully planned, and including two feints at the Upper Town
wall to distract the defenders' attention, the scheme was still most
chancy. It was a complicated plan, dependent on surprise, coordination and the will to win.

At four o'clock on Sunday morning, December 31, 1775, in the
midst of a howling blizzard—ideal weather condition for surprise—
three signal rockets triggered off the attack, and the two storming
parties lurched forward through the drifts. Unfortunately, all Quebec,
it seemed, had also seen the streaking rocket flares. Church bells
clanged, drums rolled, lanterns and fireballs began to illuminate the
walls, while the garrison hurried to their posts.

Montgomery's column, scrabbling along the water's edge below
Cape Diamond, had to traverse two miles of narrow path, heaped
with ice-cakes, before it came to the blockhouse barricade. With
Montgomery himself lending a hand, the advance party cut and
chopped their way through while the Canadian picket fled. They
passed the blockhouse, deserted by its militia garrison, rounded the
point, and forced a second barricade. In the dawn, another house
loomed in front of them. Montgomery led his party—including young
Aaron Burr—in a rush for it. Inside, one of a huddled group of Canadian militiamen touched match to a 3-pounder gun trained down the
roadway. Its belching grapeshot mowed down a dozen Americans,
among them Montgomery—killed instantly. Behind them the slowly
moving column halted, irresolute. It received another blast of grape
and musketry. Colonel Donald Campbell, assuming command, ordered inglorious retreat. The New Yorkers streamed away, harassed
by a Canadian sortie as they reached the Plains of Abraham.

On the other side of town the story is really that of Daniel Morgan,
backwoods paladin. Leader of the first company of riflemen to join
Washington's army, hero of Arnold's amazing march through the
Maine woods, Morgan would prove himself to be an indomitable

combat commander. Arnold's corps, skirting the Quebec walls to reach the Lower Town, ran the gauntlet of harassing fire from the battlements before being halted at the first barricade below. Arnold, whipping his men on, went down with a bullet through his leg, and Morgan took command by sheer assertion of leadership. (There were three irresolute field officers present.)

As Arnold was helped from the field, Morgan's bull voice galvanized the men into action. A ladder was flung up and Morgan, partly stunned by a fall in his first attempt, topped the barricade on a second try. With his men following, he swept a passage into the crooked Sault au Matelot and stormed through two more barricades. By now he had fewer soldiers than prisoners, for resistance was cracking. But no one knew the way through the pitch-dark alleyways, the storm was still raging, and anyway, this was the spot where Montgomery should meet them.

So Morgan and his men waited until daylight for the Montgomery who would never come. And when they did move at last, in the dawn, Carleton's troops had concentrated to snuff out this last American threat.

Knowing that the Lower Town was his weakest point, Carleton had prepared a hedgehog defense, with barricades and sheltered embrasures lining the Sault au Matelot, where every house had become a fortlet. Into these prepared defenses the British and Canadians now poured, to open deadly fire on the Americans packed, elbow-to-elbow, below them.

One Canadian sally was repulsed, and Morgan's men, tackling the nearest barrier, won their way through, only to be met by a converging cross fire, while the bayonets of a double line of British regulars— that last remaining company of the 7th Foot—gleamed beyond.

For a time the Americans carried on a house-to-house struggle, vainly trying to break through. Then, behind them in that winding Sault au Matelot, the trap snapped shut; 200 more British, sent by Carleton from around the Upper Town, backtracked the American move. House by house, and group by group, the Americans began throwing down their arms.

But not Morgan. His back against a wall, tears of rage mingling with the blood from a head wound, Daniel Morgan, sword in hand, defied the throng of English and Canadians now closing in and calling for him to surrender or be shot. Then a clerical cassock in the crowd of bystanders beyond caught his eye.

"You are a priest? Then I give my sword to you. But not a scoundrel of these cowards shall take it out of my hands!"

And that was the end. Some sixty Americans had been killed or wounded; 426 more were prisoners in British hands. Carleton's losses were but five killed and thirteen wounded. Arnold, retaining command despite his wound, withdrew his remaining 600 men about a mile, erected ramparts of frozen snow and waited for a British attack which never came. There the Americans would cling, decimated by disease, awaiting reinforcements.

7

Guns to Boston

SINCE THE END OF OCTOBER, Washington's military machine in front of Boston had hung on dead center. And with it hung, too, the effort of the United Colonies, for—as usual in such cases—an uninformed population craved aggressive action and this Washington could not yet give them.

Skirmishing—relatively unimportant and certainly indecisive—had of course been going on. The most serious was a successful attempt on August 26 to seize and fortify Ploughed Hill, overlooking Charlestown Neck and within close range of Bunker Hill—by now a well-organized British strong point. But that was all. The British sat stolid in Boston and without heavy artillery Washington could not winkle them out.

Not that Washington had been idle; far from it. The immediate questions of ordnance, ammunition, subsistence, uniforms, shelter, training and discipline had pressed down on him at the same time as he faced the probability of serious combat. And to the best of his ability he had made do; far better than might have been expected. His army had been shaken into a formation of six brigades of six regiments each, organized in three divisions. Artemas Ward's division, the right wing, lay at Roxbury. Putnam commanded the center, in and about Cambridge, and Charles Lee had the left wing, at Prospect Hill. Some 17,000 strong (on paper), the army was reasonably well fed—due to the exertions of his commissary general, Joseph Trumbull. Horatio Gates, the adjutant general, with his past knowledge of British military administration, had brought some order out

of chaos. But clothing, blankets and fuel were in short supply, as
was ammunition.

As a partial remedy to these shortages, Washington extemporized
a navy, following the sporadic example of Rhode Island, Massachusetts and Connecticut. All three colonies had fitted out armed vessels
to provide in some fashion for the protection of their coasts from
British aggression. The British cooped up in Boston drew all supplies
by water—from the West Indies, from southern American ports and,
above all, munitions of war from England. Not expecting any naval
harassment from the colonies, these supply ships sailed without arms
or naval protection.

So in September Washington had commissioned a shipmaster serving in Glover's regiment of Marblehead fisherman, one Nicholson
Broughton, a captain in the army, and sent him out in the armed
schooner *Hannah*. Broughton promptly brought in a British vessel
well laden with provisions and naval stores. Congress then authorized
further action. By the end of October six schooners were preying on
the transports. The biggest catch was the brig *Nancy,* captured at
the very entrance of Boston harbor—a windfall of a huge 13-inch
brass mortar, 2,000 muskets, 100,000 flints, 30,000 round shot and
30 tons of musket balls. These guerrillas of the sea, commanded now
by Commodore John Manley and locally known as "Washington's
Navy," garnered no less than 35 prizes in all.

Admiral Graves and his warships seemed to be incapable of coping
with these fast craft. The best Graves could do in reprisal was send
two ships to "burn, destroy and lay waste" the northeast coastal settlements as far north as Machias. They put in at Gloucester, decided
it would be difficult to burn the town, and moved on to Falmouth
(now Portland, Me.) where the entire settlement was set ablaze
October 17, after giving the inhabitants two hours to get out.

So the months drifted on, until, in mid-November Washington
sent his prospective chief of artillery, jovial, rotund Henry Knox,
up to Ticonderoga, with orders to bring down the heavy cannon
lying useless there since Ethan Allen had captured the place. "The
want of them is so great," the Commander-in-Chief instructed Knox,
"that no Trouble or Expence must be spared to obtain them." So
Knox, first going to New York, disappeared into the north country.

On the face of it, then, as November drew to an end, the prospect for the future for Washington's army was far from black. The catch was that by the end of December, when its enlistments would expire, this army would cease to exist. So George Washington's most pressing problem now was how to keep any army at all in the field after December 31.

The Congress had authorized a new army of 30,732 officers and men: 26 regiments of infantry, plus riflemen and artillery, to be enlisted for one year—despite Washington's ideas for a long-term soldiery. But to obtain volunteers from amongst his troops was something else again. Parochial interest, the lure of bounties which the respective colonies were offering their own short-term militia, the lucrative prospects of privateering, jealousies and homesickness, were among the factors limiting re-enlistment.

Despite coaxing and haranguing, as December came in only 3,500 men had re-enlisted. New recruits were arriving in driblets only and on December 10 the Connecticut troops, whose enlistments expired on that date, marched out of camp for home, flatly refusing to stay one moment longer. The bottom was dropping out of the army.

As a stop-gap, appeals to the Committees of Safety of Massachusetts and New Hampshire brought results—5,000 militiamen from Massachusetts and 2,000 from New Hampshire—to serve until January 15, when it was hoped the recruiting campaign would have brought results. Meanwhile, on December 22, Congress had passed a resolution urging an assault on Boston.

Outwardly, Washington faced the situation with superb *sangfroid*. On January 1, 1776, he ordered a new flag to be broken out from the tall pole at American headquarters on Prospect Hill in Somerville, Mass. It was hoisted, as General Orders No. 1 proclaimed, "in Compliment to the United Colonies." The flag bore thirteen alternate red and white horizontal stripes, and its canton was the Union Jack of Britain. If, as someone reported, the British over the way in Boston thought it for the moment a signal of American surrender, they were sadly mistaken.

For the order announced as preamble that "This day giving commencement to the new army, which, in every point of view, is Continental, the General flatters himself, that a laudable Spirit of emulation will now take place and pervade the whole."

Actually, Washington was whistling in the dark, for he was back

where he had started in July. He did have a new army that New
Year's Day, the initial Continental Army; but it was a hodge-podge of
re-enlisted veterans, raw recruits and short-term militia, with a paper
strength of 8,212, of whom only 5,582 were present and fit for duty.
With them, the Commander-in-Chief proposed to take the offensive
as soon as he had heavy artillery with which to bombard Boston.

"Search the vast volumes of history through, and I much question
whether a case similar to ours is to be found; to wit, to maintain a post
against the flower of the British troops for six months together, without
powder, and at the end of them to have one army disbanded and another
to raise within the same distance of a reinforced enemy. It is too much
to attempt. What may be the final issue of the last manoeuvre, time
only can tell. . . . We are now left with a good deal less than half
raised regiments, and about five thousand militia, who only stand in-
gaged to the middle of this month; when, according to custom, they
will depart, let the necessity of their stay be never so urgent. Thus it
is, that for more than two months past, I have scarcely immerged from
one difficulty before I have plunged into another. . . ."

Thus George Washington in a letter to Joseph Reed, President
of the Continental Congress, summed up the problems facing him
just a few days after that formal flag-raising.

It was a pretty grim situation. Fortunately, in Boston, General
Howe, who assumed command there on October 10—Gage having
been ordered home—was facing one still grimmer. The British force
had by this time been augmented to about 11,000 men, and the
defenses of the city well prepared. At Bunker Hill on the Charlestown side, and at Boston Neck on the Dorchester side, elaborate
works had been constructed; so heavily gunned and manned as to be
impregnable to any assault the Americans could make.

But inside those bristling defenses the garrison was rotting with
scurvy and smallpox. They were short of all food but salt meat, dried
peas and—occasionally—fish. Some of the many cargoes of food-
stuffs sent from England mildewed and spoiled on the long voyage;
others were captured by the little American cruisers. With the chill
of a New England winter came shortages of fuel. Churches, houses,
wharves, trees and old ships were ruthlessly broken up for firewood,
and still the redcoats shivered; the hospitals overflowed with sick men.

General Clinton, urging a shift to New York, expressed the consensus that no military advantage could be gained in Massachusetts; victory there, be it "ever so compleat," would lead nowhere. Howe and the authorities in London were also in agreement that Boston should be evacuated, and that the garrison must be accompanied by the Boston Loyalists, who on no account should "be exposed to the rage and insults of the rebels, who set no bound to their barbarity." Unfortunately, Howe calculated that more than 35,000 tons of shipping would be needed, and he had little more than 23,000 available. Thus he and his garrison would have to stand fast in Boston until spring.

The scenes of war were in reality about to shift, but in a direction unexpected by Howe and Clinton, for London's eyes were looking to obtain a decision far south of New York. To implement the new orders from England, on January 20 Clinton, with two companies of light infantry, sailed south from Boston, escorted by a frigate. Washington, fearful that New York was threatened, hurriedly detached General Charles Lee, with a battalion of riflemen, to prepare for its defense.

It was a weird stalemate in Boston. Howe and Washington were each generally aware of the other's weaknesses, yet each was convinced of his own inability, unaided, to force a military decision. There was, however, one radical difference in the two soldiers' outlook. Howe had accepted the inevitable and was prepared to evacuate of his own volition; Washington chafed for the opportunity to deliver a vital stroke which would compensate for the depressing news of the disaster before Quebec, and boost colonial morale.

An express from Springfield in mid-January brought matters to a head. Knox and the guns from Ticonderoga were debouching east of the Berkshires! How they had gotten there deserves the telling.

Bustling, cheerful Henry Knox, fashionable bookseller of Boston and amateur artilleryman in a local militia company, combined terrific leadership drive with a profound knowledge gained by incessant reading. His particular bent, it seems, was the technique of war. Like his crony Nathanael Greene, he delved into military history—particularly fortification, field engineering and gunnery. He came to Washington's attention first as the constructing engineer of two outworks at Roxbury. Washington needed an artillery chief. Knox looked good, and John Adams endorsed him; he got the job. It appears

certain that during their initial conversations Knox recommended that
the guns at Ticonderoga be brought to Boston to fill the need for
ordnance. In any event, Washington sent Knox to get them—with
$1,000 cash to defray expenses. How the task would be accomplished
was up to Knox, who took his younger brother William along.

Arriving at Ticonderoga on December 5, Knox sorted out some
59 usable cannon: long guns, short guns, and dumpy mortars,
ranging from 4- to 24-pounders. The smallest pieces weighed 100
pounds each, the largest 5,500 pounds. Just how these clumsy weights
were hauled up the gorge to Lake George and manhandled onto
a large scow is not of record. It must be remembered, however,
that the rural American of that day was well acquainted with rudimentary mechanical requirements—juggling great logs and shifting
huge stones. The forests furnished rollers, levers, skids and wedges,
all to be had for the chopping. In any event, the toilers—soldiers of
the garrison and hired help, plus oxen and horses—did the job. By
December 9 the guns, together with 23 boxes of lead and a barrel
of flints, were on board the scow and moving up the still unfrozen
lake for Fort George. There Knox had arranged for the construction
of 82 "exceedingly strong" sleds and provision of 80 yoke of oxen
to draw them. Off Sabbath Day Point the scow with its more than
six-ton load of ordnance, swamped and sank. Fortunately it was in
shallow water and in some fashion—the details of Knox' trek are
exasperatingly vague—it was bailed out and put afloat again.

General Schuyler, who had arrived in Albany to take command
on December 7, characteristically set about aiding the move, authorizing the detail of soldiers, with relays of horses, sleighs and team-
sters. When the snow came, on December 17, Knox' caravan hit the
road. His report to Washington, of that date, noted his expectation
to present him "I hope in 16 or 17 days . . . a noble train of
artillery."

Knox was too optimistic. The caravan bogged down in all-too-
heavy snow not far below Saratoga (now Schuylerville), December
26. By the 31st, 124 pair of horses with sleighs were rushed up to
his help by Schuyler, together with additional men. Meanwhile Knox
and an advance party were testing crossings of the frozen Hudson
near Albany, where the train arrived January 5. The crossings were
hair-raising. The heaviest guns were snaked over to distribute the load

—each team going far ahead on a long tow rope, a man with a sharp axe beside it, to cut the horses free if the cannon and sleigh broke through.

Despite all precautions two big guns did break through—one at a crossing near Waterford, the other near Albany itself. Each time luck was with Knox, for the breakthroughs occurred in the shallows. Floundering men braved icy water to fish tackle about the guns, and oxen and horses dragged the pieces ashore again.

Safe at last on the old Post Road, the caravan heaved its way from Greenbush through Kinderhook to Claverack, and squared away for its last test—the haul through the Berkshires. The path followed in general what is now Route 23, through Great Barrington and east to Springfield. It was hard enough to get up the west face, but the eastern descent was even harder, with drag-chains and poles pushed under the sled-runners to check them, and, on the steepest slides, snubbing ropes made fast progressively from tree to tree, lest runaway sleds overwhelm the teams and men ahead.

But they made it, passing through Westfield, where the populace turned out to see this monstrosity of movement and were rewarded by the salute of a blank charge fired from the biggest gun of all—a 24-pounder nicknamed "Old Sow." Perhaps the fact that the villagers had plied all hands with cider and whiskey in celebration had something to do with the salute.

At Springfield, thaws checked the movement. There, too, Knox discharged his New York civilian drovers and dickered with Massachusetts men to lug his cannon further. Obliging frost soon hardened the ground once more and by January 25 the great trek ended at Framingham. Knox spurred on to report to Washington. Within a week, some of the precious cannon were emplaced, the remainder ready to be moved into action.

Washington now would brook no further delay. He had prevailed on the Committees of Safety for another draft of short-term militia—ten regiments—to fill his ranks. At a council of war held February 16 he actually proposed a hazardous assault across Back Bay, but was dissuaded. Instead, the council voted to seize and fortify Dorchester Heights; an attempt, as Washington wrote Reed, "to try if the enemy will be so kind as to come out to us."

The point was well taken. An American fortification on the Heights, mounting heavy guns, would play hob not only in Boston itself, but to its precious shipping and to Castle William at the harbor mouth. It would also completely dominate the British defenses on Boston Neck.

To such a threat the British must respond, even as they had to the earlier Breed's Hill threat, much less dangerous to them in fact. Like that affair, a British response must also come by water, for in this case they could not afford the delay of a protracted assault across narrow Boston Neck.

To secure surprise, the enemy must be presented with a *fait accompli;* a fortification thrown up secretly in a single night; again, even as at Breed's Hill.

But how accomplish in Boston wintertime what had been easy in June? The ground on Dorchester Heights was frozen now to a depth of eighteen inches or more.

Colonel Rufus Putnam offered a solution: build *on,* not *in* the ground; his scheme was a prefabricated fort, composed of "chandeliers" (heavy timber frames), into which ready-filled fascines (bundles of logs), gabions (baskets of earth), and bales of hay could be stuffed. A facing *abatis* (frieze of sharpened stakes), could be hewed from the plentiful fruit trees in the adjoining orchards. And on the crest in front, Putnam proposed rows of earth-filled barrels which would not only give appearance of strength, but—should the British assault—could be rolled down the steep hillside upon the attackers.

Immediately accepted, Putnam's plan was feverishly implemented. The materials were prepared, the heavy guns gathered at Roxbury. At the same time Washington detailed the brigades of John Sullivan and Nathanael Greene—4,000 of his most reliable men—under Israel Putnam, to counter any British assault by attacking the Boston Neck defenses from the rear across the Back Bay. Two floating batteries and 45 bateaux, each capable of carrying 80 men, were secreted in the Charles River to lift this amphibious effort. D-day was set for March 4, by which time all the militia from the neighboring towns were expected to join the Continental forces.

On the night of March 2 the American batteries at Lechmere's Point and Cobble Hill on the Cambridge side opened sporadic fire to attract British attention. They repeated it the following night. And on March 4—Washington was squandering his precious ammunition purposely—they racked the darkness with a really thunderous bombardment, eliciting nervous British rejoinder.

Under cover of the noise and commotion, Brigadier General John Thomas, with a working party of 1,200 men, supported by a covering force of 800 more, moved out of Roxbury to the Heights. Behind the column creaked 360 oxcarts laden with the prepared construction material and trundling cannon.

There, on the mile-long peninsula, the workers—like busy ants—swarmed over traces of redoubts already staked out on the hard-frozen ground. The timbered chandeliers fell into place, willing hands stuffed into them the gabions, fascines and hay bales. Axemen swept through the orchards, while working details hurried behind them to gather and weave the *abatis* ringing the redoubts. All through the night the workers toiled—the original party relieved by a new gang at three o'clock in the morning—while the slow-moving oxcarts came and went with successive loads.

With dawn Howe indeed faced a *fait accompli;* complete in surprise and shocking in impact. Two substantial redoubts crowned the Heights. Adding to the shock was the stuffy but patently unanswerable announcement from Rear Admiral Molyneux Shuldham—Graves' successor—that he could not and would not risk His Majesty's ships in harbor under this new threat. Howe must evacuate the place or storm the Americans out from their new stronghold.

Howe tried bombardment, but his guns could not be elevated sufficiently to reach the new redoubts. As we know, he had already determined on an evacuation, but it was not in the nature of the man tamely to tuck his tail between his legs. So he ordered an assault to be delivered that very night. Five regiments—some 2,200 men—would go by water to Castle William, thence to the extreme tip of the Dorchester peninsula. At the same time the grenadier and light infantry battalions and two additional regiments would also move by flatboat to the north side of the peninsula. The assaults were to be simultaneous and with cold steel only.

The preparations could not be concealed. On the American side the working parties continued strengthening the redoubts, where some 20 guns were now mounted. Five battalions of riflemen reinforced the garrison. Over on Cambridge Common, Putnam's divisions paraded, ready for the Back Bay counterattack.

But Nature stepped in. A fierce storm broke that night and continued through the next day, with thunderous surf churning the shoreline. Howe called off his planned attacks. When the weather cleared, the jig was up. The Dorchester fortifications were completed, the heavy cannon in place. Howe ordered immediate evacuation.

Washington watched them go; saw the ships move out to anchorage beyond reach of his guns, saw the processions of boats and lighters moving to and from the wharves. He hurried them by sporadic cannonading, and by extension of the works on Dorchester Heights, but spared the city itself. Howe had assured a delegation of terrified Bostonians he would not burn the city unless the Americans attacked his troops. Washington took no formal note of this promise, but tacitly both sides reduced hostilities to a minimum—an interesting example of mutual restraint in limited war.

The evacuation was a mess; hospital ships crammed with the sick and dying; some 150 transports and warships loaded to capacity with human freight. The more than 1,000 Tory men, women and children who accepted Howe's offer of transshipment to wherever the army was bound, suffered most, perhaps. Abandoning all they possessed, they huddled in stinking steerage, doomed forever to exile. Vessels had been alloted to them, but they had to find and pay sailors to man them. Typical was the case of one Benjamin Hallowell, former commissioner of customs, into whose cabin were crowded 36 individuals in addition to himself—"men, women and children; parents, masters and mistresses, obliged to pig together on the floor, there being no berths."

In the city, British stores were abandoned; some of the army's cavalry and artillery horses left behind. Shops and storehouses were plundered.

By nightfall on St. Patrick's Day, March 17, the last cannon had been spiked, the last British soldier was on shipboard. The fleet lay anchored some five miles below the town in Nantasket Road, while suspicious Washington pondered on the delay, wondering if some trick was in progress. Cautiously, American scouts entered the lines, followed by detachments. At Bunker Hill, sentinels still seemed to be on the ramparts, but these turned out to be dummies. By the 20th, the Continental Army was in full possession of Boston, and Washington, convinced that Howe was bound for New York, had

ordered Heath, with five regiments of foot and two companies of
artillery, to march overland to assist in defending that city.

On the 27th the British fleet, having completed taking on water
and adjusting the cargoes so hurriedly shipped, broke out its canvas
and stood north. It was bound for Halifax, Nova Scotia, but Washington didn't know that. By the beginning of April the Continental
Army, less five regiments left in Boston under Artemas Ward, was
marching fast for New York.

8 ★ ★ ★ ★ ★

Preliminaries in the South

THE FIRE OF REVOLUTION BURNED FIERCELY in many Southern hearts in 1775. But the difference in social structure, based upon a plantation and slaveholding economy, prevented the flames from spreading as rapidly as in the North. Loyalist sentiment was widespread, particularly amongst the wealthy planters, who were naturally conservative, dreaded riot and rebellion, were loyal to a régime which had enriched them, and were suspicious of "hot-headed radicals" like Virginian Patrick Henry, and the Rutledge brothers of South Carolina. In the Carolinas, furthermore, there were sharp and intensive political and hereditary cleavages amongst clannish groups of diverse backgrounds. These differences automatically made Loyalists of those whose natural enemies had earlier joined the patriot cause. In North Carolina, in particular, most Scots followed the popular leadership of Allan and Flora Macdonald in loyalty to the king.*

For these reasons, royal authority was not so immediately nor so directly challenged in the Southern colonies as in the North. Patriotic rebels moved cautiously, even after the Continental Congress virtually declared war upon the British Crown in June, 1775.

During that summer, however, Charleston patriots began to move more boldly against the new governor, Lord William Campbell. Led by John Rutledge, the citizens established a Council of Safety, openly

---

* This was an amazing switch for the Macdonalds. In 1746 Flora, as a young girl, had helped Prince Charles Edward Stuart—"Bonnie Prince Charlie"—escape from Scotland after the Battle of Culloden. In 1773 she and her husband Allan emigrated to America, and from ardent Stuart supporters, turned into loyal and enthusiastic subjects of the once-hated Hanoverian king.

raised provincial regiments, and commissioned a provincial warship —which then seized a cargo of gunpowder in Charleston harbor. Shortly after this the governor took refuge on the sloop-of-war HMS *Tamar*. The patriots thereupon declared the independence of South Carolina, and elected Rutledge as President (or Governor).

About this same time Governor Josiah Martin of North Carolina was also forced to flee to the safety of a British man-of-war. The two royal governors maintained contact with many of the loyal citizens of their rebellious colonies, and jointly conferred with the Earl of Dunmore, Governor of Virginia, also a refugee on a warship in Hampton Roads. Meanwhile, in the three colonies, unrest seethed between suspicious patriots and Loyalists, although the numerically preponderant patriots had seized the reins of government.

Late in 1775 Britain decided to send an expeditionary force to re-establish royal control in the Southern colonies. Recommendations from the three governors undoubtedly contributed to the decision. The British plan was to send an amphibious force to North Carolina, under the command of Admiral Sir Peter Parker, convoying seven army regiments, commanded by Major General the Earl Charles Cornwallis. The armada was to leave Cork, Ireland, in December. At Cape Fear, North Carolina, they would be met by a small contingent from Boston under Clinton, who would take command of the land force of the expedition. Parker and Clinton would then decide whether to initiate their operations in Virginia or the Carolinas.

In November, Dunmore strengthened anti-royalist sentiment in Virginia by rash and hasty actions. He raised some Loyalist units, which became involved in several clashes with patriot militia and newly established Virginia Continental forces. On November 7 Dunmore declared martial law, and began to gather his Loyalist troops at a base in Norfolk. Ten days later, promising freedom to all slaves who would desert their masters and join the Loyalist cause, the governor began to raise "Lord Dunmore's Regiment of Ethiopians." This completely alienated all undecided Virginia planters, and caused many former Loyalists to join the rebels.

A force of some 900 Virginia and North Carolina Continentals under Brigadier General William Woodford, joined by some volunteer riflemen, marched against Norfolk. They found Dunmore's Loyalist force of 900 whites and 300 Negroes at Great Bridge, nine miles south of Norfolk. Both sides threw up entrenchments and faced each other for several days. Then on December 9, Dunmore's troops—strengthened by about 200 regular soldiers, Royal Marines, and sailors—attacked the rebel earthworks overlooking the bridge. The Continentals repulsed the attack, then drove Dunmore's men back to Norfolk. In fright, Dunmore and his troops took refuge on four British warships in Hampton Roads. The rebels seized the town on December 14.

On New Year's Day, 1776, vengeful Dunmore ordered the warships to shell Norfolk with red-hot shot. As the flames spread, British raiding parties landed to set fire to buildings close to the shore, then returned to their vessels. Norfolk was gutted. With it, Dunmore had destroyed almost every vestige of Loyalist sentiment in Virginia.

Early in February Governor Martin issued a manifesto for all North Carolina Loyalists to rise against the rebel regime. Expecting the early arrival of Sir Peter Parker's expedition, Martin instructed his Loyalists to assemble at Cross Creek. By February 18, nearly 2,000 Loyalists, mostly Scots, had gathered under the command of Donald McDonald, who was appointed Brigadier General by the Governor. His second-in-command was Colonel Donald McLeod.

While the Loyalists were rallying, a rebel force of about 2,000 men assembled nearby, under Colonel James Moore, commander of the 1st North Carolina regiment. Moore sent half of his troops under the command of Colonels Richard Caswell and Alexander Lillington, to block the road between Cross Creek and Wilmington.

Late in February McDonald's force began to march toward the coast, where he hoped to join forces soon with the British expedition. Many of the Scottish Loyalists were dressed in kilts, and bagpipes skirled as they marched proudly towards the sea. On February 27 they found their route blocked at Moore's Creek, a swampy stream flowing into the Black River about eighteen miles above Wilmington. Caswell and Lillington had had their men remove most of the timbers from the bridge, and had then built an earthwork overlooking it.

McDonald was ill, but McLeod—without reconnaissance or plan of maneuver—ordered an immediate charge to seize the bridge and to drive the patriot force from its earthworks beyond. The cheering Highlanders came to a sudden halt at the end of the floorless bridge.

They hesitated to scramble down the high banks to try to ford the sluggish stream. A few brave souls attempted to cross the bridge stringers, but were promptly shot. The rebel troops then poured several volleys into the milling mass of Tories on the opposite bank. Hardly a shot was fired in return. Within three minutes all of the Loyalists were in flight.

Losses were light: 30 Loyalists were killed or wounded; only two patriots wounded. The next day General McDonald and 850 of his men surrendered; the remainder had dispersed back to their homes. Loyalist sentiment in North Carolina had been greatly dampened by the swampy waters of Moore's Creek.

Along the frontiers of the Carolinas, too, the early enthusiasm of England's Cherokee allies was waning. Friction between settlers and Cherokees had long been endemic in this western mountain region, and little English inducement had been required to spur the Indians to raids against the frontier settlements in early 1776. The frontier militiamen, aided by friendly Catawba Indians, reacted promptly, to devastate the Cherokee villages and farmlands. The Creeks, from whom the Cherokees had expected assistance, decided to stay neutral, and so frontier activity subsided for three years, while the Cherokees licked their wounds, and awaited another opportunity to gain revenge.

Meanwhile, at Cambridge, as we know, Washington had learned of British plans to send an expedition south from Boston. It was not clear to him whether the British objective would be New York or Virginia. Not yet aware of the British plan for Southern operations, and fearing for the safety of New York, Washington sent his second-in-command, enigmatic Major General Charles Lee, to strengthen the defenses of New York.

Clinton sailed from Boston with a few companies on January 20, stopping briefly to pick up Governors Martin and Campbell, who were then on board British warships anchored off Sandy Hook. At Hampton Roads, he and the two governors stopped again to confer with Dunmore. Early in March Clinton arrived at the mouth of the Cape Fear River, where he awaited the arrival of Parker and Cornwallis.

Evidence of increasing Royalist interest in the South caused the Continental Congress in late February to appoint General Lee to command the Southern Department, which included Virginia, the Carolinas, and Georgia. Leaving New York, Lee arrived at Williamsburg, Virginia, in March. He sent detachments to keep an eye on Clinton's small flotilla anchored in the Cape Fear River, while at the same time he attempted to improve the coastal defenses of Virginia.

At about this time a Virginia privateer intercepted, and delivered to Lee, a letter from Lord George Germain to Governor Robert Eden of Maryland. Written on December 23, the letter informed the governor that "seven regiments and a fleet of frigates and small ships" would soon leave for "the southern colonies . . . in the first place to North Carolina, and from thence either to South Carolina or Virginia as circumstances . . . shall permit."

The long-delayed British expedition was already on the high seas. It had sailed from Cork on February 13, comprising 2,500 troops, in 30 transports, and escorted by eleven warships. Dispersed by a storm en route, the ships straggled to Cape Fear between April 18 and May 3. Lee now moved down to Wilmington, whence he directed the skirmishing of American troops against British foraging parties.

On May 30 the British armada sailed from the Cape Fear River. Despite the entreaties of Lord Dunmore, Parker and Clinton had decided that the Royalist cause would best be served by the seizure of Charleston. The flotilla arrived off the Charleston bar on June 4.

Lee arrived in Charleston the following day with 1,900 Virginia and North Carolina Continentals, bringing the total defense force to about 6,600 men. He found that the citizens of Charleston were expecting attack, but were confident that they would repulse it.

To Lee's experienced military eyes, however, this was highly doubtful. At the time they had expelled Governor Campbell, the South Carolina provincial troops, under the guidance and inspiration of Colonels Christopher Gadsden and William Moultrie, veterans of the Cherokee War of 1760-61, had strengthened the existing defenses of Charleston, and had begun to build more. But the work had gone slowly, and the fortifications were far from complete. The most important of these, in light of the approach of the British armada, were existing Fort Johnson, on James Island, and new Fort Sullivan on the opposite side of the harbor mouth, on Sullivan's Island. Fort Johnson was garrisoned by approximately 400 men under Gadsden. Moultrie, with nearly 450 more, was in unfinished Fort Sullivan.

Lee immediately agreed with the South Carolinians that Fort Sullivan was theoretically the key to the harbor defenses of Charleston.

It was a square structure, with bastions on the southeastern and south-western corners, facing the harbor mouth. But Lee was disturbed by the low, unfinished walls facing to the west and north. That on the north could be attacked by British troops who could be landed on the northern end of Sullivan's Island. The open western side was vulnerable to naval fire from just inside the harbor entrance. Lee urged immediate abandonment of the fort, to prevent loss of the entire garrison to a British combined land and sea attack.

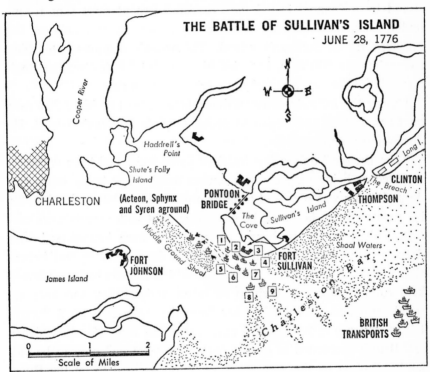

THE BATTLE OF SULLIVAN'S ISLAND
JUNE 28, 1776

Key to British ships: (1) *Active*, (2) *Bristol*, (3) *Experiment*, (4) *Solebay*, (5) *Acteon*, (6) *Sphynx*, (7) *Syren*, (8) *Thunder*, (9) *Friendship*.

Governor Rutledge and Colonel Moultrie emphatically disagreed. The completed southern and eastern walls were composed of parallel palisades of palmetto logs, 12 feet high, with 16 feet of sand between them. The South Carolinians, sure that these were proof against any naval guns that could be brought to bear, insisted that they could defend even the unfinished walls against any possible attack, and were so vehement that Lee gave in. He then devoted considerable time and attention to improving the readiness of the garrisons, and to preparing a floating bridge across "The Cove" between Sullivan's

Island and the mainland, so that Moultrie's garrison would have a line of retreat.

Annoyed by Lee's patronizing and arrogant attitude, many of the Carolinian militiamen refused to obey his orders. Rutledge quickly solved the impending crisis by placing all South Carolina forces under Lee's command.

On June 9, Clinton sent a force of 500 men ashore from the fleet to seize the southern end of Long Island, separated from Sullivan's Island by a channel called the "Breach." Lee at once sent troops under Lieutenant Colonel William Thompson to entrench on the northern tip of Sullivan's Island. Thompson's command, totalling approximately 800 men, included his own 3rd South Carolina Regiment, 200 Continentals, and some other detachments.

During the following week Clinton landed most of his 2,500 men on Long Island, and began to probe towards Sullivan's Island. He discovered unexpected difficulties.

"The Breach," only a few hundred yards wide, had been variously reported as being only eighteen inches deep, or as being seven feet deep. Clinton was prepared to cross either by boat or by fording. To his consternation, however, he discovered that both reports were correct. Ridges or shoals, barely under water, were interspersed with deep trenches or holes seven or more feet deep. Fording was impossible and even flat-bottomed boats—of which Clinton had very few—kept running aground, then to be taken under heavy and accurate small arms and light artillery fire from the Americans on Sullivan's Island. After a rather spirited engagement on June 19—in which a few British succeeded in getting across the "Breach" only to be violently repulsed by the Americans—Clinton decided to let the Royal Navy have the honor of forcing a passage into Charleston harbor.

Sir Peter Parker meanwhile had been preparing for this eventuality. To get his two 50-gun vessels * over the shallow bar, he was forced to dismount their guns, then remount them in the harbor entrance. This took about two weeks. By the evening of June 27, however, Parker was ready.

Early next morning, under the cover of 10-inch shells from the mortar ketch *Thunder,* Parker's squadron approached Sullivan's Is-

---

* Heavy frigates or small ships of the line. See Appendix II.

land. One frigate protected the *Thunder,* and two more were with the transports off Long Island. Standing in boldly towards the shore, the British vessels opened fire as they dropped anchor, apparently so close that they were within extreme small arms range of Fort Sullivan's walls—probably about 200 yards. Ignoring the fire which they were receiving from the 25 guns of the fort, the British ships rigged springs on their cables—to bring their broadsides fully to bear —in the order: *Active,* 28; the flagship, *Bristol,* 50; *Experiment,* 50; and *Solebay,* 28. A few hundred yards farther out from shore, and anchored in the intervals between the first line of ships, were the *Acteon,* 28, *Sphinx,* 28, and *Syren,* 28.

In reply to this intensive bombardment from eight warships, the guns of Fort Sullivan replied slowly and deliberately. Moultrie was short of ammunition, having barely 30 rounds per gun at the outset of the action. Although Lee rushed him additional ammunition during the battle, Moultrie and his artillerymen never had enough to feel that they could waste a single round. As a consequence, the Americans laid their guns carefully and accurately, remaining amazingly cool despite the intensity of the British fire.

Fortunately for the defenders, Moultrie's confidence in the staunchness of his palmetto walls was soon substantiated. Hardwood, such as oak, would have shattered under the hammering, but the cannon balls simply penetrated the soft, sponge-like palmetto wood to become imbedded in the sand behind. A few projectiles entered the embrasures, but casualties and damage were light from these rare shots. Hardly any of the *Thunder's* mortar shells exploded; either falling into a marsh in the center of the fort, or into the soft sand paths behind the brick gun platforms.

The British were at first surprised, and then dismayed, by the accuracy of the American fire—which was concentrated mostly against the two larger British vessels, both of which suffered severely. If the Americans had had more ammunition, one or both of these ships would probably have been sunk before the close of the day.

Early in the fight the *Bristol's* bow cable was shot away and she swung with the tide to expose her quarterdeck to the Americans. Immediately every American gun concentrated on the helpless ship, raking her several times before her small boats could tow her back into line. Every officer was killed or wounded. For a time Admiral

Parker—slightly wounded—was the only man left standing on the quarterdeck. Her main topmast was shot down, and her mizzenmast was so badly shattered that it had to be cut away.

After the first hour of the bombardment had failed to have any noticeable effect on the fort, the three frigates of the second British line weighed anchor and began to advance slowly into the harbor. Recognizing that the western face of the fort was incompleted, the British intended to move around the island far enough to bring fire to bear against the exposed flank and rear of the American gunners. Had they been able to do this, Lee's original forebodings would have been fulfilled; the fort undoubtedly would have become untenable.

The rough handling which they had been receiving from the American guns, however, caused the three British vessels to keep a respectful distance. As a result, all three ran aground on the Middle Ground Shoal just inside the harbor entrance. In their efforts to pull away, the *Acteon* and the *Sphinx* ran into each other, the latter losing her bowsprit. During the afternoon, by kedging, the *Sphinx* and the *Syren* were able to pull themselves off, and limped back out of the harbor entrance to repair their damage. The *Acteon,* however, could not be budged.

During the morning Clinton made one more half-hearted effort to get troops across the "Breach" to Sullivan's Island. Thompson's men repulsed the effort easily. Lee, however, was fearful that the British would make another effort, so he sent a regiment of Virginia Continentals, some 500 strong, to reinforce Thompson. Clinton's failure to push more aggressively, or to work out plans for a truly coordinated action with the navy, are evidence of serious lack of energy and of preparation. Evidently this led to later recriminations from Admiral Parker.

Shortly after noon General Lee arrived to inspect, and was amazed by the staunchness of the defense under "the most furious fire I ever heard or saw." Lee praised Moultrie and his men for their "coolness and intrepidity." He then turned to Moultrie and said, "Colonel, I see you are doing very well here. You have no occasion for me. I will go up to town again."

The ship-shore engagement lasted past dusk; the last British shot was fired at about 9:30 P.M. An hour and a half later the British vessels quietly slipped their anchor cables and withdrew out of range of the fort. The Battle of Sullivan's Island was over.

Early the following morning the *Acteon's* crew set their vessel afire, and returned to the fleet in small boats. The frigate exploded a few hours later.

Total reported British casualties were 195 killed and wounded, mostly on the *Bristol* and the *Experiment*. This figure must be questioned, however, since a British army surgeon who helped to take care of the casualties wrote in his diary that the *Bristol* alone had lost over 300 men.

American losses were seventeen killed or mortally wounded, and twenty wounded. This relatively light loss is a testimony to the staunchness of the palmetto-walled fort. The British apparently fired some 10,000 rounds during the day; about 7,000 cannon balls were retrieved on the island after the battle.

During the following weeks, Parker's fleet was engaged in repairing the terrible damage it had suffered. Early in July Clinton re-embarked his troops from Long Island, and then took his convoy northward, to join General Howe's force preparing to assault New York. Parker's fleet completed its repairs on August 2, and sailed to New York as well. This ended formal warfare in the South for more than two years.

9 ★ ★ ★ ★ ★ ★

Defeat in the North

FROM JANUARY TO MAY OF 1776 the ghost of an American army, held together by Benedict Arnold's fiery leadership, worried through a howling Canadian winter in front of Quebec. Then, unexpectedly, Arnold's men found themselves in the path of a juggernaut, as England mustered her resources to extinguish the rebellion.

As envisaged somewhat vaguely in London, the English plan was to strike three blows: an invasion from Canada south through the Hudson valley, a massive sea-borne occupation of New York, and a thrust into the Carolinas. The first two moves would split New England—hotbed of revolution—from the other colonies. The third would arouse what was believed to be predominant Tory sentiment in the South into an irresistible backfire.

Clinton, as we have noted, had moved towards the Carolinas prior to the evacuation of Boston. Howe, after reorganizing his demoralized forces in Halifax, would join a powerful amphibious expedition already under sail for New York under the command of his brother, Admiral Lord Richard Howe. Burgoyne, who had gone back to England from Boston, was returning with an expedition to reinforce Carleton in Canada for the push from the St. Lawrence River into the Hudson valley. Not only was the cream of England's regular army in the transports crossing the Atlantic, but also some 17,000-odd Brunswick and Hessian troops, hired from their impecunious rulers with British gold. Before the war was ended, 29,875 of these hired German soldiers would have come over.

Meanwhile Arnold was grimly hanging on south of Quebec. One

can hardly designate his stand a blockade. At no time during the winter did Arnold have more than 700 men, a good half of whom were smitten by smallpox. Behind Quebec's fortified walls and 148 cannon, Carleton had 1,600 able-bodied soldiers, while in the river below lay a frigate, a sloop of war and several smaller vessels. Carleton, however, sat snug and inactive.

Arnold's pleas for more men and supplies had led Congress, as early as January 19, to vote him reinforcements "with all possible dispatch," and sent him $28,000 in "hard" money. But neither wheezing old General David Wooster at Montreal nor Schuyler at Albany had men or supplies to spare, and Washington at Cambridge had troubles of his own. So Arnold's wretched men shivered, their short rations supplemented by what they could loot from a not-too-hospitable countryside.

In April Wooster did come up in person with reinforcements, bringing the American strength to 2,000, while Arnold, his leg wound aggravated by a fall from his horse, returned to Montreal. A momentary flurry of activity followed, as Wooster attempted a bombardment (quickly checked by Quebec's superior firepower), and made an unsuccessful attempt to burn the British ships. Then energetic Brigadier General John Thomas, replacing Wooster in May, found himself faced by disaster.

Carleton, with Burgoyne's expedition moving up the St. Lawrence, bestirred himself to end the "siege" of Quebec. A vigorous sortie on May 6 crashed into the American lines; 900 infantry with four field guns. Thomas could rally but 250 men to oppose it. Then his entire force disintegrated into a mob that would not halt until Sorel, at the mouth of the Richelieu, was reached.

On June 2 Thomas died of smallpox at Sorel just as reinforcements arrived. Washington sent Brigadier General William Thompson from Boston with a brigade of Continentals—2,000 strong. Brigadier General John Sullivan arrived from New York with 4,000 more. Sullivan, who had been appointed to command, also brought food, ammunition, small arms and cannon.

"On to Quebec" once again became the slogan. Overconfident Sullivan, whose directive from Washington was to press down the St. Lawrence as far as possible, sent Thompson with 2,000 men to take Trois Rivières, midway between Montreal and Quebec. He believed that some 800 British and Canadians, under Maclean, held the town. What he didn't know was that Burgoyne's 8,000 troops were also concentrating in the vicinity. So Thompson's men—the fine Pennsylvania rifle battalions of Anthony Wayne, Arthur St. Clair, William Maxwell and William Irvine—landed in darkness early on June 8, some three miles above Trois Rivières, to poke into a hornets' nest.

Misled by their Canadian guide, they stumbled through swamps and thickets to debouch, long after sunrise, into a clearing where a British covering force awaited them. Wayne led a piecemeal attack, driving the enemy outposts back to reveal a most unwelcome surprise —an entrenched British camp. Then British vessels on the river opened a flanking fire. The American attack broke up, recoiling into the woods. A three-day running fight followed, as Thompson's command—cut off from their bateaux—were harried by Indians and Canadian irregulars. Fortunately the Pennsylvania riflemen were crafty forest fighters, too. The expedition got back to Sorel, but had lost some 400 men killed, captured and missing. Carleton and Burgoyne pressed after them vigorously.

Sullivan at once evacuated Sorel for St. Johns. It was touch and go, for the British river flotilla arrived almost on the heels of his scurrying bateaux. As the British continued up the St. Lawrence towards Montreal, Arnold, waiting near Chambly till the last minute, hurried his garrison over to join Sullivan.

In a sorry huddle of sick and despondent men, the Americans left St. Johns for Ile aux Noix in boats provided by Schuyler. There they writhed in indescribable misery for a few shelterless days, subsisting on raw salt pork and flour. Of 8,000 men, 2,000 were smallpox cases, and another 1,000 stricken with dysentery or malarial fever. Men died like flies, their bodies flung in open pits. Then the survivors, the sick and the half-sick, hurried away from that pesthole on the last lap of their *via dolorosa,* as fast as enfeebled muscles could pull oar. June saw them back at Crown Point.

As soon as the generals saw the condition of the refugee army, they immediately realized that no further attempt to invade Canada was possible in 1776. On the contrary, the shoe was on the other foot, for Carleton, in overwhelming force, was poised in the St. Johns-Ile aux Noix area. Immediate British invasion was to be expected. Where and how could it best be opposed?

A council of war, held at Crown Point July 5, with Schuyler, Gates, Sullivan and Arnold present, rejected any attempt to hold that place; its defenses were in complete ruin. Ticonderoga, they believed, could be held. But control of southern Lake Champlain, at least, was vital, and for that a naval flotilla must be built.

So the sick were sent on to Fort George, the remainder of the army concentrated at Ticonderoga, with one regiment remaining at Crown Point as a covering force, and General Arnold—"perfectly skilled" for the job, as Gates put it—was ordered to build a navy.

In hand were three armed schooners and one sloop. Around them, Arnold planned to build a flotilla of gunboats. Timber, of course, was in abundance, and three small sawmills existed. But tools, rigging and all the other materials for shipbuilding just weren't there. And if they had been, there still would have been no artisans to use them.

Arnold, an experienced salt-water sailor, threw himself into the task with his usual vim. Frantic calls for skilled workmen and for materials went out to the coastal states, whose own shipyards were now humming with activity fitting out privateers. Meanwhile, wielding axes supplied in quantity by Schuyler in Albany and Governor Trumbull in Connecticut, soldier working parties swarmed in the forests, felling trees.

Attracted by promises of the unheard-of wages of $5 a day in "hard" money, some 200 ship carpenters—in four companies of 50 men each—came up from Massachusetts, Connecticut, and Rhode Island, with a few from as far south as Philadelphia. They brought their tools with them. Lured by the same promise, blacksmiths, sailmakers, riggers and oarmakers drifted in.

Skenesboro (now Whitehall) at the head of the lake became the birthplace of the inland navy. Brigadier General David Waterbury, Jr., of Connecticut, was in charge of the construction effort, while Arnold shuttled back frequently from Ticonderoga, giving—to quote Gates again—"Life & Spirit to our Dock Yards."

Two types of craft were built; row-galleys and gondolas. The round-bottomed row-galleys, approximately 80 feet long and eighteen feet in beam, were lateen-rigged with two masts, supplementing their 36 sweeps. Each was to carry ten or twelve guns—two each in bow and stern, the remainder in broadside—and a crew of 80 men. The flat-bottomed gondolas, also rowboats, 45 feet long, each carried a mast with two square sails, used only before the wind. They carried each three guns and a crew of 45 men. As fast as one was constructed it was sent to Crown Point.

Meanwhile, at Ticonderoga itself the dilapidated troops shook themselves again into some semblance of an army. Militia gathered. Continentals from Massachusetts arrived. A new fortification rose on the east side of the narrow lake neck: Fort Independence, on the hill-mass of the same name. A heavy boom, with a footbridge paralleling it, linked the twin forts and barred the narrow southern end of the lake.

Even so, the gathering strength of the defenders, five brigades, was not sufficient to man the extensive works. They mustered on paper more than 9,000 rank and file, twenty regiments in five brigades, but only 6,000 were present and fit for duty. Ordnance, too, was insufficient. Knox, when he stripped the post, had left 120 guns of light caliber, but mounts could be provided for only 43 of them, and Arnold had earmarked others for his navy.

But bread was being baked, and twenty head of beef on the hoof were coming in each week, over the rough trail blazed eastward from Independence to Hubbardton which linked the fortress with New England; the "Military Road," they called it. Sutlers, too, were daring its ruts and snags, to offer more varied fare to soldiers lucky enough to afford it. *Per contra,* sectionalism was rife. So hard was the feeling between the New Englanders and Pennsylvanians that the latter were quartered in Fort Ticonderoga itself, while the others bivouacked across the lake in Fort Independence.

On July 29 the garrison was mustered for a memorable occasion: reading of the Declaration of Independence by recently promoted Brigadier General Arthur St. Clair. And on August 20 Arnold put out from Crown Point with the major part of his makeshift squadron; the remainder would join him shortly, piecemeal.

Up north, all this while, Carleton had been concentrating in the Chambly-St. Johns-Ile aux Noix area. His total ground strength was something like 13,000 men; Burgoyne's 8,000 English and German regulars, plus Canadian militia, and Indian allies. And St. Johns itself had become a shipyard, for Carleton, too, had at once recognized the necessity for command of Lake Champlain. His task, like that of Arnold, was prodigious, but he could draw on the resources of the

St. Lawrence river towns, and of the warships and transports which had brought Burgoyne's troops over.

Up from the St. Lawrence came the 18-gun sloop *Inflexible*—a three-masted square-rigger—and two schooners. At Chambly these vessels were knocked down and transported overland to St. Johns, bypassing a ten-mile strip of rapids. It took only 28 days to rebuild the *Inflexible*. Ten gunboats, each mounting one bow-gun, had been brought out from England, knocked down. These, too, were reassembled, and ten additional gunboats constructed on the spot. Carleton's squadron also included a gondola captured from the Americans in the St. Lawrence. The crowning element of this array was a monstrous *radeau* christened the *Thunderer*—a flat-bottomed floating battery carrying six 24-pounders, six 12-pounders and two small howitzers.

By October 4 the flotilla, commanded by Captain Thomas Pringle, R.N., stood out from the Richelieu River mouth. Trailing behind were 28 longboats, carrying supplies; four of these mounted field guns in their bows. The three salt-water ships and the *radeau* each carried a company of the 29th Foot as marines.

Arnold was waiting, half-way up the lake. He had cruised as far north as Isle la Motte, exchanged shots with Carleton's Indians scouting along the shoreline, and had then retired behind Valcour Island, which sat south of Cumberland Head; a mile and a half long, steep and heavily wooded.

Here Arnold had moored his vessels in a half-moon, in the 900-yard stretch from the west shore to the southern tip of the island. They were screened from the gaze of south-bound vessels passing up the main channel; two schooners, a sloop, eight gondolas and four row-galleys, their broadsides facing south. From the soldier's point of view this was a perfect ambush; a deep-water navy man might have had misgivings.

Arnold, in the *Congress* galley, held the center. Waterbury in the *Washington* galley commanded the right wing, and Colonel Edward Wigglesworth of Massachusetts in the *Trumbull* galley commanded the left. Up north of the island the schooner *Revenge* was scouting. Arnold's firepower was only about half that of Pringle's; actually the *Inflexible* alone, with her eighteen 12-pounders and her maneuverability, was a match for the entire American flotilla.

Pringle's squadron, the *Inflexible* leading, rounded Cumberland Head in the early morning of October 11. The weather was fair; the wind blowing up the lake from the north. The *Revenge,* spotting them, fled back to warn Arnold, who decided to await them in position.

Unwitting, for Pringle had neglected to send any scout boats ahead, the British squadron, sailing on the wind, passed east of Valcour Island. They discovered the American squadron on their starboard quarter only after they cleared the southern tip of Valcour.

Consequently, Pringle had to come about and beat back to close with his enemy, to whom he had surrendered the advantage of the wind—a grave error in windjamming days.

Arnold, who had originally planned a defensive battle, now changed his mind. He ordered the schooner *Royal Savage* and the four row-galleys to attack. But as they stood out of the line he changed his mind again and ordered them back. Due to the ineptitude of her amateur crew, the *Royal Savage,* trying to beat back to her station, drifted hard and fast ashore.

This mishap, however, was offset by Pringle's original error of incautious advance, for the mighty *Inflexible* and the schooner *Maria,* Pringle's flagship, found it impossible to beat back against the wind and close. They had to anchor and content themselves with long-range fire. Clumsy *Thunderer,* the floating battery; and the galley *Loyal Convert,* never even got into the fight.

But the sharp-pointing schooner *Carleton,* 12, fully sustained the honor of the Royal Navy. Her skipper, Lieutenant J. R. Dacres, by noon had clawed against the wind to within 350 yards of the center of the American line. There he dropped anchor with a spring on his cable enabling him to haul his vessel broadside to his foes, and opened with his six 6-pounders. Beside him, seventeen of the little one-gun English gunboats drew into line, their cannon rating from 9- to 24-pounders. A slam-bang fleet gun-duel began.

Over on the American left flank, where the *Royal Savage* had grounded, British army Captain Simon Fraser (cousin of the brigadier of the same name who led Burgoyne's light corps) got his Canadian irregulars and Indians ashore and took the galley under musketry fire. Her crew abandoned her. A boat party from the *Thunderer* boarded and turned her guns against Arnold's line, but was in turn driven off by American fire. Then a boarding party from the *Maria* set her on fire.

But the main gun fight centered on the *Carleton,* whose nearest antagonist was Arnold's *Congress.* Converging American fire hulled the *Carleton* again and again. The spring line on her cable was shot

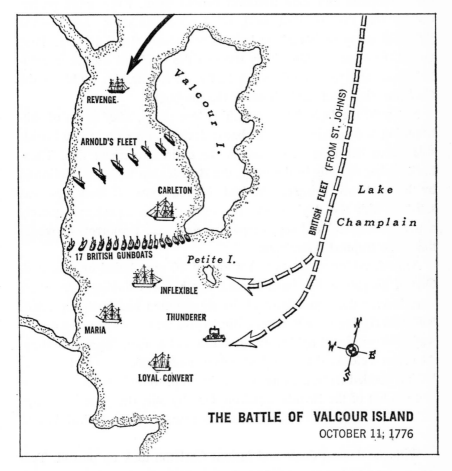

REVENGE.

Valcour I.

ARNOLD'S FLEET

CARLETON

17 BRITISH GUNBOATS

Petite I.

INFLEXIBLE

THUNDERER

MARIA

LOYAL·CONVERT

BRITISH FLEET (FROM ST. JOHNS)

Lake

Champlain

THE BATTLE OF VALCOUR ISLAND
OCTOBER 11, 1776

away and she swung head-on into the wind, to be raked incessantly. With her captain, Dacres, knocked senseless, Midshipman Edward Pellew * took command. Climbing out of the schooner's bowsprit, he tried to spread her jib to catch the wind—to swing her back into line—but without success. Two longboats came up to help. Pellew,

---

* Pellew would live to become one of England's great admirals, Lord Exmouth.

daring a shower of musket balls, managed to pass them a line, the schooner's cable was slipped, and the crippled *Carleton* was slowly drawn out of the fight. Half of her crew had been killed or wounded, and she was making water fast.

Such conduct was to be expected from professional naval men, with discipline and long tradition behind them. Even more praiseworthy was the steadfast work of Arnold's amateur sailors—"the refuse of every regiment" as he had previously dubbed them. They served their guns unflinchingly through the melée of a close-in artillery duel, and they didn't do so badly, either; besides drubbing the *Carleton,* they had sunk three of the gunboats.

Not until the *Inflexible* got within close range, after hours of sail-trimming and coaxing, was the battle decided. Five successive broadsides from her long 12's silenced the entire American line. Then, backing her topsails in the dusk, the British ship withdrew, followed by the gunboats. Pringle, who had suffered some 40 casualties, was satisfied with the day's work. He anchored his squadron squarely across the channel and began repairing damages. Tomorrow he would finish the trapped Americans.

Arnold, taking stock, tallied a loss of 80 men killed or wounded. One of his galleys had been burned, another was sinking, two others were heavily damaged. Most of the ammunition had been expended. Sails and rigging were in tatters. But to give up hope was not Arnold's way. The wind still held from the north and a night fog was settling. At seven o'clock, the *Trumbull* galley made sufficient sail to move. With a hooded lantern on her stern, she crept south between the shore and the left of the British squadron. One by one, the American ships followed, with Arnold's *Congress* the last vessel out, in typical Arnold fashion.

With the dawn Pringle and furious Carleton took up pursuit. Two American schooners, a galley and a gondola got clear away to reach Crown Point. But the *Inflexible* and two British schooners overhauled the cripples, one by one. Waterbury's *Washington* was forced to strike. Arnold, in the *Congress,* with four gondolas, slugged it out in a two and a half hour running fight. Then, with his galley battered into a sinking shambles, he ran his five wrecks ashore in Buttonmould Bay below Split Rock Point and set them on fire. He held his men on shore until the ships blew up, their flags still flying, then led the

200 survivors—46 only were left of the *Congress'* original 73—to Crown Point, ten miles to the south. Next day its garrison burned the untenable post and with Arnold and his survivors retreated to Ticonderoga.

Lake Champlain had been transformed into King George's duck pond; the way cleared for a determined British thrust on Fort Ticonderoga. Be it on land-locked lake or mighty ocean, the effects of sea power are the same. So long as Arnold was able to boast a splinter squadron it was a "fleet in being." Carleton could not advance until it was eliminated. By the time that happened, he felt that it was too late in the year to exploit the success.

Winter was approaching fast. Cautious Carleton dreaded dangling at the end of a frozen communications line reaching back more than 200 miles to Quebec. So, on November 3, the British expeditionary force, abandoning all its territorial gains, started back to winter quarters in Canada.

Alfred Thayer Mahan would later comment that the American victory at Saratoga in 1777 "was due to the invaluable year of delay secured to them in 1776 by their little navy on Lake Champlain, created by the indomitable energy, and handled with the indomitable courage of the traitor, Benedict Arnold."

★ 10 ★ ★ ★ ★ ★

Munitions Flow through Troubled Seas

NOT UNTIL OCTOBER 13, 1775 did the Congress get around to authorizing a Continental Navy, although—as we know—"Washington's Navy" of 1775 had already dared Britannia's naval might in New England waters.

Congress now faced up to the fact that war could not be waged without munitions and these must be sought via the high seas—either through purchase, in Europe's trade with the already gathering munitions peddlers in the West Indies, or wrenched from the enemy. Time was of the essence. Accordingly, although the construction of thirteen frigates began, the first reliance of the new Navy was upon converted merchantmen.

On February 17, 1776, the infant nation's first squadron put to sea from Delaware Bay, Commodore Ezek Hopkins, 58-year-old Rhode Island sea captain, commanding. His objective was a raid upon the island of New Providence in the Bahamas, where a large quantity of powder was said to have been stored for British supply.

Hopkins' fleet consisted of the ships *Alfred* and *Columbus,* both 24; the brigs *Andrew Doria* and *Cabot,* both 14; the slooprigged *Providence,* 12; and the schooner *Wasp,* 8. Among the hurriedly commissioned personnel was one John Paul Jones, first lieutenant in the *Alfred.*

Taking advantage of a heavy gale, Hopkins cleverly avoided British blockaders in the Chesapeake and off the Carolina coast, and rendezvoused off Abaco, Bahamas, March 1. Two days later, a task force of 200 marines and fifty bluejackets under Marine Captain Samuel Nicholas of the *Alfred* was landed without opposition at the eastern end of New Providence, and marched towards Nassau, the capital, defended by two forts and a garrison of 200 men.

Nicholas informed the British governor of his intention to seize all "warlike stores" without, if possible, "touching the property or hurting the person of any of the inhabitants." After token resistance, Nassau was peaceably occupied and 71 cannon, fifteen brass mortars and 24 casks of powder captured—a neat contribution to Washington's military necessities.

Unaware that the British had hidden 150 additional casks of powder during the landing, Hopkins sailed for home, capturing two small British armed vessels and two merchantmen off Block Island. He failed, however, in a night encounter on April 5, with HMS *Glasgow*, 20; the British sloop beat off attacks of both the *Cabot* and the *Alfred*, whose inexperienced crews could not match the British gunnery.

Hopkins reached New London with his precious cargo after having executed an important task with initiative and responsibility. His reward was to be dismissed a few months later for alleged disobedience of orders in not first operating against the British blockaders in the Chesapeake at the start of his cruise. Before suffering this injustice, however, Hopkins protected the water transport of part of Washington's army from New London to New York—a most valuable bit of cooperation. Hopkins deserved better from his country.

It was during Hopkins' Bahamas cruise that privateering was authorized by the Congress on March 19, unleashing a continually growing flock of sea-guerrillas who would in their own fashion play hob with unprotected British commerce during most of the war. The other side of this coin was an immediate and continuous competition between American private enterprise and government for able-bodied seamen. As is usual, the lure of prize money and comparative freedom from harsh, regular discipline offered to the privateersman would sadly hamper recruiting for the Navy all through the struggle. In addition, state navies in Massachusetts, Rhode Island, Connecticut, New York, Pennsylvania, Maryland, Virginia, and the Carolinas came into being to harass enemy shipping and to drain further the new nation's limited maritime resources away from a coordinated effort.

Like the privateers, the Continental Navy was forced to resort to a *guerre de course* (hit-and-run commerce destruction) since its vessels were no match for the superior numbers and ships of the line of the Royal Navy. Cruising individually or in small company, the daring American seamen compelled the employment of many times their number in British ships for blockading and for convoy, while at the same time forcing up insurance rates to plague the British merchant marine and British merchants.

A few of the many cruises are well worth noting. There was, for instance, that of the brig *Reprisal*, 16, Captain Lambert Wickes, in July, 1776, carrying as a passenger William Bingham, newly appointed commercial and naval agent to the French West Indies. En route, Wickes convoyed thirteen American merchantmen out of the Delaware and later captured three prizes. Arriving off St. Pierre, Martinique, with his official passenger, Wickes fell in with HM sloop *Shark*, 16, just clearing the harbor. After a brief but inconclusive action the Britisher stood off and Bingham, safely landed, began his most important task of organizing and controlling the rapidly growing arms trade.

In October, Wickes and his *Reprisal* sailed across the Atlantic in support of another diplomatic effort; he was carrying Benjamin Franklin to France to begin the first and one of the most notable of American diplomatic missions overseas.

Franklin having been landed, Wickes proceeded to shove the war right under King George's royal nose. Cruising into the English Channel, out of St. Nazaire, the *Reprisal*, during January, 1777, captured three brigs, one snow (or barkentine) and a ship.

While the British Ambassador to France, Lord Stormont, was loudly protesting this illegal use of French ports, Wickes sold his prizes, securing not only prize money for his crew but funds for spreading his endeavors. He purchased and fitted out the schooner *Dolphin*, which he turned over to Captain Samuel Nicholson. Joined now by the Continental brig *Lexington*, 16, under Captain Henry Johnson, Wickes led his little trio in May on a brilliant raiding cruise around the Irish coasts, gathering eighteen prizes in all.

Then Wickes headed for the English coast. Off Ushant, June 26, he met more than he had expected; HMS *Burford*, 74. The little American squadron scattered like three frightened birds. The big ship of the line, running on the wind after the *Reprisal*, showed surprising speed. An eight-hour chase brought her near enough to open with her light bow guns. Wickes, making for the French coast, heaved overboard his entire battery of eighteen guns without increasing his distance. Fortunately, the Englishman's marksmanship was poor. By dusk, with a rocky lee shore in sight, he gave up the chase. Wickes, clawing off in turn, made St. Malo and a hospitable welcome.

While insurance rates in England soared and Stormont stormed in Paris, Wickes calmly refitted in an efficient French shipyard. Not until he was shipshape once more, including a new battery, did the French—in lip-service to British protests—order him to sea again. On September 14, 1777, the *Reprisal* left for America. She never got home. After eluding several British cruisers she foundered with all on board in a gale near the American coast. Had it not been for this disaster, the name of Wickes might today be revered in the United States Navy beside that of John Paul Jones.

During May and June, Captain Nicholas Biddle, in the *Andrew Doria*, also cruised from New England ports to garner twelve prizes, including two troop-transports. And John Paul Jones, commanding first the *Providence* and then the *Alfred*, harried the Nova Scotia coast. Before he was through he had captured a score of prizes and had outwitted and outsailed in turn the British frigates *Solebay* and *Milford*.

Captain Gustavus Conyngham, commissioned by the American Commissioners in Paris, for a while continued nautical depredations off England's coasts. First in the lugger *Surprise*, 10, then in the cutter *Revenge*, 14, he operated out of Dunkerque and—later— from Ferrol, Spain. He captured a number of prizes in the North Sea and along the Atlantic coast.

Meanwhile, other vessels of the little Continental Navy afloat attempted the work of obtaining war munitions from British Army supply ships and from the West Indies, which was rapidly becoming an essential entrepôt for munitions from Europe. Also, though sporadic at first, the efforts of American agents abroad and of enterprising foreign commercial firms to guide a flow of munitions to the American cause had now become big business.

King Louis XVI of France on May 2, 1776, decreed a secret grant to the patriots of one million *livres* (approximately $200,000) for the purpose of arms procurement. The King's action was a result of the recommendation of his secret service agent Beaumarchais, who in December, 1775, urgently recommended steps be taken to assist the colonies in their struggle with England. Concurrence of the foreign minister, Vergennes, brought matters to a head. At the same time Vergennes sounded out Spain's foreign minister, Jerónimo Grimaldi, on the possibility of joint action. Charles III of Spain then matched the French gift with another million *livres.*

Organizing a dummy company—Rodrigue Hortalez et Cie., with himself at its head—Beaumarchais went into action, in close communication with Silas Deane, one of the American Commissioners in Paris, and later with Benjamin Franklin. Almost instantaneously, it seemed, a generous flow of arms, ammunition, uniforms and other military supplies began moving across the Atlantic to the West Indies in French bottoms, consigned to Hortalez at Martinique, at Cap François (Cap Hatien) in Haiti, and in Holland's St. Eustatius. In cold fact, Beaumarchais, pyramiding upon the original two million *livres,* eventually furnished munitions many times more in value than the initial capital. And in Martinique William Bingham, as agent for the Continental Congress, directed the redistribution and shipment to the United States. Legitimate foreign firms—French, Dutch and Spanish —participated. Even some canny English merchants were in fact coppering their bets, so to speak, countering trade losses resulting from the war by judicious and lucrative participation in the munitions game—and at the same time contributing to the death of many of their country's soldiers, and helping to frustrate their nation's war effort.

Whatever the motives, it was indeed big business. Beaumarchais' own record shows that Hortalez' first shipment included 300 "thousands" of gunpowder, 30,000 muskets, 200 cannon, 100,000 bullets and 13,000 bombs. In addition, 30,000 sets of uniforms went in the eight vessels chartered to carry the goods.

Naturally, not all these essentials ever reached America; the British blockade was too vigilant. But sufficient got through, by bits and pieces and in intermittent gushes, to ensure the prosecution of what would otherwise have been an unsuccessful revolution.

Before the war closed, French aid had reached a peak enormous for those days: the equivalent of $1,996,500 in subsidies, and $6,352,-500 additional in loans. Spanish subsidies amounted to $397,230, with another $248,098 in the shape of loans.

Both the French and Spanish governments were, of course, gambling in cold blood for high stakes: to cripple England. For them there would be agonizing moments as the fortunes of war fluctuated and the Revolutionary cause teetered several times on the verge of disaster.

Holland's part in this European aid program was slightly different in motivation. The Dutch Republic was unofficially allied to Great Britain both through its Stadtholder's blood ties and because of a long-continued policy of mutual assistance. But Holland was both a maritime and mercantile nation with munitions of war for sale, and in her West Indian possession of St. Eustatius a huge traffic in munitions was building up, too lucrative to be passed up by thrifty Dutch merchants. So Holland long preserved a tenuous neutrality, skating on thin ice. As early as November, 1776, St. Eustatius' Governor Johannes de Graaff saluted the new Stars and Stripes flown from USS *Andrew Doria,* drawing a lusty protest from Britain. In any event, the arms trade was officially denounced but unofficially welcomed; a situation unchanged until December, 1780, when Rodney's ships of the line seized both St. Eustatius and St. Martin and choked the Dutch supply line.

Late that year, with the Netherlands finally at war with England, France borrowed ten million *livres* from the States General for the United States, guaranteeing repayment. In 1782 John Adams, minister plenipotentiary, obtained a direct loan of five million *guilders,* at 5 per cent interest from a consortium of Amsterdam bankers. All in all, Dutch monetary aid furnished the United States in the latter part of the war and during the first struggling years of the following peace amounted to approximately $9,000,000. It should be noted that after the war, all the foreign loans—French, Spanish and Dutch—were gradually repaid in U.S. bonds.

There is, unfortunately, no room in these pages to discuss more fully the diplomatic intrigue in Europe's council chambers and counting-houses caused by the War of the Revolution. Before the frantic European jugglings to upset England ended, Austria, Prussia and even remote Russia also became involved in one way or another with matters of neutrality and the sanctity of commerce on the high seas. Neutrals' rights became the bone of contention that would gradually and inexorably transmute the rebellion of the colonies into an almost-World War. As we shall see, American liberty became perhaps as dependent upon the outcome of armed clashes between England and the Franco-Spanish alliance on the world's oceans, as upon those fought by Americans on the North American continent.

All this aid was, of course, entirely separate from any popular and individual good-will accorded by the peoples or governments of Europe to the colonies' struggle for liberty. Only in France was there any really popular sympathy for the colonies in their struggle for liberty; a sympathy amazing in the warmth displayed both by the people and the king, distinct from the cynical motives of the French Cabinet.

As for individual sympathy, expressed by actual participation in the war, many Europeans flocked to the American cause, but again a sharp division in motivation separated the comparatively few generous souls—like France's Lafayette, de Kalb, and Fleury; Prussia's von Steuben; and Poland's gallant Kosciuszko and Pulaski—from the horde of soldiers of fortune who gravitated from overseas to America, seeking their own advancement. With Europe in comparative peace, professional soldiers out of jobs were a dime a dozen in 1776-77, and Silas Deane in Paris was dangling generalcies in the Continental Army with spendthrift generosity. This, as it would turn out, was much to George Washington's embarrassment, to the rage of competent American officers, and to the detriment of the cause.

11 ★ ★ ★ ★ ★

A Declaration Frustrates the Howe Brothers

DURING THE WINTER OF 1775-76 the English government of Lord North completed its plans to suppress the rebellion in the colonies by concentration of overwhelming force. Army and navy recruitment in Britain was disappointing, however, in the latter months of 1775, partly as a result of sympathy for the colonists' cause, and, to an even greater degree, public apathy regarding a war 3,000 miles away. Recruiting problems played a major rôle in delaying Sir Peter Parker's expedition to the Carolinas for two months.

Accordingly, the British made treaties with the German principalities of Brunswick, Hanover, Hesse-Hanau, Hesse-Cassel, and Waldeck, to hire approximately 17,000 German troops for operations in America. Including these mercenaries, they expected to be able to deploy upwards of 50,000 troops in America in 1776. Lord North and his ministers had little doubt that this would be sufficient force to suppress the rebellion.

New York had been selected as the principal target of the coming British offensive even before General Howe's evacuation of Boston in mid-March, 1776. There were several reasons for this choice. New York was centrally located on the Atlantic coast, and its superb harbor would provide a naval base for further coastal operations, and at the same time an army base for an advance up the Hudson River, which would split the thirteen colonies in two parts. Furthermore, Loyalist sentiment was strong among New York merchants, and this was expected to facilitate occupation of the town.

The British government selected Admiral Lord Richard Howe as the commander of the great land and naval force being assembled in England for the purpose of seizing New York. When Howe's fleet and troop convoys arrived near New York, he was to be joined by his younger brother, General Sir William Howe, who would sail from Halifax with the troops recently evacuated from Boston. At the same time, the reinforcements under General Burgoyne, which had been sent to Carleton in Canada, would press southward down the Richelieu River and Lake Champlain to the northern Hudson valley, to meet the Howe brothers somewhere near Albany.

The Howes, both being relatively liberal Whigs, and known to have been sympathetic with colonial grievances, were specifically empowered by King George III to act as peace commissioners as well as military commanders. They were authorized to treat with individual rebel leaders, and to offer general and liberal terms for the surrender of rebellious forces and for the re-establishment of loyal, representative colonial governments. With a few notable exceptions, the brothers were empowered to pardon and protect from Loyalist retribution those colonial leaders who abandoned the patriot cause. They were specifically forbidden, however, to enter into political negotiations while rebel armies remained in the field, undispersed and armed.

The British plans, as well as the military and political mission of the Howe brothers, were of course unknown to the Continental Congress or to General Washington when Boston was evacuated on March 17, 1776. Washington, however, immediately assumed that New York was the most likely place for the next British action. He had already sent General Charles Lee in February to prepare New York for defense, but Lee had later been ordered by the Continental Congress to take over the military command of the Southern colonies.

This left New York's defense in the hands of Brigadier General William Alexander, Lord Stirling (a Scottish title recognized in Edinburgh but disallowed by the House of Lords in Westminster). Before the end of the war Stirling would have proven himself to be a stout soldier and one of Washington's most trusted subordinates. But at this time all the Commander-in-Chief knew about him was that he was from New Jersey, son of a Scottish Stuart supporter who had fled from persecution; also that he had had some military experience in the French and Indian War, was a harsh disciplinarian, and—rumor had it—was over-fond of the bottle. So Washington hurried Israel Putnam to New York to assume command. Putnam, with some reinforcements, arrived from Boston on April 4.

Washington himself reached New York on April 13, and was soon followed by most of the Continentals who had been under his command outside of Boston. He immediately set about improving the readiness of the city's defenses.

During Lee's short tenure of command there, he had developed a rather comprehensive defensive plan, based on the reasonable assumption that if and when the British really wanted to take the port, seapower would enable them to do so. So Lee's plan was one of deterrence rather than a last-ditch stand. Earthworks and barricades were in construction all around lower Manhattan Island, blocking waterfront approach to all principal streets. On Brooklyn Heights, Long Island, dominating the lower tip of Manhattan, fortifications were also begun, primarily to prevent the heights from falling into enemy hands, secondarily to assure that American guns could still dominate the city were it captured.

Washington now approved Lee's plan, although he believed it would require larger forces than the existing garrison of some 4,000 men. By the end of the month, however, with the arrival of more troops from Boston, Washington's force in New York had grown to more than 8,000. All of these were soon busily engaged in completing the fortifications planned by Lee, but which had not been too energetically pursued meanwhile.

During the late spring and early summer the American fortifications grew in strength and number under the supervision of young Colonel Henry Knox. By the end of July these included some twenty redoubts and major batteries, with about 130 artillery pieces of varying calibers, most of which had been brought by Knox from Boston or Ticonderoga.

Since it was essential that British warships be prevented from entering either the Hudson or East rivers from New York Bay, and thus flanking Manhattan Island, the mouths of both waterways were

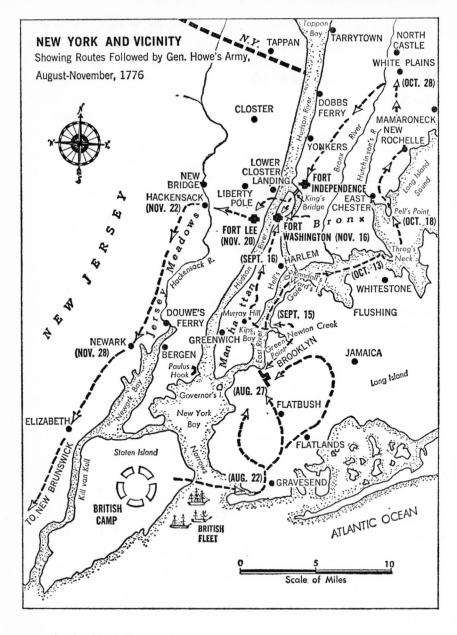

NEW YORK AND VICINITY
Showing Routes Followed by Gen. Howe's Army,
August-November, 1776

strongly fortified. Protecting the Hudson entrance were guns at the
"Battery" of Fort George, on the southern tip of Manhattan, and at
Paulus—or Powle's—Hook (now Jersey City) across the way. Further up-river were Forts Washington, in Harlem Heights, and Constitution (later Fort Lee) opposite on the New Jersey Palisades.

The East River—no river at all, but a gulf linking New York Bay and Long Island Sound—presented a more complicated problem. Governors Island loosely stoppered its bay mouth, with Buttermilk Channel passing to its east along the Brooklyn shore, while the main channel skirted its northwest side, between the island and Manhattan. Each channel was swept by short-range cross fire of batteries emplaced on the opposite banks. Additional guns were scattered along Manhattan's shores, and at Hell Gate a battery defended the east mouth of the Harlem River against any British approach from Long Island Sound. Just north of the Harlem River, at King's Bridge, Fort Independence guarded the only land road to Manhattan from the mainland.

Because of the importance of Brooklyn Heights to the defense of the city, and because Long Island offered the most feasible land approach to the city, additional works had been built near Brooklyn. To protect the rear of the batteries overlooking Buttermilk Channel and entrance to the East River, a line of five redoubts, connected by entrenchments and *abatis,* extended from the Gowanus Marshes to Wallabout Bay (present site of the Brooklyn Navy Yard).

While all this work was going on, Washington established a lookout on the heights of Staten Island, to observe the British blockading squadron which was anchored near Sandy Hook. Lord Tryon, the Royal Governor of New York, a refugee on one of the ships of this squadron, kept up an undercover correspondence with Loyalist sympathizers in the city.

Tryon's activities included a program for enlistment in Loyalist military units which were being clandestinely raised on board the British ships. At the same time he was apparently supporting and abetting a more serious Loyalist plot within the city itself. One of the principal participants in this plot, evidently, was David Matthews, the mayor of the city. When, on June 22, Matthews was arrested for suspicious activities, an intensive investigation soon revealed plans for a Loyalist uprising which would be coincident with a British attack. At this time Washington and other leading American generals were to be assassinated. Implicated in the plot were several Continental soldiers, including one Thomas Hickey, actually a member of Washington's personal bodyguard. Hickey was court-martialed, and was executed on June 28. This appears to have greatly dampened the enthusiasm of other Loyalists for continuing subversive activities. Though Matthews' direct connection with the assassination plot was never proven, he was kept in jail.

Meanwhile, on June 25 a large convoy of transports and warships arrived at Sandy Hook, bringing General Howe, and approximately 9,000 men, from Halifax. On the 28th the armada sailed close to the Narrows between Staten Island and Long Island, causing immediate alarm in New York. Next day, however, Howe contented himself with a landing on Staten Island, where he stayed to await reinforcements.

These were not long in coming. On July 12 more than 100 additional British ships from England arrived in New York's lower bay. This was Admiral Lord Richard Howe's expedition, with almost 10,000 British troops, and more than 1,000 Germans. These troops also landed on Staten Island.

Meanwhile, in Philadelphia, an event took place which would have the utmost significance to the watchful armies observing each other across New York Bay, and to their respective commanding generals. On July 2 a committee of the Continental Congress had presented to that body a document written by Thomas Jefferson of Virginia, with the assistance of Benjamin Franklin of Pennsylvania and John Adams of Massachusetts. Entitled "The Unanimous Declaration of the Thirteen United States of America," this noble document, after summarizing the injustices suffered by the colonists at the hands of George III—"a Tyrant . . . unfit to be the ruler of a free people"—concluded "that these United Colonies are, and of Right ought to be FREE AND INDEPENDENT STATES." By their resolution endorsing this Declaration of Independence, the members of Congress joined with their drafting committee in asserting that "for the support of this Declaration, with a firm reliance on the protection of Divine Providence, we mutually pledge to each other our Lives, our Fortunes, and our sacred Honor." This concept was later expressed somewhat more pithily by Benjamin Franklin, when he signed the document: "We must all hang together, or assuredly we shall all hang separately."

Two days later, July 4, 1776, Congress approved the publication of its Declaration of Independence to the American people and to the world. America was now a nation—*if* it could defeat the armed might of the most powerful nation in the world.

On July 9 Washington received official notification of the signing of the Declaration of Independence. He assembled his army and had the Declaration read to them. The ceremony ended with a brief exhortation from the Commanding General for his men to be worthy supporters of the newly independent nation whose uniform they now wore. After the troops were dismissed, many of them joined with local townspeople in pulling down the statue of George III on Bowling Green.

The proximity of some 20,000 British regular troops on Staten Island caused Washington, who had barely half that many, to suggest to Congress that their Declaration would be meaningless unless he received reinforcements. As a result, Congress called for more troops from the States, and by mid-August Washington's strength had grown to about 20,000. Of these, however, only about 10,000 were relatively reliable Continentals, the remainder being short-term militiamen. Of this total force, probably about 1,500 were riflemen; the remainder were armed with muskets or fowling pieces. An additional 10,000 militia from Pennsylvania, Maryland, and Delaware were assembled in a "flying camp" at Amboy. Most of the Jersey militia was spread through that state on home defense tasks.

Washington reorganized his army into five divisions, under Generals Putnam, Spencer, Sullivan, Heath and Greene. Greene's division held the fortified Brooklyn Heights, while the others manned defenses around the perimeter of Manhattan Island.

There was no cavalry in the army, and contemporary and later historians have severely criticized Washington for his failure to provide for sufficient mounted men to carry out reconnaissance, screening, and harassing missions in the event of operations on Long Island. This criticism is at least partially justified, though it does not prove—as some historians have averred—that Washington had no understanding of cavalry. In July he had received a cavalry regiment of some 500 men from Connecticut. Washington refused to accept these men, however, because they claimed that the laws of Connecticut excused them from guard, fatigue or any dismounted duty. Because of this, and because forage was short on Manhattan Island, he sent them back to their homes.

Despite severe punitive measures, Washington had considerable difficulty in maintaining discipline. Civilians complained incessantly about the men's drinking and wenching, and in addition there were many desertions. The militia gave Washington the most trouble, but his newly raised Continentals were not immune to the attractions of a city of 25,000 people.

In addition, the collection of so many units from the different states led to considerable friction. On August 1 Washington was forced to issue a general order to the troops, entreating them to lay aside their regional and factional "jealousies and et cetera," appealing to their patriotism and to their soldierly instincts; urging them to consider only the "honor and success of the army."

Because of his administrative headaches, Washington probably would have welcomed some overt move by the Howe brothers. Nevertheless, he took advantage of their apparent lethargy to improve and extend the fortifications of the city.

The British leaders, however, were extremely busy during the latter part of July and the early days of August, despite the inaction of their troops. Endeavoring to carry out their conciliation mission, they tried to enter into private negotiations with leading members of the Continental Congress. Since as loyal British officers they could not recognize Washington's military rank, and since Washington refused to enter into any discussions unless his status and the independence of his nation were recognized, the first peace efforts came to naught. Lord Howe, however, did have an informal discussion with Benjamin Franklin, John Adams, and Edward Rutledge at his brother's headquarters on Staten Island. Nothing came of this, either, since Howe could not recognize the independence of the United States, and since the three congressmen—even had they been so inclined—could not abjure the Declaration of Independence. The Howes' peace mission became hopeless after the Congressional resolutions of July 2 and 4.

★ 12 ★ ★ ★ ★ ★

Defeat on Long Island

WHILE THE HOWE BROTHERS WERE VAINLY TRYING to carry out their function as peace commissioners, they also completed their preparations for military action. On August 1 Generals Clinton and Cornwallis returned from the unsuccessful expedition against Charleston, adding 2,500 more troops to Howe's command. On August 12 another large fleet of warships and transports arrived from England, with 2,600 British troops, and 8,000 Hessians. This brought General Howe's total force to a strength of approximately 32,000 professional soldiers, the largest expeditionary force which Great Britain had ever sent from her shores up to that time. At the same time Lord Howe's fleet of ten ships of the line, and twenty frigates, plus several hundred transports, was manned by an additional 10,000 British seamen.

While waiting for these reinforcements, Lord Howe had on July 12 made a significant probe of the defenses of New York by sending the frigates *Phoenix*, 40, and *Rose*, 32, accompanied by three unarmed vessels, up the Hudson River. The American troops—who should have rushed to their batteries as soon as the alert was given—seemed to think that the spectacular movement of five British vessels up the river was merely a show for their edification. A few American guns did open fire, however, and the festive aspect of the event quickly ended when several British broadsides hammered the city and its defenses, creating a panic in the civilian population. Next day Washington issued a stern rebuke to the troops for having failed to respond adequately to the alert.

For more than a month the two British warships remained anchored in the Tappan Zee north of the city. Here they disrupted communications between New York and the northern army. On August 3 an American force under Lieutenant Colonel Benjamin Tupper attacked the British vessels in a few small boats, but was beaten off. On the 16th an American fire raft attack was also repulsed, but came so close to success that the little British squadron decided to withdraw. On August 18 the ships again successfully passed the American batteries along the North River, suffering very little damage. Washington was again mortified, but other events soon took his mind off this relatively minor activity.

Washington agreed with Lee's view that New York would be untenable if Brooklyn Heights were in the possession of the British. On the other hand, to defend Brooklyn Heights, and still be able to oppose a direct British attack on New York, he would have to divide his army between Manhattan and Long Island, with the two portions separated by the East River: an arm of the sea accessible to British warships from New York Bay and Long Island Sound. Even more dangerous was the now-demonstrated fact that British ships could fight their way up the Hudson River to land British troops either on northern Manhattan Island, or in the Bronx, to cut off the American army from all possibility of escape to the mainland. Thus, so long as he defended Manhattan or Long Island, Washington recognized that there was great danger that all or part of his army might be destroyed by the combination of overwhelming British land and naval strength.

On the other hand, Washington well appreciated the serious strategic implications of a British capture of New York. It is clear from his correspondence that this was the basis of his apparent belief that it was worth the effort and the risk to endeavor to defend the city. In any event, having clearly pointed out to the Continental Congress the dangers to his army, he loyally and energetically attempted to carry out the Congressional resolutions directing him to hold New York. In retrospect, Washington as Commander-in-Chief would have been justified in disregarding instructions from the Congress which in fact threatened the very existence of his army. In light of his own uncertainties, however, he determined to carry out the mission as best he could. This required him to divide his army on both sides of the East River—a decision severely criticized by military and civilian historians.* Under the circumstances, and in light of his mission as he saw it, his defensive plan was probably as sound as could have been devised.

Washington took all possible precautions to prevent the British fleet from sailing up either the Hudson or East rivers, and to assure the security of communications between Brooklyn and Manhattan. He strengthened the fortifications and the batteries on Governors Island. The repulse which had been suffered by Sir Peter Parker's fleet at Charleston is an indication that the mutually-supporting batteries on Governors Island, at the tip of Manhattan, and on the Brooklyn shore would probably have been able to prevent the British fleet from moving up the East River. To render such an attack even more difficult, Washington had hulks sunk to obstruct Buttermilk Channel and the East River. Thus the fundamental strategic error of attempting to hold New York was greatly minimized. On the other hand, as we shall see, these sound defensive measures were to a large extent nullified by tactical mistakes which Washington and his subordinates soon afterwards made on Long Island itself.

On August 22, protected by warships in the Narrows and in the southern portion of the upper bay, General Howe and his army brilliantly executed a well-prepared plan for a landing on Long Island. In a few hours 15,000 troops, plus artillery and stores, were moved from Staten Island in flat-bottomed boats to Gravesend Bay.

Observing the crossing on the Long Island side was the 1st Pennsylvania Continental Regiment of Colonel Edward Hand. Recognizing that his few hundred men could do nothing to prevent the landing, Hand withdrew, burning all of the crops in the southwestern position of Long Island, and slaughtering as many cattle as he could find.

The leading British elements, under Lord Cornwallis, advanced to seize Flatbush. American sharpshooters, concealed in cornfields, attempted to ambush the advancing redcoats, but the concealed positions were betrayed by Loyalists or deserters. Flushing the skirmishers from the cornfields, the British advanced to make small arms contact with American outposts holding the Long Island Heights (Heights of Guan) beyond. Cornwallis set up his own pickets opposite Flat-

---

* See Appendix V.

bush and Bedford passes. Behind him the main body of the army established encampments from Gravesend to Flatlands. Two days later, about 5,000 Hessians under Major General Leopold von Heister joined the other troops on Long Island, bringing Howe's total force there to slightly more than 20,000 men. The remainder of his army he kept on Staten Island to be available for a possible move against New York, or to act as a reserve for the main army, as the situation might dictate.

Active British reconnaissance and patrolling soon gave Howe an accurate picture of the American dispositions. This was amplified by intelligence flowing in from Loyalist spies behind the rebel lines. Extending eastward from Gowanus Bay lay the rugged, heavily wooded Heights of Guan, a spine separating northern Long Island from the southern plains. This ridge was tightly held by American skirmishers, while substantial units protected the crossing points at Gowanus, west of the ridge, and at the Flatbush and Bedford passes. A mounted patrol observed Jamaica Pass, further east. Behind this strong outpost line lay the formidable line of fortifications that Lee had begun, and Washington had strengthened, protecting Brooklyn Heights and the batteries covering Buttermilk Channel and the mouth of the East River.

While the British were reconnoitering and preparing for further action, the Americans were having some command problems.

On August 20, General Greene, down with a fever, was replaced by Sullivan, recently returned from Canada, and unfamiliar with the situation on Long Island. The day after the British landing, August 23, Washington visited Sullivan and observed skirmishing going on south of Long Island Heights. Apparently he became doubtful as to Sullivan's ability to defend Long Island, and so on the 24th he sent General Putnam, with substantial reinforcements, to take overall command. Sullivan was to retain Greene's division, and be second-in-command to Putnam. Washington still kept more than half of his army on Manhattan, fearing that the landing on Long Island was merely a diversion, and that Howe's main effort would come as a direct assault on the city. On the 25th, after the arrival of the Hessians, Washington sent additional troops to Putnam.

On August 26 there was a change in British dispositions. General von Heister's Hessians moved to Flatbush and the English troops of

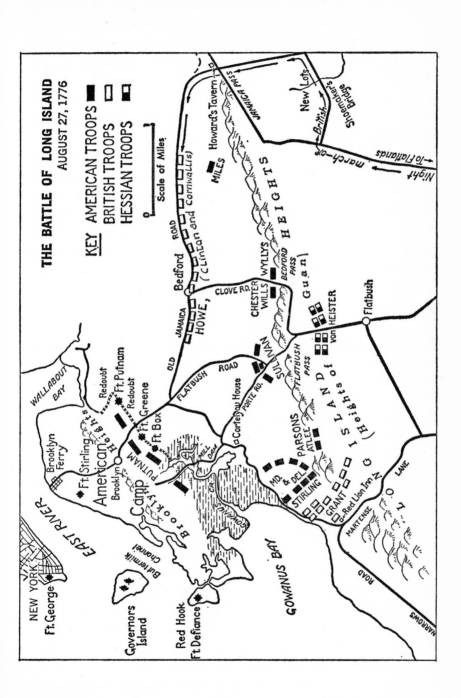

THE BATTLE OF LONG ISLAND
AUGUST 27, 1776

KEY AMERICAN TROOPS
BRITISH TROOPS
HESSIAN TROOPS

Scale of Miles

Lord Cornwallis shifted southeast to Flatlands. The American outposts in the Long Island highlands observed the movements but did not consider them significant. During the day, more reinforcements were sent from Manhattan to Long Island by Washington, bringing the total force under Putnam's command to 10,000 men or more. Washington himself again spent most of the day on Long Island, observing dispositions and discussing the probable course of operations. He expected an English attack on the 27th.

Putnam, retaining his own headquarters within the fortified lines of Brooklyn, put Sullivan in command of 3,500 troops manning the outpost line along the Long Island Heights. Sullivan in turn assigned to Lord Stirling responsibility for covering the Gowanus Road on the extreme right of the American position. He assumed personal command of the regiments covering the Flatbush and Bedford passes, assigning to Colonel Samuel Miles of the Pennsylvania Regiment of Stirling's brigade the responsibility for the left of the outpost line, east of Bedford Pass.

Evidence is contradictory as to whether Miles was specifically given the responsibility for covering or observing Jamaica Pass. Later Sullivan stated that he was; Miles insisted that he was not. Subsequent actions of both officers showed that while both felt some sense of responsibility for the Jamaica Pass, neither of them took this responsibility seriously enough. Whatever his instructions to Miles may have been, Sullivan seems to have established an officers' patrol of five young mounted militia officers to observe the pass.

Washington does not appear to have seen any need for his own personal intervention in the decisions or pre-battle preparations of his two principal subordinates. He toured the line, and seemingly was satisfied. There is no evidence that he paid any particular attention to Sullivan's left wing; if he did he appears to have seen nothing with which to find fault. Putnam, it seems, did not even check the dispositions or orders of his outpost line commander.

At approximately 1:00 A.M. of the unseasonably chilly morning of August 27, General Stirling's outpost near the Red Lion Inn, on the Gowanus Road, opened fire on British troops advancing in the dark. A spirited fire fight broke out all along the line of American outposts, as British Major General James Grant's division pushed steadily, but slowly, against them. About the same time von Heister's

Hessian artillery opened up on the defenders of the Flatbush and Bedford passes.

Word of the skirmishing near the Red Lion Inn evidently reached Putnam before Stirling was notified; Putnam himself roused Stirling sometime before 2:00 A.M., and ordered him to advance with his brigade to meet the threat—whatever it might be. This appears to be the only order Putnam issued that day to his subordinate commanders outside the Brooklyn line of fortifications. Thenceforward he was merely an interested, but ineffectual, spectator of events.

Stirling promptly roused his regimental commanders and was advancing with his two reserve regiments to join his outpost forces by 3:00 A.M. By dawn his brigade was deployed east of Gowanus Bay, about midway between Gowanus Creek and Red Lion Inn. Covering his exposed left flank was a small force under Brigadier General Samuel Parsons, west of Flatbush Pass, on the Long Island Heights. Shortly after dawn, about 6:00 A.M., British infantry, supported by artillery, began to probe Stirling's position. Stirling's Maryland and Delaware Continentals stood fast. Though skirmishing and cannonading continued for several hours, particularly on the inland flank, the British were seemingly stopped by Stirling's determined stand.

Meanwhile, soon after dawn, Sullivan had ridden out from the Brooklyn fortifications to assume personal command of his troops at Flatbush Pass. He arrived there shortly before 8:00 A.M. The Hessian cannonading was continuing, but the German infantry had not advanced. Sullivan seems to have sent an aide to check on the situation at Bedford Pass, and was satisfied with the report he received.

Still further east, at about 7:00 A.M., for reasons which have never been satisfactorily explained, Colonel Miles appears to have suddenly become concerned about his obscure responsibilities for the security of Jamaica Pass. Whether he heard noise, or saw dust, or merely had some inner premonition, is not clear. He marched east toward the pass with his entire regiment—some 500 men—following trails along the crest of the wooded Heights. He arrived at the pass at about 8:00 A.M., to find himself unexpectedly in the midst of the main body of Howe's army.

Howe's orders, issued early on the 26th, had prompted the activity which the Americans had noted around Flatbush and Flatlands. The plan was simple, and sound. It was carried out perfectly by the experienced professional British and German officers and their disciplined troops. The midnight advance of Grant's division had been a diversion, as was the Hessian bombardment of Flatbush and Bedford passes. Three hours earlier, at about 9:00 P.M., more than 10,000 British soldiers had begun a silent march northeastward from Flatlands toward Jamaica Pass. Clinton led the van, guided by three Tory farmers. Following him came the reserve, under Cornwallis, and the main body, under Lord Percy. Howe was with Percy.

Taking a side road, as they approached the pass at about 3:00 A.M., Clinton's men surprised and captured the five young militia officers without a shot. Continuing on, Clinton secured the pass, then the entire British army halted to rest for an hour or two. After a cold breakfast from their knapsacks, the British resumed the advance toward Bedford at about 7:00 A.M. They marched cautiously westward down the Bedford Road, not seeing and unseen by Miles' Pennsylvanians, who were at this time moving in the opposite direction through the wooded heights, a few hundred yards south of the British column.

The Americans and the British were equally surprised by the sudden confrontation at the pass. After a brief exchange of musketry, Miles was overwhelmed; he and most of his men were captured. The noise of the brief fire fight was muffled by trees and hills, and not a sound reached the ears of Sullivan or Putnam or their men. But a few of the Pennsylvanians escaped through the wooded hills west of Jamaica Pass. Several of these seem to have hastened back to the main Brooklyn fortification, to report to General Putnam that the British were marching through the Jamaica Pass in great strength and were rapidly approaching Bedford. Putnam took no action upon receipt of this report, and made no effort to send the information to Sullivan. It was then nearly 9:00 A.M. It is not clear whether Washington had reached Putnam's headquarters when the refugees reported Miles' disaster; if not, he did arrive shortly thereafter. Sullivan and his troops at Flatbush and Bedford passes had no intimation that the British were behind them until Clinton had two signal guns fired at Bedford, about 9:00 A.M. Sullivan immediately recognized that his rear was threatened, and rushed one of his regiments back towards Bedford. These troops ran into the British van, and were thrown back to the south.

At about the same time von Heister's Hessians, responding to the signal guns, promptly advanced northward into the Flatbush Pass, and stormed the American barricades there at the point of bayonet.

In vain did Sullivan attempt to rally his troops. Caught between the inexorable pressure of the British and German professionals, the raw Americans broke and fled, despite individual and unit exceptions of gallantry. Sullivan was last seen by some of his fugitive men caught between the two lines of converging foes with a smoking pistol in each hand. In fact, although the Hessians were mercilessly bayoneting many of the cowering Americans, Sullivan and several hundred of his surviving troops were taken prisoner and sent to the rear. Clinton and Heister pursued the fugitives to within musket shot of the Brooklyn fortified line. Cornwallis swung southwest, with his right on the Gowanus Road, moving to the sound of firing still continuing between Grant's and Stirling's commands.

On the extreme left of the British line General Grant had also heard the signal guns, but deferred his attack for almost an hour, while waiting for a replenishment of ammunition which he had requested after the heavy artillery and musketry duel of the early morning. Receiving this ammunition at about 10:00 A.M., as well as a reinforcement of some 2,000 Royal Marines sent to him by Lord Howe, Grant ordered an advance. To the surprise of the British, Stirling's brigade stood fast, and for a while these 1,500 men stopped the 7,000 British in their tracks.

Shortly after this Stirling heard heavy firing to his left rear. For the first time he realized that British troops were behind him, and had cut off his line of retreat to the Brooklyn fortifications. Stirling's situation looked hopeless. To the front Grant's troops were bearing down in a renewed attack. To his immediate left Parson's force was being smashed in an envelopment by Grant's right wing. To his left rear were Cornwallis' advancing columns. To his right rear were supposedly impassable Gowanus Creek and the Gowanus Marsh.

Stirling seems to have made an estimate of the situation, and reached a decision, in less than a minute. About an hour earlier he had noticed a detachment of his men carrying some wounded back to the Brooklyn fortifications by a trail through the marsh. Here was the only possible line of retreat—but even this would be cut off unless Cornwallis could be stopped. He ordered two of his three regiments to fall back slowly in front of Grant, and then to withdraw across the marsh as best they could. At the same time Stirling led Colonel William Smallwood's Maryland Continentals—some 500 men—in a spirited charge to the northeast against the advancing British. He apparently hoped to cut his way through to reach the Flatbush Road and the center of the Brooklyn fortifications, while gaining sufficient time to enable the other two regiments to get back across the marsh.

Five times Stirling's and Smallwood's men attempted to cut their way out, and five times they were thrown back. Finally, as Grant came up from the south, wounded Stirling and the survivors of his command were completely surrounded and forced to surrender. Meanwhile, from hills inside the Brooklyn fortifications, Washington saw Stirling's main body fall back toward the marsh. He immediately rushed some troops to the high ground overlooking the creek and marsh, to cover the withdrawal. This musketry and artillery fire forced Grant's left wing units to halt their pursuit of the withdrawing Americans. It was evidently while observing this withdrawal, and Stirling's gallant charges against Cornwallis, that Washington made the statement attributed to him: "Good God, what brave men must I lose this day!"

This virtually ended the Battle of Long Island, at about noon. Though reports are conflicting, it seems that the Americans lost about 1,500 men—Washington's subsequent report of less than 1,000 was due to poor American records. About 1,100 were captured; many of them wounded. Another 100 wounded had been evacuated to the Brooklyn fortifications. Probably 300 had been killed. British losses were about 370 killed and wounded, plus 23 men captured by Stirling's brigade, and brought back in that remarkably steady withdrawal across the Gowanus Marsh.

Exultant, the British troops pressed up to the Brooklyn lines in the early afternoon, expecting orders to assault the American fortifications. When such orders were not forthcoming, some commanders actually pleaded to be permitted to attack. But Howe and Clinton had had enough experience in assaulting prepared American fortifications at Bunker Hill, and at Charleston. They had no desire to relearn these costly lessons. Making a quick reconnaissance of the defense line with his chief engineer, Howe decided to make a siege approach, and issued orders to this effect. He hoped that naval assistance from his brother's fleet would then make the task of attacking Brooklyn Heights a relatively easy one.

Washington, belatedly taking over full command responsibility for his forces in Brooklyn, had also expected a British assault that afternoon. If it were successful, he knew the result would be disaster. Forced back to the East River, all the troops in the lines—now at least half of his army—would be killed, drowned or captured. His only hope was to hold on to the fortified line at all cost. He had nearly 7,000 fresh troops that had not been engaged in the morning's battle, and though they had been somewhat shaken by the impressive demonstration of British tactical skill and power, he believed that from the security of their trenches and redoubts they had a good chance of stopping even the British and Hessian regulars. He was also confident that the British fleet would be stopped by the formidable batteries and obstacles covering the approaches to the East River from New York Bay.

Having quickly decided to hold on at all costs, Washington sent his handful of wounded back across the river, with a messenger ordering more reinforcements from Manhattan to Brooklyn. Then he rode along the lines to check the disposition of his forces, and to stiffen his men. In this he was assisted by Putnam, who, though worthless as a field commander or tactician, was a fiery and inspirational leader of troops in positions selected by someone else.

Reinforcements began to come over during the afternoon and early evening. More arrived on the morning of the 28th, bringing Washington's total strength in the Brooklyn fortifications to nearly 12,000 men. Confident now that his position was at least temporarily secure, Washington could breathe more easily, and could consider his next move.

Although the situation was no longer desperate, the American army was still in a precarious position. About three-fifths of Washington's troops were now in Brooklyn; the remainder on Manhattan. The British fleet could not get up the East River, but it could move up the Hudson, and some or all of General Howe's troops could be shifted by water to land on upper Manhattan, behind the Americans. Or, were the combined forces of the Howe brothers to undertake a deliberate siege of Brooklyn, it was doubtful if Sir William's land assaults, supported by Lord Richard's naval guns, could be stopped,

And if a strong British naval squadron were to circle Long Island, and approach by way of Long Island Sound, they could then cut Washington's line of communications across the East River. All day on August 28, and into the night, Washington pondered his problem. He probably reached a decision before daybreak.

During that night the British had begun to dig parallel and approach trenches.* Seeing this evidence of a deliberate preparation for a siege and assault, Washington realized what he should have known even before the start of the campaign. British sea power and the enormous British numerical and qualitative superiority in land forces was a combination which had from the beginning doomed his chances of permanently holding on to Brooklyn Heights.

Having finally come to this conclusion, Washington made the prompt and proper decision to withdraw from Brooklyn. This would unquestionably be a very ticklish maneuver. Were the British to learn of the withdrawal before it was complete, a determined attack could break through the thinly-manned defenses and annihilate that portion of Washington's army still on the Long Island side.

Consequently, although Washington made up his mind early on the morning of the 29th, he did not reveal his decision even to his most trusted subordinates until late that afternoon. Too much secret information had already reached the British through unsuspected Loyalist spies. Meanwhile all of the many measures he took, and the activities which he started, were for the ostensible purpose of moving still further reinforcements to Brooklyn. Every available boat was assembled on the New York side of the East River, and units there were alerted to move. To man the boats collected, Colonel John Glover's regiment of Marblehead men, seamen all, were assembled.

Then, in the afternoon, Washington assembled his generals for a council of war, ostensibly to obtain their collective views on a course of action; actually to inform them of his decision. He ordered that the troops manning the lines were to be informed that reinforcements were arriving to take their places in the line, and that therefore they should expect to be relieved during the night. At the same time, all supplies and all of the artillery (save for five old and very heavy pieces) were to be prepared for evacuation.

---

* For discussion of 18th Century fortifications and siegecraft, see Appendix IV.

To hold the defenses after all the other units had withdrawn, and to cover the embarkation, Washington selected five units of proven discipline, commanded by reliable leaders. These were Colonel John Haslet's Delaware regiment, the Pennsylvania regiments of Colonels John Shee and Robert Magaw, a Connecticut battalion under Lieutenant Colonel John Chester, and the survivors of Smallwood's Maryland regiment. In command of this picked group was Brigadier General Thomas Mifflin.

The evacuation began at dark, and—thanks to Washington's preparations—moved with amazing speed and smoothness. A rising wind threatened to interfere with the boat movement, but this soon subsided. Continuing rain, while making the troops uncomfortable, tended to dull British alertness.

Before 2:00 A.M. Mifflin was informed by one of Washington's temporary aides-de-camp that the boats were ready for his embarkation. Mifflin at first refused to believe that this was Washington's order, since he did not think the embarkation could have been completed so quickly. When the aide insisted, however, Mifflin ordered his units to move quietly from their trenches and to report to the ferry. When he arrived there, he found great lines of troops still waiting to get on the boats.

Washington, as close to despair as he ever came during the war, stalked up to Mifflin and said, "Good God, General Mifflin, I am afraid you have ruined us by unseasonably withdrawing the troops from the line!" Briefly explaining how the mistake had occurred, Mifflin ordered his units to return to their trenches. That they did so, under the circumstances of the time, was a tribute to their own courage and discipline, as well as to the care of their selection by Washington.

Finally, shortly after 4:00 A.M., Mifflin received the authentic message to withdraw. Pulling back quickly and silently, the troops reached the river, and began to embark, just as dawn was breaking. Fortunately the aftermath of the storm had left a heavy fog over Brooklyn. Though the British had already begun to suspect that the American lines were unusually quiet, they could not observe what was going on.

British patrols probed forward, and soon after 4:30 discovered that the American lines had been abandoned. Moving ahead cautiously, they reached the ferry shortly before 7 o'clock, to find the last boat just pulling away. They opened up with muskets, and with a light field piece, but they scored no hits.

This was fortunate for the rebel cause, since the last man to get onto the last boat had been General George Washington. Sleepless for more than 48 hours, he had given the closest possible personal supervision to every detail of the brilliantly planned evacuation, and had by his calm presence and deliberate energy, inspired, calmed, and reassured his men.

The skill and brilliance of the withdrawal could not undo the damage caused by Washington's earlier strategical and tactical mistakes in attempting an impossible task, and by his failure to exercise adequate command supervision and control of the forces on Long Island. But it did demonstrate that Washington could learn from his mistakes, and that he possessed potentialities for higher military leadership that, even to this day, have rarely been recognized. Thanks to him alone, Long Island, instead of being the final battle of the war —which it might well otherwise have been—became merely another setback to the Revolutionary cause.

As British military historian Trevelyan has well put it, the evacuation was "a master stroke of energy, dexterity and caution, by which Washington saved his army and his country." *

---

* Few single operations have caused more controversial Monday-morning quarterbacking than has the Battle of Long Island and its aftermath. For a critical analysis of the actions and decisions of both Washington and the Howe brothers, see Appendix V.

★ 13 ★ ★ ★ ★ ★ ★

Struggle for New York

THE DEFEAT ON LONG ISLAND and the following evacuation came close to completely demoralizing the poorly disciplined American army. Washington, while striving to oppose the next likely British move, found himself plunged also into administrative problems—to check plundering, drunkenness and desertion. The trouble was not confined to the militia alone; many Continental units were unravelling, and in some instances officers were as derelict as their men. In addition, lack of confidence in Washington and his leadership was growing, even among some of the better officers. Nor did the fact that pay was two months in arrears help the dwindling American morale.

News of an audacious underwater attack against the British fleet anchored off Staten Island briefly aroused enthusiasm, and gained deserved encomiums for Captain David Bushnell and for Sergeant Ezra Lee. Bushnell was inventor and builder of the *Turtle,* the world's first working submarine; Lee was its one-man crew. But though the attack alarmed the British fleet, no vessels were sunk, and British sea power was unaffected.*

In the first days of September Washington reorganized the army into three divisions, disposing his forces to meet the most likely of Howe's possible moves. Since the British were shifting troops north-ward along the western shore of Long Island, and had already seized Ward's and Randall's islands, Washington was particularly concerned about northern Manhattan and the southern Bronx. Should the British

---

* See Appendix VI.

seize or block the one crossing from northern Manhattan over the Harlem River at King's Bridge, the entire American army would be bottled up by the combination of British sea and land power.

Even before the withdrawal from Brooklyn, Washington, due to his army's precarious situation, proposed to burn New York to prevent its use as winter quarters by the British, and then to withdraw north of the Harlem River. But Congress, rejecting his recommendation, informed him on September 2 that the city should not be damaged, even were he forced to abandon it temporarily.

Accordingly, Washington put the majority of his more reliable units in Heath's division of 9,000 men, deployed in northern Manhattan and holding a bridgehead at King's Bridge across the Harlem River. Putnam's division, approximately 5,000 strong, garrisoned the city itself. Between these two forces Greene's division (Brigadier General Joseph Spencer commanding during Greene's illness), some 5,000 men, stretched along the East River from New York to Harlem.

On September 5 Greene, resuming his duties, immediately urged the evacuation of Manhattan. Washington called a council of war on the 7th. Its consensus was that the city was indeed untenable, but in light of Congress' wish that it be held "at every hazard," Washington's dispositions were confirmed.

This decision Washington reported to Congress; his letter also expressed his sound concept that the war strategy "should be defensive. . . . We should on all occasions avoid a general action, or put anything to Risque, unless compelled by necessity, into which we ought never to be drawn." He made clear his personal feeling that an effort to try to hold New York could result in the loss of the entire army. In response, Congress quickly declined to accept responsibility for possible disaster, informing Washington that he should judge whether the town could be held or not, and take action accordingly.

After receiving this reply, and following continued urging from Greene, on September 12 Washington held another council of war. Almost unanimous decision was reached to evacuate the city as soon as the army's stores could be moved out. All possible wagons and horses were pressed into service, while small boats, hugging the western Manhattan shore, carried supplies north to Dobbs Ferry.

On August 30 the Howe brothers had made one more effort to negotiate with the Congress, hoping to find the Americans more amenable after their defeat on Long Island. Captive General Sullivan, on parole, was sent with a message to Washington and to Congressional leaders. But when it became obvious that this effort would be no more successful than the earlier ones, General Howe prepared for a move across the East River. On September 13 British warships and transports began to move up the East River, while British guns on Brooklyn Heights engaged the American batteries on Manhattan in a long-range artillery duel. With more British troops being observed opposite Hell Gate, Washington, confirmed in his belief that Harlem would be the British objective, moved his headquarters to Harlem Heights. He had Heath's men intensify their work upon entrenchments across the narrow northern portion of Manhattan Island, and overlooking the Harlem River.

During the morning of Sunday, September 15, militia units manning the shallow entrenchments along Kips Bay (roughly between modern East 20th and 40th Streets), noted ominous British naval and land preparations. During the night a line of five frigates had drawn up along the center of the East River, anchored fore and aft with springs on their cables. Considerable activity was noted in Green Point, on Long Island, and shortly after 10:00 A.M. a number of British flatboats, loaded with soldiers, began to emerge from Newtown Creek. No one seems to have thought of advising Washington at Harlem of these activities, since his first intimation of possible attack was the distant sound of an intensive cannonade from the British warships at about 11 o'clock.

This bombardment continued for almost two hours, while more than 80 flatboats laden with soldiers massed behind the frigates. About 1:00 P.M., just as Washington and a few staff officers were galloping to the edge of the bay, the British fire lifted and the flatboats began to race towards the Manhattan shore (near the foot of modern East 34th Street).

The American militia defenders, already shaken by the bombardment, were completely unnerved by the sight. As the British grenadiers and Hessian jägers jumped from their boats onto the shore, the Americans—officers as well as men—abandoned their trenches and fled wildly inland.

Washington rushed forward into the midst of the panic-stricken mass. He shouted to them to halt, and to take cover in the nearby cornfields, and behind the stone walls. The frightened men ignored him completely.

"Are these the men with whom I am to defend America?" someone heard the general say. With his riding crop he struck fleeing soldiers and officers trying to get them to stop. But it was hopeless. The infection spread to a brigade of Connecticut Continentals holding the second line, a few hundred yards inland. These, too, began to run.

Washington was seen to take his hat off and throw it on the ground. Suddenly he was alone, with a line of British and Hessian infantrymen approaching him, bayonets fixed. Either because he was temporarily overcome by despair, or because he was too furious to realize how dangerous his situation was, the General sat there on his horse, immobile. Two of his aides rushed forward, one grabbed the bridle of his horse, and turning, they led the reluctant general from the field, amidst a flurry of musket balls from the cheering British soldiers.

Quickly Washington recovered his composure, and issued orders to save what he could from the disaster. Brave, energetic, stupid Putnam was sent galloping off to the south to lead his troops out of New York and up to Harlem Heights as fast as he could, before the British could cut him off by advancing all the way across the island to the Hudson River. A messenger was sent north to Heath, ordering him to man the entrenchments along the Harlem Heights. Then Washington slowly followed his broken, fleeing troops northward.

With commendable speed and vigor, Putnam got his soldiers on the march out of New York City. It was a terribly hot day, and many straggled. There were few things that Putnam could do well, but his own cheerful, energetic, encouraging demeanor, as he galloped up and down the line, worked wonders. But as might be expected, Putnam had made no efforts to reconnoiter the route in advance, and although he had been in New York for five months, he did not know the roads. He came within an ace of leading his troops directly north to Murray Hill where the British were already reorganizing and preparing for a further advance. But his aide, Captain Aaron Burr, turned the column to the left at the last moment, and led them up a little-known road on the west side of the island.

The initial British landing force had been about 4,000 men, of whom three-fourths were British light infantry, grenadiers, and Foot

Guards; the remainder were Hessian jägers. Lord Cornwallis was in command of this leading division, but General Howe accompanied the assault wave. Reaching Murray Hill (about 39th Street and 4th Avenue) the cautious British commander ordered a halt, fearful that if his relatively small attacking force were overextended, the much more numerous Americans might rally and drive him back into the river. Possibly he was right, but it is doubtful if anything could have rallied the Americans that afternoon.

There is a legend that Mrs. Robert Murray served tea to the British generals, and so beguiled them with her charming company and small talk that they temporarily forgot the war, and thus permitted Putnam and his men to get away. It is a pretty, patriotic legend, but the British halt was for purely military, and not social, reasons.

Meanwhile the 84 British flatboats had returned to the Long Island shore, had reloaded with more British and Hessian soldiers, and returned. Apparently this movement was not done as energetically and expeditiously as it should have been. The Hessian division did not begin to reach Murray Hill until 5:00 P.M. Howe immediately began a pursuit north toward Harlem Heights with the bulk of his army, while sending several battalions southward to seize abandoned New York. During the march northward, along a route approximating modern Fifth Avenue, the British column was marching parallel to, and in the same direction with, the last units of Putnam's division, who were about half a mile further west. Neither column sighted the other.

As the leading elements of the British main body reached McGowan's Pass (near the northeast corner of modern Central Park) at dusk, they came under long-range fire from the Americans entrenched on Harlem Heights. Howe halted for the night.

Casualties in killed and wounded on both sides that day can only be estimated. It is doubtful that the British lost as many as ten men. Probably not more than three times that number of Americans were killed or wounded. More than 350 men, however, and about 55 abandoned cannon, were captured in New York, as well as much ammunition and considerable quantities of supplies not yet evacuated.

During the late afternoon and early evening Washington labored mightily to reorganize his army. At this time he had perhaps 16,000 men. Of these, he left approximately 6,000 to protect King's Bridge against a turning movement through the Bronx—still his greatest worry. The remainder manned three lines of entrenchments extending in depth roughly between 130th and 150th streets. Extremely discouraged, Washington doubted if his men would stand up against another British attack, despite the protection of earthworks, and the advantage of the high and rocky ground on which these were situated. Next morning, however, he would regain some of his lost faith in American soldiers.

Shortly after dawn, a battalion of Connecticut rangers, some 150 strong, commanded by Lieutenant Colonel Thomas Knowlton,* began to reconnoiter across the then-wooded valley through which West 125th Street now runs. At that time the depression was called "the Hollow Way." Working their way through the underbrush, and up the uneven, bouldered height on the south side of the Hollow Way, the Americans were approaching the high ground where Grant's Tomb now stands, when they were met by at least two British battalions. Knowlton drew his men back in good order, and arrived back on the high ground on the north side of the Hollow Way (about 130th Street) just as Washington, with his adjutant general, Lieutenant Colonel Joseph Reed, arrived. At this moment also, the English came out on the rocky spurs on the far side of the valley, jeering at the withdrawing Americans. Some British buglers blew the fox hunter's call announcing that the fox has gone to earth.

To American aristocratic fox hunters, like Washington and Reed, nothing could have been more insulting. Washington, furious, decided to teach the Englishmen a lesson. Amongst the troops holding this part of the American line was Colonel George Weedon's Virginia Regiment. Washington ordered Knowlton, accompanied by three Virginia companies under Major Andrew Leitch, to go back across the Hollow Way, further to the east, and move across Vandewater (now Morningside) Heights to get around behind the Britishers. At the same time, the remainder of Weedon's regiment, and other troops in the line, were to attract the attention of the British from the front by heavy musket fire and a feigned advance. Washington sent Colonel Reed with the enveloping force, which was probably about 300 men. One other senior American officer—who was never later directly

---

* Whom we have met previously at Bunker Hill, see p. 46.

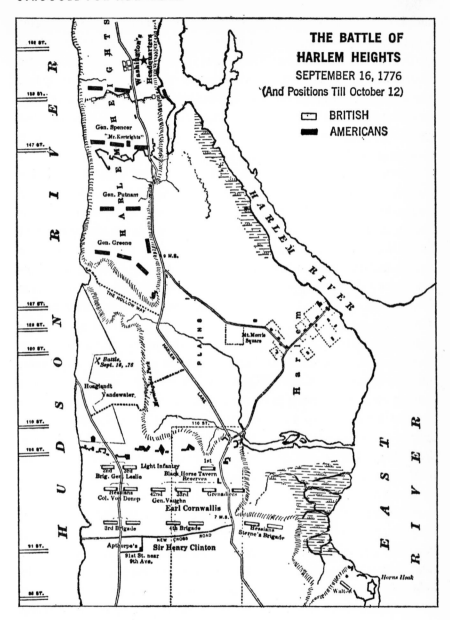

THE BATTLE OF HARLEM HEIGHTS
SEPTEMBER 16, 1776
(And Positions Till October 12)

☐ BRITISH
■ AMERICANS

identified by either Washington or Reed—accompanied the column as a self-appointed volunteer. Apparently it was either Putnam or equally stupid and industrious Brigadier General George Clinton. It was by this time nearly noon.

The holding attack quickly accomplished its purpose. As Weedon and his men moved forward into the Hollow Way, the challenge was answered by the British, who began to advance to make contact in the valley. Suddenly, to Washington's annoyance, firing broke out on the British right flank on Vandewater Heights. The general had hoped that Knowlton and Leitch would work their way completely around behind the British. Reed later reported to Washington that, despite his protests, the accompanying general officer had ordered Knowlton to open fire prematurely.

Although the results of the envelopment were thus less decisive than Washington had hoped, the British immediately fell back to the high ground south of the Hollow Way, pressed vigorously by Knowlton, Leitch, and Weedon. It was at this time that both Knowlton and Leitch fell mortally wounded. Fearful that the impetus of the drive would slacken with the loss of these two energetic leaders, Washington sent a Maryland regiment and some New England units to bolster the enveloping force. Despite reinforcements rushed to the front by British Brigadier General Alexander Leslie, the American advance continued, and the British regulars were forced to fall back.

By now there were close to 5,000 troops engaged on each side, and through his glasses Washington could see additional British units moving up. To prevent a premature general engagement, Washington ordered his troops to halt and to fall back. He was pleased that, despite the enthusiasm of the chase, his troops responded and withdrew in good order. By the time the advance ceased, the Americans had reached about to modern 108th Street, approximately a mile from the initial point of contact in the Hollow Way.

Again casualty reports were conflicting and vague. Apparently, however, the British had lost 70 killed and 200 wounded in the six-hour fight, while the Americans had 30 killed and 90 wounded. A relatively minor action, this Battle of Harlem Heights did much to help American morale. Some of the men who had taken part in the action had been New Englanders, who had run from the British the day before at Kips Bay. Though its strategical and tactical results were nil, the engagement had an important effect upon the remainder of the New York campaign. Howe and his subordinates were amazed by the American resiliency and determination, and became most cautious in their subsequent actions.

Although Harlem Heights had given Washington's army a reprieve from incipient dissolution, his administrative and disciplinary problems were little improved. Plundering and desertion were still the major difficulties. Washington properly attributed these derelictions particularly to the militia, and to the poor quality of all of his officers. In letters to Congress in the latter days of September he repeated earlier comments on the unreliability of the militia, and upon the need to increase the regular establishment. He also urged strengthening the Articles of War and measures to improve the officer corps by attracting good men to the colors. He suggested inducements which would include adequate pay and enhanced prestige for officers. Congress, on the very day of the Battle of Harlem Heights, had voted to follow one of his earlier recommendations about raising an army for the duration. They established a standing army of 88 battalions "to serve during the present war." Later Congress acted to strengthen the Articles of War, to improve the status of officers, to provide re-enlistment bounties, and the like.

These measures undoubtedly were helpful, but were rather late. Washington knew that the terms of service of many of his men would expire at the end of November, and that he would lose most of his remaining Continentals at the expiration of their year's service on the last day of December, 1776. Possibly the new laws passed by Congress would help to strengthen the army in subsequent years—but as things were going there might not be another year of the war.

A lull of several weeks now followed while cautious General Howe prepared for his next move. As usual, he was determined to avoid a frontal assault against American marksmen in prepared entrenchments. His slow-moving timetable was still further set back by a great fire which broke out in New York on September 20, and which raged for nearly two days. Despite extensive damage, the British saved enough of the town to permit its use for winter quarters. Howe and his officers, furious, assumed that the fire was deliberate sabotage— and it may have been, though this has never been proven. Washington certainly had no hand in it, though he was not displeased to learn of the damage.

One demonstration of Howe's fury was his summary sentence of death to a young American spy, Connecticut Captain Nathan Hale, who was captured on Long Island on September 21. Without benefit of a trial, Hale was hanged in New York City the following morning.

He gained the admiration of his British captors by his calm courage and dignified bearing, and by his last statement, just before the noose was slipped over his head: "I only regret that I have but one life to lose for my country."

During the last days of September, and early October, substantial militia reinforcements, and a few Continental units from the south, joined Washington's army. But the desertion rate was so high that the actual combat strength of the American army was little changed. One consolation, during this period, however, was the return of fighting Generals Sullivan and Stirling, as a result of a prisoner-of-war exchange.

On October 12 Howe finally, and belatedly, began the movement which Washington had expected and feared. Leaving about 10,000 troops to garrison New York, and to hold the lines opposite Washington's Harlem Heights positions, Howe took 10,000 more up the East River, convoyed by his brother's warships. They landed at Throgs Neck, at the southeast corner of what is now the Bronx, only four miles from King's Bridge. Howe intended to advance along the road leading from Throgs Neck to King's Bridge, hoping to trap Washington's army in northern Manhattan.

Again Cornwallis commanded the leading British division, some 4,000 English and Hessian light infantry. Boldly risking a passage through the racing waters of Hell Gate in fog and darkness, the British sailors put the troops ashore at Throgs Neck just after dawn. Here Cornwallis discovered, however, that though Throgs Neck appeared as a peninsula on the map, a marsh and brook made it more like an island.

A handful of Americans, from the 1st Pennsylvania Rifle Regiment of Colonel Edward Hand, had removed the planks from a bridge in a causeway over the marsh. The skeleton bridge, as well as the nearby ford, were then covered with accurate rifle fire from a protected position behind some wood piles. Deterred by the deadly accuracy of the American riflemen, the British paused and prepared for an assault. During this lull, Hand was reinforced by Colonel William Prescott's 7th Massachusetts Continental Regiment, and some New York Continentals, bringing the total defending force to a strength of about 1,800 men. The British assault was repulsed; Howe and Cornwallis found themselves bottled up in an area hardly a mile square.

But it was obvious to Washington that the British setback at Throgs Neck could only be temporary; they would inevitably obtain a better foothold some place on the north shore of the East River, or Long Island Sound. King's Bridge was still threatened. At a council of war on October 16, therefore, he decided to abandon the Harlem Heights position and to withdraw most of his army to White Plains on the mainland, where he could block a British turning movement from the shore of Long Island Sound.

Washington decided to leave approximately 2,000 men at Fort Washington on Manhattan, however, since retention of this fortification, and Fort Constitution (soon renamed Fort Lee) on the Jersey shore, complied with a Congressional resolution to the effect that Fort Washington, and the obstacles in the Hudson River, were to be maintained "if it be practicable, by every art and at whatever expense. . . ." Approximately 3,000 more men were sent across the river in and around Fort Lee. These two fortifications he placed under the command of his most reliable subordinate, Nathanael Greene.

On October 17 Stirling's brigade was rushed to White Plains, to make sure of holding that place, while the rest of the army and its stores moved more deliberately north from Harlem Heights. Next day Spencer's division followed, and took up positions behind the west bank of the Bronx River—facing east—to protect the passage of the remainder of the army, and of the stores which Washington had begun to move north from King's Bridge.

That same morning—October 18—Howe again bestirred himself. Cornwallis' light division was shifted northeast three miles from Throgs Neck to Pell's Point (now a part of Pelham Bay Park, where the topography has been greatly changed by earth fills).

Once more the British turning movement was thwarted by American vigilance and determination. Colonel Glover of Marblehead, with a small brigade of four skeleton Massachusetts regiments—some 750 men—was at Eastchester, where the Boston Post Road crossed Hutchinson's River. Observing the British arrival, Glover posted his men about one mile inland, behind stone walls. Their fire stopped the British for a while, but as more of Cornwallis' troops landed, Glover was forced back, permitting the British to reach the Post Road. Howe quickly pushed up to New Rochelle, sending famed Major Robert Rogers, and his Loyalist rangers, to protect the right flank at Mamaroneck. During the engagement Cornwallis was slightly wounded, but quickly recovered, and continued to lead his troops vigorously.

The British now paused for several days to build up a base and a store of supplies at New Rochelle. Keeping a close eye on them, Washington continued his deliberate withdrawal to White Plains. On the night of October 22 Haslet's Delaware Regiment, reinforced by some Virginia and Maryland units, attempted a surprise attack on Roger's Rangers at Mamaroneck, with partial success.

Upon the arrival of General Lee from the Carolinas in mid-October, Washington decided to reorganize his army again. This time it was into seven divisions, commanded respectively by Greene, Lee, Heath, Sullivan, Putnam, Spencer, and Benjamin Lincoln. Except for Greene's division at Forts Washington and Lee, the others were with Washington, comprising approximately 14,500 men. They concentrated at White Plains between October 23 and 26.

Howe's failure to strike the American army as it was moving north from Harlem may have been his most serious mistake of the campaign. In his defense, however, it should be noted that he could not very well expect to advance inland in force until he had established an adequate supply base in the New Rochelle area. So long as the Americans held Fort Washington, an overland line of communications was not possible. Thus he was forced to rely upon a water supply route through the East River, and past turbulent Hell Gate. Furthermore, although Howe and his subordinate commanders could move vigorously and rapidly on the battlefield, they were professional soldiers of the eighteenth-century tradition. Rapid strategic movements were unusual, despite the recent examples of Frederick the Great. Also, Howe's force in Westchester was outnumbered by the Americans—who now held interior lines between the two divided portions of the British army. Despite the superior quality of his troops, the recent experience at Harlem Heights caused Howe to decide to wait for reinforcements.

On October 23 a slow, five-day British advance began, culminating in a skirmish against American outposts four miles south of White Plains on the morning of the 27th. Washington and his generals, just

started on a reconnaissance to select a better defensive position, decided now to stand fast and await the expected British attack. It did
not come that day, however, Howe contenting himself with thorough
patrolling and reconnaissance.

The American position was on a line of low rolling hills just south

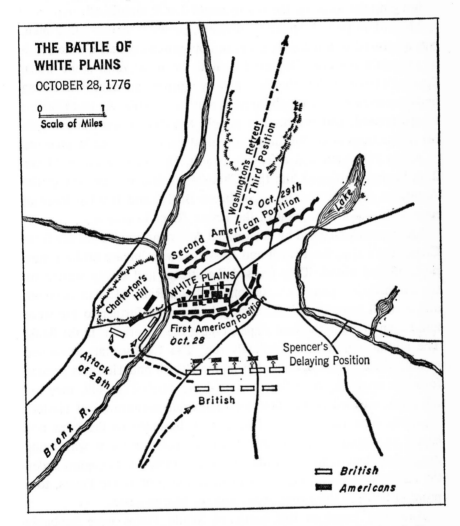

of the village of White Plains; the right flank protected by the shallow
Bronx River, the left on a millpond. Washington had been considering
moving to a new position because the right of the American line was
dominated by higher ground west of the Bronx River, known as
Chatterton's Hill. Two small militia regiments under Colonel Rufus

Putnam were entrenching an outpost there, but late on the 27th, when he noted British interest in Chatterton's Hill, Washington decided to reinforce them. Shortly after dawn on the 28th he sent over Colonel John Haslet's Delaware regiment, and then, possibly as an after-thought, followed this with General Alexander McDougall's brigade —bringing the force on the hill to about 1,600 men in all.

Meanwhile part of Spencer's division, probably about 1,000 men, was advanced to a delaying position approximately half a mile south of the main position. Deployed behind the usual farm stone walls, Spencer's troops halted the British early morning advance with strong and concentrated fire, which inflicted many casualties. As more British troops arrived, and prepared to attack, Spencer, in accordance with his instructions from Washington, pulled back to the main position.

Again Howe avoided a frontal assault. His reconnaissance of the 27th having convinced him that Chatterton's Hill was the key to the American position, he sent a combined British and Hessian force of more than 4,000 men west of the Bronx River to take it.

Momentarily checked by determined American small arms fire from Chatterton's Hill, the British and Hessians, with intense artillery sup-port, pressed ahead. They crossed the stream and slowly started up the south slope. Meanwhile, Colonel Johann Rall's Hessian regiment and a small force of British cavalry had moved further to the west, and began to climb the west slopes, taking the Americans in the flank. The militia regiments immediately ran. The Continentals attempted to hold the crest for a while, but as the British and Hessians pressed forward, extending their flanks around the base of the hill, they too fell back, covered by the slow and deliberate withdrawal of Haslet's regiment. The Hessians and British now hastened to the crest and began to organize for further advance while artillery was being dragged up behind them. In the face of this threat, Washington ended the battle by withdrawing his right flank north of White Plains, to a position between the Bronx River and St. Mary's Lake.

American losses in this battle of White Plains were probably slightly more than 250 men, of whom some 50 were killed. British losses were approximately 240, with 50 killed. The Hessian troops suffered about one third of these casualties.

For three days the two armies faced each other, while Howe's army received reinforcements from Manhattan and Staten islands, bringing its strength up to about 20,000. During the night of October 31-November 1, therefore, Washington made a night withdrawal to higher and more commanding ground on North Castle Heights. A pause of several days followed, while the British, moving into White Plains, probed cautiously against the American defenses.

With his usual distaste for frontal assault of American entrenchments, Howe saw no further reason for operations northward into Westchester. He decided instead to clear the Americans from Fort Washington and the north tip of Manhattan Island, thus opening up a land line of communications. Then, after consolidating the area on both sides of the lower Hudson, he intended to put his troops into winter quarters around New York, in preparation for what he confidently felt would be the culminating campaign against the rebels in 1777.

During the night of November 4-5, therefore, the British made a night withdrawal to the southwest. Though many of his troops were prematurely jubilant at this apparent British retreat, Washington realized the likelihood that Howe was planning an attack on Fort Washington, and then an advance into the Jerseys.

Fort Washington, located on a bluff 230 feet above the Hudson, was formidable principally because of its location, and the extremely rugged, rocky slopes which it overlooked. It was a simple, open pentagonal earthwork, with a bastion at each corner. Washington doubted that the fort could hold out against an intensive British attack, but Greene, Putnam, and Colonel Robert Magaw, the garrison commander, were all confident of its strength. Washington's doubts were intensified on November 7 when three British warships moved upstream, successfully avoiding the obstacles in the river which Forts Washington and Lee were intended to protect. Despairing now of any possibility of preventing the British from using the river, Washington could see little reason for maintaining a garrison of 2,000 men in a relatively precarious position on Manhattan. However, since Greene was on the spot, and better able to assess the situation, he left the decision to him.

Washington meanwhile began to shift his main army to meet the two major likely British threats. Because of the dangerous possibility of an advance by Howe up the Hudson to Albany, Washington left General Lee with approximately 7,000 men at North Castle to block a possible British advance northward, while Washington personally led some 2,000 men to join the equal number Greene had around Fort Lee on the west bank. To hold the Highlands region of the Hudson and maintain communications between these two major portions of his army, Heath with approximately 4,000 men would move northwest toward Peekskill. Sending Stirling on ahead to cross the Hudson on November 9, Washington led his contingent from the North Castle lines the next day. Heath moved out to the north at the same time.

This decision of Washington divided his already weak army into four major groups (his own and Greene's west of the Hudson, Lee to the northeast, Heath the north, and Magaw at Fort Washington). This left Howe on interior lines, able to concentrate against any one of these contingents. Yet, with the one exception of leaving Magaw's detachment isolated on Manhattan Island, the decision was not so bad as most critics have averred. Experience had shown Washington that the British would not move rapidly. His dispositions did allow for forces sufficiently substantial to delay any British move to the north or west, and by securing the Hudson Highlands crossings he felt that he would be able to concentrate his army rapidly once Howe's intentions had been clearly indicated. Having properly decided upon a defensive strategy, there was not much else that Washington could have done under the difficult circumstances.

Still worried about Fort Washington, on November 12 he visited Greene at Fort Lee to discuss the situation. Despite Greene's confidence in the impregnability of the fortress, Washington remained undecided. Evidently Washington and Greene were rowed over to Fort Washington to inspect Magaw's defenses on the 14th, and the General still found his better judgment completely contradicted by the enthusiasm and confidence of his subordinates. So he again postponed a decision to abandon the fort.

By November 15 it was obvious that Howe had concentrated substantial forces against the extensive outworks of the fortress. These extended across the island from the Hudson to the Harlem rivers, and from the old entrenchments overlooking the Hollow Way almost to King's Bridge in the north. To permit Magaw to hold such a line, Greene reinforced the garrison to a strength of nearly 3,000 men—

evidently done without consulting Washington, who still believed its strength to be less than 2,000.

That afternoon Howe's adjutant general, Lieutenant Colonel James Patterson, came to the fort under a flag of truce to demand surrender. When Magaw declined, Patterson threatened that all defenders would be put to the sword at the conclusion of a successful assault. Magaw responded that he intended to hold at all cost, and that in the event of unexpected catastrophe he was confident of the humanity of the English. Magaw sent a report of this conference to Greene and to Washington.

At dawn next morning—November 16—Washington, accompanied by Generals Greene, Putnam and Hugh Mercer, again had himself rowed across the river to inspect the fortress personally and to make a final decision whether to hold it or abandon it. Just as he was leaving the Jersey shore, heavy firing broke out from south and north of the fort, but Washington continued across the river. Arriving at the fort, he found that British and Hessian troops were attacking the outworks from north and south. He decided that his presence was merely an embarrassment and an encumbrance to Magaw, who had a battle to fight. Restraining his impulse to take personal command, Washington returned across the river to Fort Lee with the other three generals, to await developments.

Howe had assigned 8,000 troops to assault the fort. The main effort was to be made from the north, by some 3,000 Germans under Knyphausen. To the east, two small columns totalling another 3,000 men, under Generals Edward Mathew and Cornwallis, were to make assault crossings over the Harlem River, and then drive westward against the face of the fort. Lord Percy was advancing from central Manhattan with a mixed British-Hessian force of 2,000 men.

Percy had opened the action shortly after dawn with an intensive bombardment across the Hollow Way, followed by a general advance all along the line. The thinly spread out Americans were quickly pushed back, but Percy halted when he discovered that Cornwallis and Mathew were having troubles getting started on the other side of the Harlem River. Meanwhile, shortly before 10:00 A.M., Knyphausen's Germans had begun their assault through the wild and rocky area in the northern portion of Manhattan. Despite stubborn resistance, the Germans pushed forward aggressively. For more than three hours, the hardest fighting of the day raged amidst the boulders and ravines north of Fort Washington.

Shortly before noon Mathew and Cornwallis overcame the administrative difficulties which had delayed their movement, and successfully assaulted over the Harlem River, despite heavy American fire from the west bank heights. Now all four British columns began to forge ahead, and by early afternoon Rall's Hessian regiment was close to the fort itself, on the crest above the Hudson. As the other three columns continued to close in, Rall now demanded Magaw's surrender.

From the ramparts of Fort Lee, Washington and his companions had heard the firing grow in volume, and approach the fort from both directions. From the sound, it was apparent that other British forces were advancing against the fort from the east, having crossed the Harlem River. By early afternoon it was obvious that the British were within musket range of the fort itself, and action could be observed near the river banks. Washington, now convinced that the fort could not be held, sent a message to Magaw, ordering him to cling to his remaining positions until nightfall, and then to evacuate to the other side of the river. Washington had Greene collect boats and make preparations for the evacuation.

Meanwhile Magaw, to gain time, had attempted to discuss surrender terms with Rall. By this time he realized that while he had too few troops to hold his extensive outworks, he had far too many to be crowded safely into the relatively small, open area of Fort Washington itself.

The German, refusing discussion, insisted that Magaw either surrender at once, or deal with General Knyphausen personally. Knyphausen then sent an equally adamant demand, threatening immediate assault. Magaw, fearful of the casualties which artillery fire would cause amongst the crowd of troops huddled in the fort, now agreed to surrender. It was at this moment, probably near 3:00 P.M., that he received Washington's message to hold on until nightfall. Magaw responded to Washington that he had so committed himself to surrender that he could not with honor obey the order. So fell Fort Washington.

American losses were 53 killed, 96 wounded, and 2,722 unwounded captured. The British lost 77 killed, 374 wounded and 7 missing; nearly three-fourths of these casualties were Hessians. They captured 43 artillery pieces, and great quantities of artillery and small arms ammunition.

The loss of nearly 3,000 men was serious to Washington, while the relatively easy capture of the supposedly impregnable fortress by the British struck another sharp blow at American morale. Greene, realizing that his insistence had caused Washington to agree to the defense of the fort, was particularly broken up by the catastrophe.

The blame, however, must rest upon Washington himself. His estimate of the situation had been that the fort was indefensible. His disposition of the remainder of his forces had been such as to make the retention of the garrison of Fort Washington on Manhattan not only unnecessary, but dangerous. A firm decision had been necessary, and Washington had vacillated. He was soon to face the consequences.

★ 14 ★ ★ ★ ★ ★

The Month that Tried Men's Souls

On THE NIGHT OF NOVEMBER 19-20, Cornwallis crossed the Hudson River with some 4,000 men at Closter, about five miles above Fort Lee. As dawn was breaking the British troops began to march down the Palisades toward Fort Lee. Greene, alerted by a patrol, was barely able to get his troops out of the fort and back to Washington's position at Hackensack before the British took the place. The hasty evacuation of the fort resulted in 30 more cannon and large stores of ammunition and food falling into the hands of the British.

The arrival of Cornwallis' division on the west bank of the Hudson, quickly followed by additional British forces, convinced Washington that Howe intended to seize at least part of New Jersey, and even possibly to press on to the American capital at Philadelphia before going into winter quarters. Accordingly he appealed to Congress and to New Jersey for reinforcements. He also sent a message to Lee, suggesting that he bring his command west of the Hudson to join forces with Washington somewhere in the Newark-New Brunswick area. Washington had already sent Stirling on to New Brunswick. On November 21, he withdrew the remainder of his 3,000 men from the exposed position at Hackensack, and pulled back to Newark to wait for Lee.

To his dismay, Washington soon learned that Lee did not believe that he should yet cross to the Jersey side of the Hudson. Lee did not consider Washington's politely worded suggestion as a direct order. As the days passed, and as Washington continued to send more strongly worded messages—but never couched in terms of a direct order—Lee continued to procrastinate east of the Hudson, and to send evasive, and somewhat patronizing, replies.

What was going on in Lee's mind during the last week of November and the first two weeks of December has never been completely clarified. He has been accused of both treason and cowardice, and in light of subsequent events neither of these possibilities can be completely discounted. It is more likely, however, that Lee was convinced that Washington's mistakes, failures, and defeats since the Battle of Long Island would soon result in his being relieved from command by the Continental Congress. He, Lee, a professional officer with a high reputation gained in operations in Europe and America, was the only logical successor. His criticisms of Washington, many of them well-founded, became more outspoken. Possibly he was avoiding obedience to Washington's orders deliberately, to assure Washington's downfall and his own appointment to overall command. Or, it may simply have been that he had become so contemptuous of Washington's decisions, that he felt that his ideas as to the proper strategy were better than Washington's.

Howe held up Cornwallis' division near Hackensack, while he completed his plans for the winter. He had decided that he would not press very hard into New Jersey, but would spend the winter in New York, and complete the suppression of the rebellion during the spring of 1777. He then visualized simultaneous operations in New England, and either up the Hudson or Delaware rivers. Having selected Newport, Rhode Island, as the base for operations in New England, on November 27 he sent Clinton with some 6,000 men there by sea, where they were to spend the winter. Then, to complete preparations for an advance either across New Jersey, or up the Hudson, the following spring, he ordered Cornwallis to drive Washington out of eastern New Jersey.

On November 28 the British van entered Newark, on the heels of Washington's departing rear guard. Washington continued to New Brunswick, where he stopped briefly. There 2,000 men of his Maryland and New Jersey brigades left the army—their period of service expired. The New Jersey men, apparently, felt no concern that their departure still further reduced Washington's chances of defending their state. Washington sent an urgent message to Schuyler to send back all of his Pennsylvania and New Jersey Continental regiments from the Northern Department.

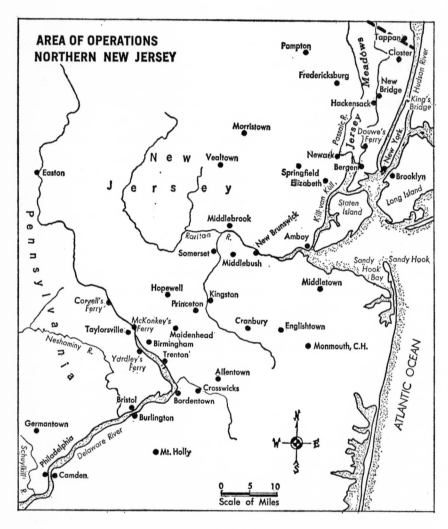

Cornwallis pressed on against the dwindling American army, now only 3,400 strong, and on December 1st there was skirmishing at New Brunswick, while Washington's troops destroyed the bridge over the Raritan River. That day Washington ordered all small boats along

the Delaware River, for 70 miles north of Philadelphia, to be collected on the west bank of the river. Leaving Stirling at Princeton,
on December 3 he marched on to Trenton, to prepare for an evacuation of all of his remaining troops to the far bank of the Delaware
River. Leaving a detachment there, on the 7th he returned to join
Stirling at Princeton, where his total force was now little more than
3,000 men.

Upon orders from Howe, Cornwallis stayed in New Brunswick for
six days. Sir William, fearful of becoming overextended, had originally
intended to have his winter outpost line along the Raritan. Evidently,
however, after urgings from Cornwallis, he decided to move his
outposts as far as the Delaware River.

On December 7, therefore, just as Washington was rejoining Stirling, intending to harass the British along the Raritan, he discovered
that the British were approaching Princeton. He thereupon withdrew
to Trenton, leaving a trail of wrecked bridges and felled trees behind
him. Washington personally stayed with the rear guard to supervise
these destructive and delaying measures.

Next day, December 8, Washington shifted his small army westward across the Delaware River. Cornwallis arrived at Trenton at
2:00 P.M., just as the last American boats were in midstream. American artillery on the far shore fired on the British van, to cover the
evacuation. Upon reaching the Pennsylvania shore, Washington found
he had been reinforced by 2,000 Pennsylvania militia and a few
Continentals sent him by Congressional order. This brought his
strength on the west bank of the Delaware to nearly 5,000 men.

On December 2, meanwhile, Lee and 4,000 men had belatedly
crossed the Hudson. Washington urged Lee to join him as quickly
as possible, but that general, still arrogant and confident in his superior
professional ability, decided to come more slowly. He would, he
claimed, harass the British flank and rear. Yet as he continued his
painfully slow advance westward across New Jersey, he undertook
no offensive action. On the night of December 12 his command was
encamped at Vealtown, southwest of Morristown.

Leaving the troops under Sullivan's command, Lee and a small
guard spent the night three miles away in a tavern. Why he did so
has never been satisfactorily explained, though there is some sus-

picion of an amorous adventure. In any event, he took sufficient time while at the inn to write his close friend, Horatio Gates, describing Washington as being "most damnably deficient."

Early on the morning of December 13 a detachment of Lieutenant Colonel William Harcourt's British cavalry regiment, under Lieutenant Banastre Tarleton, swooped down on the tavern. Lee's aide-de-camp, Captain James Wilkinson, escaped, apparently carrying Lee's letter to Gates. But the general and the remainder of his party were captured. Ironically enough, his captors belonged to the regiment which Lee had commanded when he made his reputation in Portugal, some years earlier.

On top of the disasters which had been suffered by the American army, the loss of the man generally regarded as their most capable, competent professional officer was a further shocking blow to the American people, and to the army. Washington himself felt the loss keenly, though he had begun to lose faith and confidence in Lee. Sullivan, however, marched promptly to join Washington and on December 20 brought his remaining men—now barely 2,000—into Washington's camp west of the Delaware.

In such fashion, by mid-December, 1776, the struggle for American liberty moved apparently to its last gasp. This was the view of many members of the Continental Congress when they met in Philadelphia on December 12. They did not see how Washington, after all of his defeats, with a handful of troops still remaining to him, could stop Howe's victorious army from crossing the Delaware and capturing Philadelphia. Figuratively washing their hands of the military situation, Congress voted a vague resolution giving Washington "full power to direct all things relative . . . to the operations of war," and then adjourned to reconvene in Baltimore on the 20th. Most of the congressmen immediately scuttled southwards.

To Washington this apparent honor was an empty gesture. For it was useless to him without an army. On December 14 he wrote to Gates to join him as rapidly as possible with seven regiments he had brought south to Peekskill from Schuyler's northern army. But Washington knew that on the 31st the enlistments of these, as of most of his other regular and militia troops, would expire. Even counting the outlying detachments in New Jersey, he could not expect to have more than 1,400 men on January 1.

Washington's depression following his defeats in and around New York, and the humiliating retreat across New Jersey—combined with the frustration he felt in the face of the prospective dissolution of his small army—were revealed in the letters which he wrote to Congress, and to others, during those dark days of December. On the 17th he wrote: "The unhappy policy of short enlistments and a dependence on militia will, I fear, prove the downfall of our cause. . . . Our only dependence now is upon the speedy enlistment of a new army. If this fails, I think the game will be pretty well up, as from disaffection and want of spirit and fortitude, the inhabitants instead of resistance are offering submission and taking protection from Gen. Howe in Jersey." Three days later he bluntly added: "Ten more days will put an end to the existence of our army."

Howe apparently shared Washington's view of the future prospects of the cause of independence. On November 30 he and his brother, Admiral Lord Howe, in their joint role as peace commissioners, issued a proclamation granting pardon to all citizens taking an oath of allegiance to the British Crown in the next 60 days. Some of Washington's most bitter comments during the following weeks were reserved for the thousands, in all walks of life, who hastened to avail themselves of this opportunity, now that they were convinced that the revolution had failed.

General Howe had apparently considered continuing on across the Delaware to seize the rebel capital at Philadelphia. But when he discovered that Washington had moved all of the boats from the east bank of the river, and with the weather turning cold, he gave up the idea. At this late period in the season he was not prepared to shift his entire army from New York, and despite realization of Washington's weakness, he was reluctant to spread his forces any thinner. On December 14 he issued an order closing the campaign.

After Clinton's departure for Newport, Howe still had approximately 23,000 men based on New York City. About half of these were east of the Hudson, in and around New York itself. The remainder, under the command of Major General Grant, occupied east-central New Jersey, with advanced posts at Princeton, and along the Delaware at Trenton and Bordentown. In accordance with the custom of the day, Grant's Hessian division, about 3,000 men, was placed on the left of his line, across the Jerseys. This division was commanded by Colonel Carl von Donop, whose own brigade of nearly 2,000 men, including one Highland regiment, was at Mount Holly, with detachments in Burlington and Bordentown. The other Hessian brigade, about 1,400 men under Colonel Johann Rall, was at Trenton. Donop was somewhat concerned about the exposed location of his two brigades. He entrenched his positions at Mount Holly, Burlington and Bordentown, and ordered Rall to do likewise at Trenton. Rall, however, could see no possibility of danger from the disintegrating American army. His views were corroborated by letters from General Grant, who made clear his total contempt of the colonials, and told both Donop and Rall that they were in no danger from the Americans, who were "almost naked, dying of cold, without blankets, and very ill supplied with provisions."

This estimate of Washington's capabilities and future prospects was not too different from his own. Nevertheless, he had not given up hope. And at least one other American felt the same way. Thomas Paine, who had served as a volunteer with the American army during the retreat across New Jersey, wrote *The American Crisis,* which was published in Philadelphia on December 19. From the way in which Paine referred to Washington in the text of his essay, the General was obviously, at least in part, his inspiration. In turn, Washington drew strength from Paine's words, particularly the well-known lines:

> "These are the times that try men's souls: The summer soldier and the sunshine patriot will, in this crisis, shrink from the service of his country; but he that stands it *now* deserves the love and thanks of man and woman. Tyranny, like Hell, is not easily conquered. Yet we have this consolation with us, that the harder the conflict, the more glorious the triumph."

15

★ ★ ★ ★ ★ ★

Laurels on the Delaware

THE POSSIBILITY OF STRIKING AN AUDACIOUS BLOW at the English had begun to form in Washington's mind as early as December 8. The appearance of Paine's pamphlet a few days later quite possibly confirmed that determination. In any event, he saw to it that the stirring words were read to every man in the army during the following week.

In retrospect, it is hard to see how a general in Washington's circumstances could have considered offensive action. Even on December 20 with the arrival both of Sullivan, with the 2,000-man remnants of Lee's command, and of Gates with 600, the paper strength of the army was only 7,600. The effective strength was considerably less than 6,000. These were spread out more than 20 miles to cover the nine ferry crossings near Trenton and Bordentown. Washington with the main body, about 2,500 men, was bivouacked between Taylorsville and Yardleyville. Brigadier General James Ewing had less than 1,000 opposite the river bend between Trenton and Bordentown. Colonel John Cadwalader, of the Pennsylvania militia, had slightly more than 2,000 in the vicinity of Bristol. Barely half of this effective strength consisted of the gaunt and dispirited survivors of the Continental units which Washington had led in retreat across the Jerseys. The rest were raw militia.

By December 23, however, Washington had decided to cross the Delaware and to strike one or more blows against the British in their winter quarters in New Jersey. Without some sort of dramatic success to electrify the country, and to inspire his troops, he had no hope of holding an army together during the winter, or of recruiting more men before the next spring campaign. If successful, a blow at Trenton, possibly followed by a raid on the main British supply depot at New Brunswick, would gain supplies of clothing and ammunition for his men, and give them some concrete and tangible basis to hope for the eventual success of their cause. Failure, of course, as Washington well knew, would mean the end of the Revolution, as well as complete disaster for himself. This, however, would also be the likely consequence of inaction.

Washington issued orders making clear to his officers and men that something was afoot. Rations were to be cooked for three days; ammunition, and new flints were distributed to the troops. The following evening—December 24—he called a council of war to reveal his plans, and to issue his orders.

The plan was to cross the Delaware River on Christmas night, at McKonkey's Ferry, nine miles north of Trenton, with the bulk of his effective Continentals—2,400 men and 18 cannon. This force, under Washington's personal command, would constitute the main effort, attacking Trenton at dawn the next morning. Ewing was to cross the river later that night, just south of Trenton, with 600 to 800 Pennsylvania and New Jersey militia, and was to seize the bridge across Assunpink Creek, to cut off the enemy line of retreat from Trenton south towards Bordentown. To prevent Donop from interfering at Trenton, Acting Brigadier General Cadwalader, with nearly 2,000 mixed Continentals and Pennsylvania militia, was to cross the river near Bristol, and to demonstrate against Mount Holly and Bordentown.

Plenty of boats were available for these crossings, because of Washington's earlier foresight in sweeping the east bank of the river clean, and collecting them on the west bank. These were substantial, sturdy "Durham" boats, averaging about 50 feet long, especially built for Delaware River ferrying work, and able to carry up to fifteen tons each. Glover's Marblehead regiment, the amphibious fisherman-soldiers who had handled the evacuation from Long Island, were assigned to man these boats for the main crossing. This Washington expected would be completed by midnight of December 25-26, giving plenty of time to organize the columns for an advance on Trenton, nine miles away. He expected to reach the town, and to attack, about an hour before dawn. The password was "Victory or Death."

Washington's troops assembled in a sheltered valley just west of the ferry, shortly after 3:00 P.M. on Christmas afternoon. Each man had forty rounds of ammunition, a blanket, and in his knapsack the three days rations. As they paraded in front of him, on their way to the ferry, one can only wonder about the emotions which struggled behind the impassive, austere features of the big man, on his big horse.

These were men who had fought well—and sometimes poorly—from Long Island back through Manhattan to White Plains, and then on the bitter retreat across the Hudson and Delaware rivers. They were gaunt, their haphazard uniforms were ragged and torn; many had no shoes, wrapping their feet in rags; some were even barefoot; few had overcoats. But though he knew his mission was possibly a forlorn hope, Washington realized that through the bitter process of elimination which had begun in August and had continued on into December, these were the most reliable, most steadfast soldiers that a general could ask for. And though he was still dissatisfied with his officer corps in general, he knew he could count on most of the brigadiers who saluted so formally with their swords as they passed by, leading their men towards the ferry.

Greene and Sullivan, despite their mistakes at Fort Washington and on Long Island, were men on whom he knew he could rely to do well as his two division commanders. In Greene's division Hugh Mercer and Lord Stirling were also men of proven competence, if not brilliant. He was less certain of Adam Stephen, a former political adversary in Virginia, but he unquestionably felt some stirrings of regional pride as Stephen's stout Virginia Continentals passed in front of him. An unknown factor was the recently-arrived Frenchman, Roche de Fermoy. In Sullivan's division of three brigades, Glover had long ago proved his reliability, and both Arthur St. Clair and Colonel Paul Sargeant had shown promise. Following them came youthful, brilliant, dependable Colonel Henry Knox, leading his artillery. To Washington's knowledgeable eye, the glowing coats of the sturdy horses showed the attention which they had received from Knox, his officers, and men. Among the three battery commanders young Alexander Hamilton again caught the General's eye; there was a man who should go far.

It was dark when the small column arrived at the ferry, about 5:00 P.M. The wind was rising, and a few flakes of snow were beginning to fall. The river was roaring swift; filled with ice cakes that bumped and crunched against the boats, and sent chilling spray over their shivering occupants. Snow fell steadily during that cloud-shrouded, bitter night until, at about 11:00 P.M., it changed to sleet.

The crossing had already been going slower than Washington had hoped for, largely because of the difficulties of poling the boats through the ice. Now, with the wind rising, and the sleet-laced wind ripping through tattered clothing, and cutting exposed hands and faces, the work went even more slowly. Particularly difficult was the loading and unloading of the guns, and getting the unshod horses onto slippery decks. Instead of midnight, it was after 3 o'clock in the morning when the last group of wet, shivering men pushed the last gun up the river bank on the Jersey shore.

Washington stood silently on the bank as this gun trundled by him to be hitched up to its team of horses. Then he walked ahead to where Greene and Sullivan were getting their columns ready for the march. Though his impassive exterior did not reveal it to his subordinates, his heart sank at the continuing delays as the officers herded the sodden, freezing men into their formations, and as the artillery batteries slowly moved into their assigned positions in the column. It was nearly 4 o'clock before Greene's men were actually starting down the road toward Birmingham.

"This made me despair of surprising the town," Washington wrote later, "as I knew well we could not reach it before the day was fairly broke. But as I was certain there was no making retreat without being discovered and harassed when repassing the river, I determined to push on at all events."

Some time after 5:00 the column was halted briefly at the Birmingham crossroads; the men were told to fall out to gulp down a cold breakfast from their knapsacks. Mixed rain and sleet were still falling; nevertheless many of the soldiers seized the opportunity to snatch a few moments' sleep. As the officers came around to shake them awake and get them on their feet again, shortly after 5:30, two men could not be roused. They had frozen to death.

The army trudged ahead, Greene's division turning left at the crossroads, to approach Trenton from the northwest by way of the Pennington Road. The remainder, under Sullivan, continued along the River Road. Washington stood by the crossroad, his cloak wrapped around him, ignoring the stinging sleet in his face, peering into the gloom as his troops slid and slipped past on the icy road. As he listened to the monotonous plop, plop, plop of feet, punctuated by the muffled rumbling of gun wheels wrapped in rags, an aide approached him. General Sullivan reported that the storm was wetting the muskets, and that most were now unfit for firing.

We can only guess at Washington's thoughts at this time. Certainly despair must have struggled with determination as he realized that he had brought his thin-clad, freezing, ill-shod men to battle across an ice-packed river, on this stormy Christmas night, only to find that they could not use their weapons. After a moment's hesitation, Washington turned to speak firmly, but without emotion, to the aide.

"Tell General Sullivan to use the bayonet. I am resolved to take Trenton!"

Having made clear his determination to himself, as well as to his subordinates, the General swung into the saddle, as the first dim light of morning lightened the clouds to the east. He trotted ahead to pass Greene's column and to join that doughty general with his leading brigade.

Just after dawn—about 7:00 A.M.—the point of Greene's advance guard shouted an alarm and began to deploy across the road. Trenton was still more than a mile away. The column halted. Seeing a small body of men advancing towards them, Washington and Greene galloped forward to the point, where they discovered that this was a company of Stephen's brigade. Washington was dismayed to learn from the captain that with Stephen's permission he had come across the river the previous day to scout around Trenton, and that he had carried out a raid against the Hessian outposts during the night. Now certain that all chance of surprise had been lost, Washington expected the Hessians to be waiting in formation at the outskirts of the town. For the first time Washington revealed his emotions, and delivered a brief, stinging rebuke to Stephen, the leading brigadier, for having had the temerity to send a patrol across the river without authority. But the damage could not be undone. The advance must continue.

Though the record is not clear, it is evident that Washington kept close touch with Sullivan's advance, by means of messengers or aides. With Trenton in sight, and Stephen's brigade beginning to deploy at the head of Greene's column, Washington received word that Sullivan was also preparing to attack. It was almost 8 o'clock, an hour after dawn.

The storm that had delayed the American advance had equally discouraged the Hessians from patrolling the roads. Major Friedrich von Dechow, of the Knyphausen regiment, who was officer of the day, had called off the regular pre-dawn patrol, because of the weather. Disciplined Hessian sentries were at their posts, at the outskirts of the town, but it is evident that their backs were turned to the north wind, to keep the stinging sleet off their faces.

In the town itself, despite the lateness of the hour, few of the troops were astir. Christmas had been a day for celebration; the men had eaten well, and drunk much beer. The officers, in particular, had partied into the early hours of the morning, entertained by one of Trenton's leading Tory citizens. There had been a flurry of excitement in the early hours of Christmas evening, when a small band of marauding Americans had attacked an outpost, and had wounded six men of the picket company, before being driven off. But after this, the merriment of officers and men had been undisturbed. Near midnight an unidentified man tried to see Colonel Rall, and when the Colonel refused, he had scribbled a note which was to be delivered to the Hessian officer. A servant handed it to the Colonel, who stuffed it in his pocket, apparently unread. The note reported that the American army was marching against the town.

Rall's brigade consisted of three Hessian regiments—Rall's, von Knyphausen's and von Lossberg's—plus a company of 50 jägers and a detachment of 20 British light cavalry. The total strength was more than 1,400 men, and six cannon.

Simultaneously, Greene's and Sullivan's divisions bore down on the Hessian sentinels. The outpost pickets fired a few shots, then ran. The picket company guarding the Pennington Road was on the job. Deploying promptly, the Germans opened fire against the advancing Americans. Then, as the Continentals slipped and slid towards them on the run, the outnumbered Hessians drew back slowly and calmly, taking advantage of trees and houses to keep up a steady fire which snubbed but did not stop the American advance. Farther south, at the River Road, the jägers fell back more quickly, hotly pursued by Colonel John Stark's New Hampshire regiment.

Trenton's two main streets, King and Queen, ran north and south, with their northern tips converging at the junction of the Pennington Road and the "Old Road" to Princeton. Stephen's brigade quickly pushed down King and Queen streets, as Stirling and Mercer's troops filed off to the right in accordance with the plan. Fermoy led his brigade past the road junction to take up a blocking position on the Turnpike, or Post Road, which led northeast from Trenton to Princeton.

At the southern end of town, skirting Assunpink Creek, which emptied into the Delaware, several cross streets cut east and west across both King and Queen. The Hessians were quartered mainly in this area where the houses crowded close together between the narrow streets. This was the objective of Sullivan's corps, advancing from the River Road. Although St. Clair's brigade had promptly seized the bridge over the Assunpink, and had established a blocking position south of the stream, Sullivan's other two brigades, like those of Greene, were now meeting more stubborn resistance.

The Hessians, undoubtedly groggy from their Christmas celebration, were still soldiers. They came dashing out of the houses, arms in hand. In the confusion, with American artillery balls already whistling down the narrow streets, and thudding into the sides of houses, there was not much time for a very orderly assemblage. Nevertheless, detachments formed rapidly, and the officers and non-commissioned officers led them toward the western edge of town, or up King and Queen streets. But the American artillery, the guns jammed wheel-to-wheel just below the Pennington Road intersection, were now sweeping both main streets. The ammunition had been kept dry, and cannoneers kept their hands over the touch holes, to keep freezing rain from dripping down into the guns' powder chambers. Now, instead of ball, Captain Hamilton's and Captain Thomas Forrest's guns were spraying canister.

Quickly two Hessian cannon were wheeled into King Street to reply. But as they were beginning to fire Captain William Washington and Lieutenant James Monroe led their company of Virginians in a rifle charge. Though Washington and Monroe were both wounded, the guns were taken, and promptly turned against their former owners.

There was little musket fire. Save for the few Americans and Hessians who had taken refuge in houses, to dry their flints and gunlocks before firing from windows, the weapons were too wet. With fixed bayonets the Americans worked their way around behind the houses, carefully avoiding the streets where their artillery was firing. The Hessians too, after a few rounds, had also abandoned the streets and most of them began straggling eastward, to fields beyond Queen Street, where drowsy Colonel Rall was now attempting to reorganize his three regiments for a counterattack.

Early in the fighting Washington had realized that neither Ewing nor Cadwalader was on the field. He had anticipated this possibility, and expected that Sullivan's men would have seized the Assunpink bridge as quickly as possible, to cork the southern bottleneck. Seeing the Hessians beginning to form up east of the town, he ordered Greene to shift another brigade eastward to help Fermoy block the escape route towards Princeton. Greene sideslipped Stephen to the left, to comply with this order, leaving Stirling's brigade to push down King and Queen streets, while Mercer, further south, had joined Sullivan's left flank to push into the town from the west. It was a complete envelopment; the Hessians were now blocked from three directions, with the flooded Assunpink to their back.

Though still confused and disorganized, the Hessians were rallying to the beating of drums. At Rall's order, his brigade band struck up a stirring march. The brave colonel attempted to retrieve the disaster caused by his own negligence by leading two of his regiments in a counterattack. He left the Knyphausen regiment in reserve.

But the Americans were rushing in from three sides, covered by scattering rifle and musket shots from windows, and by devastating artillery fire. Rall went down, mortally wounded, and this was enough for his Hessians. The Rall and von Lossberg regimental colors were lowered to the ground, and Greene's men quickly took them prisoners. Farther south the Knyphausen regiment held out a few minutes longer against Sullivan, as their commander vainly sought a ford across the creek. Just as Washington was ordering Greene to join Sullivan in a converging attack, this regiment, too, surrendered.

It was about 9 o'clock. The battle had lasted slightly more than an hour. Twenty-two Hessians had been killed, and there were 948 prisoners, including 92 wounded. About 430 escaped, including the British light cavalry, which apparently took no part in the fight. American casualties had been negligible; there had been very little musket

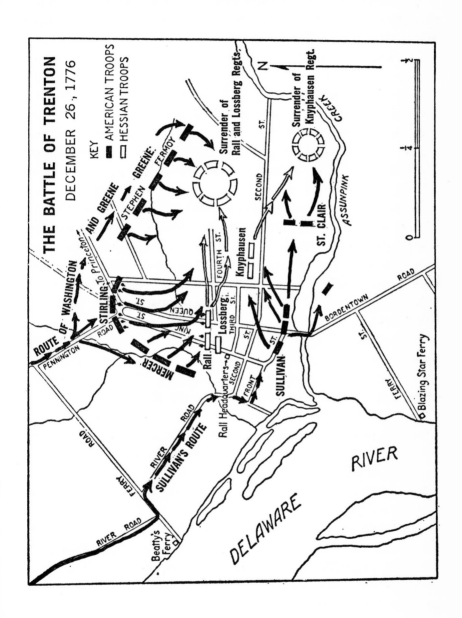

fire, the Hessians had never been able to get their artillery properly into action, and had surrendered before there was a major bayonet clash. Besides the two Americans who had frozen during the march, only two others had been wounded in the battle, in addition to Captain Washington and Lieutenant Monroe.

Considerable ammunition had been captured, together with the small arms and cannon which the Hessians had surrendered. Otherwise, the booty was not as great as Washington had expected. No great stock of supplies had been collected in Trenton, save for 48 hogshead of rum, which the American troops soon found. Before anyone could get more than a faint glow from the captured spirits, Washington ordered the casks stoven in. The thirsty troops sorrowfully watched the dark liquor flow into the rain-choked gutters.

Washington now faced another decision. By this time Donop's brigade would have been alerted by refugees from Trenton. In a few hours British and Hessian troops might be converging against him from Princeton and Bordentown, in strength considerably greater than his own 2,400 tired men. Without Cadwalader and Ewing, his situation in Trenton was precarious. He would have to return across the Delaware.

So, herding their prisoners along—accompanied by several wagonloads of booty, plus the captured cannon—the indomitable little army retraced its steps through the continuing storm, to its boats at McKonkey's Ferry. The return river crossing was as bitter as that of the previous night, save that it was in daylight. Even so, three more men froze to death. During the late afternoon and early evening, the troops reached their old bivouacks. They were exhausted by a march of nearly 30 miles, in abominable weather; yet at the same time they were as happy as only men can be who have tasted victory after months of defeat.

The results of the battle have been summed up by Trevelyan, the British historian: "It may be doubted whether so small a number of men ever employed so short a space of time with greater or more lasting results upon the history of the world." The country was galvanized; the Revolution reprieved.

Howe, dismayed by the news, found it stupefying that "three old established regiments of a people who make war a profession, should lay down their arms to a ragged and undisciplined militia." He immediately sent Cornwallis, with 8,000 men, to re-establish the situation on the Delaware.

The failure of Ewing and Cadwalader to carry out their missions during the Trenton operation had jeopardized Washington's plan. The lapse was what might have been expected from inexperienced leaders handling inexperienced men. Ewing had taken one look at the Delaware that Christmas night, had decided the river was impassable, and marched his men back to camp. Cadwalader had not been so easily deterred. Some of his troops actually reached the opposite bank below Burlington when he came to the conclusion that it would be impossible to load artillery or horses on his boats. Recalling his troops that had reached the far side, he returned to his bivouack. The next morning he wrote to the Commander-in-Chief about his efforts, adding, "I imagine the badness of the night must have prevented your crossing, as you intended."

When he later realized that he had penned this letter at the very time that Washington's men were fighting their way through Trenton, Cadwalader was stung into action. Without requesting permission, and without even informing Washington of his intentions, he took his 2,000 men across the river on December 27. The passage was no easier than it would have been on the 25th, but now Cadwalader and his men knew that it could be done, and they hoped that perhaps they could share some of the glory. Pushing inland, he discovered that the Hessian garrison at Bordentown had withdrawn into central New Jersey. Advancing to Crosswicks, he sent a message urging Washington to join him. This belatedly bold, and exceedingly rash, move now placed the General on the horns of an entirely new dilemma.

To recross the river, and to support Cadwalader would be extremely dangerous. Washington's men, without rest or tangible reward for their magnificent effort, might well still refuse to re-enlist. And even if they did, he would still have insufficient force to oppose the strong effort which an indignant and powerful enemy was bound to make, to avenge the humiliating defeat at Trenton.

On the other hand Washington knew that if he ordered Cadwalader to withdraw, this might be considered as an ignominious retreat on the heels of a brilliant victory. Fear of such a psychological blow, combined with his continuing desire to harass the English, led Washington to decide to go back. First he made sure that his men had as much rest as possible, with a good Christmas dinner on the 27th. The captured Hessian officers dined with Washington. Then, on December 29, with 1,500 men, he crossed the Delaware for the third time in four days. The remainder were sick or exhausted from their exertions. He reoccupied Trenton, and organized a defensive position south of the town on Assunpink Creek's farther bank. He sent messages to Heath at Peekskill, and to McDougall at Morristown, to join him, and to harass British communications en route.

On December 30 and 31 Washington personally went to each of his Continental regiments in Trenton to make a last-minute plea for re-enlistment. He sent staff officers to his other detachments. An offer of $10 bounty, and appeal to patriotism in terms similar to those Thomas Paine had used in *The Crisis,* brought better results than he had hoped for. More than half of his able-bodied Continentals, buoyed up by their Trenton victory, agreed to serve for six more weeks. Thus, by evening of December 31, 1776, Washington found himself with a hard core of some 1,600 veterans; a new contingent of Philadelphia militia under General Mifflin brought his total effective strength to almost 5,000 men.

Washington was troubled by the fact that in offering a bounty from public funds he had exceeded even the blanket authority recently given him by Congress. Ever meticulous in his deference to Congress, particularly in budgetary affairs, Washington justified his action to himself on the grounds of military necessity, which could be explained frankly to Congress in due course. He was both amazed and pleased, therefore, when later that day he received a message from Baltimore, forwarding a Congressional resolution of December 27 which specifically authorized the action he had taken.

But the resolution had not stopped at empowering Washington "to use every endeavor, by giving bounties and otherwise, to prevail upon the troops whose enlistment shall expire at the end of this month to stay with the Army so long after that period as its situation shall render . . . necessary." The Congress went on to state that, "having maturely considered the present crisis; and having perfect reliance on the wisdom, vigour, and uprightness of General Washington," he was granted for a period of six months "full, ample and complete powers" to raise sixteen independent battalions of Continental infantry, plus supporting artillery, cavalry and engineers; he was authorized to commandeer whatever supplies "he may want for the use of the army"; he was empowered to appoint and promote officers, and to fix rates of pay. He had, in fact, been appointed a military dictator in the tradition of the Roman republic.

Next day Washington learned British reaction to his victory at Trenton. Cornwallis, about to return to England on leave, had been ordered by Howe to re-establish the situation on the Delaware. On the evening of the 1st he reached Princeton, a bare dozen miles away, with 8,000 British regulars. Washington despatched Fermoy's brigade, with some additional units, to delay the British advance down the Post Road and Old Road from Princeton. He placed Sullivan's brigade in Trenton in another delaying position. The remainder of the army was gathered from Bordentown and Crosswick, and put to work strengthening the defenses behind the Assunpink.

Washington had acted just in time. With his usual energy and vigor, Cornwallis began to advance before dawn on the 2nd. Despite effective American delaying tactics, despite roads muddied by a rain and thaw, the efficient British regulars pushed down the Post Road to within a mile of Trenton by mid-afternoon. Fermoy, who was proving himself to be a worthless commander, for all of his European reputation, had left his troops earlier in the day, and had returned to Trenton. Experienced Colonel Edward Hand, however, had taken over command of the delaying force and had done an efficient job, despite Cornwallis' firm pressure. Washington himself supervised the holding of Hand's last delaying position, outside of Trenton, ordering a withdrawal only at about 4:00 P.M. Falling back slowly and deliberately, Hand's men, now supported by Sullivan, delayed the English in the town for another hour. It was after 5 o'clock, and dark, before Cornwallis' leading troops reached the Assunpink.

Confronting Washington's gaunt, footsore, exhausted veterans, and his unreliable militia, Cornwallis had 5,500 regulars in hand, with two additional brigades, some 2,500 men, disposed in reserve a few hours away, one at Maidenhead (now Lawrenceville) and another at Princeton. Under the circumstances, it seemed to many of the American leaders that any effort to oppose this "flower of the British army" must result in the destruction of the Americans, boxed in as they were with the Delaware River to their left rear, and the Atlantic Ocean to their right rear.

This estimate of the situation was shared also by Cornwallis, aware not only of the geographical situation of the American army, but also of its limited combat effectiveness. Brigadier General Sir William Erskine was not so sure. He suggested an immediate night attack, saying that "if Washington is the general I take him to be, he will not be found there in the morning." Across the way Cornwallis could see American soldiers throwing more logs on their campfires; while the clatter of spade and pick told of feverish work on entrenchments.

"No," Cornwallis is reported to have replied to Erskine. "We've got the old fox safe now. We'll go over and bag him in the morning."

But Cornwallis woke at dawn to the noise of distant cannonading behind him, and a deserted camp across the Assunpink.

Soon after dark Washington had sent his baggage trains safely south to Burlington. At the same time, apparently, he called a council of war, in St. Clair's headquarters, near the banks of the creek.

St. Clair and others, in writing about that council of war, have implied that Washington had no plan, and that he asked his assembled officers for advice. Yet it is hard to believe that Washington, in the light of his past and subsequent record, would have deliberately taken up the defensive position on the Assunpink without a carefully pre-pared plan of action. There is other evidence that this council of war, like those which preceded the withdrawal from Long Island and the attack against Trenton, was for the purpose of issuing orders, rather than soliciting advice. The fact that the baggage movement to Bur-lington began either during the conference, or immediately thereafter, is further indication that previously prepared plans were already being put into prompt and efficient execution.

At midnight, with gun-wheels muffled in rags, and strict silence enjoined on every man, the American army began to file out of its trenches to move around the British left, and northward. Washington had selected rough and unused back roadways, whose existence was unknown to the English. Men and horses skidded and stumbled on boulders; guns frequently jammed between stumps, and had to be literally manhandled free. Otherwise the roads were practicable, and led northeast to Princeton. Five hundred men were left behind to keep the fires burning, and to hold the Assunpink bridge against a possible British night surprise attack. They were to be in readiness to scamper after the rest of the army at dawn.

Despite minor disappointments and accidents, fortune had been smiling steadily on Washington for over a week. And fortune was still favoring the brave. The weather turned cold around midnight, stiffening the muddy roads. Tired, but surprisingly cheerful, the veteran Continentals and raw militia marched steadily on. The head of the column, reaching Stony Brook, about two miles south of Princeton, just before dawn, rested briefly. Then the march was resumed, over an old road which followed the course of the brook for almost a mile to the vicinity of Quaker Meeting House. Here the old road was within half a mile of the new Post Road, Cornwallis' line of communications. The two roads then ran parallel from Stony Brook into Princeton.

At this point Washington detached Mercer's brigade of Continentals to cover the left flank. Mercer was to destroy the Stony Brook bridge on the Post Road, and then take up positions from which he could not only block any return move of Cornwallis, but also cut the westward line of retreat of British troops in Princeton. The main body of the army, headed by Sullivan's division, pushed along the old road toward Princeton.

When he had pressed on to Trenton, the day before, Cornwallis had left his 4th Brigade, about 1,200 strong, under efficient Lieutenant Colonel Charles Mawhood, at Princeton to protect his line of communications. He had also left another brigade, under General Leslie, at Maidenhead. Having discovered all of Washington's army entrenched in front of him on the Assunpink, Cornwallis had that same evening sent a message back ordering Leslie and Mawhood to move up to join him, leaving only small detachments to guard the road and supplies.

Following these instructions, Mawhood had begun to march south from Princeton at dawn with the 17th and 55th Foot, plus a cavalry detachment—some 800 men, all told. His third regiment, the 40th Foot, consisting of about 400 men, he left in town to guard military stores there.

Mawhood's men were crossing the Stony Brook bridge when Mercer's column appeared, approaching from the south. At almost the same instant the Americans saw the British. Both sides deployed promptly eastward from the brook, and each sought to gain the high ground between the two roads. The Americans reached the crest shortly before the English. Mawhood, seeing that he was opposed by a very small force, immediately attacked.

Washington, who had been observing the march of his ragged troops past Quaker Meeting House, heard the rattle of musketry from the direction of the bridge, and the high ground above it. He galloped up the road a few hundred yards to observe the developing action through the trees. Seeing that Mercer was outnumbered, he sent back for the next unit on the road, which happened to be Cadwalader's 900 militia—the Associaters of Philadelphia.

Before these could arrive, however, Mawhood had mounted a co-ordinated infantry-artillery attack on Mercer's brigade. The exhausted Continentals stood their ground briefly, but when the British charged with the bayonet and Mercer fell mortally wounded, his brigade disintegrated. The remnants streamed back towards the Meeting House, pursued by the British. At this moment, two American guns, which had gone into position in an orchard to the right of Mercer's line, opened up on the English flank. Mawhood ordered a halt, and was just about to face his troops around to take care of these troublesome guns, when he saw the advance elements of Cadwalader's militia emerge from the woods near the Meeting House. Accordingly, the Englishman fell back to the crest, refusing his left flank slightly to get it away from the American guns. Although shaken by the sight of Mercer's fleeing men, Cadwalader troops advanced on the British position. But one concentrated volley from the English regulars was enough for the Pennsylvanians. They took to their heels.

Again Mawhood was about to take care of the two artillery pieces on his flank, which were continuing their harassing fire, when he saw more American reinforcements appearing in the low ground towards the Meeting House. These were the American rear guard, Colonel Daniel Hitchcock's brigade of New England Continentals. Ordering these veterans to deploy to the right of Mercer's and Cadwalader's fugitives, Washington dashed into the mob of militia to help Cadwalader, who was vainly trying to reform his men. Raising his voice, Washington shouted: "Parade with us, my brave fellows. There is but a handful of the enemy, and we shall have them directly."

The effect was almost miraculous. Washington's presence was all that Mercer's leaderless men needed to restore them to order. Their example, and the sight of the imposing figure on his big horse, quickly

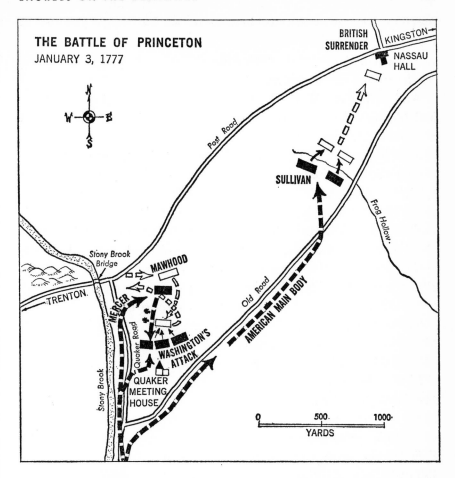

shamed the Philadelphia militiamen also to turn around and form ranks again. Mawhood's troops, now firmly established behind a fence on the ridge, saw the men they had just routed turn and begin to re-form beside Hitchcock's fresh troops. Then galloping across the fields between the two forces came the American general, waving his men forward with his hat. Across the field his stentorian voice carried: "Follow me! Hold your fire!"

As though drawn by a magnet, the militiamen and Continentals advanced behind their imposing Commander-in-Chief. About 30 yards from the British line, the General drew rein and cried: "Halt!" His men raised their muskets, awaiting his command to fire. But before he could speak, a volley rang out from the British troops, spontaneously answered by the ready American muskets. Washington, between the fires, was swallowed in billowing smoke. Frantic aides, dashing forward, fearful of what they would find, discovered their chief untouched and unruffled. "Bring up the troops!" he called. "Bring up the troops, the day is ours!"

And so it was. As Hitchcock's men began to envelop one flank, and Mercer's the other, Mawhood abandoned his guns and ordered a withdrawal. Some of the Americans had already gotten between the British and the bridge, but Mawhood led a desperate bayonet charge which cleared the way. He got his men safely across the bridge, and fell back toward Trenton. Washington, sensing an opportunity to turn this retreat into a rout, ordered a troop of the Philadelphia Light Horse to follow them. Stopping for an instant to order an aide to have the British baggage collected, and to have the bridge destroyed, the general himself clapped spurs to his horse to clatter across the bridge after the Philadelphia cavalrymen. He shouted to his aides as he left: "It is a fine fox chase, my boys!"

The unexpected cavalry charge had the effect Washington desired. Mawhood's infantrymen scattered, and ran for the woods, while the small group of British cavalry galloped down the road toward Trenton.

Reasonably assured that there would be no more trouble from Mawhood's men, Washington reluctantly gave up the pleasure of the chase to reassume the responsibilities of command. Realizing that Cornwallis would soon be coming up from Trenton, he ordered the Philadelphia cavalrymen to turn back, and he led them towards Princeton, where Sullivan was now engaged. On the way he took time personally to chase away a thief who had begun to rob a helpless wounded British soldier, lying on the battlefield. After a word of comfort to the surprised redcoat, he galloped on to Princeton, to find the town in Sullivan's control.

The British had held out briefly on the college grounds, and nearly half of them had taken refuge in Nassau Hall, where they refused an American demand for surrender. But a cannonball from one of Hamilton's guns, crashing through the wall of Nassau Hall, soon caused them to change their minds. More than 100 British surrendered. The remainder were fleeing eastward towards New Brunswick. Washington's elation was subdued when he learned not only of Mercer's mortal wound, but of the death of brave Colonel Haslet, who had deliberately deferred compliance with orders to recruiting duty in order to stay with the army in its crisis.

Quickly Washington ordered his troops to collect what they could carry from the British stores, and to destroy the rest. Most of his ragged, barefoot men were able to refit themselves with new shoes and blankets, and to gorge themselves on British rations. Cornwallis' advance guard reached the ruins of Stony Brook less than two hours after the last shot of the battle had been fired. At that very moment Washington was leading his tired but happy men northward toward Morristown, safely inland of the enemy. Cornwallis, fearful that the Americans might try to seize the lightly guarded supply depot at New Brunswick, did not tarry at Princeton, but continued back to Brunswick in a night march. A few days later Putnam, advancing from Philadelphia on Washington's orders, occupied Princeton.

The Battle of Princeton, which lasted less than half an hour, was only a skirmish insofar as numbers engaged and casualties suffered were concerned. The British loss was approximately 100 killed and wounded, and 200 taken prisoner; the Americans had about 40 killed and wounded. Actually, however, this small engagement was the magnificent conclusion of one of the most brilliant, and one of the most significant, military campaigns in history.

Strategically and politically the effects were enormous. The British had been driven from western and central New Jersey. The dying embers of an almost lost cause flamed anew; the War of the Revolution would continue. The American people and the American Army realized that they had a general at least as good as the English best. Five years later, when Cornwallis surrendered to Washington at Yorktown, the British general himself supplied an amazingly frank and glowing military evaluation of this brief campaign:

"Fame will gather your brightest laurels from the banks of the Delaware rather than from the Chesapeake."

★ 16 ★ ★ ★ ★ ★

Problems and Plans

J OHN BURGOYNE WAS A MAN OF MANY PARTS: soldier, dramatist, parliamentarian, sybarite, and gambler. He was also ambitious. Sir John had taken sail for England at the conclusion of Carleton's abortive operations in the Lake Champlain-Ticonderoga region in the fall of 1776, and laid an alluring plan before King George. The concept of splitting the Colonies would be the same as that of 1776, but this time more specific in operation. There would be no repetition of the Carolina diversion, since this would drain troops from the critical northern theater. Howe's forces, now firmly established in New York, would be the anvil upon which two hammer blows would smash the revolt.

The principal blow, as Burgoyne presented it, would strike through the Champlain-Hudson valleys to Albany. He hoped to command this primary effort. The secondary effort would come from Oswego, on Lake Ontario, down the Mohawk Valley, also converging on Albany. If Howe had not already reached that town, Burgoyne envisaged that the combined invading forces from the north and northwest would sweep down the Hudson to a junction with Howe some place above the Hudson Highlands. At the conclusion of this converging series of operations, New England would be split from the other colonies, British troops would be occupying America's heartland, and any remaining rebel forces would be dispersed and discredited. The Revolution would be over.

King George was not a very bright man; neither was Lord Germain. In February they both approved Burgoyne's scheme, with no thought of the intricate problems of coordination, concentration and supply involved in such long and widespread wilderness operations.

Even while Burgoyne's plan was still under consideration, Germain had received a quite different strategic proposal for 1777 from General Howe. Sir William had originally planned to hold New York as a base from which three forces would fan out to complete the suppression of the rebellion. One of these would sweep through New England to Boston by way of Newport; one would advance northward up the Hudson to Albany, possibly to effect a junction with forces from Canada; the third and smallest force would demonstrate against Philadelphia.

The events of the Trenton-Princeton campaign had caused the British general to have second thoughts. Such a diversion of his forces would be dangerous in the face of an opponent as active and aggressive as Washington had proven himself to be. Washington's army was now obviously and properly the major British objective. Howe rightly felt that if he could crush that army, he could crush the Revolution. An important, but secondary, objective attractive to Howe was Philadelphia, the capital of the revolting Colonies, seat of the Continental Congress and administrative headquarters for the American army. A blow struck at Philadelphia would force Washington to defend his capital, and Howe was certain that the poorly disciplined Colonials would be quickly overwhelmed in open battle by his disciplined troops. Subsequent occupation of the rebel capital would quickly bring about the dissolution of the Colonial union, and the end of the Revolution. There is some evidence that captive General Charles Lee influenced Howe's estimate along these lines, in discussions that were probably treasonable on Lee's part.

On March 3, Lord Germain approved Howe's plan to operate against Philadelphia. It has never been clear how he envisaged coordination between Howe's southward movement against Philadelphia with his expected advance northward to Albany, contemplated in the already-approved Burgoyne plan. Possibly he thought Howe could do both, either at the same time, or in quick succession. Possibly— and this would be in the nature of the man—he never thought of the inconsistency. In any event, Germain never ordered Howe to cooperate with Burgoyne.

As soon as Howe was informed of the approval of his plan by the

British government, early in April, 1777, he wrote to Carleton in Canada not to expect his cooperation in operations in the north, unless Washington were to go in that direction. It is evident from this letter that Howe knew of Burgoyne's plan, but felt that, since his own had been approved, he had complete freedom of action to operate against Washington as he saw fit. He sent a copy of this letter to Lord Germain. Burgoyne also saw the letter, which was shown to him by Carleton before his expedition started south from Canada.

Since neither Carleton nor Burgoyne offered any objection to Howe's letter, Burgoyne must then have been satisfied with Howe's promise "to have a corps on the lower part of Hudson's River sufficient to open the communications for shipping through the Highlands, at present obstructed by several forts erected by the Rebels for that purpose, which corps may afterward act in favor of the northern army." There is no basis for Burgoyne's later claim that he expected "a cooperating army at Albany;" the excuse he was to give Parliament for abandoning his line of communications through Ticonderoga.

Confident, therefore, that his plans for operations against Philadelphia had been fully approved by Lord Germain, and by King George himself, and having communicated adequately with the other major British command in America, Howe went ahead with his plans. There is no basis for the commonly accepted conclusions that Howe either deliberately failed to cooperate with Burgoyne, or that he misunderstood his orders, or that the instructions from England had not been clear. The instructions were woefully confused and inadequate, but so far as Howe was concerned, his letter to Carleton removed any ambiguity.

The closeness of the American ring around British positions in New York and eastern New Jersey created serious problems for Howe during the winter. He had approximately 13,000 men in New Brunswick and Amboy, and another 10,000 on Manhattan, or holding outworks at King's Bridge and Fort Independence. The shortage of housing and inability to obtain much food from the countryside caused discomfort to the troops. Howe, himself, however, seems to have been quite comfortable. It was common knowledge in New York that he spent much of his time, awake and asleep, with the attractive wife of his Commissary of Prisons, one Joshua Loring. That greedy functionary, it seems, encouraged the liaison for his own selfish motives.

Washington, meanwhile, was having much different problems. He had moved to Morristown on January 6, after his victory at Princeton; a secure position from which he could threaten the flank of any British thrust towards Philadelphia, without being forced to fight a disadvantageous battle in the open field. Morristown, on a plateau in the Watchung Mountains, could be approached from the east or south only through relatively narrow defiles in several chains of hills, while passes leading westward were available both for retreat and for access to farmlands in the upper Delaware Valley. Not only did Morristown overlook the central New Jersey plain between New York and Philadelphia, it was also convenient to the Highlands, in the event of any British moves northward up the Hudson. Thus Washington decided to stay there through the winter, alert for any possible British move in either of the two most likely directions.

A week later, upon urging from Washington, Heath marched south from Peekskill with 3,400 men against Fort Independence, just north of King's Bridge on the Harlem River. Washington hoped that a surprise move would eliminate the English bridgehead north of Manhattan, or, at the very least, so harass the foe as to prevent him from reinforcing his troops in Jersey. The British garrison of Fort Independence ignored Heath's summons to surrender in twenty minutes or else suffer the consequence. He waited ten days for an answer, which finally came in the form of a determined sortie by the garrison of 2,000 men. Heath's militiamen panicked, and he returned to Peekskill, the laughing-stock of the British and of his own army. Washington wrote him a stinging personal letter of reprimand, but took no other action. He realized that Heath was a loyal, mediocre officer, who was simply doing his best to carry out a responsibility beyond his capabilities. And there was no one available to replace him.

Washington's most immediate problem was the perennial one of how to hold his army together. In mid-February the extended enlistments which he had obtained in the last days of 1776 expired. His strength quickly dwindled to less than 1,000 Continentals, augmented by shifting contingents of militia, rarely totalling more than 2,000 men. Despite Washington's efforts, and his constant prodding of the administrative offices in Philadelphia, his tiny army was constantly short of food, equipment, clothes and ammunition. Thanks to Robert

Morris—one of the few Congressmen to stay in Philadelphia during the dark days of December, 1776—Washington was able to obtain sufficient money and supplies to hold his army together, despite severe hardship and austerity. Financier Morris, who took seriously his duties as a member of the Congressional Committee of Secret Correspondence (and munitions procurement), risked his own personal credit to borrow the money needed to obtain the bare minimum of supplies for Washington's army.

The outbreak of an epidemic of smallpox in central New Jersey added further to Washington's worries. To the consternation of the local citizens, he required the inoculation of everyone in Morristown, military and civilian. (The process of inoculation in the late eighteenth century was much more grim than today's simple vaccination.)

Washington was particularly bitter about the failure of Congress, and of the states, to cooperate in recruiting the forces which Congress had approved. Thus, when Congress urged him to plan for an early spring offensive, he pointedly replied that first they would have to furnish him with troops. It will be recalled that in September, 1776, Congress had called upon the states to raise 88 battalions; and then on December 27, at the time he was granted his dictatorial powers, Congress specifically permitted Washington to raise an additional 16 battalions. But when he tried to get his veterans to re-enlist in their own units, and sent out officers to recruit the independent battalions, they soon discovered that the $20 bounty which Congress had authorized had little effect.

The states, in their own half-hearted efforts to raise their quotas, were adding their own bounties to entice men to enlist in new Continental units. Even worse, the states were also raising their own home guards in first priority, and most offered better pay for these more comfortable and less dangerous posts. Thus enlistment in the independent battalions was the fourth choice for an adventurous young man who would be more likely first to consider the lucrative opportunities of privateering, next the relatively well paid and only slightly dangerous duties in the state home guard, or finally the higher bounties for enlisting in the Continental battalions raised by his state. In addition, some men had been enlisting, accepting their bounties, and then deserting—sometimes to repeat the process in other communities. Washington's stern measure of shooting deserters was only a marginal deterrent to this practice.

Nevertheless, despite a shortage of troops and the inadequacies of supplies and equipment, Washington was able to present a bold front to the British. With the unexpectedly enthusiastic support of the New Jersey militia, his troops incessantly harassed British outposts, and particularly their foraging parties. The support of the local populace, and of the local militia, was largely the consequence of British and Hessian outrages against civilians during the short time they had controlled central Jersey, and in their continuing raids from New Brunswick and Amboy.

One of the most serious of the American shortages, that of weapons, was eased somewhat in March when two ships arrived from France, carrying a total of about 20,000 muskets, with considerable powder and other items of ammunition and equipment. Although most of this matériel was quickly dissipated by being issued to the militia, some of it went to the new Continental regiments beginning to take shape in the states. In April and May some 43 of these new regiments began to arrive at Morristown, though they averaged less than 200 men each.

With these new arrivals, by the middle of May Washington's army on paper consisted of nearly 9,000 Continentals, though his effectives were only about 6,000. In light of the augmentation, Washington reorganized his army into five divisions commanded by Greene, Stephen, Sullivan, Lincoln and Stirling. As the army began to swell, Congress became bold enough to return to Philadelphia from Baltimore. The members made clear to Washington, however, that he must devote adequate attention to the defense of the capital.

The arrival of spring increased foraging and skirmishing activities on both sides. On March 23, 500 British troops were landed by ship at Peekskill, where they seized many valuable stores, and burned most of the rest, as well as destroying the American barracks. The acting commander in the Highlands at that time was Brigadier General Alexander McDougall (Heath having recently been shifted to command the inactive Massachusetts region, after Artemas Ward had resigned.) With the assistance of Colonel Marinus Willett, commander of Fort Montgomery, McDougall was able to drive the British back to their ships, but not before they had accomplished most of their mission.

A month later General Howe sent a similar expedition to demolish the large magazine of American stores at Danbury, Connecticut. This force, consisting of nearly 1,300 men—British regulars, plus a small Tory contingent—was commanded by Major General William

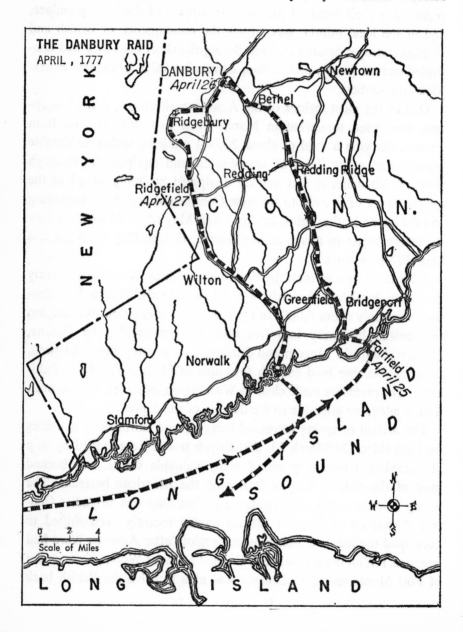

THE DANBURY RAID
APRIL , 1777

Tryon—the royal governor of New York. Convoyed to Norwalk by two frigates, Tryon's men debarked on April 25, and marched inland unopposed. The Continental garrison at Danbury—about 250 strong —retired precipitously. The British collected as much booty as they could gather, then put the remainder of the magazines to flame, destroying large quantities of food, clothing and tents, as well as much of the town. After spending the night at Danbury, the British troops started back for their ships.

News of the raid reached Benedict Arnold, who was at that moment on leave, sulking at his sister's home in New Haven, and contemplating resignation. Despite his brilliant services, Congress had passed him over for promotion to major general, when Stephen, Lincoln and Stirling had been promoted. News of the British raid at Danbury caused him to leap at the chance for a fight. Joining old General David Wooster (who commanded Continental troops in Connecticut) and militia Brigadier General Gold Silliman, Arnold initiated a movement of 100 Continentals and 500 militiamen to intercept the departing British.

On April 27, Arnold with 400 men blocked the British advance at Ridgefield, while Wooster with the remainder attacked Tryon's rear guard. Successful at first, the old general was mortally wounded, and his men scattered. At Ridgefield, after a brief fire fight, Tryon's regulars encircled the American flanks. Arnold withdrew his men in good order, but was almost captured when his horse was killed. Shooting his way out, Arnold reassembled his small force and tried again. In a melée at the embarkation point, the American militia were driven off by a British bayonet charge, and Tryon got his men aboard ship without further difficulties.

It was a small affair; but nearly 200 British were casualties, while the Americans lost about 20 killed and 80 wounded. And Congress could not ignore the widespread praise of Arnold's vigor and leadership. He was made a major general, and Congress bestowed upon him the gift of a charger. Still rankling at the original injustice, which had put five juniors above him, Arnold was dissuaded from resigning only by Washington's persuasion. When the Commander-in-Chief sent Congress a letter suggesting that Arnold, "an active, spirited officer," be sent north to the forces opposing Burgoyne, Arnold cooled down and consented to serve under Schuyler.

During the spring of 1777, another problem began to plague both Washington and the Continental Congress. Silas Deane, special representative of the United States in France, had been over-eager in carrying out one of his missions; that of attracting volunteers from among the European corps of officers. Without bothering to check very seriously into their records, their characters, or even their basic military qualifications, Deane was sending to the United States anyone who claimed to have had military experience. To each of these he gave written promises of high rank and high pay. As one member of the Continental Congress later put it, the result was that Philadelphia was "swarming with Frenchmen."

At first, to the consternation of Washington and of his officers, Congress unhesitatingly accorded these foreigners all that Deane had promised them. American colonels, who felt that they had qualified themselves for promotion by staunch service during 1776, were incensed to find foreign officers granted commissions as brigadier generals, and then assigned to commands which the Americans felt that they had earned. All too often these foreign officers proved themselves incompetent or uninterested in their duties. One such was Roche de Fermoy, whose disappointing conduct in the Princeton campaign was soon to be compounded in the north.

The growing discontent among American officers reached a crisis when a French officer named Philip C. T. du Coudray, an experienced but undistinguished French artilleryman, arrived with a written promise from Silas Deane that he was to be made a major general and put in command of all American artillery, or other equivalent position, and that his date of rank was to be as of August 1, 1776. Greene and Sullivan were both incensed, since this would have given du Coudray precedence over them; Knox, only a relatively recent brigadier general, was equally furious, since he felt that he had already proven himself as Washington's chief of artillery. Washington was annoyed, not only because he didn't want du Coudray, but because of the effect of the affair upon three of his most capable officers.

All three of these generals wrote letters to Congress stating that they would resign if du Coudray was appointed a major general of the line. The congressmen, in turn furious at having this pressure placed upon them by the three officers, rebuked them, but not so severely as to make them carry out their threat. Soon disenchanted by the imperious and arrogant attitude of du Coudray, Congress compromised by making him a major general in the staff, with the title of Inspector of Ordnance. When it was pointed out to the three dissident American generals that this would keep him from being over them in a line position, they reluctantly withdrew their threatened resignations.

Du Coudray, however, did not accept the compromise, and kept pressing for field command. The du Coudray case continued to simmer throughout the summer, causing Washington headaches even during his campaign against Howe. It was settled, however, in September by an accident in which du Coudray was drowned in the Schuylkill River. John Adams wrote, with obvious relief, that this was a "dispensation that will save us much altercation."

Coping with his many problems with amazing patience, yet with unswerving determination, and at the same time smoothing the ruffled feathers of various subordinates, Washington had, nonetheless, been able throughout the winter of 1776-77 to devote considerable thought to the strategic aspects of the coming campaign. He had no illusions, of course, as to the possibility that he might be able to seize the strategic initiative.

To a degree unmatched by any of his American contemporaries —and indeed by very few Englishmen—Washington recognized the tremendous advantage which sea power gave to the British. Accordingly, during the winter, and particularly as reinforcements began to arrive in the spring, he strove to dispose his three major field forces in such a way as to be able to provide one another as much mutual support as possible against any of the more likely British moves. He saw how the St. Lawrence River permitted the English to extend far to the rear of the coastal settlements of the thirteen states. Thus he felt it essential that there be two major American forces in areas where Britain could apply its sea power advantage most effectively: the Lake Champlain region, guarded by Schuyler's northern forces, and the Hudson-Delaware lowlands, where his own army faced the Atlantic.

His concern regarding the northern army was demonstrated during the winter and spring primarily in his efforts to provide Schuyler with able, experienced subordinates, amongst whom Gates, Arnold and St. Clair were the most outstanding. In addition, he continuously exhorted Congress and the New England states, as well as the Continental commanders in those states, to provide adequate forces for Schuyler's requirements.

At the same time, and particularly after the new Continental regiments began to appear, he built up his force in the Highlands. This he placed under Putnam in the spring, after Heath had been shifted to Boston. He visualized the Highlands command as a mobile reserve, available not only to block British moves up the Hudson, but to provide support either to his own or to Schuyler's army—or both— depending on which of the many possible strategies the British selected.

In the light of Carleton's penetration into the Lake Champlain area in the fall of 1776, Washington expected some kind of British movement from St. Johns against Ticonderoga and Crown Point. He also recognized the possibility of an advance up the Hudson by Howe, in cooperation with such a move from Canada. There is nothing in the record, however, to indicate that Washington realized how much of an effort the British intended to make from Canada, in pursuance of Burgoyne's plan. It was probably not until late May or early June, 1777—when he learned of the arrival of Burgoyne's army in Canada—that this became a major consideration in his mind. Until then, he seems to have expected that Howe's principal objective would be Philadelphia.

By the end of May Washington felt that he had prepared himself and his two major subsidiary field forces—within the serious limitations on available manpower and material resources—as best he could to meet either of the most likely British moves. He now felt strong enough to undertake more active campaigning. With an army augmented by militia to a strength of about 9,000 men, on May 28 he marched to Middle Brook, in the hills eight miles north of New Brunswick. The move from Morristown was undertaken as much to break the monotony of the long winter camp sojourn, and to provide some activity and field experience for his new soldiers, as it was for any intention of harassing the British.

In any event, he soon saw action, for the British were coming, on both fronts.

17

Crises in the North

On MAY 6, 1777, JUST AS THE ST. LAWRENCE ICE was breaking up, Burgoyne arrived back at Quebec, a happy man. He was to lead the invasion from Canada in accordance with the plan he had sold to King George. Germain's instructions to Governor General Carleton were explicit, even insulting in tone. Carleton would stay in Canada with 3,770 men. Burgoyne, with nearly 7,500 men, would "proceed with all possible expedition to join General Howe and put himself under his command." Carleton was also to detail from his own troops Lieutenant Colonel Barry St. Leger (temporary brigadier general) with 675 men, plus "a sufficient number of Canadians and Indians" for the Mohawk Valley operation; this force would also be under Burgoyne's command. Everyone was happy except Carleton, who found his role reduced to that of garrison commander and general housekeeper. However, smarting Carleton nevertheless gave Burgoyne loyal support. (Having done his duty, he would later submit his resignation, which was promptly accepted by his arch-enemy, Lord Germain.)

Burgoyne concentrated his troops at St. Johns; St. Leger's force, assembling at Lachine, near Montreal, we leave for the moment, to follow "Gentleman Johnny" up Lake Champlain, Ticonderoga-bound.

Burgoyne's expedition started from St. Johns in June 1777—an imposing amphibious array on that wilderness waterway. The naval flotilla led: two full-rigged ships (HMS *Royal George,* constructed at St. Johns during the winter, was added to the *Inflexible*), two schooners, six big row-galleys and 28 gunboats. Behind them came the troops, embarked in a multitude of bateaux and longboats, with the great floating battery *Thunderer* in their midst; above it streaming the royal standard. Ahead darted the canoes of the irregulars—Indians, Canadians and Tories. The glittering bayonets and variegated uniforms, the blaring field music, and the occasional whoops of war-painted Indians added to the spectacle. A brave show, indeed; well-attuned to Burgoyne's sense of the dramatic.

Except for the irregular contingent—some 250 French-Canadians and Tories commanded by British Captain Simon Fraser, and 400 Indians under the unsavory Canadian characters Louis St. Luc de la Corne and Charles de Langlade—this was an aggregation of well-disciplined fighting men, led by professionals. Burgoyne, for all his many faults, was nevertheless experienced, active, firm and courageous; above all, he had the confidence of his men, for he was far ahead of most of his European military generation. He believed that his soldiers were men, not cattle, and his nickname of "Gentleman Johnny" was their accolade in return. Of like military mould was Major General Baron Friedrich Adolph von Riedesel, his titular second-in-command and leader of the German Brunswick corps. He, too, took seriously the well-being of his men, and he had a background of twenty years of distinguished combat service.

The army was organized in two divisions—British and Brunswick (German). Each division consisted of an advanced corps and two brigades of line troops. In the British division, commanded by Major General William Phillips, the advanced corps was led by temporary Brigadier General Simon Fraser (not to be confused with his cousin and namesake, Captain Fraser), Master of Lovat. Fraser, alert, determined and battle-wise, was a light infantry commander *par excellence,* brought up in the hard school of the Royal Americans (60th Foot, now the King's Royal Rifle Corps). His advanced corps was in every way a *corps d'élite.* The line brigades of the division were commanded respectively by Brigadier Generals Powell and Hamilton. The total divisional strength was approximately 4,000 officers and men.

In the Brunswick division, lately arrived from Germany, the advanced corps was commanded by Lieutenant Colonel Heinrich C. Breymann. The line brigades were led, respectively, by Brigadier Generals Specht and Gall. In division reserve was a battalion of Brunswick dragoons, dismounted. Total division strength was a little more than 3,100 officers and men. Except for von Riedesel, whose rotund, jovial exterior covered an agile, adaptable mentality, most of the German officers, brave but dumb, appeared less than mediocre in comparison with their British colleagues, and completely incapable of coping with the problems of open-order combat over broken terrain.

Burgoyne's 42 artillery pieces, of varied caliber, were divided between the two divisions. They were manned by a mixed complement of Royal Artillerymen, the Hesse-Hanau artillery company, and drafts from the British infantry.

In all, this army of Burgoyne's numbered more than 7,400 regular fighting men. But it dragged behind it also an enormous amount of excess baggage and a sad rag, tag and bob-tail of camp-followers, not the least number of whom were women and children. The feminine contingent ranged from drabs to high-ranking ladies—lights o'love and honest women, too—the most prominent of the latter being the vivacious and gallant Baroness von Riedesel, who with her three little daughters shared her husband's fortunes in campaign.

There, too, was Lady Harriet Acland who, when her wounded husband was captured during the Saratoga campaign, would follow him into Gates' camp under flag of truce to nurse him. There was the wife of Major Henry Harmage, and there was Anne Reynal, the young bride of Lieutenant Thomas Reynal (he would be killed in action in the last days of Saratoga). And we have Baroness von Riedesel's diary as evidence that Burgoyne throughout the campaign was "amusing himself with the wife of a commissary, who was his mistress." One can almost hear a swish of contemptuous skirts in the Baroness' terse comment that Burgoyne's lady friend "was as fond of champagne as himself."

Approximately 500 of these women were "on the strength"; that is, they were soldiers' wives—from three to five per company—carried on the returns and drawing rations in return for laundering, cooking and like chores. The remainder were, like the officers' wives, the charge of their respective protectors.

Henry Belcher remarks of this feminine element in the British army: "It would seem as if all warriors of the correct model went on campaign with sword in one hand, a lass on the disengaged arm, and a bottle knocking up against his cartridge box . . ."

David Wier, Commissary of the British Army in America, notes in his report for May, 1777 that the women and children belonging to each regiment "are indeed very numerous beyond any Idea of imagination."

The morale of the British was high. They had passed a comfortable winter; they were well fed. Their uniforms were worn—no new clothing had been sent out from England—and it had been necessary to clip their coat-tails short for patching purposes. Their cocked hats, too, had been trimmed down into caps. But their arms were bright and their discipline excellent. The patient, well-drilled German cannon-fodder, whose principal affliction was homesickness, were also a bit shabby in appearance, for the Duke of Brunswick had sent them out originally in worn uniforms and old shoes, which passage of time had not bettered. Perhaps the greatest handicap the Germans suffered was the absurdity for wilderness campaigning of their awkward and all-too-tight clothing and equipment. The dragoons—who were serving dismounted—were in the worst way, with high cocked hats, leather breeches, gauntlets and heavy jack-boots to hamper them, while they trailed long broadswords and shouldered heavy carbines. But to compensate, there was plenty of food, beer and tobacco.

Sweeping majestically up the lake, the expedition began deployment at Crown Point. General Fraser's advanced corps, with the Tories and Indians attached, started south June 26, the remainder following more slowly, and heralded by a bombastic proclamation. Burgoyne called upon all Loyalists to rise, threatening to loose his Indians upon recalcitrants. His vengeance would fall upon them with "devastation, famine and every concomitant horror that a reluctant but indispensable prosecution of military duty must occasion." He also had harangued his Indians. The proclamation, which would later occasion ridicule and censure in London, both inflamed and scared the New Hampshire Grants (Vermont).

Three miles north of Fort Ticonderoga, the main body of the expedition disembarked June 30, the British on the west shore, the Germans on the east, to face Major General Arthur St. Clair, commanding the fortress complex of Ticonderoga.

Scottish-born St. Clair, British Army veteran of the French and Indian War, had served with credit at Louisburg and Quebec. Settling

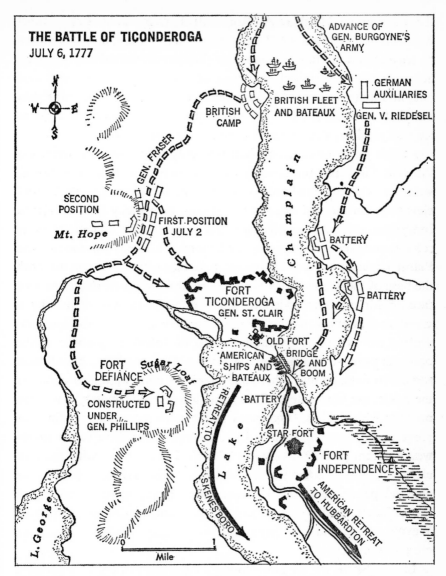

THE BATTLE OF TICONDEROGA
JULY 6, 1777

ADVANCE OF
GEN. BURGOYNE'S
ARMY

GERMAN
AUXILIARIES

GEN. V. RIEDESEL

BRITISH FLEET
AND BATEAUX

BRITISH
CAMP

GEN. FRASER

SECOND
POSITION

FIRST POSITION
JULY 2

Mt. Hope

BATTERY

C h a m p l a i n

FORT
TICONDEROGA
GEN. ST. CLAIR

BATTERY

OLD FORT

AMERICAN
SHIPS AND
BATEAUX

BRIDGE
AND
BOOM

FORT
DEFIANCE

Sugar Loaf

CONSTRUCTED
UNDER
GEN. PHILLIPS

BATTERY

RETREAT TO SKENESBORO

L a k e

STAR FORT

FORT
INDEPENDENCE

AMERICAN RETREAT
TO HUBBARDTON

L. George

0   1
Mile

in Pennsylvania, he became a colonel of militia. Responding to the
call for the original rifle companies of the Continental Army, he distinguished himself in the invasion of Canada, and later at Trenton
and Princeton. A major general now, he had been specifically appointed by Gates to the Ticonderoga command, arriving on June 2.
On June 20 Schuyler had come up and discussed the defense of the
fortress with him and his three less than mediocre brigadier generals—

the Frenchman Matthias A. Roche de Fermoy, John Patterson of Massachusetts and Enoch Poor of New Hampshire. Gates was absent on leave, down in Philadelphia stirring Congressional animosity against Schuyler. The uninspired consensus of the council of war was that men and matériel were both insufficient to defend the entire complex, but that Ticonderoga and Independence in turn should be held as long as possible, with retreat by water as a last resort.

At this point Lake Champlain was only a quarter-mile wide. On the west bank the promontory of Ticonderoga jutted, blunt-nosed, with the original French star-shaped stone fort crowning its 70-foot elevation. On the east side lay the 50-foot high rocky bluff of Mount Independence, with an eight-pointed star redoubt citadel, recently rebuilt, enlarged and improved by Colonel Thaddeus Kosciuszko, the Polish engineer officer. Out-works and block-houses protected both the base of the Ticonderoga promontory and the northern and eastern face of Mount Independence, which in addition was skirted by a creek and swampy morass. Behind the boom and footbridge connecting the two posts lay the remnants of Arnold's squadron of the previous year—two schooners, a sloop and two galleys. In addition some 200 bateaux and other small working craft were also clustered there. On the land side of Ticonderoga a barbette battery had been built on Mount Hope, two miles to the northwest, commanding the gorge and connecting road to Lake George. But a mile to the southwest a vacant precipitous conical hill called Sugar Loaf, with 750-foot elevation, stared directly down onto both the Ticonderoga plateau and Independence across the lake. Gates, in the 1776 revamping of the defenses, had tossed aside the recommendation of Trumbull, Wayne and Arnold that Sugar Loaf be fortified; he assumed that its crest was inaccessible.

In a nutshell, the situation topographically consisted of a fortified position dominated by an unfortified crest. In addition to this defect, to man the elaborate defense system adequately would necessitate a garrison of at least 10,000 men. St. Clair had ten thin one-battalion Continental regiments in three brigades: Poore's, Patterson's and Fermoy's; and also two militia regiments. These, with scouts, artificers and artillerymen, totalled about 2,500. By July the alarm of Burgoyne's approach resulted in the arrival of two additional ill-armed, untrained militia regiments, bringing total strength to 3,500. The entire force was poorly clothed, inadequately armed and equipped, and racked by disease and malnutrition.

It was not a pleasant prospect for St. Clair, particularly as he knew that popular opinion both in New England and in the central states cherished the fiction that Ticonderoga was the impregnable guardian of the Northern gate. If he stood, he would be licked; if he retreated he would be damned as a coward and possibly as a traitor.

On July 1 the British advanced corps, reinforced by Phillips' brigade, moved down on the Mount Hope outpost, whose garrison promptly set its log works on fire and dashed back into the main position—the old French lines at the base of the promontory. The British approached cautiously through the trees. St. Clair ordered fire held until an assault was actually launched, but one drunken British soldier weaved out in the open. A trigger-happy American fired and the entire American force manning the outworks blazed away. The artillery joined the uproar, and the British fell back. The drunk who had caused all the rumpus was brought in unscratched by an American patrol. Meanwhile Riedesel, on the east shore, advanced on Fort Independence until he drew fire, then halted.

Next day, Burgoyne consolidated his position while he sent his engineer officer to investigate Sugar Loaf. The engineer came back with word that the crest dominated Ticonderoga at 1,400 yards range, and Independence at 1,500 yards. Better still, he guaranteed the building of a road and the emplacement of artillery on the hill within 24 hours. So, while the working parties set out, "Gentleman Johnny" shifted forces. Riedesel was given the Tory and Indian contingents to assist his reconnaissance.

St. Clair, on the morning of July 5, was shocked to observe redcoats on the top of Sugar Loaf (the British christened it Mount Defiance) and to see the glinting barrels of two 12-pounder guns in process of mounting. The jig was up. In accordance with the good old rule of thumb that he who fights and runs away will live to fight another day, St. Clair determined to save his army by an evacuation under cover of darkness that night.

The sick, the baggage and as much of the artillery and stores as possible, would go up-lake to Skenesboro, using the plentiful water transport, with Colonel Pierce Long's New Hampshire regiment—some 400 men—as escort.

The stout log boom, St. Clair fondly thought, would hinder British movement by water. The rest of the command, assembling in Fort Independence, would strike across country via the "Military Road," through Hubbardton to Castleton and rendezvous with the train at Skenesboro.

St. Clair's decision was later received with scorn, invective and blind rage amongst patriots in the Northern states. It was nevertheless strategically correct. The invader had to destroy both St. Clair's and Schuyler's commands—the only American armies in being in the region—to ensure success. Rightly, St. Clair had refused to play into his hand.

So with nightfall the evacuation started, in a bedlam of haste, much misdirected energy and—particularly among the raw militia levies—fear. There was some anger, too, among men who felt they ought to stand and give the British a fight. Meanwhile a continuous American cannonade covered the move. Fermoy contributed little to the deception. He—drunk or stupid, one will never be sure—set fire to his quarters on Mount Independence and the roaring blaze caused speculation in the British ranks. Not, however, until three American deserters ran into his lines was General Fraser sure.

By that time it was half past four, July 6, and the last American had scurried out of Fort Independence 30 minutes previously. The last, that is, except four men left to sweep the footbridge with two ready-loaded cannon should the British try to cross. Unfortunately someone—was it Fermoy?—had dropped a puncheon of Madeira wine nearby, and when Fraser, whirling through deserted Ticonderoga with a scratch force of his advanced corps, rushed the bridge, he found the four in drunken stupor beside their silent guns.

Energetic Fraser gathered up his corps. Kicking a few half-drunken Indians out of the looting horde of soldiery to act as scouts—Fraser had a low opinion of Indians in general—he went pounding up the rough, rutted, stump-sprinkled "Military Road" in hot pursuit of the Americans. Three hours behind him, at Burgoyne's direction, plump von Riedesel booted up his own advanced corps and followed in support. Riedesel himself took the lead—he, too, could move fast in emergency—with a company each of jägers and grenadiers.

Meanwhile, with the daylight, Burgoyne brought up his warships, blasted a gap in the boom, and sailing up to Skenesboro, surprised

LAKE CHAMPLAIN–HUDSON RIVER–
MOHAWK RIVER
AREA OF OPERATIONS

Long as he tried to land. The entire train of the American army was
captured; Long and his 400 men got away in a running fight—during
which they badly roughed up the British 9th Foot at Fort Anne, ten
miles south of Skenesboro.

On the road to Hubbardton, pursued and pursuers pushed on at
a remarkable pace through heat that after sunrise became almost
unbearable on the tree-enclosed trail. St. Clair's militia, terrorized,

overran the plodding Continentals again and again, despite his frantic efforts to bring them under control. Rumors of a British ambuscade didn't help matters. It was, in fact, only a marauding party of Indians and Tories, wandering down from Crown Point, who would later be brought to bay and driven off down at Castleton. But at the moment it aroused the militia to a frenzy of fear.

At Hubbardton, St. Clair, who had placed his most reliable troops in the rear guard—Colonel Ebenezer Francis' 11th Massachusetts and Colonel Nathan Hale (no relative to the man who had "but one life to lose for [his] country") and his 2nd New Hampshire regiment —added Colonel Seth Warner and his Green Mountain Boys battalion of Continentals to the rear guard, charging Warner with the command. Then he hastened on to Castleton with the main body. Warner was to join him there that night.

But Francis was delayed in sweeping up the many stragglers, so Warner decided to bivouac at Hubbardton. Early next morning Fraser —who had been only four miles behind the previous day—whirled into the American rear guard. Hale's regiment, surprised at breakfast, stampeded. Warner snubbed the British advance and Francis counterattacked on Fraser's left flank.

A bitter hour and three quarter-long fire fight ended with the death of the gallant Francis and the complete dispersal of St. Clair's rear guard. But Warner had accomplished his mission, for Fraser's force had been badly punished. He had only won the fight when von Riesedel in person, with his own advance detachment, came bustling in on his left. The British being unable to advance for 40 hours, St. Clair escaped to Rutland and thence—the long way round—to join Schuyler at Fort Edward on July 12.

American losses at Hubbardton, out of some 700-odd engaged, were 96 killed and wounded, and 228 taken prisoner (this includes Hale's regiment, which surrendered with its colonel in a body after the fight was over). Fraser, of 850-odd men, lost 50 killed and 100 more wounded; the Brunswickers, ten killed and fourteen wounded. Remarkable, as usual, was the number of officer casualties in Fraser's command—in all, two killed and sixteen wounded; a tribute to American marksmanship.

The action at Hubbardton has gone practically unnoticed by most historians. It was there, as one of Burgoyne's officers remarked, that "the Advance Corps certainly discovered that neither were they invincible, nor the Rebels all Poltroons." The two little American armies opposing Burgoyne were still in the field and as he later said, "the New Hampshire Grants . . . now abounds in the most active and rebellious race of the continent, and hangs like a gathering storm on my left."

Burgoyne lay at Skenesboro from July 9 to the 25th. His immediate goal was Albany, where he would meet St. Leger. At Fort Edward, 25 miles below Skenesboro, Schuyler lay in insignificant strength; a minor obstacle to be crushed or brushed aside. But should he strike directly south, through wilderness, or—retiring to Ticonderoga— shift to a more leisurely boat trip to the head of Lake George and only ten miles of road to Fort Edward? A retirement now might dull the effect of his victory.

Burgoyne straddled. His artillery and heavy baggage, with his gunboats, went via Lake George. The foot troops pushed into the wilderness. Burgoyne was in a hurry to meet St. Leger and to whirl down the Hudson to New York and a triumphal reunion with Howe.

He need not have hurried; St. Leger would never join him.

Lieutenant Colonel Barry St. Leger, 34th Foot, was one of the British Army's gay bloods; his place in history assured by the fact that in 1776 he founded one of England's horserace classics—the St. Leger—since run annually at Doncaster. Less than a year after that momentous occasion, he found himself a temporary brigadier general in command of a task force in the wilds of northern New York state; a force bizarre in composition and fantastic in objective.

St. Leger's mission, as we know, was to strike 150 miles down the Mohawk Valley—from Lake Ontario to Albany—and join Burgoyne. Thanks to a battling Knickerbocker Dutch colonel of Continental infantry and a stubborn, pipe-smoking militia general of German Palatinate extraction, St. Leger would fail dismally.

His theater of operations—Tryon County—was sparsely populated with whites—some 5,000 men, women and children. The settlers were mainly of Rhenish Palatinate and New Amsterdam Dutch extraction, with elements of Irish, Scotch-Irish and Scottish Highlanders intermixed. A remarkable family—the Johnsons—exerted strong Tory influence not only over the settlers but also over the great Indian population fringing the area to the westward—the Iroquois of the Six Nations. Sir William Johnson, patriarch of the family and twice married to daughters of Indian chieftains, had been until his death in 1774 for many years British Superintendent of Indian Affairs, admired and revered by the Indians.

An honorary sachem of the Mohawks, and a major general in the British provincial forces, Sir William had rallied the Six Nations for England in both King George's War and the French and Indian War. He took a prominent part in every British expedition against French Canada. His baronial mansion, Johnson Hall (on the site of Johnstown, N.Y.) was a mélange of European splendor and Indian squalor; a veritable medieval castle, garrisoned by armed retainers: local Highlanders and Mohawks. With the outbreak of the Revolution, his son, Sir John, his nephew Colonel Guy Johnson, and son-in-law Daniel Calus, together with an allied family, the Butlers—Colonel John and his son Walter—had now become right-hand men of Carleton. Together with Joseph Brant (Thayendanegea), brilliant English-educated chief of the Mohawk tribe, whose sister was old Sir William Johnson's widow, this little coterie rallied four of the Six Nations—Mohawks, Senecas, Cayugas, and Onondagas—into alliance with England (the Oneidas and Tuscaroras sided with the colonists).

The Tory rule in this broad area was now being contested with some success by 50-year-old Nicholas Herkimer, a brigadier general in the New York militia. Herkimer, wealthy landowner and son of a Palatinate emigrant, in early 1776 had taken a force of 3,000 militiamen—at Schuyler's order—to Johnson Hall, and captured Sir John, who gave his parole not to engage in hostilities against America. Then Johnson, gathering a number of his tenants and other Tories, broke parole and fled to Montreal, organized a two-battalion regiment—the Royal Greens—and was commissioned a colonel. John Butler likewise raised a Tory corps, known as Butler's Rangers. Before the Revolution was ended, the names of Johnson, Butler and Brant would become synonyms in American ears for ferocious savagery.

St. Leger thus was entering a region divided in sentiment, with neighbor arrayed against neighbor, quite similar to the conditions in the Carolinas.

St. Leger's troops, first assembled at Lachine, were a mixed bag; 100 regulars each from the 8th and 34th Foot, contingents from Johnson's Royal Greens and Butler's Rangers, a battalion of Hesse-Hanau jägers, and some bits and pieces of Canadian irregulars, supported by four light field guns and four small mortars, handled by 40 artillerymen. At Oswego, Joseph Brant and 1,000 Indian warriors joined the 750 whites.

St. Leger left Oswego on July 25. His proposed route was over a well-established trail up Wood Creek to the so-called Great Carrying Place—a portage to the Mohawk River—the key to the Mohawk Valley. At this portage stood Fort Stanwix (Rome, N.Y.), dilapidated relic of the French and Indian War. So far as St. Leger knew, the place was in ruin and garrisoned only by a handful of Americans. What he didn't know was that in April energetic 28-year-old Colonel Peter Gansevoort of Albany, with his 3rd New York Continentals —550 strong—had arrived and had reconditioned its bastions, glacis, covered way and outer ditch. St. Leger did hear, though, of a convoy of food and reinforcements on the way, and accordingly rushed an advanced detachment—200 Indians under Brant, and a handful of regulars—to cut it off. They reached the fort on August 2, just too late. The convoy and its stores, with 200 Massachusetts reinforcements, got safely in after a brush. St. Leger and his main body arrived next day. To intimidate the Americans, he reviewed his troops in plain view of the garrison—perhaps not a wise move, for the presence of the horde of painted, whooping Indians about to descend on their homes in the valley aroused the defenders' determination.

A pompous demand for surrender receiving no answer, St. Leger set about a loose investment of the place, which was patently too strong for assault without his artillery. It took him several days to clear the road for his cannon and heavy stores. Meanwhile firing was exchanged between the jägers and the defenders.

Herkimer had early learned of the coming invasion. His proclamation on July 17 aroused the countryside. On the 30th he ordered militia mobilization at Fort Dayton, on the Mohawk, some 30 miles below Stanwix. By August 4 they were ready to march to Stanwix' relief, 800 strong, with a train of oxcarts behind them, and 60 Oneida

Indians scouting before them. Messengers carried word to Gansevoort of the approach, proposing a diversionary sortie when the relief column came up, and requesting a three-gun acknowledgement. By nightfall on the 5th, Herkimer had made 22 miles. Next morning he held a council of war. No gun signals had been heard. Should they advance or wait?

Herkimer's suggestion of caution was poorly received by his subordinate commanders. All were for going on. So they did, the Oneidas ahead. Herkimer on a great white horse, led 600 men in double file. Then came the squeaking oxcarts, followed by a rear guard 200 strong. Six miles short of Stanwix, near the hamlet of Oriskany, as they traversed a deep, wooded, rocky ravine, the skies fell in on them.

St. Leger, learning of the relief column, had conceived the perfect ambush. He had almost to denude his investing lines before Stanwix, for many of his men were working on the line of communication. But he used all his Indians, under Brant, and detachments of the Royal Greens and Rangers. Colonel Johnson was in command. Hidden in the woods, the Tories blocked the western end of the ravine, while the Indians waited on the flank until Herkimer's column had entered from the east. It was caught in the center of the hollow. The Indians whirled down on the wagon train, the Tories in front opened fire.

The rear guard, just outside the trap, fled. The main body, encircled, stood and fought. Herkimer himself, his horse shot beneath him, got a bullet through his leg. Carried inside the circle, he was propped up on his saddle and, pipe alight, calmly directed his men to form behind cover for all-round fire. Perhaps because they knew this kind of combat, perhaps because there wasn't any place to run anyway, or perhaps because of both, Herkimer's men gave as good as they received, for three-quarters of an hour. A sudden heavy rain then drowned the musket primings, bringing an impromptu cease-fire for a good hour.

Herkimer, still puffing on his pipe, counseled his men to fight by twos—one man loading while the other fired. When the sun came out and firing started again, they were in this formation. There was a bit of hand-to-hand fighting when a reinforcing detachment of Royal Greens tried to barge in, but that was soon checked. Thus far it had been a nasty fight, much of it at close quarters—a kill-or-be-killed affair—with few prisoners taken. St. Leger's Indians now began to lose interest; an ambuscade where the victims refused to be victimized was not at all their dish. They melted away and the outnumbered Tories soon followed suit.

Herkimer's men were only too glad to see them go. All thought of relieving Stanwix forgotten, they gathered up their wounded, including doughty Herkimer—who would die shortly afterwards—and went home. No accurate statistics of the Battle of Oriskany exist. We know that 50 wounded Americans were picked up. On the field lay somewhere between 150 and 200 more of their dead. Indian and Tory losses must have been about 150.

Meanwhile, Herkimer's messengers had reached the post during the morning, the three-gun signal had been fired (never heard down Oriskany way), and Lieutenant Colonel Marinus Willett, with a 240-man detachment from the 3rd New York and 9th Massachusetts, had made a sortie. Finding the Tory and Indian camps deserted, the Americans tore through them, destroying or carrying away everything movable—arms, ammunition and camp gear, including the Indians' deerskin sleeping wraps—and got safely back before St. Leger could muster sufficient men in his own regular bivouack to oppose them. Adding insult to injury, Colonel Johnson's private papers were now in Gansevoort's hands.

All this was a stiff blow to St. Leger, but by now his little ordnance train had arrived. So, placating as best he could the indignant Indians and sulky Tories, he set about a formal investment. His light guns had no effect on the sod-covered bastions, but trenches and parallel approaches slowly grew nearer. Another formal demand for surrender, threatening massacre otherwise, not only of the defenders but also of the entire patriot population in the valley, was rejected by Willett, speaking for the commander. He told the envoys—Butler and two other officers—that they had brought a "message degrading for any British officer to send and disreputable for any British officer to carry."

Still, the situation was serious for the defenders, whose food and ammunition could not last forever. Willett, with one other officer, bravely sneaked through the lines with an appeal to the Tryon County militia to help. Both men got safely to Fort Dayton, to learn that help was indeed coming: Benedict Arnold with a strong force from Schuyler's army.

Down at Stillwater, Schuyler had been torn between two threats
—Burgoyne's advance and St. Leger's move into the Mohawk Valley.
An attempt to relieve Gansevoort at Stanwix would weaken his already
inadequate strength to oppose Burgoyne. His officers, suspicious of
their commander, opposed any such weakening. Schuyler took the
bull by the horns. He called for a general officer to lead a volunteer
relief column down the Mohawk.

Benedict Arnold leaped at the chance. Volunteers rushed to follow him. By August 21 he was at Fort Dayton with approximately
1,100 men. There he learned the danger to Stanwix was grave; St.
Leger's saps were close to the fort. On the 23rd Arnold started on
a forced march. But several days ahead of him had gone a peculiar
individual with a peculiar mission. A whodunit writer of today might
entitle the escapade the "Tale of the Brilliant Half-Wit."

Hon Yost Schuyler—a nephew of Herkimer—was one of those
mewling, dribbling unfortunates occasionally found at large in rural
circles. To the Indians he was, of course, one of the sacred ones of
the Great Manitou, accorded awe and respect. In some way Hon Yost
had become involved in a Tory recruiting plot. Arrested by the local
Committee of Safety, he lay at Stillwater, condemned to death. Arnold
promised him pardon if he would spread the rumor in St. Leger's
camp of the approach of a relief force overwhelming in strength.

Hon Yost fired several bullets through his coat and hurried off to
Stanwix, with one Oneida Indian companion. He got there on August
21. He had come, he told St. Leger's Indians, to warn his red brothers
of imminent danger. Not only were thousands of American troops on
the way, but their commander was the man most feared by both
Indians and British in the North—Benedict Arnold. The Oneida assistant then drifted in to confirm the tale. Hon Yost, brought before
St. Leger, told of his escape from American hands and showed his
bullet-riddled coat to prove it.

St. Leger may not have been impressed, but Brant's Indians were.
They rioted in panic, they began looting British officers' supplies; their
disgruntled chiefs demanded immediate retreat. St. Leger, to whom
his allies had now become, as he later reported, "more formidable than
the enemy!" threw up the sponge. The entire expedition decamped
for their boats on Wood Creek on August 22. Behind them they left
their tentage, their cannon and ammunition, their stores.

The Mohawk Valley was saved, and one of the legs of Burgoyne's three-legged stool lay shattered. He didn't know that, yet, but by this time other events caused him to realize that he was in serious trouble.

Major General Philip John Schuyler during the summer of 1777 was fighting in his own backyard. He had marched and fought over all northern New York in the French and Indian War; his military experience earning him one of the first four major generalcies in the Continental Army. Wealthy and most influential—Schuyler's vast estates included a mansion at Albany and a country seat at Saratoga (now Schuylerville)—he was an exception to most of his compeers. He was an ardent and high-minded patriot, who from the beginning had thrown himself into the struggle.

An excellent administrator, Schuyler lacked the spark of combat leadership; a serious defect in his present situation, for a sizable proportion of the troops in his skeleton army awaiting Burgoyne's advance were New Englanders—filled with the hatreds and suspicions of the internecine New York-New Hampshire Grants feud—and Schuyler was a New Yorker. The Ticonderoga disaster aggravated general resentment against him. To counteract this sectional antagonism, Washington hurried two New Englanders to aid Schuyler; Major Generals Arnold and Lincoln. In the absence of Gates, Arnold became Schuyler's second in command; Lincoln took charge of the New England militia.

St. Clair's battered remnants joined Schuyler at Fort Edward on July 12. A few days later the combined force wisely fell back further. Meanwhile Schuyler, with his knowledge of the terrain, had done the one thing open to him—he had laid waste the country over which the British would have to travel. He did it well. His axemen had felled the forest trees in interlacing heaps across the road, ripped out some 40 bridges over creeks and rivers, created new bogs and swamps by rough dams. Most of the settlers obeyed his call to burn their standing crops and to scatter their cattle.

He did more, too, as we know; his decision to succor Stanwix and to stop St. Leger was sound. Schuyler's reward was to be relieved from command. The American cause had been shaken by the fall of Ticonderoga. With rumors of treason rumbling in its ears, plus Gates' shrewd prodding, the Congress reacted. Later it would get around to investigating both St. Clair and Schuyler (both men would be acquitted by courts martial). But at the moment Gates had been appointed to command the Northern army on August 4. He arrived on the 19th and Schuyler bowed out, to resume department command at Albany.

While this behind-the-scenes upheaval in the American camp was in process, Burgoyne was inching his way at the rate of a mile a day through Schuyler's obstacle course—the welt of scorched earth gashing the valley down to Stillwater. Ahead of Burgoyne's toilers, St. Luc de la Corne's Indians brought murder and rapine against the few settlers who had not heeded St. Clair's warnings to leave.

Among the victims was pretty, 23-year-old Jane McCrea, fiancée of a Tory serving with Burgoyne. At the cabin of elderly Mrs. McNeill of Fort Edward village, Jane, dressed in her Sunday best, on July 27 awaited the arrival of the British and her lover. A group of Indians rushed the cabin and carried off both women. Old Mrs. McNeill, stripped naked, later found herself safe in the hands of her cousin, British General Fraser, but all of Jane that arrived was her long, black hair. The Indians had quarreled over her. One of them, Wyandot Panther, shot her to end the argument, then scalped her.

The outrage was but one of many such instances. But the hand of fate singled out Jane McCrea to become a *cause célèbre*. Burgoyne was stirred to arrest and condemn the murderer to death. Then St. Luc de la Corne, in cold-blooded effrontery, threatened the general with the immediate departure of all the Indians if his warrior died. And Burgoyne, to the amazement and disgust of most of his British soldiery, pardoned the culprit.

Gates, on his arrival, would seize on this precious bit of potential propaganda value. His angry protest to Burgoyne, publicized throughout New England, transformed Jane McCrea, the unfortunate Tory girl, into a symbol and a martyr to British savagery—a most potent stimulant to patriot recruiting.

Having thus callously and stupidly provided propaganda for his enemies, Burgoyne on July 29 reached deserted Fort Edward on the east bank of the Hudson. There he paused to take stock and await his artillery, supplies and boats to join him from Lake George. The joy of having reached the Hudson at long last was tempered by the disconcerting news that Howe had left New York, Philadelphia-bound. Howe's letter, informing him of that fact, and dated July 17, reached Fort Edward on August 3, as Burgoyne was plotting methods of replenishing his larder locally and investigating how to mount his cavalry —the booted, spurred but horseless Brunswick dragoons.

Burgoyne, informing no one of the news from Howe, determined to push down the Hudson to Albany and his date with St. Leger. Meanwhile, with Riedesel, he had planned an expedition which he hoped would give him much-needed horses—both riding and draft— as well as wagons, cattle, and recruits for his Tory contingent. The foray had, in fact, a most amazing conglomeration of objectives, for Burgoyne expected also to levy taxes, seize hostages and generally harass the countryside west of the Connecticut River—an odd method of soliciting good will. Colonel Philip Skene, prominent New York Tory landowner (Skenesboro was included in his domain), who was Burgoyne's political advisor, was to go with the expedition to "distinguish the good subjects from the bad."

Lieutenant Colonel Friedrich Baum—who incidentally spoke no English—would lead the expedition. His force would consist of 170 of his own jack-booted dragoons, a detachment 100 strong of Breymann's jägers and grenadiers, a 50-man corps of British regular "marksmen" under Captain Fraser, some 300 Tories, Canadians and Indians, and two 3-pounder guns served by a handful of artillerymen. Counting officers, non-coms, musicians—for this "secret expedition" had a band with it—and batmen (soldier servants), Breymann's force came to a round 800 men.

The plan had been brewing for some time and all of Burgoyne's general officers had discussed it. There was no doubt in anyone's mind that something must be done to relieve dependence upon the 185-mile long line of communications through the wilderness back to Montreal. There was no doubt, either, that the cavalry must be mounted. But General Fraser (again we must distinguish him from his namesake Captain Fraser) had his qualms about this particular venture. For that matter, Riedesel himself was uneasy about it. Apparently the resistance both had encountered at Hubbardton had not been without effect. This particular apprehension was reflected in a warning contained in Burgoyne's meticulous instructions to Baum;

instructions originally drafted by Riedesel. "The corps of Mr. Warner, now supposed to be at Manchester" was to be either avoided or attacked, at Baum's discretion. However, Burgoyne had no doubts of success, nor had Skene, who envisioned Tory sympathizers flocking in to swell the British ranks.

So on August 11, Baum's expedition moved east. Schuyler by this time had withdrawn to the mouth of the Mohawk River. Last-minute instructions from Burgoyne changed Baum's objective from Manchester to Bennington, where it was reported great stores of American supply had been collected. Burgoyne's intelligence also reported that but 300-400 American militia lay in that vicinity. Riedesel, it appears, was not too happy about this change in direction, which left Warner's Green Mountain Boys on Baum's left flank. But neither he nor anybody else knew that New Hampshire was now coming into the campaign in a big way, with John Stark leading.

Stark, of course, had fought at Bunker Hill, in Canada, at Trenton and at Princeton. In April, 1777, when Congress began making a flock of new generals, Stark, like Arnold, had been passed over. So Stark threw up his colonel's commission and went back to his New Hampshire farm. When Burgoyne's invasion rocked New England, New Hampshire authorized a brigade of militia, enlisted for two months, and asked Stark to command it. He agreed on one condition —this would be a New Hampshire organization and his responsibility would be to the General Court (the New Hampshire legislature) alone—neither Congress nor the Continental Army command was to have anything to do with it. They took him at his terms, on July 18, and the ink on his commission was hardly dry before a round 1,500 men had flocked to his call; ununiformed but eager to follow John Stark, and each man carrying his own firearm.

By early August, Stark had his brigade at Manchester, where Seth Warner and the Green Mountain Boys lay. Schuyler, who had learned of the new organization, sent Lincoln to order Stark to join him. Cantankerous Stark flatly refused. Leaving Warner at Manchester, Stark then shifted his force on August 8 to Bennington, where a depot of stores had been accumulating.

Unaware of this shift, Baum had moved up the Battenkill, then across the hills to Cambridge and over to the Hoosick River; his Indians ranging wide on a spree of looting and destruction that absolutely defeated any effort to collect voluntarily either supplies or animals. At Van Schaick's Mill, Baum's advance guard ran into resistance—a detachment sent down by Stark at word of the Indian raids. The Americans, only 200 strong, fired one volley and then decamped. Baum's pursuit was hampered by a wrecked bridge, but he learned enough to send word back to Burgoyne that an estimated 1,500 to 1,800 rebels were at Bennington. Optimistically, he stated that the Americans were "supposed to leave at our approach." He would, he added, "fall on the enemy tomorrow early."

Stark by this time knew the invaders were in force. He moved out from Bennington to meet them, at the same time calling on Warner at Manchester to join him. Four miles west of Bennington, on August 14, the opposing forces sighted one another, halted, and bivouacked with the Walloomsac River between them. Next day, pouring rain prohibited combat. While Baum disposed himself for defense, Stark —with Warner, who had rushed down in advance of his 500 Green Mountain Boys—planned attack.

Baum's dispositions were in plain view of the Americans. He had put his dragoons and half of Captain Fraser's "marksmen," with one of the 3-pounders, behind log breastworks on a height a half-mile north of the river. A bridge directly in front was guarded on both banks by the Canadian militia. Half of the Brunswick infantry and the rest of Fraser's detachment lay with the remaining 3-pounder near the bridge on the north bank. On the south bank, the bridge approach was defended by a makeshift entrenchment held by 150 Tories. The rest of the force was sprinkled about between the river and the main position, while the Indians clustered on a plateau behind. A more preposterous formation could hardly be imagined. Baum, with his 800 men scattered over a square mile of terrain, could never have gathered more than a tithe of them in any one spot for mutual support.

Stark and Warner evolved a most ambitious double envelopment. Stark now had about 2,000 men, for some Vermont and Massachusetts militia had come in, together with a body of Stockbridge Indians. The Walloomsac was fordable. Colonel Moses Nichols' regiment would circle wide to the enemy's left and rear, north of the river, while Colonel Samuel Herrick's command would swing well to the west on the south bank and then come in on Baum's right.

Meanwhile a frontal demonstration by Colonels David Hobart and

Thomas Stickney, coming down the Bennington road, would threaten the Tory position in front of the bridge and distract attention. All three of these forces were approximately equal in strength—between 200 and 300 men. Behind all, Stark would launch the main body in a straight frontal attack as soon as the encirclers opened fire. It was a complicated scheme, with success dependent upon timing and concentration of widely separated elements of untrained soldiery. The amazing thing is that it worked.

Baum was, perhaps, overconfident, that morning of August 16, when the rain stopped. He had twice sent back word of unexpectedly strong resistance but he knew that somewhere in his rear—they couldn't be more than ten miles away—the rest of the Brunswick advanced corps under Breymann, 700 men and two field pieces, were hastening up the mud-slicked road. From his log-ramparted citadel he observed the flanking movements in the distance, but he jumped to the surprising conclusion that these must be Americans scurrying in retreat. Even when little clumps of men in civilian clothing began to infiltrate his flanks he was not alarmed, for Skene assured him these must be Tories coming in to help; they moved with muskets clubbed—that is, shouldered, butts up. Acland could have told him that that same ruse had deceived his grenadiers at Hubbardton, but Acland wasn't there.

Then Nichols' and Herrick's men brought their firelocks down and began firing. At the sound, Hobart and Stickney rushed the Tory emplacement in front of the bridge, with Stark's main body moving in behind them. The Tories ran through the Canadian bridge defenders, who joined them, pell-mell. As for the Indians, they had simply vanished at the first shot, with slimy St. Luc de la Corne leading their flight.

Baum's thin-skinned alignment blew up in his face like a pricked balloon. In a few moments the fighting had shifted into a swirling all-round assault on the main Brunswick position, where the dragoons and Fraser's red-coated marksmen stood and gave battle in a fire fight for nearly two hours. Higher and higher the American tide lapped upward on the slopes. Then an ammunition cart—Baum's sole reserve—exploded. In the face of a final American rush the dragoons, at Baum's order, slung their carbines, drew their long swords and tried to hack their way out of the press. Then Baum went down,

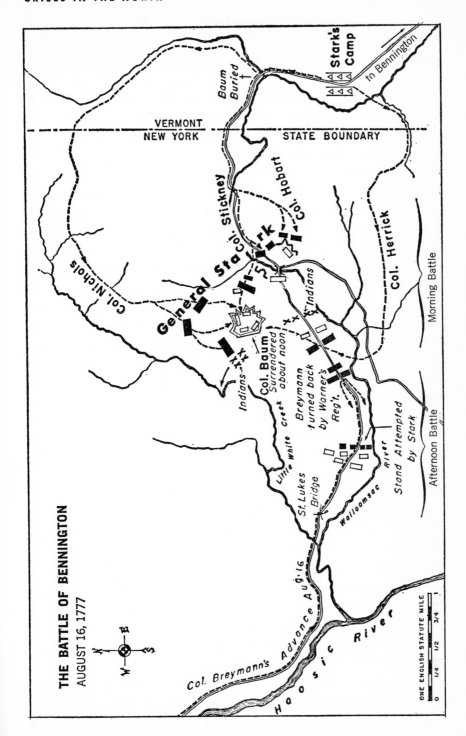

THE BATTLE OF BENNINGTON
AUGUST 16, 1777

ONE ENGLISH STATUTE MILE
0   1/4   1/2   3/4   1

mortally wounded, and the Brunswickers flung away their blades in surrender.

Flushed with victory and with spirits—a hogshead of rum broached by Stark, and other liquor discovered in their plundering of the enemy bivouacks—Stark's rustic soldiers relaxed. They had fought a good fight under a scorching August sun. They didn't know—until a sputtering of musketry down river near Van Schaick's Mill brought warning—that they would have to fight again.

Von Breymann's grenadiers and jägers, muddy, water-soaked and stifled in their heavy uniforms, were on the last lap of a cruel march in rigid formation. It was half-past four in the afternoon when they first clashed with some of Stark's men, and brushed them off. With their drillmaster commander continually dressing their ranks, the serried, pompous advance continued, thrice beating off hurriedly assembled formations of tired Americans.

Then they met the Green Mountain Boys. Warner's outfit, temporarily led by Lieutenant Colonel Samuel Safford, had made a long march, too, from Manchester, as they hastened after their commander. They had halted at Bennington to drop their packs, draw ammunition and drain a rum ration. Then they spat on their hands and hiked out over the original battlefield to deploy in front of Breymann's path a mile to the west, in low, swampy open ground. Stark's fragments rallied with them, as Warner resumed command of his own men. He pulled them back from the swamp to a wooded height north of the road.

Breymann, who knew by this time he had a fight on his hands, attacked, seeking to turn the American right. But the Green Mountain Boys had a score to settle—that fight at Hubbardton. Warner threw half of his regiment to his own left and outflanked the flankers; the remainder, with Stark's troops, extended to the right. Breymann, checked, brought his two guns into action and kept up a fire fight until his ammunition ran low; his men had carried only 40 rounds each into the action. Then he tried to withdraw.

Abandoning their guns, the Brunswickers recoiled to the westward, at first in good order. But the Americans still had plenty of ammunition, and they were in their element now—an open-order harassment of a slowly moving enemy. Breymann's formation began to crumble. The withdrawal turned into a disordered retreat. Breymann, still dreaming of eighteenth-century European warfare, had his drummers beat a long roll—the signal for a parley. But to the Americans this was just a silly noise; their fire continued.

Thus, in the dusk of evening, a disorganized horde of defeated men went staggering down the road, with Breymann himself—although wounded—bravely holding together a small rear guard. Stark, at nightfall, called off the pursuit. About two-thirds of the Brunswickers got away.

The spoils were rich on Bennington field. In the two actions 207 of the enemy had been killed; 700 more, including some 30 officers, made prisoner. Four guns, 250 broadswords, four ammunition wagons and hundreds of muskets and jäger rifles, all had been garnered. Stark's losses were probably less than 20 killed and about 40 wounded.

Several interesting points stand out in this battle. About 2,000 Americans, hurriedly raised, most of them untrained, had met and defeated in detail 1,500 disciplined regulars, who had four cannon, well served. In each fight, true, the Brunswickers had been badly outnumbered; it is not at all certain what the result would have been had Baum and Breymann been concentrated in the beginning. On the other hand, military history is rife with instances where a command—flushed and disorganized as was Stark's in victory—has been swept away by an unexpected second assault delivered by troops arriving fresh on the field.

Tactically, strategically and psychologically, Bennington was an important American victory. Not only did New England's spirit soar, but also that of the entire American cause—sadly buffeted by events further south.

As a minor relief, the Congress—whose tartly worded resolution had just chided New Hampshire for Stark's refusal to join Schuyler—now hurriedly voted him its thanks and the commission of a brigadier general in the Continental Army.

★ 18 ★ ★ ★ ★ ★ ★

Washington Attempts the Impossible

MEANWHILE THERE HAD BEEN MUCH ACTIVITY in the lowlands of the Hudson and Delaware valleys. Two weeks after Washington had advanced from Morristown, Howe responded by assembling 18,000 men at New Brunswick. On June 14, 1777, he sent approximately half of this army under Cornwallis towards Somerset, and the remainder under von Heister to Middlebush. His two objects were to entice Washington to combat, and to cut off a detachment under Sullivan at Princeton. Washington, adhering to his principle of avoiding combat against British regulars except under the most advantageous circumstances, withdrew into the foothills near Middle Brook, just north of the Raritan River, and ordered Sullivan back as well. There followed two weeks of maneuver, in which Howe vainly endeavored to trick Washington into combat by feigned retreats, rapid changes of front, and night marches. Although Washington maintained close contact with the British, and despite a number of brisk skirmishes, the Americans successfully avoided the engagement which Howe was endeavoring to bring on, while at the same time continuously harassing British flanks, outposts and encampments. Finally, on June 28, Howe began a withdrawal from Amboy to Staten Island. By the end of June all major British forces had been withdrawn from New Jersey; quite a change from the situation seven short months earlier.

By this time, of course, Washington had received information of Burgoyne's advance southward from St. Johns. Washington assumed that Howe's withdrawal was a preliminary to an advance up the Hudson to meet Burgoyne, and so returned to Morristown, while shifting Sullivan's division to Pompton, nearer to the Hudson. At the same time he alerted Putnam's 4,000 men in the Highlands, but also warned Putnam that he might have to send many of these troops northward to help Schuyler meet Burgoyne's advance.

Washington's estimate of Howe's intentions was not changed on July 8, when he learned that British troops were beginning to embark on ships at New York. He had expected that the move up the Hudson would be by ship at least as far as the Highlands. On July 10 the dismaying news that Ticonderoga had been abandoned confirmed Washington's belief that Howe's "designs . . . are most unquestionably against the Highlands." Accordingly on the 12th he shifted most of his army to the region between Haverstraw and West Point.

Then on July 24 Washington learned that Howe's army of about 16,000 had set sail the previous day—not up the Hudson, but out to sea from Sandy Hook. The armada consisted of 245 transports and supply ships, escorted by 16 warships under the command of Admiral Howe. A garrison of about 7,000 was left to hold New York.

For Washington, this was the beginning of a month of uncertainty, doubt and concern. As he expressed it himself, "the amazing advantage the enemy derive from their ships and the command of the water keeps us in a state of constant perplexity and the most anxious conjecture." Still believing that the eventual main effort would be up the Hudson to assist Burgoyne in splitting the Colonies, he knew that at the same time he must be ready for any other of the numerous possibilities available to the Howe brothers. One of these, of course, would be an advance up the Delaware River against Philadelphia. The Continental Congress and the administrative military facilities in Philadelphia made this a particularly sensitive target, and the congressmen would not let him forget it. Yet the Howes could also be heading southward, to the Carolinas, or could be returning to New England. Uppermost in Washington's mind, however, was the likelihood that Howe was making a feint towards Philadelphia, for the purpose of causing Washington to move his army south of the Delaware, and that the British fleet would then suddenly reappear in New York Bay and sail up the Hudson River.

Nevertheless the disappearance of the British army and fleet forced Washington to respond to Congressional pressures by shifting his army closer to Philadelphia. By July 28 his main body was on the Delaware River just north of Trenton, while Sullivan's division stopped at Morristown. Thus Washington could still move either way, and concentrate before Howe could complete disembarkation. It was at this time that Washington wrote that "Howe's in a manner abandoning General Burgoyne is so unaccountable a matter that till I am fully assured it is so, I cannot help casting my eyes continually behind me."

Meanwhile from the north had come the discouraging news of Burgoyne's steady advance down the invasion route to the Hudson Valley. On July 24, as we know, Washington sent General Benjamin Lincoln, one of his division commanders, to take command of the poorly coordinated Continental and militia forces in New Hampshire and the Hampshire Grants, under Schuyler. He ordered Putnam to rush most of his remaining troops to upper New York and urged Heath to arouse the New England states to react with new levies against the danger. He also detached some reliable units from his own army to hasten north to stiffen Schuyler's crumbling forces. Of these the most important was Daniel Morgan's superb corps of riflemen, who left for the north in mid-August.

On July 30, Washington learned that Howe's fleet had been sighted off the Delaware Capes. He immediately went to Philadelphia, and started his army in that direction, only to learn next day that the fleet had again stood out to sea, with no further indication whether it had gone north or south. Once more Washington could not help suspecting that this whole movement had been for the purpose of enticing him away from New York, and so he started his army back slowly toward Trenton, anxiously awaiting further news.

While he took care of some administrative matters in Philadelphia he met a young French nobleman, the first foreigner who did not seem to be trying to gain fame and fortune at American expense. The Marquis de Lafayette, barely twenty years old, charmed both the suspicious congressmen and Washington himself, with his protestations that he wished no financial rewards, and desired no command for which he was not worthy. "I am here to learn," he said disarmingly, "and not to instruct." Congress gave the young Frenchman the honorary title of major general, and Washington adopted him as a staff officer.

On August 10 word reached Washington that the British fleet had been sighted off the east coast of Maryland. Once again he halted his army's movement, and established an encampment on the Neshaminy River, twenty miles north of Philadelphia, and twenty miles west of Trenton. Howe's actions were still inexplicable to him, as he wrote that day: "I had no doubt in my own mind but that [Howe] would have pushed up to [the Hudson] River, to cooperate with General Burgoyne." Because the malaria season had begun in the Carolinas, he felt that it was unlikely that the British were going to Charleston, though this was a possibility that could not be ignored. The only other possibilities would be a move into Virginia or Maryland, or up the Chesapeake for the purpose of approaching Philadelphia from the southwest.

By August 22 it had become obvious that this last was Howe's intention. Howe's reasoning, apparently, was that a move against Philadelphia from the upper reaches of Chesapeake Bay would avoid the defenses which the Americans had built along the Delaware River between Chester and Philadelphia. But Howe had not really thought this through. He could have landed at New Castle, or at Chester, some 30 miles south of Philadelphia, instead of at the head of Chesapeake Bay, where he was over 55 miles from the city. The overland approach to Philadelphia would have been practically identical in either instance, save for the additional 20-odd miles. Furthermore, he would have begun land operations against Philadelphia nearly a month earlier, and these operations probably would not have lasted half as long as those which he actually was forced to undertake. This was probably the most serious mistake that Howe made during his two years of command in America.

On August 23 Washington's army began to move south from his camp on the Neshaminy. He sent for Sullivan—who had the previous day been repulsed by the British garrison of Staten Island in an abortive attempt to cross the Kill Van Kull. On August 24 the little American army paraded through Philadelphia. Probably about 10,000 men took part in this parade, since at that time Washington's army, including Sullivan's division, was close to 13,000 men in effective

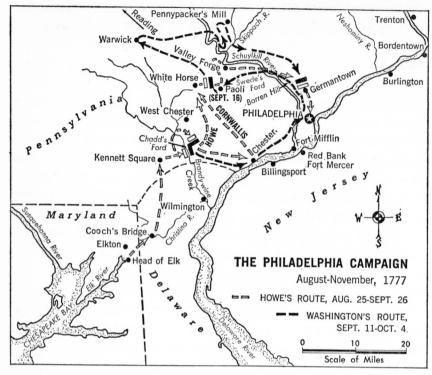

THE PHILADELPHIA CAMPAIGN
August-November, 1777

━ ━ HOWE'S ROUTE, AUG. 25-SEPT. 26

━ ━ WASHINGTON'S ROUTE,
SEPT. 11-OCT. 4.

strength. Washington personally then hastened on ahead, to reconnoiter. On August 26 he was within two miles of Head of Elk (Elkton) where the British had begun debarkation the previous day. He returned to Wilmington on the 27th.

Washington had hoped to be able to assemble a larger and more experienced army for the defense of Philadelphia than that which was now deploying west of Wilmington. But continuing bad news from the north had forced him to keep the large strategic picture in mind, and prevented him from devoting himself singlemindedly to Howe's threat. Some of his best generals and most experienced Continentals had already been in the northern theater and he had reinforced these strongly at the expense of his own army. Although Washington was unhappy about the bitter dispute between Schuyler and Gates, it had for a while seemed that Gates' return to Philadelphia would at least permit him to use Gates to command Lincoln's division in the forthcoming campaign. But Gates, through his friends in Congress, had succeeded in having Schuyler removed, and had returned north to take command against Burgoyne.

Thus, as the British advanced slowly northward from Head of Elk, in the last days of August and the first of September, Washington's army, though reinforced by Pennsylvania militia, comprised no more than 15,000 men. Of these, less than two-thirds were Continentals, organized into five principal divisions of two brigades each, commanded respectively by Greene, Sullivan, Stephen, Stirling and Maxwell (senior brigadier of Lincoln's division). In addition, General John Armstrong commanded the principal Pennsylvania militia contingent, about 3,000 men.

While holding his main army near Wilmington, Washington sent Maxwell's light infantry brigade to the Christina River to delay the British. On September 3, Maxwell's troops were engaged by the van of Cornwallis' corps of Howe's army in a sharp fight at Cooch's Bridge. In accordance with his orders, Maxwell withdrew after a short skirmish forced the British to deploy.

Howe, meanwhile, had been advancing very slowly. His troops, after six weeks cooped up on shipboard, needed time to regain their land legs and to absorb some of the fresh meat which they found in abundance on the fertile and well-stocked Maryland farms. The British were also handicapped by a shortage of cavalry and draft horses. Many had died during the voyage, and the rest were in very poor condition. Adequate replacements were obtained from the countryside, but it took some time to break these into military service. By September 19, however, when his army reached Kennett Square, Howe believed it to be ready for action. His effective strength was about 13,000 men.

Meanwhile Washington decided that the most advantageous site for a defensive battle would be along the banks of Brandywine Creek, a tributary of the Delaware, which flowed in a southeasterly direction a few miles north of Wilmington. The main road to Philadelphia from the South—Howe's logical route—passed through Kennett Square and thence across Chadd's Ford on the Brandywine. The creek formed a substantial obstacle, although it was traversed by several fords. Its valley was deep and narrow and troops on the east bank could overlook the far side of the valley and the fords which the British would be most likely to use from heights rising some 200 feet.

Washington planned his main defense at Chadd's Ford. South of Chadd's was Pyle's Ford. To the north, in a five-mile reach, were, in succession, Brinton's, Jones' (also called Painter's), Wistar's and Buffington's Fords.

Armstrong's militia held the easily defended rugged cliffs overlooking Pyle's Ford. Next, opposite Chadd's Ford, came Greene's division and Wayne's brigade. The army's right flank was held by Sullivan's division, deployed between Brinton's and Jones' fords. Sullivan posted Colonel Moses Hazen's "Canadian" regiment to cover the next two fords to the north—Wistar's and Buffington's, respectively one and two miles above Jones' Ford—with a battalion at each. Behind Greene and Wayne respectively at the Chadd's Ford position lay Stephen's and Stirling's divisions, in support and reserve.

Outposting the position west of the creek was Maxwell's light infantry, athwart the main road. Further north, Colonel Theodorick Bland's 1st Dragoons in front of Jones' Ford had the task of screening the front generally from Welch's Tavern up to Buffington's Ford. On the far right, security beyond the Brandywine was entrusted to one Major Spear with a body of local Pennsylvania militia.

It does not appear that any real effort was made to reconnoiter the creek and its fords north of Buffington's, nor to study the road net—particularly the Great Valley Road, which ran north from Welch's Tavern, paralleling the Brandywine for some six miles, then crossed it at Jeffries' Ford, a good mile above Buffington's.

Sullivan, who moved into his position late in the afternoon of the 10th, had had no opportunity for extensive reconnaissance. He went to Washington's headquarters, a mile east of Chadd's Ford, to inquire about the situation to his right. He was given the incorrect information that no fords existed to the north beyond Buffington's for twelve miles. He was also informed of the security missions of Bland and Spear on the far bank. The information appears to have been given by a staff officer in Washington's presence.

Howe and his two corps commanders, Cornwallis and Knyphausen, were thoroughly reconnoitering west of the Brandywine on September 10, with Loyalist guides. This, plus cavalry patrol contacts and, undoubtedly, information from Tory spies, seems to have given Howe a fairly good picture of the American dispositions. He determined to repeat the tactics which had been so successful on Long Island.

Knyphausen, with some 5,000 men, would engage the American attention at Chadd's Ford, while Cornwallis, with about 8,000 men, would envelop the American right flank. Cornwallis' route, recommended by local Loyalists, would be northward on the Great Valley Road, across two small fords over the west and east branches of the Brandywine above Buffington's Ford, turning southward then to get behind Washington's army near the Birmingham Meeting House.

The British advance began at dawn, September 11. Knyphausen's corps, in the lead, surprised a patrol of American horse about 8:00 A.M., while they were having a drink at the bar of Welch's Tavern. Soon after this, the alert British advance guard ran into Maxwell's brigade near Kennett Meeting House, about three miles west of Chadd's Ford. After two hours of brisk skirmishing, Maxwell fell back slowly across the ford and took a position between Wayne's brigade and Greene's division.

Knyphausen's men advanced promptly and deployed on the heights west of the Brandywine between Chadd's and Brinton's fords, while

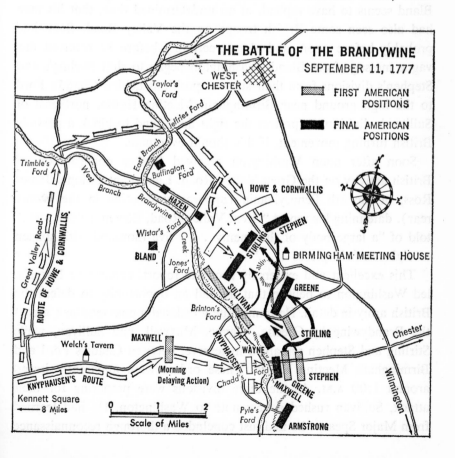

THE BATTLE OF THE BRANDYWINE
SEPTEMBER 11, 1777

FIRST AMERICAN POSITIONS

FINAL AMERICAN POSITIONS

skirmishers approached the riverbank. There was a spirited exchange of artillery and musket fire for the next two hours, but very little damage was done on either side.

By half-past ten activity about Chadd's Ford had slowed to a sporadic exchange of cannonry. Meanwhile, Cornwallis was plodding north up the Great Valley Road, his redcoats hindered only by the summer heat. At about 11:00 A.M. Sullivan relayed to Washington a message from Hazen at Wistar's Ford: a large British column was marching to the northward on the Great Valley Road, west of the creek.

Evidently this situation reminded Washington of the opening phase of the Battle of Long Island, when a British holding attack distracted the Americans from Howe's enveloping force. He immediately sent a message to Colonel Bland, of the dragoons, specifically requesting him to "send an intelligent, sensible officer" to investigate this report. Bland seems to have replied, at an undetermined time, that his men had also seen some British troops on the Valley Road. Sometime probably before noon, and almost certainly before he received this vague message from Bland, Washington began to shift Stirling's and Stephen's divisions from their support positions behind Chadd's Ford to the high ground near Birmingham Meeting House, northeast of Sullivan's division, to protect the right flank, and to block a possible British turning movement, if this should eventuate.

Soon after noon Washington received further confirmation of British activity on the Great Valley Road. Lieutenant Colonel James Ross, of the 8th Pennsylvania (apparently scouting in the enemy rear), datelining his report "Great Valley Road, Eleven o'clock A.M.," told of "a large body of the enemy . . . five thousand with sixteen or eighteen field pieces . . ."

This excellent and extremely accurate report, confirming Hazen's, led Washington to believe that he had an opportunity to defeat the British army in detail. He immediately ordered a counterattack across the Brandywine by Greene, Wayne, Maxwell, and Sullivan, while Stirling and Stephen remained in reserve, between Chadd's Ford and Birmingham Meeting House. These orders were apparently issued around 1:00 A.M. As the three divisions were preparing for their attack, Sullivan rushed a new note to Washington. He had learned from Major Spear, who had just concluded a thorough reconnaissance west of the Brandywine, that no British troops had been seen around the upper fords. Therefore, concluded Sullivan, "Hazen's information must be wrong."

It was probably about this time, shortly after 2:00 P.M., that a local citizen, Squire Thomas Cheney, galloped up to Washington's headquarters, demanding to see the General. Washington's staff reluctantly brought him before the Commander-in-Chief. Cheney reported that the main British army was east of the Brandywine, and marching south towards Birmingham Meeting House. Washington was incredulous; he did not see how the British could have reached that far, particularly in light of the recent information from Sullivan, and without any report of such a movement from the light cavalry. But Cheney was so vehement that Washington called off his planned attack. He was apparently on his way to investigate personally, when he received a report from Bland, written at 1:15 P.M.: the British were then about half a mile north of Birmingham Meeting House!

Sullivan had received the same information from Bland, which he reported to Washington. He seems to have begun shifting his division to the right rear even before Washington's orders confirmed this movement. Washington also ordered Stirling and Stephen to resume their march toward Birmingham Meeting House as rapidly as possible, and to deploy on the high ground nearby. Sullivan would command this new right wing. The Commander-in-Chief decided to stay with Greene, to await further developments.

An hour later, probably between 4:00 and 4:30, Washington heard the sounds of heavy cannonading from the right. As the volume of artillery and musket fire grew, he realized that the British attack was in great force. He decided therefore to pull back Greene, leaving only Wayne's and Maxwell's brigades to hold Chadd's Ford. With a local guide, Washington and Greene hastened northward; Greene's two brigades followed, marching abreast on parallel roads.

Shortly before this, Sullivan, shifting his division to the southwest of Birmingham Meeting House, and seeking room to deploy, ordered Stephen and Stirling to shift to the right. While this movement was taking place, the British struck, making their main effort on their right, toward the creek. After a brief, sharp fight, Sullivan's deploying brigades began to break, despite his efforts and those of his brigade commanders. As Sullivan's division was beginning to crumble, Weedon's Virginia Brigade, of Greene's division, arrived at the left, in time to restore the situation, and to retard the British pursuit. Sullivan's troops fell back through the Virginia regiments, in considerable confusion, but not in panic. The British were also pressing vigorously against Stirling and Stephen, between Birmingham Meeting House and Dilworth, but their progress was slow, and they were unable to break the American lines.

Cornwallis' men were exhausted from their hot, sixteen-mile march, followed by two hours of sharp fighting. Recognizing after the arrival of Greene's division that there was no prospect of a quick success, and with darkness falling, Howe halted his weary troops for the night.

Meanwhile, at the sound of Cornwallis' cannonade, Knyphausen at Chadd's Ford had sprung into action. Under cover of intense artillery fire, his assault columns gained the east bank, reformed, and pushed on vigorously. The American artillery, keeping up fire to the last, was overrun; eight guns being lost in all. Wayne and Maxwell, however, managed to withdraw their infantry in good order, and this portion of the battle also ended with nightfall.

During the night the American army withdrew in considerable confusion, but not in flight, to Chester. By midnight, Washington, with the assistance of his division commanders and his staff, had reorganized the troops into some semblance of order, and the army bivouacked until dawn.

The records of American losses are extremely vague and unreliable. There seem to have been about 200 killed, probably another 700 or 800 wounded, and nearly 400 prisoners. British casualties were reported as 89 killed, 488 wounded, and 6 missing; less than half of the American loss.

The American troops were not greatly depressed by this defeat. They had stood up remarkably well against the determined attacks of regular English and Hessian soldiers, and they believed that they had inflicted more casualties than they had suffered. And so, as the army marched north from Chester towards Germantown on the 12th, the men were surprisingly cheerful.

The Brandywine battle may be summed up in eleven words: an amateur army and an amateur general were defeated by professionals. Faulty reconnaissance, inadequate patrolling, and—back at headquarters—faulty analysis of information received, combined to spell defeat. Primarily, the fault lies at Washington's door. He had apparently made no prior reconnaissance of the creek north of Chadd's Ford, though there appears to have been plenty of time for this—or at the very least, to have had some of his trusted staff officers do it. Sullivan, by gratuitously endorsing one negative against two positive reports on enemy locations, must share some blame.

On the other hand Washington took reasonable efforts to clarify this confused situation by sending at least one urgent message to the ineffectual Colonel Bland, prodding him into belated action. Washington's order moving Stirling and Stephen's divisions to the right rear was correct and proper, and apparently made in good time. Because of this, and because of the prompt reactions of both Washington and Sullivan after the British turning movement was definitely identified, the Battle of the Brandywine was only a defeat, and not a disaster.

At Chester, Washington realized that an energetic British advance could pen the American army into a cul-de-sac between the Schuylkill and Delaware rivers. Early on the 12th he got his army on the march, back across the Schuylkill. As he retreated north, past Philadelphia and Germantown, he received information that he had again been given dictatorial authority by the Continental Congress, for a period of 60 days, and within a radius of 70 miles from his headquarters. Congress then hurriedly left Philadelphia, reconvening a few days later at Lancaster, and after that at York.

Having replenished his supplies from magazines north of the Schuylkill, Washington recrossed that river at Swede's Ford on September 15, to block the British advance on Philadelphia. Fortunately for the Americans, Howe was as dilatory after his victory at the Brandywine as he had been in his movements near New York almost exactly a year earlier. Thus, by September 16, his army had just reached White Horse Tavern, barely ten miles north of the battlefield. His objective, as Washington had guessed, was apparently Swede's Ford.

With the British army stretched out in marching column, Washington was presented with an excellent opportunity. The American army deployed near Warren Tavern, against a portion of the British army, which hastily prepared to meet the unexpected attack. But before either side could engage, a torrential downpour suddenly flooded the countryside, turning roads and fields into mud, and rendering muskets useless. By evening of the 16th Washington discovered that because of leaky cartridge boxes the rain had ruined the ammunition of most of his men. Realizing that the British cartridge boxes were watertight, he knew that he would be in a hopeless situation in the event of battle next day, so hastily withdrew westward to his principal supply depot at Reading Furnace (Warwick) to replace the 400,000 rounds of ruined powder.

Again Howe had an opportunity to march into Philadelphia, since he was nearly twenty miles closer to that city than Washington. But as he advanced slowly toward Valley Forge, Washington, his ammunition supply replenished, promptly recrossed to the north bank of the Schuylkill on September 19, and moved down opposite Valley Forge to block the expected crossing.

Washington's withdrawal to Warwick had not left the approach to Philadelphia quite as open as might appear. Expecting the British to take more advantage of this opportunity than they actually did, he had left Wayne with his brigade and a brigade of militia—1,500 in all—hidden in a forest near Paoli. This was Wayne's home country, and Wayne had assured the General that he would be able to hide from the British and attack them in the rear as they crossed the Schuylkill.

For three days Wayne and his men remained securely hidden in their thickets near Paoli. But Wayne had not counted on local Loyalists. His presence was reported to General Howe, who ordered Major General Charles Grey to make a surprise night attack on Wayne with five battalions.

Grey ordered his troops to use the bayonet only. To make surprise certain, he ordered the flints removed from every musket. As a result, he was known forever after in the British army as "No Flint" Grey.

Had Wayne not posted his guards and kept them constantly alert, his entire command probably would have been wiped out, as the English, directed by Tory guides, unexpectedly came slashing in with the bayonet. As it was, the hastily aroused Americans fought manfully against the charge, and Wayne was able to withdraw his troops, with all four of his artillery pieces, having lost only about 150 men killed, wounded and captured. Grey had only seven casualties.

Word of this grim demonstration of British skill with the bayonet spread rapidly amongst the militia of Washington's army; most of them accordingly found pressing business at home. By September 22 the disappearance of the militia had reduced Washington's overall effective strength to less than 10,000. Washington sent an urgent call for reinforcements to Putnam, who promptly sent Brigadier General Alexander McDougall's Continental brigade, and other units, totalling about 2,500 men. By forced marches, McDougall joined the army on September 27.

Meanwhile, late on the 21st, Howe began a rapid movement northwestward, toward Washington's supply depot at Reading Furnace. Moving immediately to block this threat, Washington discovered that Howe had merely been feinting, in order to draw him away from the Schuylkill fords. Having accomplished this neatly, on the 22nd the British crossed the river, thus interposing themselves between the American army and Philadelphia. Four days later, after a leisurely march, Howe's troops occupied the half-deserted American capital.

By this time Howe's main body was in Germantown; some 8,000 men encamped in an approximate order of battle. He had decided against entrenchments, since he felt that this would be an indication of uncertainty and moral inferiority. Cornwallis, with approximately 3,000 men, was in Philadelphia itself, while detachments totalling nearly another 3,000 were scattered along the Delaware to the Jersey shore, to cooperate with Admiral Howe's fleet in operations against the American forts blockading the Delaware River.

Washington had rebuilt his army to approximately 8,000 Continentals and 3,000 militia. He believed that the British dispersal of forces, and Howe's lack of fortifications in Germantown, provided an opportunity for a surprise blow. He knew the region well; his army had been in and around Germantown two or three times in the past month, and he had considered the possibility of defending Philadelphia in approximately the same area where Howe now was encamped. And from his well-established espionage system, he had a good picture of the British dispositions. Accordingly, with the assistance of his staff, he drew up a plan for a night march and surprise attack on Howe's army.

Sprawling Germantown lay about five miles northwest of Philadelphia on the road toward Reading and Bethlehem. Center of the town was the Market House, where the main north-south road—which was also Germantown's Main Street—was intersected at right angles by a road which was called Church Lane to the east, and School House Lane to the west. Howe's main army was encamped just south of these two lanes, and astride the main road. The left flank of the long British bivouack area extended almost to the Schuylkill River; its right was covered by Wingohocking Creek, an insignificant obstacle. Howe had substantial outposts covering the two main approaches to Germantown from the north and northeast, with another outpost east of Wingohocking Creek to protect the exposed

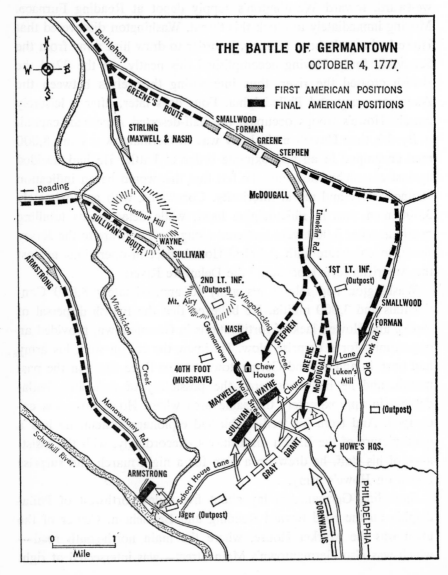

THE BATTLE OF GERMANTOWN
OCTOBER 4, 1777.

FIRST AMERICAN POSITIONS
FINAL AMERICAN POSITIONS

right rear of his army, and one at the junction of the Schuylkill and Wissahickon to cover the left front.

The British outpost covering the Bethlehem and Reading Road was at Mount Airy, just beyond so-called Beggarstown—the straggling northward extension of Germantown—and about two miles along Main Street from the Market House. Here the 2nd battalion of light infantry was bivouacked just east of the road, with a picket post just north of Mount Airy's scattered houses. In support, a few hundred yards to the south and west, lay the 40th Foot. About a mile and a half to the east, covering the Limekiln Road which approached Germantown from the northeast, the 1st light infantry battalion was holding another outpost.

Washington, who planned to attack generally down these two principal roads from the north and northwest, was well aware of the locations of the outposts, and knew that British patrols were active for several miles further north. On October 2, therefore, he advanced along the Bethlehem (or Shippack) Road from Pennypacker's Mill to the vicinity of Metuchen Hill (now Centre Point), about 15 miles north of Germantown. He was afraid that any closer daylight movement would be discovered by the British. He planned to march during the night of October 3-4 to the vicinity of Chestnut Hill, about two miles north of Mount Airy. Here the troops would rest briefly until 4:00 A.M., when they would move out to overrun the outposts at precisely 5:00.

Because of the road net, and in hopes of achieving a surprise double-envelopment of the British, Washington divided his army into four principal elements for the attack. On the extreme right the Pennsylvania militia, under Armstrong, would move along the Manawatamy Road, beside the banks of the Schuylkill, to get around the British left flank. The right wing of the main army, under Sullivan, would strike the British left and center, just west of Germantown Main Street. The left wing, under Greene, would make the main effort, its axis of advance being down the Limekiln Road, to envelop Howe's right, and to force the British back against the Schuylkill. Still further to the left was a turning column of New Jersey and Maryland militia under Generals Forman and Smallwood, who were to proceed down the Old York Road, to get behind the right rear of the British army.

The night march began at 7:00 P.M. on October 3, in two parallel columns. Sullivan's wing, consisting of his own division and Wayne's independent brigade, took the Manawatamy and Reading Roads to Chestnut Hill. Sullivan was followed by Armstrong. Greene's wing, consisting of his own and Stephen's divisions, plus McDougall's brigade in the lead, followed the Bethlehem Road almost to Chestnut Hill, then turned southeast to reach the Limekiln Road. Following Greene's wing were Smallwood's and Forman's commands, while Stirling's division—the army's reserve—brought up the rear. After Greene, Forman and Smallwood turned off to the left, Stirling was to continue along the Bethlehem Road to its intersection with the Reading Road at Chestnut Hill; here he would be able to support either of the two wings of the main army.

Washington, aware of much Congressional criticism of Sullivan for presumed responsibility for the Brandywine defeat, decided to accompany the right wing, not only to protect Sullivan, but to exercise personal command supervision if necessary. Since the attack was to begin in the dark, he issued orders that each man was to have a piece of white paper pinned to his hat for identification.

Although Washington thought he had allowed plenty of time for the approach march, permitting nearly two hours' rest before the planned time for attack, his troops were unable to keep to the schedule. With very little time taken out to rest, Sullivan's division, with Conway's brigade in the lead, was not in position to move down the Bethlehem-Reading-Shippack Road, against the Mount Airy outpost, until about dawn, 6:00 A.M. Though Washington did not know it, Greene's guide had lost his way, and the American left wing was at this time still more than half an hour away from its jumping-off point against the Limekiln Road outpost.

As the leading regiment of Conway's brigade deployed just north of Mount Airy, even though the sky was beginning to lighten in the east, there was nothing to suggest to the Americans that they would not be able to surprise and overwhelm the British pickets with the bayonet, as Washington intended, without firing a shot. In fact, however, the van of Sullivan's wing had been seen by British patrols northwest of Chestnut Hill almost three hours earlier. Howe had been informed, and though he and his staff assumed that this was merely an American reconnaissance party, he had nonetheless alerted his outposts. Evidently some, but not all, of the remaining British army units in Germantown were also informed.

Thus the silent advance of Conway's van was met by the fire of the Mount Airy picket, which then began to fall back in good order. Conway's men pushed after them, only to be surprised by a British volley. The 2nd light infantry had formed up at the first shots, and had immediately advanced to support the picket. Following its volley, the British battalion counterattacked. Recoiling from this surprise, the more numerous American van rallied to force the British battalion back into Mount Airy. As the remainder of Conway's brigade deployed to meet this unexpected resistance, the American advance was resumed, only to be thrown back in confusion by an even more intensive British volley, followed by another bold charge. Lieutenant Colonel Thomas Musgrave had brought up his 40th Foot to form a line of battle across the road, beside the Light Infantry.

Despite surprise, bordering on dismay, at this formidable opposition again, the Americans rallied, and as the rest of Sullivan's division, with its artillery, entered the fight, charged in their turn. Even though elements of two more British brigades now joined the fight, the numerically superior Americans could not be denied. Probably within twenty minutes of the first shots, the Americans were steadily pushing their way into Beggarstown.

Howe, hearing the firing, rode forward personally, and was shocked to find his light infantry falling back in confusion. "For shame, Light Infantry," he is reputed to have cried. "Form! Form! It's only a scouting party!" At this moment, to the unconcealed delight of the retreating redcoats, a volley of American grapeshot smashed through nearby trees, dropping leaves and branches onto the general's shoulder. Sir William apparently wasted no more time in trying to rally his outpost troops. Realizing that this was a full-scale American attack, supported by artillery, he galloped back to his camp to prepare for battle.

By this time the American attack, rolling up the collapsing British outpost line, had advanced more than a mile. The early morning mist, however, was now thickening into heavy fog, reducing visibility to about fifty yards. As they pushed after the retreating English, Sullivan's men were discharging their muskets at every fence post and tree that loomed in the fog. Worried by this needless expenditure of ammunition, Washington sent word to Sullivan to curb the firing, but the orders were not effectively enforced amongst amateur soldiers who were still encountering scattered English resistance.

Washington and Sullivan now realized that there was no firing to their left. Greene had obviously failed to attack as scheduled. So Sullivan shifted Wayne's brigade to the east of the highway, where the Pennsylvanians quickly deployed, then plunged south through the fog to try to catch up with Sullivan's rapidly advancing troops. Thus the weight of Sullivan's attack was shifting—as happens so frequently in battle—away from the British left, its original objective, and was now directed toward the center of Howe's encampment.

Meanwhile, English Colonel Musgrave, battling manfully to rally his troops, found himself near a large stone mansion, the Chew House, just east of the road, and about a mile north of the center of Germantown. In the fog he managed to gather into it elements of six companies of his command—some 120 men—while the Americans streamed past the house on both sides. Musgrave and his redcoats worked feverishly to transform the Chew House into a fortress, barring doors, filling the hallway with furniture, and poking portholes in shuttered windows on both floors.

Unaware of this activity, Washington had reached the vicinity of the Chew House sometime before 7:00, still worried by lack of noise from the east. Concerned about the possible consequent danger to Wayne's left flank, and realizing that Sullivan's right was also exposed by the shift in direction of its attack, Washington decided to commit Stirling's reserve division. Maxwell's brigade, in the lead of this division, was to follow Sullivan's advance, echeloned to the right rear, while Nash's brigade would move forward behind Wayne's left. In this way Sullivan's wing would be protected against envelopment, and would also have the additional weight of the two fresh brigades.

As Maxwell's brigade began its deployment, under Washington's supervision, close to the Chew House, the grim mansion suddenly blazed with musket fire. Washington, shocked by the surprise, was undecided whether to disregard or to smother this unexpected ulcer within his lines. Knox, just then joining the small group of officers around Washington, persuaded him that it would be unwise to leave "an occupied castle" in his rear. So Washington ordered Maxwell to storm the house before moving on in support of Sullivan. Nash, apparently, kept his brigade in column along the road behind Maxwell, waiting for the stronghold to be overwhelmed.

For half an hour a fierce struggle raged around the house. Musgrave and his men comported themselves with great gallantry and distinction, throwing back every American assault. Knox brought up a battery of artillery, but the gunners were unable to aim accurately in the fog. Most of the cannon balls bounced harmlessly off the stone walls, and few penetrated doors or windows. The American assaults were apparently poorly coordinated; casualties mounted. After half an hour Washington realized that he had made a mistake. Maxwell's men were badly needed to support Sullivan further south, where the roar of battle was increasing. Stirling was ordered to keep a small force in observation of the Chew House. Washington then galloped forward to observe the main action. It was probably about 8:00 A.M.

Meanwhile Howe's line of battle had hurriedly formed north of School House and Church Lanes, astride Main Street and barring Sullivan's and Wayne's advance. By this time, however, Greene was also moving rapidly into Germantown from the northeast, driving back the Limekiln Road outpost and two more battalions which Howe had advanced to cover his right front. Not till he had reached the edge of the British camp was Greene's advance snubbed by Howe's main body. In the confusion and fog, part of Muhlenberg's Virginia brigade—of Greene's division—actually pushed through the British line, into the heart of Howe's camp. Here they were surrounded, and though some were able to fight their way out again, most of the 9th Virginia Continentals were captured by the British.

As Washington approached the battle line, he was met on the road by Sullivan, who politely but firmly insisted that the Commander-in-Chief must withdraw out of musket range. Reluctantly Washington fell back a few yards, unhappy that he was unable to direct the confused struggle now going on in the fog to his front. Nevertheless, the sound of Greene's musketry to his left, which now clearly extended deep into the British encampment, caused him to believe that his army was on the threshold of victory.

Then, alarmingly, came the sound of more firing, to the right and to the rear. Because of the confusion which pervaded this fog-shrouded fight, it has never been possible to ascertain exactly what had happened, or the sequence of events. But the Chew House fight was unquestionably a primary cause for what occurred.

The noise of Maxwell's vain attacks against Musgrave had caused the first shadows of alarm among the officers and men of Sullivan's wing. Wayne had slowed down his advance, and had sent back some units to the rear to investigate. At the same time Stephen, who had apparently been bolstering his courage with rum, had swung his division away from its appointed position on the right of Greene's wing, to blunder directly across country toward the sound of the firing at Chew House. Arriving there after Maxwell had pushed on, apparently some of Stephen's units began a renewed assault against the stronghold.

At about this same time Wayne's rear security detachments arrived in the vicinity. Mistaking each other for English in the fog, Stephen's and Wayne's men began fighting one another east of Main Street.

It was about this same time—nearly 9:00 A.M.—that the British main army, which had never been so near defeat as Washington thought, began to counterattack. General Grant, taking advantage of the gap which Stephen's diversion had left between Wayne's and Greene's front line units, started to push forward in the center. At the same time tough General Grey was working his way around Sullivan's exposed right flank.

Sullivan's and Wayne's men, now having expended most of their ammunition, hearing the sound of battle coming from all sides, seem now to have concluded that they were surrounded, and broke. They streamed past Washington and Sullivan, pointing to their empty cartridge boxes, as both generals tried vainly to rally them.

As this confused mass reeled north toward Mount Airy and Chestnut Hill, Greene found himself faced by superior numbers, now augmented by three battalions that Cornwallis had hastily led from Philadelphia. Greene ordered a withdrawal, manfully saving his guns from almost certain capture. The Battle of Germantown was over.

Both of the proposed encircling efforts had also failed. Armstrong, on the extreme American right, had waited hesitantly near the mouth of Wissahickon Creek, deterred from further advance by the small but determined Hessian outpost. When the Hessians had the temerity to attack, Armstrong and his far more numerous militia fled. On the extreme left Smallwood's and Forman's men had been even more delayed than Greene, and had barely arrived near Luken's Mill, on

Greene's left, in time to join his retreat to the north. Recognizing the inevitable, Washington ordered a general withdrawal.

The audacious American plan had been well-prepared, but it was much too complicated. Success was dependent upon perfect timing and coordination between commanders intimately conversant with the terrain, with highly-trained, well-rehearsed troops. Lacking these basic qualifications, it is a tribute to Washington's leadership that the American army came as close to success as it did. The fog, of course, was impartial, and perhaps impeded the British as much as the Americans. It did, however, reduce what little chance there was for coordination of Washington's four converging attacks. And it combined to facilitate the action of stout-hearted Musgrave at Chew House, and to add to the confusion of a befuddled Stephen.

By noon the American divisions were pretty well rallied in the vicinity of Chestnut Hill. The British, evidently still unable to overcome their surprise at this amazing American offensive spirit, seemed perfectly content to let the Americans go without pursuit. Washington now led his troops on a long twenty-mile withdrawal, back beyond the Metuchen Hill encampment to a previous bivouack at Pennypacker's Mill. By the time they arrived there, that evening, they had completed a round trip march of between 36 and 40 miles, in addition to fighting a battle. Though they had been beaten, this was a creditable showing for a citizen army opposed to the finest professionals in the world.

Again the Americans erroneously thought that they had inflicted more casualties than they had received. Though figures are only approximate, the British lost about 70 killed, 450 wounded, and 14 missing. American losses were 152 killed, 521 wounded, and nearly 400 missing.

For the next two weeks the armies remained relatively inactive, approximately twenty miles apart. On October 18 Howe decided to withdraw from Germantown into Philadelphia, which he then began to fortify by a chain of redoubts, linked by a strong stockade. Though he had won the only two major battles of the campaign, this withdrawal, and his resort to strong fortifications, showed that he had changed his mind about prestige symbols.

While most of Howe's troops were busy fortifying Philadelphia, he now devoted considerable attention to opening up a line of communications through the Delaware River. A combination of American fortifications and warships had the river channel blocked between Chester and the mouth of the Schuylkill. The survival of the British army depended upon re-establishing a free line of communications to the open sea, and to Lord Howe's fleet.

The American river defenses had not been completed when Lord Howe returned to the Delaware early in October, after depositing his brother's army at Head of Elk. Midway between Chester and the mouth of the Schuylkill, but on the opposite, New Jersey, shore, was a still-unfinished redoubt at Billingsport. Its guns covered a double-line of *chevaux-de-frise*. These heavy timber obstructions were box-like rock cribs, loaded with stones and sunk in the water between Billingsport and Billings Island, off the Pennsylvania shore; projecting from the cribs were iron-tipped beams, pointing downstream, and projecting to within four feet of the surface at low tide. Any seagoing vessel attempting to pass these obstructions would have its bottom ripped out.

About three miles further north, below the mouth of the Schuylkill, were three or four more lines of *chevaux-de-frise,* stretched across the ship channel. These were protected by the guns of Forts Mercer and Mifflin. Fort Mercer, at Red Bank, on the Jersey shore, was a substantial earthen-walled structure with fourteen guns. Fort Mifflin, on Port (or Mud) Island, close to the Pennsylvania side, presented an even stronger, stone-faced wall to the river side, but on the west and northwest it was protected only by some small wooden blockhouses, palisades and ditches.

Between the forts and Philadelphia lay a small American naval squadron. This included the two Continental frigates *Delaware,* 32, and *Montgomery,* 28, and the Pennsylvania navy, comprising four small sailing vessels, thirteen row-galleys, two floating batteries, and an assortment of fire-ships and fire-rafts. Congress had placed the two frigates under the command of Pennsylvania Commodore John Hazelwood.

On September 27, the day after the British occupied Philadelphia, the *Delaware,* accompanied by the sloop of war *Province,* 18, moved up to attack batteries which Cornwallis had raised along the city's waterfront. The *Delaware* ran aground and was forced to surrender, after a severe hammering from the British guns.

On October 2, three days before his brother's fleet reappeared in the river, General Howe sent two regiments across the Delaware to attack the Billingsport redoubt. Unfinished as it was, the small garrison spiked their guns and departed. British blockading vessels removed the *chevaux-de-frise*, permitting the later passage of warships to take part in a combined land and naval assault against the next line of fortifications.

Fort Mercer was attacked on the afternoon of October 22. The land element consisted of Colonel von Donop's Hessian brigade, 2,000 strong. The Germans advanced against the fort under the cover of fire from an artillery battery, and an awesome naval bombardment from a British squadron consisting of one ship of the line, three frigates, a sloop of war, and a large floating battery.

Defending the fort were two small Rhode Island regiments, totalling some 400 men, commanded by Colonel Christopher Greene, cousin of the general. They were supported by long-range fire from the American fleet above the fort. Undaunted by the bombardment, Greene's men held their own fire until the charging Hessians had forced their way through a line of *abatis* and into the ditch around the land face of the fort. Then, at short range, repeated murderous grapeshot and musket volleys turned the ditch into a bloody shambles. In a few minutes approximately 400 Hessians were killed or wounded. Vainly trying to rally his troops, Donop was mortally wounded, and captured.

While the defeated Hessians were withdrawing, the British naval squadron also suffered disaster. At least three of the attacking ships went aground on a mudbank below the fort and two of them—HMS *Augusta*, 64, and the sloop *Merlin*, 18, could not be floated. Early next morning the guns of both American forts concentrated their fire against these ships, while Commodore Hazelwood sent fire-rafts down the river against them. The *Augusta* caught fire, and blew up when the flames reached her powder magazine. The *Merlin* was set afire by her own crew, and abandoned.

It was three weeks before the British were ready to renew their attacks against the two staunch forts. Meanwhile they had erected numerous batteries along the west bank of the river overlooking the vulnerable land side of Fort Mifflin. From November 10 to 15 these batteries, plus the guns of two British ships of the line, three frigates, a sloop and a floating battery concentrated overwhelming fire on the fort.

For six days the garrison of 450 men endured what may have been the most concentrated bombardment of the 18th Century. The commander, Lieutenant Colonel Samuel Smith, was wounded—one of more than 250 casualties. Every night the wounded were evacuated by water, and small boats brought reinforcements and supplies to the garrison. On the morning of the 15th, when only two guns were still able to fire from the fort, the British intensified their bombardment, firing at a rate of about 250 shot per minute throughout the entire day. A large proportion of the damage was done by HMS *Vigilant,* 16, which worked its way into the channel between the fort and the mainland, then hammered the fort with her 24-pounders at a range of less than 100 yards. The last two guns were overthrown, the walls, palisades and blockhouses destroyed. That night Major Simeon Thayer, who had succeeded Smith, evacuated about 300 survivors to Red Bank, after one of the most memorable defenses in American military annals.

Cornwallis now crossed the river with 2,000 of his best troops, to attack Fort Mercer. The reinforced British fleet moved up to take it under fire from the river. On November 22 Colonel Greene evacuated the fort, while the blockaded American flotilla was burned. The Howe brothers were secure in their possession of Philadelphia and the lower Delaware River.

★ 19 ★ ★ ★ ★ ★

Saratoga

WHILE THESE OPERATIONS HAD BEEN TAKING PLACE around Philadelphia, decisive and dramatic events were occurring in the north. On September 13, two days after the Battle of the Brandywine, obstinate "Gentleman Johnny" Burgoyne crossed to the west side of the Hudson River, dismantling his bridge of boats behind him two days later. One by one, he had seen his supporting prospects crumble. Howe was not coming up the Hudson, St. Leger had been driven back. Chances of local replenishment—as well as a good portion of his Brunswick corps—had been shattered at Bennington. He was on his own, with Albany still his goal, and a maximum of 30 days' provision on hand for his troops—now reduced to an overall strength of perhaps 6,500 men.

Previously Burgoyne still had a choice. He could have given up his plan and fallen back into Canada. After crossing the river, it was Albany or nothing, for he could neither survive through the winter where he was, nor be supplied from Canada. He had had, up until that moment, another option, too. Gates lay on the west bank, blocking the way south. The road on the east side was open. But Albany lay west of the river; Gates would probably move to confront him anyway, and a crossing near Albany might be difficult and dangerous.

So Burgoyne went south, paralleling the river, bringing his boats along. He was purblind, now, for most of his Indians had slipped away, including their malodorous leader, St. Luc de la Corne. Burgoyne didn't learn of Gates' whereabouts until a foraging party was ambushed by an American patrol, between Stillwater and Saratoga.

Gates, he then found out, was entrenched on Bemis Heights, three miles north of Stillwater. Burgoyne elected to attack him.

"Granny" Gates had moved up there September 12, and Kosciuszko had laid out the defenses. Gates' army had been swelled to a strength of some 7,000—not counting Stark's brigade. That dour individual, still smarting from his previous handling by the Congress, had finally come into camp September 18, the day his men's two-month enlistments expired; he had then turned them around and marched off again, thereby in his pique nearly missing participation in the turning point of the Revolution. Not the least important of the reinforcements Washington had sent was Colonel Daniel Morgan's crack rifle corps, with Colonel Henry Dearborn's Continental light infantry attached.

Beginning at the southerly end of a plateau rising more than 200 feet from the river, the American works lay on three sides of a quadrangle approximately three-quarters of a mile long on each face. The river façade was manned by Massachusetts men—the brigades of John Glover, John Paterson and John Nixon. Gates himself took control of this wing. Beneath this face a bridge of boats spanned the Hudson. Learned's Massachusetts brigade, plus James Livingston's 4th New York regiment held the center. On the left was Arnold, with Morgan's brigade, most of Poor's New Hampshire and New York brigade, and some Connecticut militia; all these troops were Continentals except the last.

Two ravines cut the plateau from west to east: Mill Creek, a mile in front of the American position, and the Great Ravine north of it. Most of the terrain was wooded, except for some small clearings, the largest of which was a deserted farmstead, known locally as Freeman's Farm, lying north of Mill Creek. A network of wood roads and trails laced the forest.

Burgoyne's plan was to envelop the American left and drive Gates down into the river. General Fraser's advanced corps, reinforced by Breymann's now-attenuated jägers and grenadiers—some 2,000 men —with eight guns would make the main effort, circling wide towards high ground to the west and then driving southeast. Hamilton's brigade —the 9th, 20th, 21st and 62nd Foot—1,100 strong, with six guns, would strike the center of the American front; Burgoyne accompanying them. Riedesel, with the Brunswick infantry brigade—the regiments of Riedesel, Specht and Rhetz, another 1,100, supported by eight guns of the Hesse-Hanau artillery, was to advance straight down the river road. General Phillips would accompany it. Back at Swords House, Burgoyne's headquarters, just south of Saratoga, the train, stores and boats nestled, under guard of six companies of the 47th Foot and the Hesse-Hanau regiment.*

It was a complicated maneuver designed to concentrate widely separated elements on a battlefield. Success depended on careful timing and coordination. Since intercommunication was impossible, signal guns, fired at Burgoyne's personal direction, would control the attack. To further complicate matters, Burgoyne had but an approximation of the American position. Fraser's command alone seems to

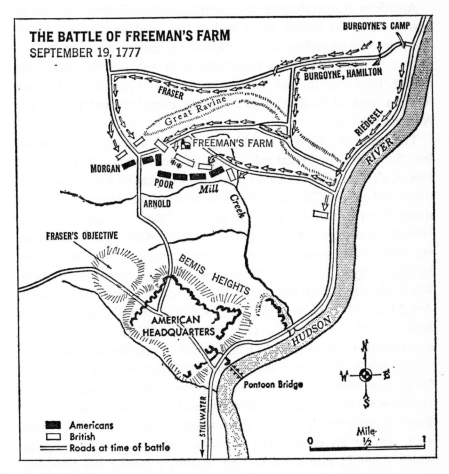

THE BATTLE OF FREEMAN'S FARM
SEPTEMBER 19, 1777

Americans
British
Roads at time of battle

---

* Burgoyne's original order of battle, both British and Brunswick, had been much modified by the detachment of troops to garrison Ticonderoga and Fort George.

have had a definite initial objective—the high ground on the west.

The morning of September 19 was clear, cool and crisp when the British moved out. Fraser struck directly west for some two miles, circling the head of the Great Ravine, then turned southward towards Freeman's Farm. Hamilton's column, Burgoyne accompanying, followed in trace, turned south after a mile of marching, crossed the Great Ravine and halting, deployed on the clearing of Freeman's Farm—the 21st, 62nd and 20th Foot, from right to left. The 9th Foot lay in reserve. Apparently it would never be used. Riedesel, delayed by broken bridges, pushed very slowly south along the river road.

American reconnaissance that morning saw sufficient evidence of movement in the British camp and on the road to convince Gates that Burgoyne was advancing to attack in several columns. He decided to wait in place behind his fortifications, despite Arnold's vehement protest. Finally Gates was induced by Arnold to permit him to push Morgan forward to develop the enemy's intentions and protect the American left flank.

The impetuous Morgan and his equally impetuous riflemen plunged into the woods, badly extended, seeking their enemy. Just south of Freeman's Farm they ran into a left flank picket of Fraser's—Canadians, Indian and Tory irregulars—most of whom were at once shot down. The riflemen, whooping in pursuit of the survivors, ran smack into the right regiment of Hamilton's brigade, drawn up in the clearing. Its volley fire broke up the riflemen, who scattered in all directions, leaving Morgan alone, twirping on his turkey call to rally them. While Morgan slowly regathered his shame-faced brush-war fighters, Arnold, closely watching, pushed in Cilley's 1st and Scammell's 3rd New Hampshire on his left. They fell afoul of Fraser's light infantry and grenadiers, were roughly handled and in turn thrown back.

Meanwhile, Burgoyne, at the farm, had given the three-gun signal for general advance. Arnold, noting a gap between Fraser's left and Hamilton's right, changed direction and threw the remainder of Poor's brigade into it, forcing Hamilton to swing the 21st Foot to the west, leaving his center—the 62nd—at the apex of a vee against which Arnold's men were beating. Fraser, retaining his grenadiers and light infantry in hand, contented himself with bolstering Hamilton's badly involved right flank by the 24th Foot and Breymann's command.

Alternate waves of assault washed the fifteen-acre clearing of Freeman's Farm for the rest of the day, with Burgoyne's silent guns—the gun crews successively picked off by sharpshooters—the focal point. Several times the accurate fire of the riflemen, many of them in tree-tops, drove the British infantry into the surrounding woods, but each time the American infantry rushed the guns the British came back with the bayonet and drove them off. In this confused struggle Burgoyne, Hamilton and Phillips—who had come up from the river front when the first noise of battle filtered down—distinguished themselves by personally rallying their men.

Burgoyne's situation was gradually worsening. He sent to Riedesel first for guns, and then for men. Arnold, with his entire division now engaged, went whirling back to Gates, impetuously demanding reinforcements. He was sure he could break the British line with additional men. Gates, snug in his own headquarters hut, refused; it would not, he said, be prudent to "weaken his line." Sharp words passed between the pair. Grudgingly, at last Gates ordered up Learned's brigade, but peremptorily prohibited Arnold from returning to the field. Learned, unguided and unfamiliar with the situation, moved too far west, tangled with Fraser's grenadiers and light infantry and was beaten off. About this time, part of Glover's brigade on the American right also became involved; it is not certain with whom. In any event, the situation at the vital center was unchanged.

Agile, brilliant Riedesel changed the fortunes of the day. Down on the river road he had heard the signal guns, noted the swelling of distant battle noise, and like a good soldier, came to its sound. He had already pulled some of his unengaged troops up on the high ground to his immediate right, and had sent out patrols to reconnoiter the approach trails leading westward. He promptly sent four of his guns forward at Burgoyne's first call. When the second came, at five o'clock, he was ready.

Leading the way, as at Hubbardton, with a two-company detachment of the Rhetz regiment, he went posthaste towards the British center. His own regiment and his remaining guns followed. Finding Hamilton in trouble, again as at Hubbardton, he simply hurled himself and his little advance party into the fight, drums beating and men shouting.

He hit Arnold's unsuspecting right flank and shocked it into recoil. The Brunswick guns came rolling in, to be manhandled through the brush by cheering redcoats. At pistol-range they opened with grape. Behind them, the plodding Brunswick infantry filed into line, blazed away with a drill-ground volley and Gates "prudence" had come home to roost. The American fire died in the dusk and the tired Continentals withdrew. The equally tired King's troops bivouacked on the field.

British losses were shockingly high, considering that less than 1,000 of Burgoyne's men had been continuously engaged: some 600 killed, wounded or captured. Hamilton's brigade took the heaviest casualties —350 men. The 62nd Foot, which had gone into action 350 strong, emerged with but 60 men and five officers. The Americans lost 65 killed, 218 wounded, and 33 missing.

Analysis of the Battle of Freeman's Farm is both simple and complex. The net tactical result was that a British attack—in reality a reconnaissance in force—had been turned into a stubborn and successful defense. The operations on both sides were piecemeal, with no overall control exerted. On the battlefield, the initiative and judgment of both Arnold and Riedesel loom large out of the hodge-podge of gallant mediocrity.

Strategically, Burgoyne had gained nothing. Gates, solidly entrenched on Bemis Heights, still barred the road to Albany, and Burgoyne's force had been weakened by the loss of irreplaceable manpower and the frustration of a check. On the American side of the ledger the factors are also contradictory. The elation of having stopped the regulars in open battle was tempered by the depressing contemplation of an opportunity lost. The casualties had been light, and replacements were obtainable. But ammunition was in shockingly short supply; most of it had been shot away. And the dissension between Arnold and Gates eroded morale. Had Burgoyne resumed his attack on the 20th, he might have punched his way through. But he didn't.

On the 21st Burgoyne received a message from Sir Henry Clinton in New York which revived his morale and changed his plans. Clinton was planning to move up the Hudson against Fort Montgomery, near

Peekskill. He intimated—or so Burgoyne thought—his intention of carrying on. Accordingly Burgoyne rushed back two messengers each bearing identical words: a plea for assistance and an intention to halt in place until Clinton approached. Burgoyne definitely set October 12 as the limiting date of his resources.

As it turned out, the first messenger never got there; the second reached Clinton too late to be of any use. Meanwhile, Burgoyne entrenched himself on the Freeman's Farm battlefield, about one mile north of Gates' position, and waited for help which would never come.

It was the arrival of reinforcements from England in late September which caused Clinton to attempt his diversion in Burgoyne's favor. His objectives lay in the Hudson Highlands, where the river ran S-shaped past the Dunderberg and Bear Mountain on the west, and Anthony's Nose on the east bank, with Peekskill nestling on its southern flank.

Opposite Anthony's Nose, Popolopen Creek empties into the Hudson from the west bank. There lay Fort Clinton on the northeast shoulder of Bear Mountain, and Fort Montgomery, north of the creek and about a half-mile distant. A great log boom and an iron chain running to Anthony's Nose blocked the waterway, and above these obstacles lay two small American frigates, one sloop and two galleys.

The forts were well planned but Montgomery was not yet entirely completed. The garrison of the two forts, under Brigadier General George Clinton, governor of New York, and his brother, Brigadier General James Clinton, consisted of a scratch force of about 600 men; some regulars, a number of militiamen and one company of Lamb's Continental Artillery.

East of the river, behind Peekskill, Putnam lay with approximately 1,200 Continentals and 300 militiamen. On the east bank, too, was little Fort Independence, opposite the Dunderberg. Some five miles up the Hudson, opposite West Point (then a wilderness), small stone Fort Constitution lay on the island of that name—separated from the mainland by a wide marsh. Fort Constitution (named in honor of the British Constitution) composed the original Hudson Highland defense; it had been built in 1775 by New York at Washington's suggestion, and was now garrisoned by some 50-odd New York militia.

Sir Henry Clinton knew, of course, the American dispositions and strength. He also was well aware of the major weakness of the defenses, predicated upon resistance to attack from the river only; the Americans deemed the mountain wilderness immediately west of the Hudson to be impassable for troops.

Leaving New York on October 3, Sir Henry Clinton's convoy of transports, flatboats and galleys carrying 4,000 British and Hessian

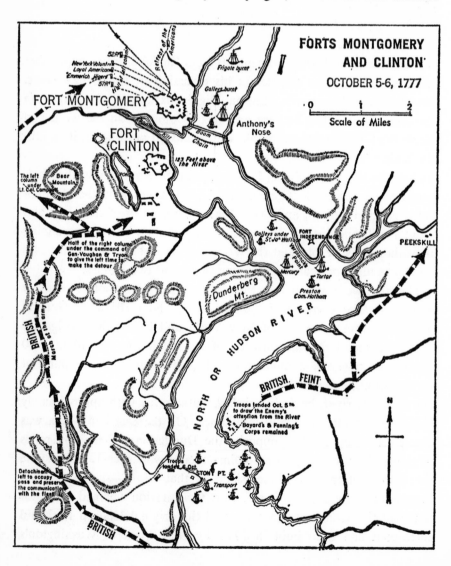

regulars and some Tory elements, escorted by Commodore William Hotham with the frigates *Preston, Mercury* and *Tartar,* arrived two days later at the head of Haverstraw Bay.

Sufficient troops—Tories—were disembarked immediately below Peekskill to alarm Putnam, who, fearing attack, withdrew into the hills to the east and sent an urgent appeal for reinforcements to American General George Clinton across the river. Then, under cover of thick fog, the British main effort landed early on the morning of the 6th on the west bank at Stony Point, five miles below Popolopen Creek, with the Dunderberg crags intervening.

The column, led by a Tory guide, marched inland over a rough road, then turned north on a trail that wound precipitously along the western slopes of the Dunderberg, to debouch at about 10:00 A.M. in the saddle between it and Bear Mountain, at the hamlet of Doodletown. Here Clinton split his forces. Lieutenant Colonel Archibald Campbell, with 900 men—regulars and Tories—swung to the left, to circle Bear Mountain and strike for Fort Montgomery. Clinton, with the main body, after a halt to enable Campbell's column to complete its long march, pushed directly east towards Fort Clinton. This force —some 1,200 strong in all, under command of Brigadier General John Vaughn—consisted of light infantry, grenadiers and line troops —regulars all. Clinton went with Vaughn. Behind, in reserve, was left General Tryon with the 7th Foot and a Hessian regiment.

George Clinton, up at Esopus (Kingston) attending a legislative session, hurried back to Fort Montgomery when the first news of the British advance was received. Meanwhile reconnoitering parties from both Forts Clinton and Montgomery, belatedly sent westward to contact the British advance, were driven in.

At four o'clock, with British forces closing in on the two American forts, British Henry Clinton called on American George Clinton to surrender. Upon his prompt refusal simultaneous attacks began. At Fort Clinton, the bulk of the attack drove directly against the southern front, with the light infantry and grenadiers heading the charge, while the 63rd Foot demonstrated on the northwest. Despite heavy fire from the defenders the assault column swept across an open space, stormed the ramparts and poured in with fixed bayonets. The defenders immediately surrendered. At Fort Montgomery Campbell's attack was three-pronged—the British regiments on the right, the Hessians in the center and the Tories on the left. Campbell was wounded in the assault. Tory Beverly Robinson, succeeding to command, carried the assault through successfully. In the gathering darkness, most of the garrison, including both American Clintons, escaped. British losses were approximately 40 killed and 150 wounded. Of the Americans, 250 were reported killed, wounded or missing. Sixty-seven guns were lost, together with a considerable quantity of stores.

In the river below, as soon as the forts were lost, the five American warships made no attempt to contest passage of the British through the chain and barricade. Attempting to flee upstream, one vessel ran aground, and all were then put to the torch.

Next day the chain and barricade were cleared and the British flotilla moved up-river. A white flag, sent to Fort Constitution to demand surrender, was fired on. Then the little garrison burned the works and fled across the swamp. Sir Henry Clinton now felt that he had accomplished his purpose of creating a diversion. So he sent a jaunty little message to Burgoyne on the 8th: *"Nous y voici* and nothing now between us and Gates; I sincerely hope this little success of ours may facilitate your operations. . . . I heartily wish you success."

Apparently Clinton was toying with the idea of striking north against Gates' rear. As a preliminary, he sent his frigates with a detachment of Vaughn's troops on board to raid and burn Esopus on the 16th. But urgent orders from Howe to send reinforcements to Philadelphia caused Clinton to give up any idea of further operations up the Hudson; instead, he evacuated the Highlands and returned to New York.

Clinton's message never got to Burgoyne; the messenger was captured. But if delivered it would have done no good, for "Gentleman Johnny" had gambled and lost the day before it was penned.

From September 21, 1777, until early October, Burgoyne confronted Gates behind a well-organized entrenched position. Meanwhile Gates was adding to his own strength at Bemis Heights. The American position had been strengthened by fortification of the high ground to the west—Burgoyne's objective in the Freeman's Farm battle.

Behind Burgoyne, Lincoln and his militia forces from the Manchester-Bennington area of Vermont had been playing hob with the all-too-tenuous line of communications from which Burgoyne had divorced himself. Skenesboro had been occupied by one of Lincoln's detachments, driving its little garrison out. Two other detachments had struck simultaneously at Forts Ticonderoga and Independence. The forts themselves—held by British General Powell with the 53rd Foot and the Prinz Friedrich regiment—had been too strong to assault, but the outworks had been scoured, 300 prisoners and 100 or more bateaux and other craft captured, and 100 American prisoners released. In addition, a force of 2,000 New Hampshire militia now sat entrenched near Fort Edward, controlling the area between it and Fort George, while 1,300 Massachusetts militia were on their way to Gates down the Battenkill, with orders to cross and bar the west-bank road north of Saratoga.

The story of Jean McCrea—circulated throughout the country—had stirred angry response in the shape of militiamen who flowed in from both New England and New York. The largest increment to Gates' command was Lincoln's contingent of 2,000 troops, now recalled from Vermont. They poured over the American pontoon bridge on September 29. By October 7 Gates mustered a total of 11,000 men with a hard core of 2,700 Continentals. Schuyler, down at Albany, had not let his animosity interfere with his efficient, patriotic administration in support of Gates. Food was plentiful, some clothing had been distributed and, best of all, there was now plenty of ammunition. So Gates, with the trumps being dealt into his hand, was content to lay inactive like a torpid cat in front of a mousehole.

It is only fair to say there was some justification for Gates' inaction. He knew Burgoyne to be a gambler; he evidently hoped for some rash move on his opponent's part. No gambler himself, he would not risk his amateur soldiers in open warfare.

But inside his fortifications sparks were flying in a private war—Gates vs. Arnold. Gates had never forgiven Arnold's impetuous, loudly voiced demands for aggressive action at Freeman's Farm. Nor had he forgiven Arnold's friends, who claimed for him full credit for the action. Deliberately, Gates didn't even mention Arnold's name in his official report—which incidentally, he made direct to Congress and not to General Washington.

Hot-tempered Arnold clashed with his commander—first in passionate personal argument, then in exchange of insulting letters. Gates relieved him of command, appointing Lincoln in his place, and barred him from headquarters. Arnold packed up to join Washington. But a round-robin—signed by every general officer except Gates and Lincoln—urged him to remain for the impending battle. He did; with Gates' consent. So when Burgoyne threw the dice once more, the second senior general officer in the American force would be merely an idler. At least, that's what Gates intended.

Unwitting of these developments, Burgoyne sat in hope long deferred, while the nights grew colder and the days more dreary for his troops. His position ran generally westward from the Hudson to Freeman's Farm. There the line angled north about the head of the Great Ravine. A deep ditch skirted the entire front, which had been cleared of trees to afford a field of fire. Behind the western angle, still on the south side of the ravine, a secondary trench system backed up the salient. To the north, a separate large horseshoe-shaped redoubt, its toe pointing northwest, anchored the western flank and protected the rear. On the eastern flank another system of redoubts crowned the bluffs overlooking the Hudson, and below them nestled all the rear echelon—hospitals, magazines, vehicles and the fleet of provision boats. Burgoyne's headquarters lay in this waterfront area. A pontoon bridge spanned the Hudson at this point.

Burgoyne could muster not more than 5,000 men, now, and desertions were melting those away. Rations, too, were dwindling fast; salt pork and flour and little of that. Local foraging was impossible; the woods were filled with roving, sharpshooting American patrols. When the last grass in the river meadows was cropped away, the horses began to die; there was no grain. Continuous night alarms and picket-baiting unravelled the nerves of despondent men whose uniforms were now as tattered as ever were Washington's Continentals, and whose belts were tightened by hunger. On October 3 rations were cut by one-third. Next day Burgoyne huddled with Riedesel, Fraser and Phillips in a council of war.

In front lay Gates, whose strength, they knew, must be increasing.

That was all they did know, for no British patrol had ever pierced his tight-woven screen of bush-fighters, and the remaining Indians were equally cowed by the sharpshooting American riflemen.

Burgoyne's council faced a stark decision. Should they attack, stay or retreat? The upshot was approval of Burgoyne's plan to make a reconnaissance in force on October 7 to test the vulnerability of the

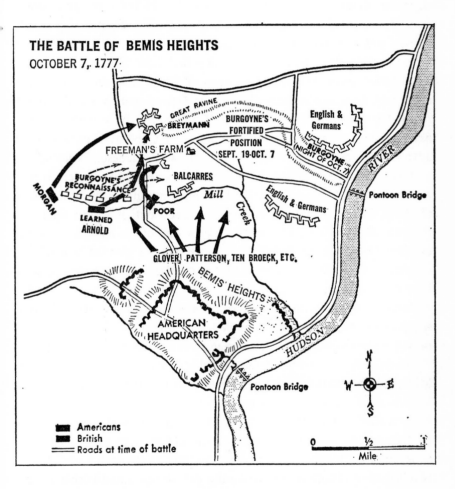

THE BATTLE OF BEMIS HEIGHTS
OCTOBER 7, 1777·

GREAT RAVINE
BREYMANN
BURGOYNE'S
FORTIFIED
POSITION
SEPT. 19-OCT. 7
English & Germans
BURGOYNE (NIGHT OF OCT. 7)
FREEMAN'S FARM
BURGOYNE'S RECONNAISSANCE
BALCARRES
Mill
English & Germans
Pontoon Bridge
MORGAN
LEARNED
ARNOLD
POOR
Creek
RIVER
GLOVER, PATTERSON, TEN BROECK, ETC.
BEMIS HEIGHTS
AMERICAN HEADQUARTERS
HUDSON
Pontoon Bridge

◼ Americans
◼ British
═══ Roads at time of battle

0   ½   1
          Mile

American left. If in the affirmative, an attack in force would follow next day. Otherwise, the army would retreat to its former Battenkill position, reopen its line of communications and there wait for Clinton's arrival. To put the troops in proper humor, twelve barrels of rum were broken out that night and distributed.

There might have been justification for Burgoyne's advance in the

Freeman's Farm battle, for that was a real reconnaissance in force. But it is hard to justify the dispositions and movements which he now ordered.

With part of his force, he emerged from the extreme right of his position that morning of October 7—against a completely undetermined objective—again in three columns closely linked. On the right was General Fraser with Balcarres' light infantry. The center column, under Riedesel, consisted of the 24th Foot (of Fraser's corps) and a conglomerate of the Brunswick units. On the left was Acland's grenadier battalion, also detached from Fraser's corps. Behind the columns trundled eight guns and two howitzers. Far to the right, as a diversion, Captain Fraser's rangers, Canadians and Indians roamed the woods. Burgoyne himself appears to have been in command. The command relationship between General Fraser—whose advanced corps had been thus scattered—and Riedesel, is not clear.

The total strength of the mobile force was about 1,600 men. It was a stupid, bungling shot in the dark, completely unworthy of a soldier of Burgoyne's experience. As matters turned out, it would squander the élite of his army and cost the life of one of his two best general officers. On the other hand, it was the frantic play of a gambler, desperate to retrieve his losses. And that, of course, was well in Burgoyne's character.

Advancing some three-quarters of a mile to a wheat field on a slight ridge, the command deployed into line and halted. Why? To permit a detachment of foragers to mow the wheat for the straw!

Gates, receiving word of the British advance from an outpost on Mill Creek, sent his adjutant general, young Lieutenant Colonel James Wilkinson, forward to investigate. When Wilkinson came galloping back with word of the enemy dispositions, Morgan urged an immediate attack against Burgoyne's right. Gates, despite his own great superiority in numbers, after some hesitation now sent forward only two brigades—Morgan's, to strike the British right, and Poor's against the enemy left. Later, still the piecemeal player, Gates released Learned's brigade to oppose Burgoyne's center, keeping most of the American army fuming behind their entrenchments.

Poor, who had at least 800 men, moved straight to the front and at half past two flung himself against Acland's grenadiers, reserving his fire until the British had blazed away. Then he charged, after delivering one close-range volley. Acland's stolid grenadiers met the Americans with the bayonet, but the very weight of the American force—four times their number—rolled them up. Acland, wounded, was captured; his men swept away.

Eager Morgan, who had further to go than Poor, by this time reached the British right. His riflemen hit Balcarres' light infantry in flank. Trying to change front to face this attack, Balcarres' men were also struck and shaken by Dearborn's light infantry of Morgan's command. An attempt to rally them failed and the entire British right wing, leaving its guns, fell back in disorder on their entrenchments.

Riedesel's command—the British center—was thus left unsupported. Against it Learned's brigade moved out slowly. And then a little man on a big bay horse raced across the field: Benedict Arnold, bound into battle. Gates had seen him gallop out of camp, had sent an aide to halt him, but the aide never caught up.

Arnold, assuming command of the attack, led Learned's men across Mill Creek and up to Riedesel's line, only to be repulsed. A second effort forced the Germans back, as Morgan's men on their right and Poor on their left came swarming in to threaten their flanks. The stubborn Brunswickers withdrew towards the earthworks, among Balcarres' men.

There Fraser, leading the thin files of his own 24th Foot, tried to turn the tide, or at least slow down the retreat. Conspicuous on a gray charger, Fraser drew the fire of one of Morgan's men, urged by Arnold to pick him off. Three times the rifleman—one Tim Murphy—drew bead, and the third shot found the mark. Fraser, mortally wounded, was carried back into the British entrenchments with the tide, and the first phase of the engagement was over, 50 minutes from the time it started.

But Arnold was not through. By this time the remainder of Gates' army, in an apparently spontaneous advance, was in the field and moving to join the attack. Arnold led Patterson's and Glover's brigades against the western salient now manned by Balcarres' light infantry. Behind their entrenchments in the angle the British regulars stiffened. Arnold, seeing Learned's brigade still moving to his own left, galloped across the field of fire and led them around the angle towards the horseshoe redoubt, where Breymann stood, his strength reduced to

200 by drafts to the morning's effort. With Morgan, on the extreme left flank, and regiments of both Poor's and Learned's brigade closing in, the redoubt was surrounded. Arnold, impetuous, put spurs to his mount, led cheering Continentals through the sallyport. A jäger's bullet knocked him from his horse with a fractured thigh—the same leg that had been wounded at Quebec. But his men weren't stopped. They swarmed over the redoubt. Breymann was killed, in last-ditch defense.

A Brunswick counterattack in the dusk failed to clear the horseshoe, and firing gradually ceased. With the horeshoe redoubt in American hands, Burgoyne's entire position had become untenable. The British commander, who had courageously exposed himself throughout the engagement, was unharmed. But he had lost his gamble. He withdrew during the night north of the Great Ravine, and next day —abandoning his wounded to American mercy—slowly retired to Saratoga, while Gates—for once spurred to action—sent a flanking force up the east bank of the Hudson while following the British closely on the west.

This second battle of Saratoga—often called Bemis Heights or Stillwater—had cost Burgoyne another 600 men in killed, wounded and captured, against an American loss of 150. All the ten guns accompanying the British gamble were lost.

Like a wounded snake, Burgoyne's army coiled up at Saratoga after taking most of three days to move seven miles. There was still fight in it, as Gates found out when his advance almost bumped into a determined delaying position on the Fish Kill. Rain was coming down hard now and both armies bivouacked under atrocious conditions. Maybe Burgoyne had the better of it, for one night at least, for he bedded down in Schuyler's own comfortable mansion—which he burned when he left.

On October 12 Burgoyne called another council of war. His army was surrounded on three sides, his boats had been captured. Riedesel had the most logical solution—to abandon baggage and artillery and march at once for Fort Edward and Lake George. The idea being approved, rations for six days were distributed, and preparations for movement—"with the greatest secrecy and quietness"—began. But Burgoyne at the last minute hesitated and next day his chance was gone. John Stark was back, with 1,100 New Hampshire militia and a battery of artillery. Crossing at the mouth of the Battenkill, he sealed Burgoyne in.

On the 13th, with the unanimous consent of his officers, Burgoyne asked for a parley. After two days of argument and quibbling, an agreement was signed and Burgoyne's army laid down their arms on the 17th, wiping one quarter of King George's forces in America off the slate. At Burgoyne's insistence, Gates weakly agreed that this extraordinary document was a "convention," not a "capitulation." As guests, rather than as prisoners of war, the defeated troops—subsisting at American expense—would march to Boston and there be taken home on British transports. It was pledged they would not serve again in North America, unless exchanged by cartel.

Gates, disturbed by reports of Clinton's activities on the lower Hudson, was in a hurry to get it over. Burgoyne, jealous of his reputation, had actually slipped him a card from the bottom of the deck, for by this means his army could be saved for garrison duty in England, releasing fresh troops for service in America. The Britisher, just before signing, also received rumors of Clinton's operation. He stalled for time while he weighed the possibility of repudiating the convention. This was too much even for Gates, who gave him one more hour. Burgoyne signed.

The surrender was carried out in all formality, and Burgoyne's army marched away towards freedom, as they thought. Actually, many of them—except for their officers, who were released on parole—would never see the Old World again. Congress, to its shame, repudiated the convention. Though rightly objecting to the leniency of the terms, it broke the pledged word of its appointed commander. The unfortunates would be herded for a year in the vicinity of Boston, then moved in turn to Charlottesville, Virginia; Lancaster, Pennsylvania; and other places. Some would be exchanged, others deserted. At the end of the war the survivors simply melted into the American population.

All this, however, would be but a footnote to a tremendous victory. The surrender of an entire army of disciplined, regular soldiers to the makeshift Americans astounded Europe. Seven general officers were included in the bag of more than 5,700 prisoners. Twenty-seven guns, five thousand stand of small arms and quite a quantity of other matériel had been garnered.

Strategically, the results were most important. All British posts to the north were withdrawn into Canada. The King's men held only the New York City area, Rhode Island, and Philadelphia.

Psychologically, the effect was enormous. In America, confidence in the patriot cause—shaken by the results of the Brandywine and Germantown—soared again. Abroad, France's Louis XVI recognized the United States, and moved inevitably towards war with England. Spain—although not recognizing the new republic—was nudged by Saratoga towards later hostilities against the British. Holland soon joined the alliance against Britain.

The turning point had been reached. But only the great-hearted leader of the Continental Army realized how long would be the path and how stupendous the obstacles still to be conquered.

★ 20 ★ ★ ★ ★ ★

Valley Forge

IN OCTOBER AND NOVEMBER OF 1777 Washington began to discern that he had enemies within the American army more dangerous to him and to the Revolution than all of General Howe's redcoats. A whispering campaign was circulating disparaging comparisons between Washington's two recent defeats and Gates' victories over Burgoyne. Some members of Congress were involved in these quiet criticisms, as well as a few disgruntled officers. Washington, busy devoting every possible effort to providing rations and clothing for a starving, threadbare army, while at the same time keeping a close watch on the British in Philadelphia, had neither the time nor the inclination to pay any attention to these murmurs.

Then, in November, loyal Lord Stirling brought to Washington's attention the fact that French-Irish Brigadier General Thomas Conway had been slandering him in correspondence with General Horatio Gates. This information had reached Stirling either through the inadvertence, or the sly machinations, of Wilkinson, Gates' aide-de-camp.

Gates, Conway, and Wilkinson had recently, in various ways, added to Washington's administrative and personal burdens. Conway, with 30 years' service in the French army, was arrogantly demanding promotion to major general, and attempting to become Inspector General of the army at the same time. There were twenty-three American brigadier generals in the army, all senior to Conway in date of rank, who were incensed that Congress would even consider promoting the foreigner over their heads.

Gates, after Saratoga, had not deigned to send a report of his victory to Washington, his Commander-in-Chief, but had instead submitted it directly to Congress. Though Washington was both hurt and insulted, he did not complain about this either to Gates or to Congress.

When Gates had sent his message of victory to Congress after Burgoyne's surrender at Saratoga, he had requested that the messenger—his aide-de-camp, Lieutenant Colonel Wilkinson—be rewarded by a promotion to brigadier general. When Congress complied, practically every colonel in the army threatened to resign. It has never been clear what part, if any, Wilkinson played in the mysterious intrigues of the following months. As his entire life was one of conspiracy and treachery, it is hard to avoid the assumption that clever Wilkinson was probably involved.

The exact nature and extent of this intrigue has never been fully established. There is no question, however, that, beginning in October, 1777, Conway was slandering Washington, as one way of suggesting his own superior military genius. At the same time he was doing everything in his power to have Washington replaced by Gates, believing this would further his own selfish ambitions. In this he seems to have been closely associated with Major General Thomas Mifflin, the Quartermaster General, who had become alienated from Washington during the summer of 1777. Many of Washington's supply difficulties during the fall of 1777, and the terrible winter months that followed, were due directly to Mifflin's dereliction in the performance of his duties. Since Mifflin had early proven himself an able and efficient man, it is hard not to believe that his shortcomings during this critical period were part of a deliberate effort to discredit Washington.

There is little doubt that Gates was well aware of what was being done and said by Conway and Mifflin, as well as by Congressmen Benjamin Rush, James Lovell, Richard Henry Lee, and (possibly) Samuel Adams. Whether these men were conspirators, or merely like-minded schemers, has never been proven. But during the early winter they all attempted to discredit Washington, and to reduce his influence. Despite Washington's known contempt for Conway as an officer and as a person, the Frenchman was promoted to major general and made Inspector General. Gates was made president of the Board of War, on which Mifflin was a member. Since this agency was responsible directly to Congress, Gates and Mifflin implied that the Board of War was completely independent of, and in a sense, superior to the Commanding General. The whispering campaign, slandering Washington's conduct of the 1777 campaign, and glorifying Gates' performance at Saratoga, grew in intensity.

Washington's enemies were misled by his initial attitude towards their criticisms. He did not reply since, as he had already pointed out to some understanding members of Congress, this would reveal to the British exactly how weak his army was. The schemers evidently concluded that if Washington were criticized sufficiently, and were insulted enough, he would resign his command in disgust. They were counting on the man's dignity, and his contempt for petty bickering, to keep him from taking any action against them.

In private correspondence then and later, Washington made it clear that if Congress and the American people thought someone else could do a better job than he as leader of the American armies, he would accept that decision, and continue in some lesser post to do all that he could for the cause. But until—or unless—he was relieved by higher authority, he was determined that no discouragement, no insult, no hardship, would be permitted to interfere with his performance of his duty as he saw it. And though very conscious of the dignity of his position, he was equally aware of both his honor and his rights as a man and as Commander-in-Chief. He had no intention of allowing his enemies to defeat him by default.

The conspirators also misjudged the attitude of the army. They had not realized the fierce loyalty to Washington among the officer corps—led by Greene, Lafayette and Hamilton, who made clear to everyone their utter contempt for the conspirators.

Without impairing his dignity, without in any way resorting to deceit or intrigue, Washington seized the initiative to defeat his enemies at their own game. Gates had attempted to justify his correspondence with Conway by suggesting in letters to Washington that he and Conway were being slandered by members of the Commander-in-Chief's own staff. He implied that these conniving staff officers had stolen or intercepted letters, then misquoted them. In an ostentatious display of his own supposedly clear conscience, and at the same time attempting to establish himself as Washington's co-equal, Gates had sent copies of his letters to Congress. Washington, on his own part, sent to Congress copies of revealingly arrogant and petulant letters he had received earlier from Conway. Then in early February he wrote a devastating letter to Gates, with a copy to Congress. In it he revealed his own complete understanding of, and contempt for Conway, in terms that made Gates and the Congressional conspirators apprehend that he was also well-aware of the campaign of vilification being waged against him. Washington also made it clear that if Gates persisted in efforts to justify such a palpably contemptible individual as Conway, then fair-minded, honorable men would be forced to draw the obvious conclusion.

Gates and the other schemers were taken completely by surprise by this stunning, irrefutable verbal counterattack. Without support in the army, and unprepared to take direct action, all scurried for cover. The so-called Conway Cabal suddenly collapsed. Gates responded to Washington in a craven letter of apology, which Washington accepted magnanimously, though obviously without illusion.

By this time Washington had his army in winter quarters on the slopes of a ridge overlooking the Schuylkill River near Valley Forge, to be as near as possible to Philadelphia, maintaining a constant threat against Howe, while at the same time establishing himself in a readily defensible position. Short of food, lacking tents, in freezing rain and frequent snow, the troops huddled in separate brigade villages of log cabins, scattered on the wooded hillside. At the same time, under the supervision of French engineer Colonel Louis Duportail, a strong system of redoubts and entrenchments was built around the base of the hill. Though members of the Conway Cabal had criticized the location and the defenses, no one had any better plan to offer.

The conditions under which the army lived that winter can be described, but can hardly be appreciated. Constant shortages of food caused understandable, persistent complaints amongst the troops. Many were the nights that Washington could hear his men calling from hut street to hut street, and from one part of camp to another, "No meat! No meat! No meat!" Some men had literally no clothes other than a blanket to cover their nakedness. Blood-stained snow eloquently proclaimed the shortage of shoes. Letter after letter, diary after diary, repeated the same grim, sad story—which was put by Greene in one stark sentence: "One half of our troops are without breeches, shoes, and stockings; and some thousands without blankets."

The circumstances of the army, the mental anguish which this created amongst all of the officers—and particularly in the Commander-in-Chief—as well as his ceaseless and tireless efforts to improve the situation are perhaps best revealed in Washington's letter to the President of Congress on December 23, 1777.

"I am now convinced, beyond a doubt, that unless some great and capital change suddenly takes place . . . , this Army must inevitably be reduced to one or other of these three things. Starve, dissolve, or disperse, in order to obtain subsistence in the best manner they can; rest assured Sir this is not an exaggerated picture, but that I have abundant reason to support what I say."

Washington went on to describe his intention of interfering with a British foraging party

"When, behold! to my great mortification, I was not only informed, but convinced that the Men were unable to stir on Acct. of Provision, and that a dangerous Mutiny [was being] with difficulty suppressed by the spirited exertions of some officers. . . .

"All I could do under the circumstances, was to send out a few light Parties to watch and harass the Enemy, whilst other Parties were instantly detached different ways to collect, if possible, as much Provision as would satisfy the present pressing wants of the Soldiery. But will this answer? No Sir: three or four days bad weather would prove our destruction.

"What then is to become of the Army this Winter? And if we are as often without Provisions now, as with it, what is to become of us in the Spring?"

By this time the troops Washington had sent north to Saratoga in the summer had returned, bringing the army to a nominal strength of 11,000, but of these, Washington reported "no less than 2,898 [are] unfit for duty because they are barefoot and otherwise naked." He then commented bitterly against his slanderers who were circulating false strength figures, and criticizing him for not attacking the British in Philadelphia.

"I can assure those Gentlemen that it is a much easier and less distressing thing to draw remonstrances in a comfortable room by a good fireside than to occupy a cold and bleak hill and sleep under frost and Snow without Cloaths or Blankets. . . . It adds not a little to my other

difficulties, and distress, to find that much more is expected of me than
is possible to be performed, and that upon the ground of safety and
policy, I am obliged to conceal the true State of the Army from Public
view and thereby expose myself to detraction and Calumny."

Among the army's many hardships were the ravages of disease. Of
these, typhus was the most prevalent, and the most deadly. During
that terrible winter nearly 3,000 men died from starvation, exposure
or disease. It is amazing that the army held together at all. That it
did can be attributed only to the amazing influence of Washington's
strength of character, will and determination. This austere man was
truly loved by his devoted officers and men. Despite a steady drain
from illness, death and desertion, by the end of February Washington
still had more than 6,000 men at Valley Forge, and of these, perhaps
4,000 had been kept fit for duty. These were the ones who took part
in endless foraging expeditions in the neighboring regions of New
Jersey, Pennsylvania and Delaware.

Yet even these expeditions were disappointing. Soon the nearby
farms were stripped bare. And although Washington was meticulous
in paying for everything obtained, the farmers were not pleased to
accept worthless Continental currency. When they could, therefore,
they saved their choicest produce and livestock for the British, who
paid in good sterling.

In Philadelphia, Howe and his troops spent a much better winter
than they had the previous year in New York, with adequate supplies
of food and drink brought in by ship. The officers, in particular, had
a winter of gaiety in the largest and most sophisticated city of North
America. The only serious alarm during the winter was the result of
another invention of the fertile brain of David Bushnell, who had
earlier created the submarine *Turtle*.

In 1777 Bushnell had designed the prototype of all naval contact
mines, by attaching a gunlock as a contact fuse to a floating barrel
of gunpowder. With one of these kegs he had sunk a British schooner
in the Connecticut River. Early in January, 1778, Bushnell released
several hundred of his mines in the Delaware River, above Philadelphia. Hampered by floating ice in the river, the kegs were detected
by the English sailors before they struck any warships. Everything
floating on the river was then taken under fire by the cannon and
small-arms from the English ships; and most of the mines were de-

stroyed. Only one small vessel was sunk. The alarmed English continued to fire at any flotsam in the river for several days thereafter, leading New Jersey Congressman Francis Hopkinson to write a ballad entitled "The Battle of the Kegs," which was soon being sung in all thirteen states—and even surreptitiously within Philadelphia itself. The quatrain which most appealed to singers and listeners was the following:

"Sir William, he, as snug as flea
"Lay all this time a-snoring;
"Nor dreamed of harm, as he lay warm
"In bed with Mrs. Loring."

Long before this, on October 28, Howe had submitted to Lord Germain his application for relief from his command in America; received while the British government was still pondering its strategy for 1778. Soon after, the British learned that France had recognized American independence and had entered into an alliance with the United States on February 6. The Revolution had become another world war. The British thereupon decided to go on the defensive in the northern colonies, to undertake a naval campaign against France in the West Indies, and then to attempt to reconquer the southern colonies later in the year. Only New York and Newport would be held as bases in the north. Thus, when Howe's request for relief was approved late in February, another message was sent to his successor—Sir Henry Clinton in New York—directing him to take over Howe's army, and then to evacuate Philadelphia.

Meanwhile Washington, in addition to his other problems, had spent many a sleepless night worrying about American strategy. Congress, favoring another invasion of Canada, had actually sent young Lafayette to Albany to command an invasion expedition. Washington was relieved when this had to be abandoned, due to inadequate forces, since he was convinced the scheme was doomed to failure.

Washington's immediate problem was how to conduct the next campaign—if he still had an army. He had no inkling, of course, that the British would be shifting to a defensive strategy, but he did believe that Howe would be replaced by a more active and more aggressive general. The great question in his mind was whether he —or anyone else—could hold the army together in active campaigning against a vigorous British opponent. No American troops had yet been able to meet the British regulars on even terms on the battle-field. The well-drilled precision, the steadiness of discipline of English and German soldiers, had always brought final tactical victory in battle, even when their generals had made mistakes. More than once, the American army had survived such defeats only because of Howe's dilatoriness. What if Howe should be replaced by a more aggressive general, such as Clinton or Cornwallis? Washington feared to answer the unspoken question.

It was clear to Washington what the deficiency was: American troops lacked those qualities of discipline and regularity which had made the British invincible in pitched battles. The American officers, capable men, knew no more of the details of discipline, drill, or of other military routine than did their men. The blind were leading the blind.

Washington had hoped that the experienced professionals among the foreign volunteers could help supply standards of training and discipline which would permit him to risk battle with some chance of success. But even the few unselfish men of ability, experience and skill among them had not been able to provide what was needed. Conway, possibly, could have done the job, had he devoted his un-questioned military talents to instruction, rather than to self-seeking criticism.

Thus it was with mixed emotions that, in late January of 1778, Washington read a letter from Benjamin Franklin introducing Lieu-tenant General Baron Friedrich Wilhelm von Steuben of Prussia. Steuben was offering his services as a volunteer, with no claim for rank or pay beyond expenses; he stated that he was prepared to impart to the American army the experience he had gained as a trusted subordinate of Frederick the Great. Washington had been disappointed so often by well-advertised Europeans that while he welcomed von Steuben cordially, he met him also with courteous restraint and keen appraisal.

As a matter of fact Steuben never had been a lieutenant general in the Prussian army. His highest rank had been captain, and Franklin probably knew this. But Franklin was a keen judge of men, and was so impressed by what he had learned and seen of Steuben that he was convinced that the man could make a unique and vital contribution to the Revolutionary cause. And since he felt sure that Congress would pay no attention to anyone who did not have a high rank, Franklin did not challenge Steuben's bogus claim.

Despite doubts suggested by recent historians, Steuben was in fact a baron, and he had served on the staff of Frederick the Great as an aide-de-camp during the Seven Years War. And he was obviously a soldier.

Washington's first reaction to von Steuben was favorable. Since the Baron spoke no English, Washington loaned him two of his own French-speaking aides-de-camp, John Laurens and Alexander Hamilton. Von Steuben was asked to look over the army in its miserable encampment and to give his frank opinion as to how its deficiencies could be corrected.

Washington seems to have been as impressed by Steuben's frank reports and cogent recommendations as he was by the glowing evaluations of Hamilton and Laurens. Also in favor of the Baron was the immediate friendship he struck up with Greene. Finally, von Steuben's martial bearing, superb horsemanship, gracious manner, keen sense of humor and incisive observations won the liking and respect of both officers and men. Satisfied by all of this, Washington appointed Steuben as his Acting Inspector General—since Conway would still officially hold the title for a few more weeks—and authorized him to initiate measures to train the army.

This was a formidable task. There were no drill regulations, there was no uniform procedure for handling weapons, nor even a commonly accepted method of marching. To the extent that there was any model, it was British, and like their English counterparts, the American officers relied upon non-commissioned officers to supervise the drilling of troops. Unlike the English army, however, there were no experienced, veteran American sergeants who could do this competently. Thus, for all practical purposes, there was no drill.

Von Steuben saw the problem in its three principal aspects, and decided to deal with each simultaneously. A system of drill must be devised. This would have to be formulated into clear regulations which could be understood by inexperienced officers and men. Also, a group of qualified instructors must be trained who could do the drilling; no one man, no matter how able he might be, nor how loud his voice, could drill an entire army—particularly if he could not even speak the language of the soldiers.

Possibly nothing else quite reveals the true genius of von Steuben better than the perception which he demonstrated in discerning that the drill regulations of the Prussian army could not be translated bodily to America, and that American soldiers could not be trained by the methods then in vogue in Europe. As he later wrote to an old German comrade-in-arms:

> "The genius of this nation is not in the least to be compared to that of the Prussians, Austrians or French. You say to your soldier, 'Do this' and he does it; but I am obliged to say, 'This is the reason why you ought to do that'; and then he does it."

Von Steuben's program was based on a simple series of movements intended to appeal to Americans, suspicious all of rigid military pedantry. He developed, for example, a manual for the musket, based upon the Prussian system, but from which more than half of the movements had been eliminated. His first great victory with American officers and men was in demonstration that a perfectly satisfactory and efficient manual of the musket could be performed with only ten commands.

Steuben began at once to write out new drill regulations, based upon the system which he was devising. He wrote this in French, so that it could be more easily translated. But he did not feel that he could afford to delay training until the entire regulation was complete and then translated. So, as soon as he had written one day's lesson, it was translated by a French assistant. The Baron then memorized the commands in English, as taught to him by Laurens and Hamilton. Night after night this continued, following a full day's labor on the parade ground.

It was on the drill field that the sturdy, jovial and shiny-domed soldier completely won the hearts of the men, and—despite an initial reluctance—the enthusiastic support of the officers. Washington authorized Steuben to select 120 men from different regiments, who were to comprise the Commander-in-Chief's bodyguard. At the same time they became Steuben's model drill company. He also selected one officer from each brigade, who was to become a brigade inspector.

These men—the bodyguard and the brigade inspectors—he drilled personally, giving his commands "in a curious mixture of German, French and English."

For a week this continued day after day, all day long. Save for outpost guards, almost the entire army—at that time a bare 5,000 men—gathered around the drill field. The audience was fascinated by the spectacle of this proud foreign general, his breast covered with decorations, drilling squads, platoons, and a single company. They were convulsed when things went wrong, and the Baron's voice rolled over the field rich with multi-lingual oaths into which he interspersed a few English "goddamns." Most of all, the audience was impressed by the remarkable results of these hours of drill; by the precision, the self-confidence, and the soldierly attitude of this company when it paraded at the end of the first week.

The brigade inspectors were then sent back to their commands, to carry the new system of training to the entire army. Infected by the Baron's enthusiasm, these officers became able instructors. As they did their job, Steuben galloped from company to company, correcting here, praising there, and generally impressing on the entire army the same force of his personality which had so magically transformed the model company. The example of a lieutenant general—as they thought—personally drilling troops, had been enough to show the junior American officers that there was no reason why this should be beneath their dignity. Thus they threw themselves into the task with the same enthusiasm which the Baron had already imparted to the brigade inspectors.

All day long, rain or shine, the army drilled under the eagle eye of the Baron; frequently with the approving observation of Washington as well. In the evenings, Steuben continued the instruction of the brigade inspectors, correcting their mistakes, and offering suggestions based upon what he had seen. Then, after these men had been dismissed, he labored into the early hours of the morning, writing out another chapter of his drill regulations, which was to be translated, copied and distributed the following day.

Steuben did not limit his introduction of regularity, precision and efficiency merely to external training and disciplinary drill. He introduced a system of inspections which he was to develop and improve during the course of the war. Every man had to be accounted for, all articles of clothing and equipment had to be laid out to be checked for serviceability, and against the property account records which Steuben demanded be maintained in each company. Companies and battalions, regiments and brigades, competed to see which could make the best impression on the keen-eyed Baron.

It is perhaps remarkable that it was a Prussian officer—from a nation noted for the inhumanity and impersonality of its military system—who taught the United States Army how to protect the dignity and welfare of the individual soldier. Steuben showed that this was not incompatible with the creation of a closely-disciplined, cohesive team. He stressed the responsibility of the officers for the care of their men and the condition of their equipment. The captain "cannot be too careful of the company the State has committed to his care," and must "gain the love of his men by treating them with every possible kindness and humanity."

During all of this time Washington paid close and favorable attention to everything that the Baron was doing. This, he knew, was the answer to his most serious combat problem. Though not relaxing for a moment his personal attention to the affairs of the army as a whole, the arrival of von Steuben had permitted Washington to devote more time to the administrative departments, to the details of improving the supply system, and to the recruitment of new troops for the coming campaign.

Upon his recommendation, on March 2 Congress appointed Greene Quartermaster General, in place of Mifflin. Greene was unhappy about leaving active field command, and Washington was sorry to lose the close counsel of the man who had been his most reliable and most capable battlefield subordinate. But it was equally obvious to both men that the army's most pressing needs now were adequate supplies of food, clothing and munitions. Washington's hopes for improvement were soon fulfilled, as Greene systematically reorganized the Quartermaster General's department, with immediate beneficial results.

Partly because of the better weather, and partly because of the increased attention which Washington had been able to give to recruiting, by late March a thin stream of new men began to flow into the encampment at Valley Forge. In April this became almost a flood. As the recruits were incorporated into their units, and supplied with uniforms and equipment by Greene's new and efficient supply system, they were immediately subjected to Steuben's new system of drill and discipline. By the middle of May, for the first time in three years of war, Washington felt that he had an army in the true sense of the word, rather than a congregation of individuals and units of varying and limited combat capabilities.

Early in April, also, Washington obtained another proven field commander, whose arrival he hoped would at least partially offset the loss of Greene. General Charles Lee was exchanged for British Major General Richard Prescott—whose capture the previous summer while in a compromising situation with his mistress had provided much merriment to both armies. When Lee arrived at Valley Forge on April 5 he was greeted with the utmost enthusiasm by Washington and his officers. Though he seemed to be still the same arrogant braggart of the past, Washington was willing to discount all of this in the light of Lee's unquestioned experience, and proven combat capabilities.

On April 23 Washington learned that Clinton would replace Howe. A week later came the electrifying news of a tremendous diplomatic success achieved by America's three commissioners in Paris—Benjamin Franklin, Silas Deane and Arthur Lee: France had signed a treaty of alliance with the United States. This extraordinary development was celebrated by a great review on May 5, in which the revitalized army displayed both its new uniforms and its new precision in drill. Washington then ordered rum issued to all men.

By this time Washington had more than 11,000 men fit for duty at Valley Forge, with a detachment of 1,400 at Wilmington, and another force of 1,800, under Alexander McDougall, in the Hudson Highlands. The British had at least 17,000 men in Philadelphia, about 10,000 in New York, and over 3,000 in Rhode Island.

On May 11 General Clinton arrived in Philadelphia, to take over the command of the British army from General Howe. The arrival was immediately reported to Washington, and in the next few days there was definite corroboration of rumors which had been circulating in Philadelphia since April. The British army would soon be moving out of Philadelphia! The evidence seemed to indicate that this would be an abandonment of the city, rather than the initiation of a new offensive campaign. Ships began to sail down the Delaware, loaded with baggage and equipment; destination apparently New York.

To obtain additional information about British activities and intentions, Washington decided on a reconnaissance in force in the direction of Philadelphia. He assembled under Lafayette a division consisting of a brigade of Continentals and a brigade of militia. This force, including a company of irregular partisan troops under the command of able Captain Allan McLane, comprised about 2,200 men. In addition to obtaining information, apparently one of Washington's purposes was also to give the young marquis an opportunity to exercise a bit of independent field command, and to gain experience and confidence, after his disappointment when the Canadian expedition was cancelled.

Lafayette's conduct of the operations appears to have been competent. Moving to Barren Hill, just east of the Schuylkill River, about midway between Philadelphia and Valley Forge, he took up a good defensive position with security outposts along all approaching roads.

News of this activity having reached Philadelphia, General Clinton decided that he would seize an opportunity which could embarrass both America and France, by defeating—and, if possible capturing— the marquis and his entire division. Before dawn on May 20 about 10,000 British troops converged from three directions on Lafayette's position, hemming the Americans against the river. Clinton came within an ace of accomplishing his objective. The militia brigade had failed to maintain its outpost security as Lafayette had directed, and a last-minute warning of the British approach was given only by the efficient Captain McLane. Lafayette skillfully and hastily withdrew from the trap, and across the river after a brief skirmish, leaving the frustrated British in possession only of the abandoned trenches on Barren Hill.

21 ★ ★ ★ ★ ★

Sunstroke in New Jersey

BY LATE MAY, 1778, IT BECAME OBVIOUS that Clinton would soon evacuate Philadelphia. Ships loaded with baggage and stores sailed down the river almost every day. Spies brought word of the assembly of a large wagon train, and other British preparations for a march. And although British officers were close-mouthed, the rumors still indicated that New York would be the army's objective. Washington sent Maxwell's brigade across the Delaware to Mount Holly, New Jersey, so as to be in position to observe and to harass the British march. At the same time he informed Brigadier General Philemon Dickenson—in the field with 1,000 New Jersey militia—of the expected British movement. To guard against a possible British surprise move to the lower Delaware or to Chesapeake Bay, Smallwood's brigade was sent to Chadd's Ford.

In June the Earl of Carlisle brought a negotiating commission to Philadelphia, to discuss peace terms with Congress. The Carlisle Commission was authorized to offer virtual autonomy of the sort later to be termed "dominion status" to the colonies. Congress, insistent on independence as a minimum basis for negotiations, refused to treat with Carlisle and his associates. The Commissioners also failed completely in their efforts to bribe leading Americans by offers of titles and wealth.

On June 17, 1778, Washington called a council of war to discuss the possible courses of action now open to the American army. Lee vehemently insisted that it would be a mistake to attempt to interfere with Clinton's anticipated movement, and that Washington should avoid any possibility of a general engagement. Lafayette and Wayne, on the other hand, felt that the Americans should not pass up any opportunity to strike the British army while it was on the march. Other opinions ranged in between. Washington then announced his intention of following the British as closely as possible, of harassing them constantly, but of avoiding battle unless a particularly favorable opportunity offered itself. Lafayette, with Wayne as his second in command, was to be ready with six brigades to pursue Clinton at short notice.

Before dawn next morning the British army began to cross the Delaware, and started to march northeastward. About 10:00 A.M., just as the last British troops were arriving on the left bank of the river, Washington received information of the withdrawal. Lafayette's brigades immediately marched out of the Valley Forge encampment, heading for Coryell's Ford on the Delaware. Except for a small force to occupy Philadelphia, the remainder of the army followed soon afterward.

Washington had hoped to have gallant and able Major General Benedict Arnold as one of his division commanders in the coming campaign, but Arnold's leg wound, received at Bemis Heights, was still not completely healed. Arnold, accordingly, was placed in command of the troops re-occupying Philadelphia.

In March Sullivan had been sent to command in Rhode Island. This left Washington with Major Generals Lee, Lafayette, Stirling and de Kalb available as division commanders. Washington also felt that Wayne was capable of such a command, but was reluctant to employ him as such, since he was junior to several other brigadier generals. Also accompanying the main army were two competent staff major generals: Greene and Steuben.

Authorities differ as to the exact strength of Clinton's army as it marched towards New York. He had sent only a few units by ship, so his total force in hand could not have been less than 15,000, and was probably closer to 17,000. Washington's army at this time, counting Maxwell's brigade and Dickenson's New Jersey militia, already east of the Delaware River, comprised approximately 14,500 men. Of these, nearly 12,000 were Continentals.

Clinton marched in two parallel columns, so as to be able to assemble his entire army quickly in the event of an American attack.

New Jersey was gripped by a heat wave, and during the last two weeks of June the temperature approached 100° every day. Scattered thunderstorms failed to break the heat, but merely intensified a muggy humidity that was well nigh unbearable. Because of this, and since they had to rebuild bridges destroyed by the Americans, the English daily marches were slow and short.

Despite the weather the American foot soldiers marched further and faster. This was in part due to the fact that they carried lighter packs than the 60 to 80 pound loads borne by the English and Hessian troops. By June 23 Washington's main army was at Hopewell, east of the Delaware, and about 20 miles northwest of Clinton, who was near Allentown. The Americans were ready to seize an opportunity to attack. Dickenson's militia were hanging on the left, or inland, flank of the British, while Daniel Morgan with 600 picked riflemen was sent eastward to harass Clinton's right-hand column. Midway between the two main armies, south of Kingston, was Lafayette's advance guard of about 2,000 men.

Next morning Washington held another council of war. Again Lee loudly proclaimed his conviction that the Americans should avoid any attack against the well-trained British regulars. Rather, he suggested, Clinton should be provided every encouragement to get out of New Jersey. Once more Wayne strongly urged attack, and was supported by Lafayette, as well as by Greene. Again Washington made clear his own unchanged concept of operations. He would not attack the numerically superior British unless a favorable opportunity presented itself—but should this occur, the opportunity must be seized vigorously. The cautious pursuit continued.

Oppressed by the terrible heat, Clinton decided to rest his tired men all day on the 27th at Monmouth Courthouse (modern Freehold). It was now obvious to him that Washington's main army was as close to New York as he was. He decided not to risk battle among the meandering waterways of the Jersey Meadows, where Washington might be able to concentrate against a portion of his army. Rather, he would turn east to Sandy Hook, where he would embark his army on ships and continue to New York by water.

Washington had anticipated this possibility, and he knew that there was only one road from Monmouth Courthouse towards Sandy Hook. With the British no longer able to march in two parallel columns, this should permit the Americans to strike a punishing blow against Clinton's rear guard. On the 26th, therefore, Washington more than doubled the strength of his advance guard, which now consisted of two echelons, the leading one still under Lafayette, the second under Lee, who, as senior, was placed in command of both bodies.

Washington had apparently been reluctant to assign this responsibility to Lee, in view of his strongly expressed opposition to any offensive action. Military custom, however, demanded that Lee, as Washington's senior subordinate, be given this important detachment of the army. Lee, after first deferring to Washington's pointed suggestion that Lafayette should command the advance guard, later changed his mind and claimed his prerogative of rank. Lee's total force, including Dickenson's militia, was over 6,000 men—nearly half of the army.

On the 27th, with Clinton's army motionless at Monmouth Courthouse, Washington believed that the long-sought opportunity would present itself as soon as the English army was spread out in march column, presumably early on the 28th. That day, therefore, in the presence of Generals Lafayette, Wayne, Maxwell and Charles Scott, Washington personally ordered Lee to attack as soon as the British were on the road the following morning. He promised to bring up the main army in prompt support. That evening Lee and Lafayette combined their forces just east of Englishtown, while the main army was concentrating between that town and Cranbury.

At 5:00 the next morning Washington received word from Dickenson that the British had begun their movement from Monmouth Courthouse at 4:00 A.M. Washington immediately sent Lieutenant Colonel Richard Meade to carry this information to Lee, and to order him to attack as soon as possible. Meade was directed to inform Lee that Washington, with the main army of nearly 8,000 men, would be hastening to join him.

Clinton had divided his army into two portions. Knyphausen commanded the leading division, which was probably about 6,000 strong. This was followed by the train of 1,500 wagons. Clinton himself accompanied the main body of the army, probably slightly more than 10,000 men, under Cornwallis. At 8:00 A.M. Cornwallis' troops began to move east from Monmouth Courthouse towards Sandy Hook.

Lee had accepted his orders from Washington the previous day without any questions. He seems to have made up his mind, however, that the attack would be unsuccessful. Quite possibly he was determined to keep it from succeeding, though this has never been proven. A few historians believe he was sincerely doubtful of the possibility of success against British regulars. Most have attributed to Lee no worse crime than disloyalty to his Commander-in-Chief. It is hard, however, to discount the possibility of treason, in the light of his numerous conferences on strategy with Howe (while he was a prisoner of war); and his subsequent cordial—though apparently innocent—exchange of letters with Clinton in early June.

Whatever the reasons, Lee, after receiving Washington's orders on the 27th, had done nothing to prepare or plan for an attack. He was slow in ordering an advance after receiving Washington's renewed orders early next morning. He held no council or discussion with his brigadiers, and he issued no orders for an attack. He simply started his troops on a relatively slow march towards Monmouth Courthouse.

Nevertheless, as they approached the rear of the British column as it was filing past Monmouth Courthouse, Lafayette and several individual American brigade commanders on their own initiative deployed and closed vigorously upon the British. It was then after 10:00 A.M. When the redcoats turned on these poorly-timed and uncoordinated thrusts, Lee still issued no orders. Generals Scott and Wayne, who led the advance, swung their brigades north of the courthouse to repulse the British counterattack. The remainder of Lee's units, however, without orders, continued to mill about in confusion near the courthouse. Wayne and Scott seem to have renewed their advance, until they saw that the units to their right were falling back. Accounts are contradictory, but Lee had apparently personally ordered one or two of his brigadiers to retreat, though he made no effort to see that the order was disseminated to the others. As a result, after a few sharp but scattered exchanges of fire, Lee's entire force began to retreat in confusion.

Clinton, who had promptly faced Cornwallis to the rear, now saw an unexpected opportunity to inflict a sharp defeat on a major portion of the American army. Directing Cornwallis to attack, he sent orders to Knyphausen to halt, and to send back about 3,000 troops toward Monmouth Courthouse. Pressing closely after the withdrawing Americans, the British soon turned the retreat into a rout. Only Wayne's brigade, falling back in good order from one delaying position to another, prevented total disaster.

It was now noon, or after. Washington, approaching Freehold Meeting House at the head of the remainder of the army, had for some time been worried because he had not heard the expected noise of battle. He became even more perplexed just before noon when he finally heard some light and sporadic firing. He trotted forward with his staff to find out what was happening. Near Freehold Meeting House he found stragglers fleeing down the road. Since there had been no sustained firing, it was obvious to Washington that there could

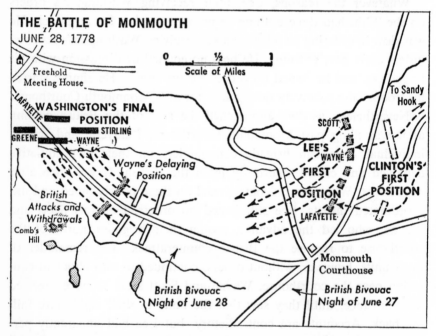

have been no serious engagement. Thus this confused retreat was incomprehensible to him. Putting spurs to his horse, he galloped through the thickening crowds of refugees, until, less than a mile east of Freehold Meeting House, he met Lee, riding calmly to the rear with a group of staff officers.

"What, Sir," asked the angry Washington, "is the meaning of this? Whence come this disorder and confusion?"

"Sir, Sir?" stammered the embarrassed Lee, who either did not understand, or was disconcerted by the glint in his commander's eye. Washington repeated his question in an icy tone of voice.

The remainder of the conversation between the two generals has been reported with many discrepancies by the several eyewitnesses who were there. Some have asserted that after hearing Lee's halting excuses, the usually composed Washington exploded in a rage as had never been seen before by his associates. Of his fury, there can be no question, though there is serious doubt whether he called Lee a "damned poltroon," or otherwise used what one observer called "a terrific eloquence of unprintable scorn." Whatever he said, he left Lee cowering and sputtering, as he plunged ahead into the motley, retreating mob to attempt to restore order. A staff officer reported that the British were only fifteen minutes away.

"I never saw the General to so much advantage," Alexander Hamilton wrote later. "His coolness and firmness were admirable. He instantly took measures for checking the enemy's advance, and giving time for the army, which was very near, to form and make a proper disposition."

Lafayette, who had apparently been endeavoring to rally the fugitives, unexpectedly found himself joined by Washington. The Marquis has also given us a description of the General's actions during these critical minutes:

"His presence stopped the retreat. . . . His fine appearance on horseback, his calm courage, roused to animation by the vexations of the morning, gave him the air best calculated to excite enthusiasm. . . . I thought then, as now, that never had I beheld so superb a man."

Washington rallied two regiments, just as Wayne and a few steadfast men pulled back to join him, a mere 200 yards in front of the redcoat skirmishers. Turning the covering force over to Wayne, Washington immediately galloped a few hundred yards to the rear, where a low ridge overlooked a meandering stream flowing through a gentle, marshy depression, locally called a "ravine." Here he was rallying fugitives when Greene arrived, with the head of the army's main body. Ignoring the fact that Greene was now a staff officer, theoretically ineligible to command, Washington immediately placed him in command of the right wing. He ordered Stirling, whose division was bringing up the rear, to move up as rapidly as possible on Greene's left, while he himself, with the assistance of Lafayette, attempted to organize Lee's refugees to form a reserve.

Wayne, meanwhile, with the assistance of artillery which Knox had rushed up to Combs Hill overlooking his right flank, repulsed a charge of British dragoons. But Clinton and Cornwallis were now advancing as rapidly as their hot, bedraggled troops could move. As the British infantry, deploying, began to attack, Wayne's two regiments fell back. Though the record is not clear, Knox must have simultaneously withdrawn his guns from exposed Combs Hill.

Washington had been keeping an anxious eye upon this delaying action, even while organizing the position of the main army. Neither Greene nor Stirling was yet completely in position, and Washington knew that he was not yet ready to face a full-scale British attack. He sent two more regiments under Brigadier General James Varnum to join Wayne.

At this time, or possibly later, Washington ordered Wayne to leave Varnum in command of the covering force, and to return across the bridge over the ravine to organize a second delaying position. On high ground, overlooking the marshy stream, Wayne found a hedgerow, between and in front of Greene's and Stirling's still uncompleted formations. Behind this hedge Wayne deployed scattered units from his own Pennsylvania regiments, with some Virginia, Maryland and Delaware units mixed in.

As the pressure on Varnum became intolerable, Wayne ordered him to fall back across the bridge and into reserve. Clinton, discovering Wayne's new position beyond the bridge, now held up his advance briefly, while the remainder of Cornwallis' division swung up into line. Separated only by the width of the ravine, less than 100 yards, the two lines now engaged in an intensive musketry and artillery duel, the clamor swelling as new units arrived in position on opposite sides of the marshy ravine. Then, seeing that Stirling's troops were still not yet fully deployed, Clinton ordered simultaneous attacks against the American center and left flank.

Washington and von Steuben—who was helping the Commander-in-Chief direct the arriving units to their posts—could now see the results of the months of training at Valley Forge. The troops already in line, though greatly outnumbered at first, stood steady as they returned the British fire, and threw back one attack after another. Lee was in nominal command on the left, but appears to have issued no orders. Stirling, who seems to have ignored Lee's presence, calmly brought up his last units on his extreme left, and then swung them in to envelop the advancing British right flank. The redcoats, who had never before encountered such opposition in open battle against the Americans, fell back in dismay.

In the center, the story was the same. Two strong attacks were thrown back by Wayne's men, and then there was a lull as Clinton reinforced his center. When the British approached for the third time, Wayne galloped up and down behind the hedgerow, encouraging his men, and ordering them to hold their fire. "Steady! Steady!", he is reported to have cried. "Wait for the word, and then pick out the king birds!" Not a shot was fired until the enemy came within 40 yards. Then, at Wayne's command, a volley rang out which staggered the advancing British cavalry and infantry, driving them back once more in confusion.

But Clinton was still determined to gain the victory. The troops he had ordered from Knyphausen were now beginning to arrive on the field. Again reinforcing his center, and shifting most of Cornwallis' remaining units to attack Greene's right wing, he made one more massive effort.

It was now obvious to Wayne that Stirling's and Greene's troops were now completely deployed, and that he could move back from his dangerously exposed position overlooking the bridge. He ordered his men to withdraw about 50 yards, into the interval between Greene's and Stirling's divisions. Mistaking this slight rectification of the line for an American retreat, the tired British came charging through the swamp and across the bridge, cheering wildly. Once more they were halted by the steady, deliberate fire of the disciplined American Continentals. Then, as British officers were endeavoring to re-form for still one more effort, Wayne counterattacked. The exhausted redcoats were swept completely off the northern slope of the ravine, and back across the marsh.

It was now after 5:00 P.M. Clinton realized at last that he could not drive the Americans from their positions. Accordingly he broke off the fight, calling his men back to a strong position a few hundred yards from the American line, out of musket range.

The artillery on each side continued to fire, however. It was probably about this time that a cannoneer named Hays (or Hayes), serving one of the American cannon, was wounded. His wife—possibly without benefit of clergy—one Martha, or Molly Hays, had been providing the thirsty cannoneers with water, carrying a pitcher back and forth from the nearest brook. Now "Molly Pitcher," as she is known in American folklore, sprang to take her husband's place, encouraging the cannoneers as much by her bawdy good humor as by her assistance at the gun.

Washington meanwhile had tested the mettle of his army, and was satisfied that they were every bit as good as the British regulars. He decided to counterattack. But only two of his brigades had not been engaged, and even these had marched more than fifteen miles in 100° heat. The troops on both sides were simply incapable of further offensive effort.

So the artillery firing died down. The opposing outposts, only a musket shot apart, kept wary eyes on each other, as the sun set. Both armies bivouacked in their final battle positions. Washington issued orders for an assault after dawn the following morning, and saw to it that food and ammunition were brought up during the night. Despite their exhaustion, the Americans were convinced that they had been victorious; the British were depressed by their failure to drive the Continentals from the field.

Clinton and his men had discovered, to their alarm and dismay, that they were faced by regulars who had shown amazing steadiness despite early panic. At midnight the British soldiers quietly marched away from their bivouack, not even making an effort to bury their dead. The next morning Washington briefly considered pursuit, but seeing that Clinton was six hours ahead of him, he was certain that he would not be able to bring on a new battle. So the British made good their escape to Sandy Hook, and thence to New York by ship.

During this hard-fought Battle of Monmouth, the records show that the Americans suffered 360 casualties, of whom 40 were deaths from sunstroke. British returns list 358 men killed and wounded, 59 being sunstroke deaths. Other, apparently corroborating, reports show, however, that the Americans buried between 217 and 249 British dead. The losses on each side were probably about twice as heavy as admitted in official reports.

On the 29th Washington apparently had time to give some thought to the action he should take about General Lee's disgraceful behavior in the first phase of the battle. He had received reports from Wayne,

Scott and others, and he knew that if it had not been for Lee, the Battle of Monmouth would have been a clear-cut American victory. Washington was still considering the matter when, early the next day, he received a letter from Lee demanding "some reparation for the injury" done to him by Washington's manner and words when they had met near Freehold Meeting House about noon on the 28th. Lee found it incredible that Washington would use "such very singular expressions" as would imply that he "was guilty either of disobedience of orders, or want of conduct, or want of courage."

Washington replied coolly to this letter—which he considered to have been couched "in terms highly improper." He was "not conscious of having made use of any very singular expression at the time" of his meeting with Lee, he wrote, but added that as soon as circumstances would permit, that officer would have an opportunity to explain "to the army, to Congress, to America and to the world in general his reasons for not attacking . . . as [he] had been directed and in making an unnecessary, disorderly and shameful retreat."

Lee shot back a letter demanding permission to retire from the army. Then a few hours later he sent another, insisting that he be given a chance to clear himself at an immediate court of inquiry or court martial. Washington did not hesitate. He sent his adjutant general, Colonel Alexander Scammell, to place Lee under arrest, and to present him with charges for trial by court martial. The court, under the presidency of Lord Stirling, deliberated in every spare moment of time from July 4 until August 9. Lee was found guilty of all three charges: disobedience of Washington's orders to attack the enemy on the 28th of June; misbehavior before the enemy by making an unnecessary, disorderly and shameful retreat; and disrespect to the Commander-in-Chief in his letters of June 30.

He was sentenced to a year's suspension from command; a verdict approved by Congress. When, many months later, the strange major general wrote an insulting letter to Congress, that body summarily dismissed him from the United States Army.

On July 1, Washington submitted a report of the battle to Congress, including only a brief, critical comment on Lee's part in the early phase of the battle. He was particularly outspoken in his praise of Wayne's conduct during the entire engagement. Meanwhile, the army marched to the vicinity of Haverstraw, to review the blockade of New York.

22 ★ ★ ★ ★ ★

Newport and New York

FRANCE'S FIRST OVERT MOVE in the new alliance with the United States for the moment eclipsed British sea power on the American coast. Admiral Charles Henri Théodat, Comte d'Estaing, had missed by ten days Admiral Lord Howe's fleet departing from Philadelphia. But his very presence changed the situation. He came in through the Delaware Capes on July 8 with twelve great ships of the line and four fast frigates.

Washington, with the capture of New York ever uppermost in his mind, at once moved his army from Haverstraw across the Hudson and down into the White Plains area, while d'Estaing cruised north, arriving off Sandy Hook on the 15th. Both commanders hoped for a joint operation which would destroy Lord Howe's fleet and bag Clinton's army.

It was not to be. For eleven days, fretting d'Estaing hung off the Hook, unable to bring his deep-laden ships over the bar and inside the bight where Howe's fleet—nine of the line with 534 guns, to the Frenchman's twelve and 834 guns—lay snug and stolid.

Washington then proposed another use of this unexpected command of the sea: capture of Newport, Rhode Island, where the British had been sitting since 1776. D'Estaing, agreeing, sailed north, arriving off Point Judith July 29, while Washington hurriedly prepared for a land attack, which Sullivan, then in command at Providence, would make.

Washington sent Lafayette with two of his best brigades—Varnum's Rhode Islanders and Glover's Massachusetts men, including the stout

amphibious Marblehead regiment. Greene, having generously consented to serve under Sullivan—his junior as a major general—Washington also sent him to assist Sullivan as a second division commander. Some 6,000 New England militia under Major General John
Hancock, were also slowly gathering.

Newport Island, in the Providence River estuary, was washed on
the west by the Conanicut (or Middle) Passage; on the east by the
Seakonnet (or East) Passage. The British fortified position lay north
of Newport village and harbor itself, on the southwesterly tip of the
island. Brigadier General Richard Pigot—of Bunker Hill fame—had
3,000 men behind strong entrenchments stretching across the island
tip. In the Middle Passage lay four small British frigates and several
lesser craft.

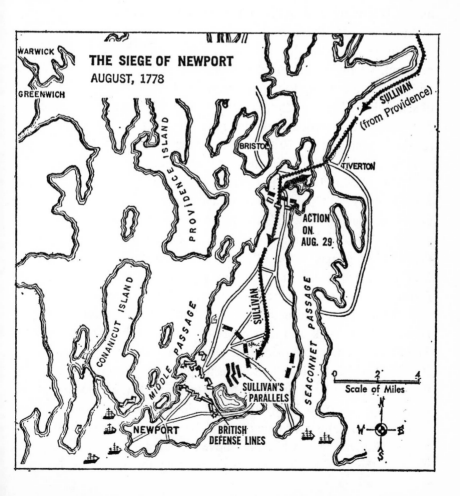

D'Estaing and Sullivan quickly agreed on a plan. The Frenchman, who had 4,000 troops with him, would land them on the west side of the island, while Sullivan made a simultaneous landing on the east, across the Seakonnet Passage—with Glover's Marblehead sailor-soldiers handling his landing craft.

A French reconnaissance—two ships of the line up the western channel and two frigates in the eastern one—on August 5, facilitated the task. The British warships, fleeing for Newport harbor, were run aground and destroyed by their own personnel. There would be no interference with the landings.

By August 8, Sullivan's Continentals were concentrated at Tiverton, on the mainland. Hancock's militia had not yet arrived, but they were coming in strength. Sullivan would soon have some 10,000 men in all. D'Estaing and Sullivan had already agreed on the next day —August 9—for the assault.

Then perverse, bull-headed Sullivan upset the applecart of military protocol. Changing his mind without consulting d'Estaing, he made an immediate crossing to the northern tip of the island, one day ahead of schedule. D'Estaing, though infuriated by this insult to his seniority, did put some troops ashore the next day, but almost immediately recalled them when a British fleet suddenly appeared in the offing.

Howe, at New York, having been reinforced by four ships of the line from Admiral John Byron's squadron, had put to sea to hunt his adversary. D'Estaing, with a favoring wind, now swept out to meet him, leaving Sullivan's troops on Newport Island uncomfortably exposed. The Englishman, declining to fight while his enemy held the weather gauge, stood off, and after two days of maneuvering, Mother Nature took a hand. A howling gale scattered both fleets, inflicting much damage. Three minor single-ship actions were inconclusive. Both admirals turned back their battered vessels for refitting— Howe to New York and d'Estaing—to Sullivan's horror—to Boston. The Frenchman, whose pride had been further injured by a derogatory statement which Sullivan had foolishly put in his general orders, now flatly refused to have anything more to do with the Newport affair, despite appeals from Lafayette and a clumsy apology from Sullivan.

Though in danger of being cut off by the arrival of British forces by sea, Sullivan meanwhile had moved in strength down the eastern-most of the two north-south roads running the length of Newport island, had come within range of the British outer defenses, and had begun siege operations. But d'Estaing's refusal to cooperate changed the situation. All but 1,000 of Hancock's disheartened New England militia decamped en masse. Sullivan—wisely as it turned out—threw up all hope for further offense with his 4,000 Continentals, and began withdrawal on August 28.

Overjoyed, Pigot at once advanced up both roads, with his main effort on the east, hoping to cut the Americans off from their landing point opposite Tiverton.

American rear guards clashed with both advances, and after being reinforced by Sullivan, threw them back. A full-scale action built up, piecemeal, as the British advanced in strength, while Sullivan halted his withdrawal, and stood. The British right was checked by Glover's brigade. After some heavy fighting the British advance was entirely halted, despite the flanking fire of three British sloops of war against the American right. Sullivan held his ground until nightfall, then succeeded in getting his entire command off to the mainland at Tiverton, thanks to the Marblehead regiment, who manned the boats. Sullivan then brought his Continentals back to Providence, where they would remain throughout the winter.

American losses in this fiasco were some 30 killed, 137 wounded and 44 missing. The British garrison lost 38 killed, 210 wounded and 12 missing.

Actually, Sullivan had narrowly escaped destruction, for a British squadron escorting 5,000 troops, with Clinton himself and Major General "No Flint" Grey, arrived at Newport from New York on September 1.

What with the disappointment of this failure, and natural resentment against d'Estaing's action, a nasty situation now affected the new Franco-American alliance. For a short time, Boston shipfitters quibbled on making the necessary repairs to the French ships, and d'Estaing's officers and men received a cold shoulder in the city. Washington, who rightly felt that Sullivan's stupidity had affronted the Frenchman, managed to calm matters down. The Congress tactfully resolved that d'Estaing had "behaved as a brave and wise officer." His ships refitted, d'Estaing betook himself and all his force to Martinique. But the memory rankled, particularly since General Grey now began a series of raids from Newport along the Massachusetts coast, burning a number of privateers and merchant vessels, and partly destroying the seaport towns of New Bedford and Fairhaven.

Meanwhile Washington, back in the area whence he had been driven two years previously, tightened the land blockade of New York, his forces lying to the north of a 40-mile wide belt of no-man's land between him and the British. The American positions safeguarded the Hudson Highlands and the vital communications between New England and the states further south. Putnam lay at West Point, which was being fortified; Gates and McDougall at Danbury, Connecticut. Between these points were de Kalb, at Fredericksburg (now Patterson, New York), and Stirling in the heights above Lake Mahopak.

The Continental army for the moment had reached a respectable strength—some 16,800-odd men fit for duty in midsummer. Washington was wary of any offensive move by Clinton. The British general, however, had no intention of advancing from New York, since he was still complying with his orders to avoid extensive action in the north, and was already preparing to send forces to the south. However, minor clashes were frequent in the belt separating the opposing forces. Not only was the area infested with both Tory and Patriot irregulars, but it was from time to time criss-crossed by patrols and raiding detachments of both armies. Three actions are worthy of note.

During the night of September 27-28, a force of British infantry under grim, efficient "No Flint" Grey repeated his Paoli exploit by surprising Colonel George Baylor's 3rd Continental Light Dragoons —"Lady Washington's Own"—in their outpost at Old Tappan, in Rockland County, New York. Covering a large foraging force of 5,000 troops under Cornwallis, Grey and his men fell on the surprisingly unalert Americans in a bayonet attack that killed some 40 men, and captured 50 more—mostly wounded, including Baylor himself. Only 37 of the dragoons escaped.

The second affray took place in New Jersey, in October. Four British sloops of war, with some smaller vessels, sailed into Little Egg Harbor, a favorite port of American privateers. Ten vessels were caught and destroyed, and the village burned.

But worse was to come. The naval attack was supported by Major Patrick Ferguson, a superb leader of partisan forces, with his Tory

3rd New Jersey Volunteers and a portion of the 70th Foot. Ferguson was informed by a deserter that Count Casimir Pulaski's Legion—three companies each of light infantry and dragoons, with artillery, lay some eight miles distant. This independent corps, then about 300 strong, was composed mainly of foreign officers and British deserters.

Ferguson, with 250 men in small boats, rowed during the night of October 14 up the coast to Mincock Island and in a surprise attack on Pulaski's light infantry bivouack bayoneted 50 men. Pulaski brought up his dragoons and drove Ferguson off, but the Britisher managed to get to his boats.

Both these incidents, of course, give proof that the Continentals still had much to learn on the subject of proper patrolling and alert picketing. Of different character was the third noteworthy clash, which occurred shortly.

Another British officer who was establishing a reputation as a leader of Tory troops was Lieutenant Colonel Banastre Tarleton, who had earlier taken part in the capture of General Charles Lee, in December, 1776. Tarleton had raised a mixed infantry-cavalry force of New York Tories, which was called the British Legion. Trained to standards comparable with British regulars, and particularly skilled in screening and reconnaissance operations, Tarleton's green-coated men were known for their ruthless bloodthirstiness.

Soon after Ferguson's massacre of Pulaski's men, Tarleton led a raid against Pound Ridge, northeast of White Plains. His mission was to surprise Colonel Elisha Sheldon, posted there with 90 men of the 2nd Continental Dragoons, and also to seize Major Ebenezer Lockwood—an ardent citizen patriot for whose arrest a British reward had been posted. But the Americans, warned by a spy, were alert and waiting. Tarleton's 360 men—mixed cavalry and mounted infantry—outnumbering Sheldon, forced him out of Pound Ridge, but Sheldon counterattacked, with the aid of local militia, and drove the raiders off.

British activities decreased with the coming of winter. In November, too, Clinton's forces were depleted by 5,000 men under General Grant, sent to take part in a combined army-navy expedition against French-held St. Lucia in the West Indies. Another 3,500 men were sent to Georgia, and a smaller contingent to Pensacola, in West Florida.

With the cold weather, Washington's army also went into winter quarters. The main army wintered again at Morristown; other cantonments were established at Middlebrook, also Elizabeth and Ramapo in New Jersey, at West Point and Fish Kill in New York and at Danbury, Connecticut. The army was better clad than it had been, for a quantity of uniforms had arrived from France. However, there never was sufficient to go around, and until they had built themselves log cabins, the lightly-clad Continentals suffered severely.

Thus rested both sides during the winter and early spring of 1778-79. With the coming of good weather the Hudson, Mohawk and Susquehanna valleys flared again.

★ 23 ★ ★ ★ ★ ★

Flaming Arrows

WHILE MAJOR OPERATIONS WERE TAKING PLACE along the coastal plain, an independent theater of guerrilla war embraced northwestern New York and northern Pennsylvania from the conclusion of Burgoyne's expedition until the close of the struggle. It was a war involving both whites and Indians on both sides; a war of neighbor against neighbor. But it also involved, during its height, the use of Continental troops in strength. Its conclusion marked the wreck of the most highly civilized Indian confederacy in North America—the Six Nations. Atrocities were the rule on both sides; malicious, frequently inhuman, brutality.

When Sir Frederick Haldiman succeeded Carleton as Governor General of Canada in 1778 he inherited the exiled Johnson and Butler clans with their two well-equipped and trained Tory outfits— John Johnson's two-battalion Royal Greens, and John Butler's Rangers —all burning to avenge themselves upon their erstwhile neighbors in the Mohawk Valley and to wipe out the stigma of St. Leger's defeat. He had, too, Joseph Brant (Thayendanegea), principal chieftain of the Iroquois, to rally the warriors of the Six Nations to England's cause and against the American settlers long trespassing upon their wide domain. Haldiman unleashed them, together with the bits and pieces of British and Hessian regulars still under his command.

The first target was the smiling Wyoming Valley of the upper Susquehanna (now Luzerne County, Pennsylvania)—particularly inviting because it had already been wracked and weakened by the internecine "Pennamite-Yankee War" of 1775, when rival settlers of Pennsylvania and Connecticut had beaten each others' brains out in a territorial dispute. Connecticut held principal control now, and a goodly proportion of Wyoming men were away in Continental service.

From Fort Niagara on Lake Ontario, in June, Colonel John Butler with 400 Greens, Rangers and Tory volunteers and 500 of Brant's Indians struck southeast through New York and entered the valley June 30.

The alarm of their first depredations brought out Colonel Zebulon Butler (no relation to the Tory Butlers), who had won the "Pennamite-Yankee War" for Connecticut. Patriot Butler had some 60 "regulars" so-called—authorized by the Congress for home defense—and between 200 and 300 militiamen. Boldly attacking the Tory force at Wintermoot on July 3, not far from Wilkes-Barre, the patriot amateurs were outflanked by the Indians, while the Tories met them frontally. In the resulting hand-to-hand melée the American force was butchered by tomahawk and knife. Only 60 men escaped. Of the others, most of those not killed on the field were captured and later tortured to death. Tory Butler, reporting his own losses as one Indian and two Rangers killed, with eight Indians wounded, gleefully added that 227 American scalps had been garnered.

Then, despite promises of Tory Butler, the Wyoming Valley was devastated. Wilkes-Barre itself was completely razed. In all, 1,000 houses as well as countless barns and mills went up in flames; cattle by the thousand were driven away. Murder, rapine and looting scourged a 20-mile strip. Most of the inhabitants were either captured by the Indians or left to die of exposure in the nearby mountains and the Pocono swampland.

Next to feel the scourge was the Mohawk Valley. Brant, with 300 Tories and 150 Indians, swept down on German Flats (now Herkimer) on September 12. They fired the town, drove off the cattle. The inhabitants, barricaded in General Herkimer's stone house, in another little blockhouse and in a stone church, resisted capture and the horde receded.

From Schoharie, in revenge, Lieutenant Colonel William Butler (no relation either to the Tories, or to Zebulon) with his 4th Pennsylvania Continentals, a detachment of Morgan's riflemen and some volunteer riflemen, moved west across the Catskills, to raze the Six Nation town of Unadilla. The Indian inhabitants had fled, but all their well-built homes, their grist- and saw-mill, their cattle and their crops, were destroyed.

The infuriated Indians and Tories struck back. In late October, Tory Captain Walter Butler, with 200 of his father's Rangers, made a 150-mile march from Chemung, near Elmira, up the Susquehanna to Otsego Lake. On the way he was joined by Brant with 500 Indians. The combined force approached Cherry Valley, a village 50 miles west of Albany.

Cherry Valley was a smiling community, whose inhabitants were protected—they thought—by Colonel Ichabod Alden and 250 men of his 7th Massachusetts Continentals. But Alden had had no experience in Indian fighting. Only part of his command was quartered in the stockade surrounding the meeting-house; the others, including Alden and most of his officers, were billeted in homes.

When rumors of impending attacks came in, the villagers clamored to move inside the fort. Alden refused to permit this, guaranteeing protection. Early in the morning of November 11, Tory Butler brought his men into town over an unguarded and unreconnoitered trail. The bloodthirsty attackers, dividing into several parties, jumped all quarters of the settlement at once. Alden was one of a score of soldiers butchered in the slaughter; 50 in all of the villagers were killed.

Butler was unable to take the stockade, where the remainder of the soldiers resisted, but he sacked the settlement, burning every structure and driving off all cattle. Then he left the smoking ruins, with some 70-odd prisoners, including 30 women and children. Hoping to secure the release of his own mother, detained in Albany when he and his father fled to Canada, Butler shortly released most of the women and children. Later General James Clinton would agree to this exchange.

It was summer in 1779 when this guerrilla war flamed again, south of the Mohawk Valley. Brant, who had brought a large body of Indians and Tories down into the Schwangunk Mountain area, between the present Port Jervis and Goshen, New York, rushed the hamlet of Minesink with a small force, burned it and made off with its inhabitants.

From Goshen, some 150 militiamen under Lieutenant Colonel Benjamin Tusten, went in pursuit. Near Port Jervis the Americans, now joined by a small group of militia under a Colonel John Hathorn, caught sight of Brant's force, tried to intercept it at a ford, and were in turn ambushed and trapped. Only 30 men of the American command escaped; the remainder were killed in action or later massacred.

So far as the patriot cause was concerned, the situation in northwestern New York had now become a running sore. Washington decided to take action. Gates having declined command of a punitive expedition into the Tory-Indian area, rambunctious John Sullivan was assigned. His instructions were to enter the country occupied by the Six Nations—from Lake Ontario to the Susquehanna and from the Catskills to Lake Erie—and effect "total destruction of their settlements and the capture of as many prisoners of every age and sex as possible" as hostages. The area was not to be "merely overrun but destroyed."

The objective, then, was the crushing of a race which had achieved a relatively high degree of civilization, as compared to the Plains Indians. They had established themselves in permanent settlements, substantially housed, had an organized system of constitutional government, and their economy was basically agricultural. They raised cattle, garnered crops of corn and other vegetables and cultivated well-kept apple, pear and peach orchards. It would appear, however, that no means other than brute force would be successful against these inveterate enemies of the United States.

Rendezvousing at Tioga with a force commanded by Brigadier General James Clinton, Sullivan was then to move north into the Indian country. Washington strained his meager manpower resources to allot Maxwell's, Poor's, and Hand's brigades to Sullivan. Added were Proctor's 4th Artillery with seven guns; a detachment of Morgan's riflemen, and an independent rifle company. This Continental division was joined by a corps of local militia. Its total strength was 2,300-odd rank and file.

Clinton's force—Continentals all—consisted of the 2nd, 3rd, 4th and 5th New York and a company of Lamb's 2nd Artillery with two small guns. Its strength was about 1,400 men. Sullivan concentrated at Easton, Pennsylvania; Clinton in the Mohawk Valley, near Canajoharie, in east central New York State.

On July 31 Sullivan's column left Easton, on the Delaware, marching northwest through the mountains towards the upper Susquehanna. Reaching Tioga in mid-August, Sullivan built a fort, where he was joined by Clinton, who had come southward down the Susquehanna from Lake Otsego. Sullivan and Clinton had both accumulated considerable quantities of heavy baggage and supplies, which caused a delay at Tioga. Washington, learning of this, was greatly annoyed, since he felt that Sullivan would lose the hoped-for advantage of surprise. In addition, he doubted that Sullivan, so encumbered, would be able to operate as the swift-moving punitive column originally envisaged. The Commander-in-Chief followed his usual practice, however, of not interfering with the arrangements of distant subordinates, and was finally relieved to learn that Sullivan's and Clinton's combined columns had started northwest from Tioga on August 26.

The first resistance was met on the 29th along the banks of the Chemung River, six miles southeast of the present Elmira; an artful ambuscade behind a stockade masked by green bushes. There lay Captain Walter Butler, with two battalions of the Rangers, a detachment of the 8th Foot, some 200 Tory irregulars and 500 Indians under Brant—approximately 1,200 men. The trap was discovered by Morgan's riflemen. Sullivan, attempting an envelopment of Butler's left, at first met with smart resistance. However, under cover of artillery fire, a thrust along the river against Butler's right was successful; all opposition gave way and the Tories and Indians fled. Casualties were small. The Americans lost three men killed and 39 wounded; Butler's troops left a dozen dead behind them, who were immediately scalped by the Americans. Two of the dead Indians were skinned to make boot legs for two New Jersey officers.

Sullivan now mowed a deep swathe into Indian territory; up through the Finger Lakes region as far as Canandaigua and Genesee, burning and destroying villages, cornfields, orchards, and anything of value his men could find. Then he returned, systematically smashing such Indian settlements and property as had been bypassed in the advance. In all, some 40 villages were razed, and an estimated 160,000 bushels of corn destroyed, together with a vast amount of other vegetables. All the Indian orchards were cut down or girdled.

Sullivan encountered very little opposition after the engagement on the Chemung, and suffered only one minor setback. On September 13 a scouting detachment of Morgan's rifles was ambushed near Genesee. Twenty-two men were killed. Lieutenant Thomas Boyd, commanding the detachment, was captured along with one of his sergeants. The two men were subjected to hideous tortures before they were finally killed.

For the most part, however, the Indians fled before the vengeful Americans. Thus, though Sullivan carried out his first mission—"total destruction and devastation"—he failed to capture any hostages. Furthermore, he had not seriously crippled the Indian combat capabilities, nor damaged their fighting spirit. On the contrary, he had kindled an even more virulent flame of revenge in the hearts of his enemies. The Tories and Indians, after retreating to Fort Niagara, would return to carry fire and sword, tomahawk and bayonet, into the American settlements. Sullivan's failure was due to his relatively unimaginative, rather ponderous movement through the Indian country, with no effort to maneuver, to encircle, or to ambush the wily foe.

The brutality attendant upon this raid was almost as barbarous as that of the enemy. However, Sullivan had shaken the Iroquois' belief both in their own and British invincibility, as well as British reliance on their red allies. Sullivan was congratulated by Washington upon his "success," and received the formal thanks of the Congress.

During this period a second, though smaller punitive expedition farther west, in the Allegheny River valley, also achieved success. Colonel Daniel Brodhead with the 8th Pennsylvania Continentals and an aggregation of militia and volunteers—perhaps 600 strong—moved out from Fort Pitt to burn several Indian towns and destroy crops, during an unopposed round-trip of 400 miles. Brodhead, too, received Congressional thanks.

Reprisals for Sullivan's raid began in April, 1780, the first being a Butler-led foray down the Mohawk Valley. From the Susquehanna Valley to the Hudson, and down into the Catskill foothills, Tory and Indian took bitter toll of the settlements. Sir John Johnson with his Royal Greens, Butler's Rangers and Indians, in May scoured Johnstown and the vicinity, burning and plundering every home not owned by a Tory.

In August, Brant and his Tory-Indian contingent spread murder and ruin through the Canajoharie settlements at Fort Plain, Fort Clyde and Fort Plank. In September Brant's painted warriors, together with Chief Cornplanter and his Senecas, united with Johnson to range through the upper Susquehanna and into the Mohawk area again. Several detachments of settlers and militia successfully defended themselves in stockaded forts, but their homes and possessions were lost.

Near Fort Plain the raiders, more than 1,000 strong, were opposed by General Robert van Rensselaer's militia and Oneida Indian allies, about 1,500 men in all. In a pitched battle, Brant's Indians were driven off, but the remainder of Johnson's force—Tories, Hessian jägers and British regulars—stood firm, and van Rensselaer's timidity prevented any decision. Johnson then retired safely to Oswego.

In 1781 Indian and Tory raids again devastated the Mohawk Valley, but as we shall see, their punch was slowing and militia and volunteers were more successful in opposing them.

24

★ ★ ★ ★ ★ ★

"I Have Not Yet Begun to Fight"

O N THE HIGH SEAS DURING 1778 AND 1779 great fleets—British, French and Spanish—struggled for a supremacy in seapower which would eventually decide the freedom of the United States. Compared to them, the efforts of the Continental Navy's dwindling handful of vessels, and the guerrilla operations of the American privateers, seem puny and insignificant. Great admirals would strut the stage—France's d'Estaing and d'Orvilliers and Britain's Howe, Keppel and Kempenfelt. Yet of all the naval names that come to mind during those two pregnant years, one flashes pre-eminent, like a meteor across history's waters: that of Scottish-born John Paul Jones, Captain, USN.

On November 2, 1777, the new US sloop of war *Ranger,* 18, left Portsmouth, New Hampshire, for France, bearing the news of Burgoyne's surrender at Saratoga. On her quarterdeck strode thirty-one-year-old Captain Jones, born John Paul in Kirkbean, Scotland, transplanted to Virginia in his youth. In his pocket was a letter from the Marine Committee of the Congress to Benjamin Franklin, authorizing the American Commissioner to purchase "one of those fine frigates that Mr. Deane writes us you can get," and to place it under Jones' command.

Making the mouth of the Loire November 30, the *Ranger* stood up river to Nantes two days later. Jones posted at once to Paris with the thrilling news of Saratoga. There he learned from Franklin that negotiations for ships from the French and Dutch had broken down. There would be no "fine frigate" for John Paul Jones. The promised ship, *Indien,* Dutch-built, was held by the Netherlands government—afraid to court English hostility. He must make do with the ship he brought over: must "proceed with her in the manner you shall judge best, for distressing the enemies of the United States, by sea or otherwise. . . ."

The news of Gates' victory did not ease Dutch fears of English retaliation, but it did tip the scales in Franklin's diplomatic negotiations with France (in which he was assisted by Deane and Arthur Lee). On February 6, a treaty of commerce and alliance was signed. Six days later Jones and his *Ranger,* sailing for Quiberon Bay, received French Admiral La Motte Picquet's salute to the new flag. They received another from Admiral Comte Louis G. d'Orvilliers at Brest March 23. On April 12 Jones stood out on the first leg of a history-making cruise, bound, as all on board knew, for the Irish Sea.

The *Ranger,* though new, was not a fast sailer. Worse yet, her crew was discontented and Jones' officers, New Englanders all, shared the general Yankee distrust for anyone hailing from Virginia. None of them, it seemed, shared his patriotism; the major preoccupation of most was with prize-money, and a cruise in British waters involved too much risk to suit them. Despite the fact that Jones had provided their first pay installments out of his own pocket, his insistence on discipline and a taut ship were galling to men who had been privateersmen.

After a severe storm, Jones captured and sank a British merchant ship in the English Channel, in sight of the coast of southwestern England. He then sailed into the Irish Sea.

Off Dublin, Jones took a valuable merchant ship and sent her in to Brest as a prize. On April 17, he ran east and attempted to make a raid on Whitehaven, England, where a large number of English merchantmen had taken shelter. Bad weather foiled that attempt, and also prevented him from entering Lochryan harbor, in southwestern Scotland. Crossing over to Carrickfergus Bay on the east Irish coast, and learning of the presence of HM sloop *Drake,* 20, Jones attempted to cut her out in a boarding operation from the decks of the *Ranger.* The plan was foiled due to the fumbling of a drunken quartermaster, who failed to drop anchor at the right moment. Jones sailed out of

AREA OF OPERATIONS
OF JOHN PAUL JONES
1778-1779

the harbor and into a gale which drove him to take shelter off the Scottish coast, an area known to him since childhood.

On the night of April 22, with the weather clearing, Jones returned to Whitehaven, brought his ship into the harbor and sent two armed boat's crews ashore. One party he led himself; the other was in charge of Lieutenant Wallingford. Jones' plan was to storm the two small stone forts on the horns of the crescent-shaped harbor, and burn the shipping inside. Both fortifications were easily taken by Jones and his party, and the guns spiked. He then turned to fire the vessels in the south basin. Whether because they had no stomach for the task, or through treachery, Wallingford's party allowed their port-fires to burn out. Someone in Jones' party was equally negligent. Dawn was breaking. Both detachments milled about until Jones procured fire from a nearby house and set one ship aflame. By this time angry townsfolk had gathered. Jones, pistol in hand, stood them off until the blaze had caught and then—releasing his prisoners, for the boats would not contain them—the indomitable captain got both boats safely away.

Jones next sailed the *Ranger* back to the Scottish shore. He landed with a boat's crew at St. Mary's Isle in Kirkudbright Bay, and attempted to kidnap the Earl of Selkirk from his ancestral home. The Earl was not at home, but his family plate was. The *Ranger's* party seized it and made off with it in lieu of prize-money. (Jones later ransomed the plate for £650 sterling, and returned it to its owner.)

While the actual damage done in this raid was small, the psychological effect was enormous. The west coast of England flamed with apprehension as gallopers spread the news. The militia was called out. Rumors of American depredations—unfounded, all of them—mushroomed. "John Paul Jones, the Pirate," became a national bugaboo almost overnight. More to the point, maritime insurance rates between England and Ireland leaped sky-high—from 1¼ to 5 percent.

Jones, knowing full well that British squadrons would soon be combing the Irish Sea for him, meanwhile had run westerly again, to Belfast Lough, still intent on capturing the *Drake*. Despite murmuring and near-mutiny—his crew wanted no more dallying in the lion's mouth—he held his course. The *Drake* came out to meet him. Shortening sail, in a masterly display of seamanship, Jones allowed the Englishman to approach, then put up his helm, crossed his enemy's bow and raked her again and again. In an hour and four minutes from the first shot, the *Drake* was partly dismasted, 42 of her complement of 175 killed or seriously wounded, including her captain and first lieutenant. She struck her flag in surrender. The *Ranger's* losses were two killed and six wounded.

Instead of sinking his battered prize and making a getaway, Jones took her in tow, then deliberately hove to, repaired her injuries, and sailed out of the North Channel. Jones had hoped to do more damage in the English Channel, but Lieutenant Robert Simpson, commanding the prize, was deliberately disobedient and sailed for France. Jones did not catch him until nearly in sight of the French coast. Putting Simpson in irons, Jones then decided to take both vessels into Brest, where he received a warm welcome on May 8. The French minister of marine suggested that Jones should remain in France to head a larger naval expedition. Jones then sent the *Ranger* back to the United States, while he sought Franklin's assistance in obtaining the larger command promised him.

Meanwhile war between England and France shaped up, despite Lord North's proposition of conciliation to the Colonies, brought vainly to America by the Carlisle Commission.* On March 13 France formally announced to England her treaty of alliance with the United States. On April 15, d'Estaing's fleet cleared Toulon for the Delaware Capes and on June 27, d'Orvilliers' 30 ships of the line, out of Brest, met Admiral Augustus Keppel's equal number in the great although inconclusive fleet Battle of Ushant off the Brittany coast.

In this struggle between the maritime giants John Paul Jones' efforts to get a new command were smothered. Not even the wily Franklin could extort a warship from France. Then, in December, informed that an elderly East Indiaman, the *Duras,* was on sale at Lorient, Jones persuaded the French Ministry of Marine to turn her over to him. Actually the ministry officials also offered him several other ships and a corps of 500 men from an Irish regiment as marines. The catch was that no French seamen could be recruited; all were needed for France's own effort. Jones, unable to man such a squadron, reluctantly declined the offer and busied himself with preparing the decrepit *Duras*—rechristened USS *Bon Homme Richard* in honor of Franklin —for sea.

---

* See p. 277.

All this while Jones had been hampered and harassed by the American Commissioners' lack of funds to pay off his own *Ranger* crew, to get them their prize money and to refit her for return to the United States. He had received no pay himself and made himself responsible for all these other expenses.

By June, 1779, Jones' unceasing effort had transformed his new command into a warship—albeit a makeshift, with a haphazard battery of ancient cannon. On her gun deck the *Richard* carried 28 12-pounders, with six or eight 9-pounders on forecastle and quarterdeck above. In the 'tween-decks below, six 18-pounders were mounted, their portholes cut so low that they were unusable except in the calmest weather.

Makeshift, too, was the frigate's crew of 380 officers and men; only 79 of them were Americans—mostly exchanged prisoners of war. The remainder, except for 137 French soldiers acting as marines, were Breton peasants and British seamen released from French jails at St. Malo and Brest—not a savory aggregation.

Through the exertions of Franklin and of an enterprising Frenchman—Jacques D. le Ray de Chaumont—three other French vessels were assigned to Jones' command: *Pallas,* 32, *Cerf,* 18, and *Vengeance,* 12. These ships were really privateers in de Chaumont's pay, although their captains carried American naval commissions.

Finally, the spanking new American frigate *Alliance,* 36, which had brought Lafayette back on a trip to France, was turned over to Jones by Franklin. She was by far the best ship in the little squadron, except for one fact: her captain, Pierre Landais, was one of Silas Deane's many "bad bargains." Landais, a cashiered French naval officer, was one of these adventurers flocking over to the United States in 1777. He had been at once commissioned a captain in the US Navy, and appointed to command of the *Alliance.* Insubordinate and treacherous, he was to be a thorn in Jones' side from the beginning to the end of the cruise.

On June 19, 1779, Jones led his squadron out of Lorient on what might be considered a shakedown cruise, convoying French merchantmen to Bordeaux. He returned after a vexatious series of minor mishaps. Landais had succeeded in fouling the *Richard* in collision with the *Alliance;* an incipient mutiny by his English seamen had been quelled with iron hand, and two chances to capture British ships in the Bay of Biscay were lost because of the *Richard's* dull sailing qualities.

Off again on August 14, Jones sailed up the Irish coast, planning to circumnavigate the British Isles, harrying coastal towns on the way. His principal objective was the annual Baltic convoy, due to approach the east coast of England. A plan to raid Leith and extort a ransom of £200,000 sterling fell through when his subordinate captains delayed so long that a heavy gale drove them all out of the Firth of Forth. Still, a few prizes were captured, and all England was in ferment. Most coastwise shipping fled for shelter, and revenue cutters were watching the movements of the bold Americans. For the moment, the Admiralty was unable to concentrate heavy ships against the raiders, for Spain had declared war on June 21, and a proposed joint Franco-Spanish operation against England was occupying the attention of the Royal Navy.

Jones, too, was having his problems. Landais was playing fast and loose with his *Alliance* in the most insubordinate manner. In fact, the only other vessel of his command loyally remaining in company with Jones was the *Pallas,* under Captain Denis Nicholas Cottineau.

However, September 23 found the squadron momentarily concentrated. *Richard, Alliance, Vengeance,* and *Pallas* were off Flamborough Head, chivvying a brigantine and a ship that fled for the shore. Then a fleet of 41 sail hove in sight: the Baltic convoy. Energetic Jones made signal for a general chase and crowded on all sail. The English convoy turned for the shore and the protection of Scarborough Castle, while its two convoying warships—HMS *Serapis,* 44, Captain Richard Pearson; and HMS *Countess of Scarborough,* 20, Captain Thomas Piercy, screened the flank.

Already warned by signals from the shore of the presence of the American squadron, Captain Pearson was eager to close. By half past five in the afternoon, the *Serapis* and the *Countess of Scarborough* had joined and tacked shoreward on westerly courses. Jones' squadron came up on their left, the *Alliance* leading. Behind were the *Richard, Pallas,* and *Vengeance.* But Landais, who was out of position anyway, thought better of it when he came within range of the English ships. Shortening sail, he fell out of line.

It was dusk when the *Richard* ranged alongside the *Serapis* and firing commenced. The *Alliance,* after a brief cannonade against the

Countess, sheered off and left her to the *Pallas;* the *Vengeance* remained far to windward, out of the fight. So the encounter boiled down to two separate ship-to-ship combats. On the very first broadside, two of the *Richard's* three starboard 18-pounders—condemned French guns—blew up, killing or wounding their crews and ripping out the ship's side and part of her main deck; a shocking and demoralizing debut.

Pearson, ably maneuvering his faster vessel, slowed down—backing his topsail to kill the ship's way—and pounded on the *Richard's* quarter. Jones attempted to check his own way. The Englishmen filled his topsails again and neatly forged ahead to rake the American ship. But Jones, who had the wind, turned sharp to starboard, hoping to close and board. Pearson backed again to avoid collision but didn't quite make it. The *Serapis'* bowsprit entangled the *Richard's* mizzen rigging and the two ships slowly swung together, head to stern. At Jones' command lashings held them fast. Meanwhile the fast-firing British 18-pounders were making a shambles of the *Richard's* gun-deck, silencing the American's main battery on that side.

Pearson, hoping to shake free, dropped his anchor, but was unsuccessful; the ships—two gladiators pinned together—simply swung into the southerly wind and tide. At this moment, the *Alliance* hove in through the smoke of battle, close inboard of the *Richard,* and Landais deliberately poured grape and cross-bar fire into his own commodore's ship, raking her stern, broadside and bow before he stood away.

All this had taken up an hour of combat. The *Richard's* gutted gun-deck was an open alley of smouldering, bloody debris. She was filling fast, and to make matters worse, her master-at-arms had released some 150 prisoners who scrambled top-side. So close were the ships that the English gun-crews were reaching with their rammers into their adversary's side to load their guns. The only American guns still firing were three 9-pounders on the *Richard's* quarterdeck, under Jones' personal command; two throwing grape and canister to clear the *Serapis'* deck, the third pounding deliberately at the base of her mainmast.

Significantly, however, up in the tops and on both poop and forecastle American sailors and French marines were pouring musketry on the *Serapis'* decks. The Franco-American topmen not only cleared the English tops, but ran across the close-linked spars to throw hand grenades down below.

What happened next can best be told in Pearson's own language later before a court-martial.

"Long before the close of the action it became clearly apparent that the American ship was dominated by a commanding will of the most un-alterable resolution, and there could be no doubt that the intention of her commander was, if he could not conquer, to sink alongside. . . ."

It was this will that turned the unruly, liberated prisoners to tamely manning the pumps; that kept marines and sailors at their stations, and that, finally, when a panicky petty-officer called for quarter and Pearson hailed to know if Jones had stuck, brought the answer: "I have not yet begun to fight!"

It was now about 9:45, in bright moonlight. Once more the *Alliance* came cruising in to rake the *Richard;* three smashing deliberate broad-sides, delivered despite hails, recognition signals, or heed of the yel-low topsides of the *Serapis* so clearly shown against the *Richard's* black.

And still the fight went on. The pounding of the persistent 9-pounder of the *Richard's* quarter-deck finally brought the *Serapis'* mainmast smashing down, to strew rigging and wreckage across the bloody deck. Then a hand grenade, dropped by a *Richard* topman, from the *Serapis'* own maintop, rebounded through a hatchway to the gun deck below, exploded and touched off the powder charges lying by the guns. Twenty British bluejackets died in the searing flame; 30 others were badly wounded. That, it seems, was the *coup de grâce.* Pearson struck his colors after Jones and his men repelled an attempt to board the American ship.

The *Pallas,* meanwhile, had won her own fight with the *Countess of Scarborough.* Cottineau handily brought his ship alongside the *Countess* and his well-served superior armament—30 guns against 20—did the rest. After a spirited fight of slightly more than an hour the British ship, with seven of her guns dismounted and 24 men killed or wounded, struck her colors.

Casualties in this famous three and one-half hours' duel can only be estimated; there are no accurate figures. By Jones' own report he lost 150 killed and wounded out of 380. Pearson's estimate, with a crew of similar size, is 49 killed and 68 wounded. The *Richard*, too far gone for salvage, sank 36 hours later, after her survivors had been transferred to the *Serapis*.

Jones, having patched up the *Serapis'* injuries and rigged a jury mast to replace the shot-down mainmast, gathered up his squadron. Cottineau in the *Pallas* was the only faithful consort. After his own successful fight, Cottineau came to Jones' help, assisting in transfer of prisoners and crew from the sinking *Richard*. The *Alliance* and the *Vengeance* merely tagged along; neither had made any attempt to raid the Baltic convoy after its watchdogs had been put out of action.

Bad weather necessitated putting in at the Texel—reached October 3—under Dutch neutrality, while British warships scoured the seas around the British Isles, fruitlessly investigating the flood of rumors which put the American raiders everywhere at once. British protests showered down upon the Netherlands, insisting that the Dutch surrender Jones as a pirate and criminal of state. While the Dutch temporized, the French government took over both the *Serapis* and *Countess of Scarborough* as their own prizes. Jones meanwhile preferred charges against Landais, and relieved him of command. Jones was also successful in obtaining the exchange of some 100 American prisoners of war.

It was December 27 when Jones, in the refitted *Alliance*, slipped his cable and stood out from the Texel in a gale, outwitting the British blockading ships still intent on bagging him.

Sailing through the English Channel "in full view of the enemy's fleet at Spithead," Jones ran south to Corunna, taking a prize on the way. A tumultuous welcome greeted the now famous commodore in the Spanish port. He put to sea January 28, 1780 and on February 10 ended his cruise at Groix.

It is hard to overestimate the effect of John Paul Jones' exploits. Certainly at the time they did much to undermine the English nation's respect for the Royal Navy, always the guardian of the waters around the "tight little island." They contributed to the entrance of both France and Spain into active war with England, and Jones' stay in the Texel despite British protests went far to precipitate England's later declaration of war against the Netherlands.

So far as the rest of Europe was concerned, not since Francis Drake had "singed the beard of the King of Spain" by his raid on the Spanish fleet in Cadiz harbor, in 1587, had anything comparable to Jones' cruises occurred.

It was the irony of fate that Jones remained in France to clear up the chicanery which deprived his men of prize money, while the *Alliance* sailed for home with Landais, by trickery, restored to command. Landais, however, was later court-martialled and dismissed from the service. Jones, arriving home in the *Ariel,* on February 18, 1781, was put in command of our one and only ship of the line, USS *America,* then building. But Congress then gave the *America* to France, as a gesture of gratitude, and John Paul Jones passed out of the Revolutionary War picture except as the prototype, and ideal forever, of the American naval combat leader.

It was well that John Paul Jones had carried the flag into English waters during those years of 1778 and 1779, for along the home coast the American navy was slowly withering.

Captain John P. Rathborne had a modicum of success in another operation against New Providence in the West Indies in 1779. Commanding the sloop *Providence,* 12, he raided the island during January, spiking the guns of Forts Nassau and Montague. He captured one ship and recaptured several vessels taken by the British.

But this was followed by disaster in February when Captain Nicholas Biddle in the frigate *Randolph,* 32, left Charleston on February 12 with a squadron of three smaller vessels of the North Carolina navy. On March 7 they fell in with HMS *Yarmouth,* 64, off the eastern coast of Barbados. Despite the disparity in armament, Biddle boldly engaged the big Britisher. His accurate gunnery brought down the *Yarmouth's* bowsprit and topmasts, but in the midst of the combat the *Randolph* unaccountably blew up with the loss of all but four of her crew of 315. The remainder of the squadron fled.

Several ships attempted to run the British blockade with indifferent fortune. There was, for instance, the *Raleigh,* 32, under Captain John Barry, which left Boston September 25, in company with the brigantine *Resistance.* They ran into HMS *Experiment,* 50, and the sloop *Unicorn,* 22. After a long stern chase, the *Raleigh* had to be run ashore in Penobscot Bay. Barry and part of his crew escaped, but the remainder were captured and the *Raleigh* was later recovered and put into British service. Slowly the American armed ships—both regular navy and privateer—fell victim to the enemy.

But the worst disaster would come next year, not too far from where the *Raleigh* met her fate.

The outbreak of war with France brought home to the Royal Navy the shocking fact that a penurious Admiralty policy had sapped its strength. Particularly was this true insofar as masts were concerned. Normal Admiralty practice had been to keep a three-year supply of mast timber soaking in navy yard mast-ponds. But the supply had been allowed to run low.

Most of the Royal Navy's masts came from the white pine forests of Maine, where the government's "broad arrow" restricted the best timber for navy use.

The outbreak of the Revolution had disrupted this traffic. Not only were the American woodsmen disaffected, but the so-called "mast ships," especially designed to carry the tall timbers, were being captured by Continental Navy ships and privateersmen.

So serious was the situation that during the spring of 1779 General Clinton was ordered to take steps to protect both the source and the flow of timber. Accordingly, in June, an expedition from Halifax, under Brigadier General Francis MacLean, occupied the peninsula in Penobscot Bay where Castine lies. There a fort was erected and a Tory colony established.

Equally aware of the importance of masts to the Royal Navy, Massachusetts and the Continental Congress undertook a joint expedition to attack the new British stronghold. The troops—Massachusetts militia under command of Brigadier General Solomon Lovell—numbered less than 1,000 men, including an artillery unit under Colonel Paul Revere. The naval contingent, commanded by Commodore Dudley Saltonstall, consisted of three Continental Navy vessels—the new frigate *Warren,* 32, and two sloops; three Massachusetts armed ships, one from New Hampshire, and twelve privateers—mounting in all not more than 300 guns.

Under Saltonstall's overall command, this motley fleet, convoying 20 transports, left Boston July 21, and arrived in Penobscot Bay on the 24th. On paper, it was a most ambitious expeditionary force; actually it turned out to be a debating society, with Saltonstall presiding over daily councils of war which included not only his naval officers and the ground force commanders but also each of the privateer skippers.

MacLean, in his still incomplete Fort George, mounting probably not more than a dozen artillery pieces, had a garrison of 600 men—portions of the 74th and 82nd Foot. In the bay were three small British naval craft, under Captain Henry Mowat, RN, mounting between them some 30 guns.

Immediate and forceful American action would have resulted in prompt victory. In fact, MacLean was almost prepared to concede defeat. Instead, timid Saltonstall frittered away the time in his endless councils of war, and less than half-hearted support of piecemeal troop landings. Meanwhile the defenses of the fort were growing stronger each day, and down in New York, British Admiral Sir George Collier was hurriedly preparing a relief expedition.

Forty-seven days of skirmishing and bickerings before the strengthened ramparts ended on August 14, when Collier in HMS *Asia*, 64, with five frigates and a sloop of war behind him, came swooping into Penobscot Bay.

Scuttling back across the beaches next day like the inhabitants of a disturbed anthill, the American militia fled to their transports. Saltonstall—for once in a lather of activity—led his entire fleet up the Penobscot River in abject flight. There all his vessels were destroyed in turn—some by British naval fire, others at the hands of their own crews. Survivors of the troops and the crews, ashore in the wilderness, made their way slowly back to the settlements. The greatest fiasco of the Revolutionary War had ended. For the moment the Royal Navy's supply source for masts was safe. No accurate returns are available, but approximately 500 Americans were lost in the campaign. British casualties in the garrison were negligible.

Back in Boston, Saltonstall was later court-martialed and dismissed from the Continental Navy. Paul Revere, convicted of negligence by one court-martial, was later cleared by a second court.

While there is no space in this book for detailed accounts of the Anglo-French-Spanish encounters which now became a concomitant part of the American Revolutionary War, these must at least be mentioned, as an element of the new global conflict.

During September and October, 1778, after the abortive operation against Newport, d'Estaing and Admiral Lord Howe continued their cautious and inconclusive maneuvering. When the Frenchman finally left the Narragansett area for the West Indies he redeemed his shaken reputation by some tough fighting. He captured St. Vincent on June 16, 1779, and Grenada on July 4. Two days later he clashed with Admiral John Byron off Georgetown, Grenada. It was an indecisive struggle; four of Byron's ships were dismasted, but d'Estaing broke off the action and sailed for Savannah, with results we shall soon note. Then he returned somewhat ingloriously to France.

During the summer of 1779 Franco-Spanish plans for an invasion of England again were thwarted—mainly through the allies' own inability to make a concerted movement. A combined fleet, under d'Orvilliers' command, rendezvoused in the Bay of Biscay—60 ships of the line. The joint expedition sailed into the Channel. Against them, under Admirals Sir Charles Hardy and Richard Kempenfelt, a British fleet of 35 ships of the line maneuvered without major clash until heavy weather drove off the allied armada and the threat abated.

In the Mediterranean, meanwhile, England was involved in another phase of the war. In August, 1779, while Jones was circumnavigating Great Britain, Spain's might closed in on the British garrison of Gibraltar. This was the opening of a three-year siege which would tax the resources of both the British Army and—above all—of the Royal Navy, whose mission it was to supply and support British General Sir George Augustus Elliot's beleaguered garrison.

All these events, it must be remembered, were to England very real and important aspects of her major problem—the subjugation of the thirteen rebellious colonies. It had become a very complicated picture from London's viewpoint, with vital European and oceanic overtones that frequently obscured momentarily the delineation of the principal land campaigns on American soil.

★ 25 ★ ★ ★ ★ ★

Westward Ho!

BEYOND THE APPALACHIANS, in 1778, the seeds of Western empire were sown by a man of destiny: George Rogers Clark, originally of Charlottesville, Virginia. Hot-blooded Clark—tall, red-headed and as ruthless as he was brilliant—was a land-surveyor, like Washington before him. He had come out to Kentucky in 1771, and had found time to gain title to large tracts of land, as well as to take part as a captain in Lord Dunmore's War against the Shawnees in 1774. Not yet twenty-five when the Revolution began, he had already won himself a reputation on the frontier as an Indian-fighter and a leader of hard men in a hard country.

For the first two and a half years of the war, the American settlements in the Ohio Valley had suffered terribly from Indian depredations instigated and directed from Detroit by British Lieutenant Colonel Henry Hamilton, lieutenant governor of Quebec. Hamilton, nicknamed "Hair-Buyer" because he paid hard cash for American scalps, incited the redskins—the Shawnees in particular—to systematic barbarity. Despite his relative youth, Clark became one of the principal American frontier leaders in this struggle for the "Dark and Bloody Ground."

Clark believed that the Achilles heel of British control of the northwest lay in three former French settlements in Illinois: Vincennes on the Wabash, and Cahokia and Kaskaskia on the Mississippi (Cahokia lay a few miles south of, and across from, Spanish-held St. Louis and Kaskaskia was opposite New Madrid). The support of the French *habitants* could be enlisted against the British, Clark believed, and from this Illinois base an offensive against Detroit could then be mounted.

Clark was elected by his fellow Kentuckians to go back to Williamsburg as their representative in order to secure support and military assistance from the Virginia government—which claimed all the Northwest territory. In late 1777 he laid his plan before Governor Patrick Henry and the Virginia legislature. They approved. Kentucky was established as a county of Virginia, and thus a responsibility of the state. Patrick Henry commissioned Clark a lieutenant colonel in the Virginia militia, authorized him to recruit 350 men for his expedition, provided more than $6,000 for ammunition and supplies, and bade him Godspeed.

Early in 1778 Clark returned by way of Fort Pitt, where in April and May he recruited 150 men—mostly tough Indian fighters—for his expedition. Here he also saw enough to confirm his strategic concept of operations in Illinois. In February, Brigadier General Edward Hand had led a small expedition toward Sandusky, but had been forced to turn back because of a thaw and resultant floods. Brigadier General Lauchlin MacIntosh, Hand's replacement, was already planning another, larger expedition from Fort Pitt toward Detroit, but Clark seems to have been doubtful of its prospects. (In fact McIntosh was forced to abandon his expedition, shortly after getting started, because of the defection of his militia contingent, and shortage of food.)

Clark, meanwhile, had embarked his own small command on four boats on the Monongahela, and then went down the Ohio River to Corn Island, at the Falls of the Ohio (modern Louisville). Here, in late May, he established a base. He then divulged to his men his plan for an expedition to Illinois. A few timorous souls deserted, but they were replaced by local frontier recruits, bringing his total strength up to 175.

On June 26 Clark's party started down the Ohio; turning into the Tennessee, they hid their boats at a ruined French fort ten miles from the river junction. A 120-mile hike through the wilderness to Kaskaskia followed. The experienced woodsmen, traveling light and fast, approached the settlement and its stone fort during the night of July 4-5 and captured it in complete surprise; not a shot was fired.

The townsfolk, at first apprehensive, became enthusiastic when they learned that France had joined America in the war against England. The half-starved invaders, who had eaten only wild berries for the last two days, were dined and feted. Although the official representative of British government, Philippe François de Rastel, Chevalier de Rocheblave (a former French officer), was recalcitrant and had to be sent back to Virginia as a prisoner, the hundred-odd other citizens of Kaskaskia took an oath of allegiance to the United States and the French militiamen became a part of Clark's command. On borrowed horses, Clark sent a detachment sixty miles across country to Cahokia, where they received an enthusiastic welcome.

At Kaskaskia the local priest, Father Pierre Gibault, became a close friend of Clark's, and volunteered to win over the people of Vincennes, which was in his far-flung parish. He was as good as his word, and returned to report that there were no English in Vincennes. In August Clark was able to send Captain Leonard Helm with a few men to take over command of the Vincennes French militia and to garrison its Fort Sackville.

Clark had attained his initial objective, but, as he soon discerned, he was far from his goal of conquest. His funds from Virginia had been expended by this time and only through the assistance and charity of Father Gibault did the expedition subsist, until Clark could establish relations with Oliver Pollock, a patriotic American merchant in New Orleans. Pollock went into debt to send supplies up the Mississippi; Clark in turn pledged his own modest fortune and vast land holdings to assist Pollock in getting credit from other New Orleans merchants.

Meanwhile, on October 7, British Colonel Hamilton started from Detroit to recapture Vincennes. Moving by canoe and overland, Hamilton, with 175 British troops and nearly 300 Indians, appeared before Vincennes on December 17. The French militia refused to fight and Helm, with his one American soldier, surrendered Fort Sackville.

Hamilton, deciding that an advance against Kaskaskia was impracticable until the next spring, sent a large detachment north to bring down supplies and settled down in winter quarters in Vincennes with his 80-odd remaining British soldiers. His Indian allies scattered to their villages, promising to return in the spring.

At Kaskaskia, Clark's force had dwindled. Many of his independent-minded woodsmen had returned to their Kentucky homes. Whether or not he could later assemble a force strong enough to resist Hamilton was uncertain. Having learned of the Englishman's present strength at Vincennes, Clark dared all; he would recapture Vincennes, now. As he wrote to Governor Patrick Henry:

"The enemy . . . could not suppose we should be so mad as to attempt to march eighty leagues through a drowned country in the depth of winter . . ."

So, on February 6, Clark, with 127 men—fifty Frenchmen had been recruited—started an amazing 180-mile march on Vincennes. His cousin, Lieutenant John Rogers, in the gunboat *Willing,* improvised from a river flatboat, had left the previous day. Turning up the Ohio and then the Wabash, he would rendezvous with the expedition near Vincennes and assist in crossing the Wabash.

Clark and his men splashed through the lowland regions where alternating thaws and freezing weather slowed progress and chilled men's bones. By the 13th they reached the Little Wabash, its basin now a five-mile stretch of water, dotted by the swaying tops of inundated timber.

They ferried that obstacle—a two-day task—on improvised rafts. They continued on through the flooded countryside, wading through water that was frequently breast-high. After crossing the swollen Embarrass River, finally on the 20th they reached the Wabash, and the rendezvous where they were to meet the *Willing,* some nine miles below Vincennes. There was no sign of Rogers and his gunboat. In fact, there never would be for—as Clark later learned—the party had been ambushed by Indians and every man killed.

Though his men were close to collapse from exhaustion, exposure and starvation, Clark knew that the only hope of survival was to press on to Vincennes. They ferried the river, then plodded wearily northward, the indomitable Clark by turns cajoling, coaxing and coercing. To combat hunger pangs they were all gnawing on elm bark.

During the afternoon of February 23, the pitiful little band arrived within sight of Vincennes. Clark did not want either the British or the French inhabitants to catch a clear sight of his scanty force of bedraggled, stumbling men. They dispersed in the edge of the woods opposite the town and waited till dusk. Then, at Clark's command, they flung themselves into the town in several groups, "with colors flying and drums brassed," as Clark described it. The colors were some twenty flags stitched for them by the women of Kaskaskia, and used by Clark to give a misleading impression of his strength.

The surprise was complete; Fort Sackville was surrounded before Hamilton knew what had happened. Revived by the luxury of a full meal provided by the rejoicing citizens of Vincennes, they entrenched within thirty yards of the fort, too close for the garrison's cannon to bear on them.

Desultory firing punctuated that night. In the morning Clark's demand for unconditional surrender was curtly refused by Hamilton. Throughout the day the sharpshooting American riflemen peppered the portholes and embrasures of the fort, silencing the garrison's fire. Hamilton then asked for a parley, trying to obtain lenient terms.

Clark refused, and to show that he meant business, several of Hamilton's scalp-hunting Shawnee Indians, captured as they returned from a scout, were cold-bloodedly tomahawked within sight of the fort walls, on Clark's order. After thinking about that, Hamilton surrendered next day. Clark then sent a detachment up the Wabash, which successfully ambushed the returning British supply train, capturing 40 men and all of the supplies which Hamilton had expected to use in his campaign against Kaskaskia.

Planning to go on to Detroit, Clark sent an urgent message to Virginia, asking for reinforcements, and received a promise of 500 men. Of these only 180 arrived. Since his own command had been still further reduced by illness and homesickness, Clark knew that it would be impossible to go to Detroit that year. Leaving garrisons in the captured Illinois towns, he returned to the Falls of the Ohio, where he established Fort Nelson, which would be his base for future operations.

In 1780 Clark's plans for an advance against Detroit were again frustrated by lack of adequate reinforcements. In May, however, he helped the Spanish repulse a British attack on St. Louis. Later in the year, with the assistance of substantial numbers of Kentucky militiamen, he undertook a highly successful punitive raid through the Shawnee country, inflicting far heavier losses on the Indians than Sullivan had done against the Six Nations the year before.

Late that year Clark returned to Virginia, and at the new capital of Richmond conferred with Thomas Jefferson, who had succeeded Patrick Henry as governor. Jefferson promised him men, made him a brigadier general of Virginia militia, and approved his plans for another attempt against Detroit. Early in 1781 Clark was elated to learn of a successful Spanish surprise attack on British Fort St. Joseph, in southwest Michigan. His hopes that this might be a preliminary to assistance for his proposed operations against Detroit were dashed, however, when the Spanish immediately abandoned their conquest, and returned to St. Louis.

In August Clark again moved southwest down the Ohio River from Fort Pitt, but he had only been able to raise 400 men. Since the British had greatly strengthened their defenses at Detroit, and with the Indians on the warpath, he knew that this would be an inadequate force for the proposed expedition. Once again he was forced to abandon his plan.

That year, British agents and their Indian allies were particularly active along the western frontier. The Shawnees were joined by Joseph Brant with Tories and Indians from the northern frontier, and the combined British-Tory-Indian forces ambushed and destroyed a force of Pennsylvania militiamen coming to join Clark for his proposed Detroit expedition. But when Brant proposed an effort against Clark himself, the western Indians and western Tories refused to join—they had seen too much of the red-headed Kentucky soldier to seek a fight with him unnecessarily.

But the Indians had no inhibitions against fighting other American frontiersmen, or even regular troops. In June, 1782, an expedition from Fort Pitt—300 Continentals, commanded by Colonel William Crawford—was defeated in a two-day battle on the upper Sandusky River by 350 Indians and 100 British and Tories, losing over 50 dead before breaking out of encirclement. The infamous Simon Girty— an American renegade deserter—took part in this battle, and gleefully supervised the slow torture of captured Colonel Crawford.

Girty also took part in a great raid of more than 300 Indians— with a few English and Tories—across the Ohio into Kentucky later that year. Their trail of slaughter, torture and rape was blocked by 200 Kentucky frontiersmen, among whom Daniel Boone was one of the leaders. On August 19, at the Battle of Blue Licks, the Indians and Tories routed most of the Americans with great slaughter, but were finally brought to a halt by the determined stand of Boone and a few companions.

In retaliation for this and other forays, on November 4, Clark again led a force of over 1,000 men into the Shawnee country. These were mostly short-term militiamen, happy to follow Clark on a punitive expedition against the Indians, but unwilling to undergo the rigors of a campaign to Detroit. He defeated the Indians at Chillicothe, inflicting so much damage on their villages that Indian interest in continued activities against the frontiersmen waned sharply.

Thus 1783 found the Americans securely in possession of the entire Ohio Valley, and much of the region to the west and northwest. The only material positions still remaining in British hands were those along the Great Lakes, of which Detroit, of course, was the most important. This situation, created almost singlehandedly by the leadership and efforts of George Rogers Clark, permitted the American negotiators in Paris to demand and to receive sovereignty of the entire Northwest Territory in the peace treaty with Great Britain.

George Rogers Clark received scurvy treatment from his government and from his people after the war. Aside from the initial $6,000 given him by Patrick Henry, there had been no financial support from the state or Continental governments. He had not even been paid. As a result he had gone deeply into debt to pay his troops and to buy their supplies and equipment. After the war neither Federal nor state governments would accept his claims for reimbursement, and neither would repay his many creditors. Most of his extensive land holdings were seized by these creditors, and the proceedings were recognized by the courts in the area which he had saved for America. The crowning blow was his subsequent dismissal from his post as Indian Commissioner in the Northwest Territory, thanks to the intrigues, treachery and guile of James Wilkinson, the same tarnished soldier who had figured in the Conway Cabal.

Putting this winning of the West in true perspective has run us perforce far beyond the tide of events in the principal theaters of war. We must turn our eyes east and southward again; to England's major efforts in the second stage of the war.

26

The British Turn South

WHEN GENERAL CLINTON WAS APPOINTED to take command of British land forces in America, early in 1778, his orders included a provision for initiating a campaign that fall to reconquer the Southern colonies. Complying, on November 27 Clinton sent a force of 3,500 men southward by ship from New York, under the command of Lieutenant Colonel Archibald Campbell. Campbell's transports were convoyed by a Royal Navy squadron under the command of Commodore Hyde Parker. On December 23 the flotilla reached the mouth of the Savannah River, where Campbell landed without opposition.

The commander of American forces in Georgia at that time was Major General Robert Howe, who lay at Fort Sunbury, a few miles south of the Ogeechee River, with 700 Continentals and 150 militiamen. Leaving a small garrison at Sunbury, Howe with most of his men marched rapidly northward to take up a position blocking the approach to Savannah from the south. Here they were joined by more local militia, bringing Howe's total strength to about 1,000 men. The old British fortifications were in ruins, but the Americans entrenched themselves along the main road southwest of the city. Campbell reached the American position December 29. With the assistance of a Negro guide, he sent a strong force completely around the American right flank, and attacked simultaneously from both front and rear. The defenders were overwhelmed, with a loss of 83 killed and 433 captured. The British, with only three killed and ten wounded, immediately occupied Savannah. With the few survivors of this brief and costly Battle of Savannah, Howe retreated into South Carolina.

Meanwhile, another and smaller British force, under Major General Augustine Prevost, had moved overland into Georgia from his base at St. Augustine in East Florida. Prevost took Fort Sunbury on January 6, 1779, and then continued on to Savannah where he assumed command over all British forces in Georgia. Campbell marched up the west side of the Savannah River, capturing Augusta on January 29.

In September of 1778, on the advice of Washington, Congress had appointed Major General Benjamin Lincoln as commander of the Southern Department. Upon receiving word of the British invasions of Georgia, he immediately repaired to Charleston, where he attempted to raise local troops to augment his small force of Continentals. Fearful of a slave uprising, the South Carolinians were holding their militia and provincial regiments at home, but Lincoln was able to obtain about 1,500 effective militiamen from North Carolina and Georgia to add to his 1,000 Continentals. With these, early in January, he advanced to Purysburg, on the east bank of the Savannah River, about ten miles north of Savannah. Shortly after this Prevost moved north to face him, on the opposite bank of the wide river, with about 3,000 men.

Prevost now began to probe across the Savannah River with a view to establishing one or more bases on the coastal islands of South Carolina. Lincoln sent Brigadier General Moultrie with 300 men to deal with a British force attempting to occupy Port Royal Island. On February 3 Moultrie defeated the British at Beaufort, and chased them back across the Savannah River.

Meanwhile Tory Colonel Boyd, with a force of 700 North Carolina Tories—mostly Scots—emboldened by the British successes in Georgia, moved south across central South Carolina towards the Savannah River. Evading pursuit by a small force under Colonel Andrew Pickens, the Tories brushed aside an American detachment guarding Cherokee Ford on the Savannah, about fifteen miles north of Augusta, and crossed into Georgia. Pickens pursued with about 300 men, mostly South Carolina militia, and a few Georgia militia. On February 14 he surprised the Tories in their unguarded camp at Kettle Creek, and inflicted a crushing defeat. Boyd lost some 45 killed and 75 captured. About 300 survivors reached Campbell in Augusta, while the remainder fled home. Pickens lost nine killed and 23 wounded.

During February Lincoln, having received substantial militia reinforcements, took the offensive. He sent General Andrew Williamson of Georgia with 1,200 men up the east bank of the Savannah River opposite Augusta. Another force of 1,400 North Carolina militia and 100 Georgia Continentals, under General John Ashe, followed Williamson with the mission of crossing the Savannah south of Augusta, to cut off Campbell and the British garrison in that town. En route, Ashe was joined by 200 militia cavalrymen. Learning of the approach of these two forces, Campbell evacuated Augusta and withdrew towards Savannah. Ashe promptly seized Augusta and pursued Campbell south to Briar Creek, where Campbell had destroyed the bridge.

While Ashe was repairing the bridge, he was suddenly engaged by about 1,500 men sent north by Prevost, under the command of his brother, Lieutenant Colonel Mark Prevost. While a small detachment made a holding attack against the Americans at the bridge, Prevost turned the American right flank with about 900 men, and moved against the rear of Ashe's position. The Americans quickly shifted to meet this new threat, but the militia then fled disgracefully without firing a shot. The 100 Continentals fought briefly, then also broke. Ashe lost nearly 200 dead (most of them drowned) and 173 captured. Only 450 of his men rejoined Lincoln's army; the remainder simply went home. The British lost only five killed and eleven wounded. Colonel Prevost reoccupied Augusta.

Despite this setback, Lincoln's forces continued to grow at his Purysburg base. On April 23 he decided to invade Georgia, with Augusta as his first objective. He crossed the river with 4,000 men, leaving General Moultrie with about 1,000 to observe the crossings over the lower Savannah.

As Lincoln advanced towards Augusta, Prevost decided to counter with an invasion of South Carolina. With 2,500 men he crossed the Savannah at Purysburg, heading towards Charleston. Moultrie fell back slowly in front of the British in a series of delaying actions.

By May 10, Prevost had driven Moultrie across the Ashley River. Repulsing cavalry attacks by Pulaski's Legion, Prevost pursued to the outskirts of Charleston, where he was faced by a series of entrenchments hastily built by the citizens and slaves of Charleston, during Moultrie's withdrawal. On the 11th Prevost demanded the surrender of the city. Moultrie and Governor Rutledge, knowing that Lincoln was hastening back from Augusta, pretended to consider Prevost's terms, and entered into negotiations. But next day Prevost, learning of the approach of Lincoln, withdrew across the Ashley River during the night.

Considerable skirmishing in the swampy islands southwest of the Ashley followed, as Prevost completed arrangements for an evacuation of his troops back to Savannah by small boat. On June 20, Moultrie attacked a British outpost in a fortified position at Stono Ferry, but was repulsed in an extremely hard-fought engagement. By the end of the month the British evacuation was complete. Prevost left a garrison of 800 of his best troops, under Lieutenant Colonel John Maitland, to hold Port Royal Island.

The remainder of the hot, steamy summer of 1779 was uneventful in the South. Lincoln was ill most of the time. The British occupation of Georgia was unchallenged. At the same time, they were too weak to consider any further action against the 7,000 or more men now under arms with Lincoln in South Carolina.

On their own initiative, Governor Rutledge and General Moultrie invited French Admiral Comte d'Estaing in the West Indies to assist by attacking the British base at Savannah. D'Estaing assented—apparently he wanted to recoup the prestige he had lost at Newport. On September 8, a French armada of 22 ships of the line, eleven frigates, and nearly 100 transports carrying over 5,000 troops, arrived at the mouth of the Savannah River. A British frigate had sighted the fleet approaching the coast, and just before the French blockaded the river Prevost was able to rush a message off by ship to New York with a request to Clinton for help.

Prevost and his men now feverishly repaired the defenses of Savannah, making use of slave labor impressed from neighboring plantations. He had about 2,500 fighting men, mostly Loyalists. Also available were four frigates and two sloops of war, which he pulled back up the river to assist in the defense. The guns were dismounted from two of these ships, and these with some other vessels were sunk below the city to block French approach to the water side of Savannah.

Prevost also sent a message to Colonel Maitland, at Port Royal Island, to return to Savannah with his 800 British regulars.

Fortunately for the British, d'Estaing was slow in the debarkation of his troops, and over-deliberate in the subsequent advance against Savannah. On the 15th, as he was approaching the town, he was joined by Count Pulaski, with his Legion of approximately 500 men: cavalry and mounted infantry.

On the 16th d'Estaing and Pulaski approached to within artillery range of Prevost's new earthworks, and demanded surrender. Prevost, knowing that Maitland was approaching from Port Royal, asked for a 24-hour truce in order to consider the terms. Foolishly, d'Estaing permitted this delay, and later that day Maitland's force arrived by boats, having completed a difficult trip through inside passages and swamps from Port Royal. That same day Lincoln, with 600 Continentals and 750 militiamen, arrived from Charleston to join d'Estaing.

When Prevost next day rejected the surrender demand, the French and Americans prepared for a siege. They were delayed, however, by the difficulties of debarking heavy guns off the ships, and then moving them up the narrow and difficult swamp roads to the lines. Meanwhile additional American militia units joined in following weeks, bringing the total investing force to more than 10,000 men.

Actual siege operations began on September 23, but the heavy batteries were not emplaced until October 3. D'Estaing by this time was getting extremely impatient. The hurricane season was at hand, and he had heard that a British fleet was en route to the assistance of Savannah. Despite the objections of the Americans and of most of his own French army subordinates, the French admiral insisted upon an immediate assault.

The attack took place on October 9, mounted by 3,500 French troops, 600 American Continentals, 250 South Carolina militia, and 200 of Pulaski's cavalry. The British, alerted by an American deserter, were ready. One French column was repulsed before it even reached the entrenchments. The principal American and French striking force was able to fight its way into a portion of the main redoubt, the key to the British position, but were there engaged by well-prepared British troops. While the battle was raging there, Pulaski and his cavalry-

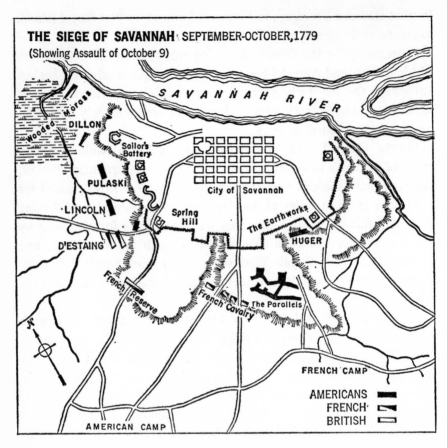

THE SIEGE OF SAVANNAH: SEPTEMBER-OCTOBER, 1779
(Showing Assault of October 9)

men attempted to break through *abatis* protecting a weakly-held portion of the British line, but they, too, were stopped and Pulaski was mortally wounded. Thrown back all along the line, the allies lost 244 men killed, and 584 wounded. British losses were 40 killed, 63 wounded, and 62 missing.

For nine more days the siege continued, until d'Estaing decided that he could stay no longer. The siege was raised on the 18th; the French withdrew to their ships, and sailed away on October 20. The Americans fell back north of the Savannah River. The successful defense of Savannah retained Georgia under firm British control, and assured the retention of a valuable naval land base in the south. The repulse also dealt a severe blow to the Revolutionary cause in the south, discouraging patriots, and prompting increased and more confident Tory activity.

These patriot reverses encouraged the Cherokees to renewed activity, and the western frontiers of the Carolinas again flared briefly in 1779. Once more, however, a punitive militia expedition laid waste the Cherokee country, markedly reducing Indian enthusiasm for continuing the war. Desultory frontier raids continued, but there was no further serious threat to the Carolinas from the Cherokees.

27

★ ★ ★ ★ ★ ★

Clinton's Problems

GENERAL SIR HENRY CLINTON WAS AN INTELLIGENT, competent and obedient soldier. He was not, however, an extremely forceful man, and though he had criticized Howe's dilatoriness in earlier campaigns, he himself became cautious and hesitant when he bore the weight of overall responsibility as British Commander-in-Chief in America. Bearing in mind the danger posed by French threats in the West Indies, the experience of the first four years of campaigning in the northern states caused Clinton to concur with the basic British strategy adopted in 1778: to go temporarily on the defensive in the north and in the Caribbean, while reconquering the Southern colonies, one at a time. He believed that this would not only progressively weaken rebel manpower and economic strength, but, in combination with the effective British naval blockade, would eventually so discourage the more populous Northern colonies that they would finally give up the struggle.

The strategy had been at least partially successful in 1778 and early 1779. Georgia had been reconquered for the Crown. French offensive moves in the Caribbean had been countered successfully. Meanwhile, Washington's army, frustrated by the impregnable defenses of the main British base at New York, had dwindled in size and—Clinton believed—in effectiveness.

Worsening relations between England and Spain, however, added further to the enormous burden of Clinton's vast, hemispheric responsibilities. Spain's demand for the cession of Gibraltar as a price for her neutrality was unacceptable to the English, and with war threat-

ening, late in 1778 Clinton followed a suggestion from Lord Germain
to send troops to Pensacola. Commanding this small force was Brigadier General John Campbell, whose mission was to protect West
Florida, and also to be prepared to move against New Orleans in the
event Spain entered the conflict.

When Spain actually declared war, on June 21, 1779, however,
the Spanish Governor General of Louisiana, Don Bernardo de Galvez,
immediately seized the initiative along the lower Mississippi and the
Gulf coast. The English Navy—overextended in a generally unsuccessful effort against French threats in the Atlantic, the Caribbean,
and the Indian Ocean—was unable to support Campbell in Florida,
and Clinton could spare no troops to reinforce him. By the close of
1779 Galvez had captured Baton Rouge and Natchez, and Spanish
land and sea forces were threatening Mobile and Pensacola.

As we have seen, the onset of summer made campaigning unpleasant and difficult in the South. To keep his troops in condition, and
to add further to the growing war-weariness in the Northern colonies,
Clinton decided to conduct a series of harassing raids in New England,
New York and Virginia—the regions where he believed combined
British sea power and land power could be employed most effectively,
with a minimum expenditure of effort, and with the least danger of
loss or failure. Major operations in the Carolinas would be resumed
again in the late fall.

Not all senior British officers in America were fully in agreement
with Clinton's strategic concept. Several of them were of the opinion
that Virginia was the political and economic keystone of the rebellious
union, and that much unnecessary campaigning in the unpleasant
swamps and jungles of the three southernmost colonies could be
avoided merely by reconquering the Old Dominion for the Crown.
The Carolinas, then cut off between Georgia and British-held Virginia, would soon be forced to submit. The most outspoken advocate
of such a Virginia-oriented strategy was aggressive, hard-fighting Earl
Cornwallis, who returned to New York from England in July, 1779,
to become Clinton's second-in-command.

Virginia's strategic location between the northern and southern
colonies was obvious, and Clinton recognized that she was economi-
cally one of the most important states in the rebel union. Her tobacco
provided much of America's foreign exchange, helping to preserve the

shaky overseas credit of the Continental Congress. Her other agricultural products contributed significantly to the food supplies of Washington's army, which also depended upon Virginia for a substantial proportion of its best Continental units.

Clinton believed, however, that he could not reconquer Virginia, and at the same time retain the American bases already in British hands, without at least 30,000 British regulars, in addition to Tory militia and his 10,000 Hessians. He refused to consider Cornwallis' suggestion that New York and Newport be abandoned in order to carry out a Virginia campaign. He was of the opinion—and probably rightly—that it would be self-defeating to abandon one powerful strategic base in order to seize another. Until or unless he received about 10,000 reinforcements from England—and this was most unlikely— he was determined to adhere to his strategy of a gradual northward expansion through the Carolinas. Not until the three southernmost colonies were firmly in British hands would he consider anything more extensive elsewhere than harassing amphibious raids.

To cripple Virginia's economy, however, and to discourage her population from their adherence to the rebel cause, that state was subjected to the first and most damaging of the raids mounted by Clinton in 1779. On May 5 a force of nearly 2,000 regulars troops, commanded by Major General Edward Mathew, had been sent from New York, convoyed by a strong naval force under Commodore George Collier. The expedition landed at Portsmouth on May 10, encountering no opposition.

From Portsmouth Mathew's troops fanned out over the nearby tidewater region, burning, pillaging and destroying everything of value. At Gosport, before abandoning the town, American militiamen burned a nearly completed American frigate, and two French vessels loaded with tobacco and other valuable supplies. But these losses were negligible in comparison to the total damage which Mathew and his men inflicted. The British destroyed or took with them some 130 coastal vessels, and over 3,000 hogsheads of tobacco, the total damage exceeding $10,000,000. Then, with transports and warships loaded with plunder, the expedition returned to New York just before the end of the month.

They were just in time to take part in another of Clinton's raiding expeditions. This was to be up the Hudson River, and was not only intended as part of Clinton's overall campaign of harassment, but also to extend British control further up that strategically important river. It is doubtful if Clinton had any intention of trying to cut New England off from the rest of the states, as has been sometimes suggested. But he did intend to make communications more difficult between New England and upper New York state, and to threaten the new American stronghold at West Point, while at the same time establishing suitable advance bases for the more extensive operations he hoped to undertake if he received sufficient reinforcements.

On May 30 Clinton personally led a force of 6,000 men—the pick of his troops in the New York region—up river from King's Bridge. Seventy sailing vessels and fifty flatbottomed boats carried English and Hessian regulars, Tory regiments and some dragoons up to the southern gateway to the Hudson Highlands just below Peekskill.

On June 1 they disembarked on both sides of the river, where an unfinished work on Stony Point on the west bank, and small but well-organized little Fort Lafayette across the way at Verplanck's Point guarded the termini of King's Ferry, the water link in the principal highway between New England and the more southerly states. Stony Point was occupied without opposition; Fort Lafayette—garrisoned by only 70 men—surrendered after investment by land and a short bombardment from the water.

Washington, meanwhile, anticipating a British assault upon the then-building vital fortress of West Point, some fifteen miles north, began concentrating his mobile troops to block any further enemy advance northward. Clinton, however, contented himself with rapidly transforming Stony Point, a natural defensive position, into an impregnable springboard for future use. A citadel with batteries capable of all-round fire, linked by trenches, rose on the 150-foot-high bare, rocky promontory. Landward, two successive rings of *abatis*—sharpened tree trunks and timbers interlaced—barred its base, just short of the broad stretch of marshland which, at high tide, transformed the promontory into an island. The sole access route was a causeway leading across the marsh in the northerly sector of the position.

The garrison consisted of a battalion of the 17th (Leicestershire) Foot, a grenadier company of Fraser's 71st Highlanders, a detachment of the Royal Americans (Tory), and sufficient artillerymen to man the guns. Lieutenant Colonel Henry Johnson commanded. Noth-

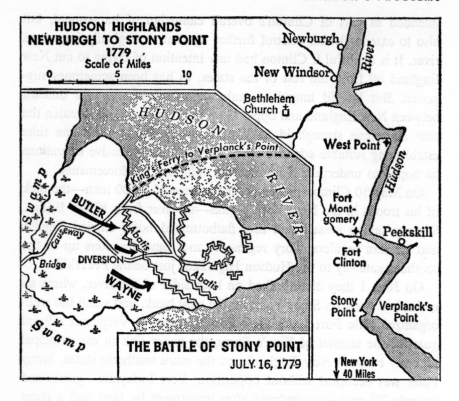

HUDSON HIGHLANDS
NEWBURGH TO STONY POINT
1779
Scale of Miles
0   5   10

Newburgh
New Windsor
Bethlehem
Church
West Point
Fort
Montgomery
Peekskill
Fort
Clinton
Stony
Point
Verplanck's
Point

King's Ferry to Verplanck's Point

BUTLER
Causeway
Abatis
DIVERSION
Bridge
WAYNE
Abatis

THE BATTLE OF STONY POINT
JULY 16, 1779

New York
40 Miles

ing but an extensive siege operation, it seemed, could dislodge the holders of this position. So Clinton, satisfied, withdrew the remainder of his expedition, having left a smaller garrison at Fort Lafayette across the river, and HMS *Vulture,* sloop of war, in the channel.

Washington had neither the means to mount a formal investment, nor was he willing to tie up his entire mobile army in such fashion. He chose another method. Brigadier General Anthony Wayne had reconnoitered Stony Point and believed he could storm it with his newly formed light corps—the élite of the Continental infantry. Though most American officers believed that an assault would be madness, Washington had confidence in Wayne. He approved.

Washington's point was well taken. For Clinton was mounting another punitive expedition into Connecticut. On July 3 a force of some 2,600 men sailed from Whitestone, Long Island, escorted by four men of war, to end the galling patriot harassment of British commerce in Long Island Sound, and to choke further Connecticut supply to the Continental army.

The British landed in New Haven harbor July 5, drove back a militia detachment and harried the town. British General George Garth, commanding, threatened to burn New Haven, but contented himself with pillage. He then re-embarked to land again at Fairfield, where the village was plundered and put to flame. The red-coated locusts moved on to Green's Farm for another sacking and pillaging affair. On the 11th they fell on Norwalk. After slight resistance by a small militia detachment the town was looted and most of it put to flame, with damage estimated at $150,000. Then the scourge moved back to New York.

But what happened on the Hudson four days later was to more than repay for Clinton's Connecticut raid.

From 1775, when Anthony Wayne had first recruited a battalion of Pennsylvania Continentals, he had stood out as a combat commander. At Trois Rivières in 1776, and as a brigade commander at the Brandywine and again at Germantown in 1777 he had proven himself. At Monmouth in 1778 he had anchored the American line and earned Washington's special praise in his report to Congress on that battle.

Wayne, a strict disciplinarian, now commanded a spick-and-span élite light infantry brigade drawn from the best in the army—men from Massachusetts, Connecticut, Pennsylvania, Virginia and North Carolina—1,300 strong. After careful reconnaissance, a study of the tide, and with well-prepared plans, he turned his corps out on the morning of July 15, 1779 at Sandy Beach, "fresh shaven and well powdered," and made the thirteen-mile march skirting west of the Dunderberg to their jump-off point, about a mile away from Stony Point. There he issued his orders.

Except for one battalion with a special mission, they would march to the assault with empty muskets shouldered and bayonets fixed. The penalty for removing a piece from the shoulder, or for trying to fire it, or for skulking, would be instant death at the hands of the nearest officer. Until the final assault, silence would be absolute. Then they would begin to shout incessantly, "The fort's our own! The fort's our own!" For identification, a piece of white paper was stuck in each man's headdress. As a matter of fact, Wayne was profiting by the hard lesson inflicted on him at Paoli Tavern in 1777 when "No Flint" Grey had surprised his troops by just such a silent night bayonet attack.

At midnight, Wayne's corps debouched from the mainland across the Stony Point swamp. Wayne himself led the right column, wading knee-deep in swamp water. Colonel Richard Butler commanded the left column, moving over the narrow causeway leading to the fort. Ahead of each column went 150 men with muskets slung, carrying axes to chop through the *abatis,* and an additional officer and twenty men who were to rush through the first openings hacked. To the first man inside the fort itself would go a prize of $500; to the next four in order sums ranging down to $100.

An alert British picket heard confused squashing and shuffling in the swamp. At his alarm the well-trained garrison rushed to arms, to see, in the first flashing of musketry and cannon, an awesome sight: close-ranked infantry moving through the mud toward the southern flank of the first barrier. Then the alarm sounded from the north— more silent, marching men, crowding the causeway.

The axemen reached the barricade, their blades began crunching deep into the timber. And at the same time a roar of musketry rose from the area between the two assaults. British Colonel Johnson, fearful for his center, rushed six companies—half his garrison—down to the *abatis* at that point. Actually, this was but a demonstration by the one battalion Wayne had permitted to carry loaded muskets.

Through rents in the *abatis* men began to squeeze. Some went down, but sufficient axemen remained to reach the inner ring and chop away once more. Through the crevices they hewed, the suicide squads of both columns raced towards the citadel, while behind them the main bodies, still keeping silence, jammed through, first in a trickle, then a tide.

Wayne went down, stunned momentarily by a glancing bullet. Clambering to his feet, and propped up by one of his men, he urged his troops on. They reached the sallyport, they topped the parapet— French Lieutenant Colonel François L. de Fleury being the first man over.

Unleashed now, Wayne's men were giving tongue, while their bayonets ripped into the confused defenders in the melée between the barricades and inside the citadel. The monotonous, repeated shouts of

"The fort's our own!" brought terror to redcoats attacked on both sides. Bewildered men, calling for quarter, began throwing down their arms. Johnson, hearing the noise behind him, tried to turn his center group—down by the outer *abatis*—back into the fight. But, hemmed in the swirling hurly-burly, they huddled and then surrendered, and Johnson flung down his sword. Up in the central log barracks a group of the 17th Foot held out for a few more minutes, then they, too, called it quits.

Thirty minutes' impetuous but planned assault had won Stony Point and—from those who didn't realize the coldly calculated and disciplined leadership involved—also won for Wayne forever the sobriquet of "Mad Anthony."

For the British, the losses had been severe: 63 killed, more than 70 wounded and 543 captured. The Americans lost fifteen killed and 80 wounded; most of them in the right column. Fifteen heavy guns and a large quantity of equipment and stores were taken.

As soon as Stony Point was captured, the guns of its river batteries were opened on the *Vulture,* lying in the stream, and on Fort Lafayette across the river. Slipping her cable hurriedly, the sloop dropped downstream out of range. Fort Lafayette didn't respond. In fact it was never taken, for a proposed attack on it was called off.

News of the storming of Stony Point broke on the American army and people with tremendous impact. A successful bayonet attack upon British regulars in a fortified position was something unheard of. Congress, voting Wayne its thanks and a gold medal, had the captured stores valued, and divided an equivalent sum of prize money among the troops. Fleury and the next four men behind him into the fort not only received the awards Wayne had promised, but other honors.

Stunned as the British were at the exploit, they not only recognized the gallantry displayed, but also pointedly commended the American clemency displayed after the surrender. Commodore Collier epitomized the British attitude with the remark:

"The rebels had made the attack with a bravery never before exhibited, and they showed . . . a generosity and clemency, which during the course of the rebellion had no parallel."

Clinton wrote later:

"the success attending this bold and well-combined attempt of the enemy procured very deservedly no small share of reputation and applause to the spirited officer [General Wayne] who conducted it."

But the affair at Stony Point, making Wayne and his light corps cocks of the walk in Washington's army, had an immediate effect on another American soldier. Major Henry Lee, Jr.—"Light Horse Harry"—might not have been jealous, but at least he wanted his share in the limelight. His scoutings down the west bank of the Hudson had revealed to him how to get it.

At Paulus (or Powle's) Hook—blunt, sandy point jutting out towards New York from what is now Jersey City (near modern Washington and Grand Streets)—the British had fashioned another fortification. Lee thought he could take it, suggested the idea to Washington and finally received a somewhat reluctant consent. It would be a hit-and-run affair, to capture the garrison and dismay the British high command; the position was too near New York for any attempt at permanent occupation.

The Hook was bounded on the land side by boggy salt meadows, crossed by but one marshy road. A creek, fordable in only two spots, gashed the bogland, and a deep ditch had been cut directly across the peninsula, making it virtually an island. A drawbridge gave access across the ditch; behind it a double row of *abatis* curtained the spit. On the water side more *abatis* and breastworks skirted the Hudson. Inside the enclosure were two redoubts mounting ten heavy guns. A blockhouse and entrenchment fortified the drawbridge entrance and another blockhouse overlooked the river. Several substantial barrack buildings were also inside the enclosure. The post was garrisoned by a part of the 64th Foot, a regiment of Skinner's Provincials (Tory regulars), a company each of Hessians and of light infantry, and a portion of an invalid battalion. A detachment of New Jersey Volunteers (Tory) was absent on a foraging expedition. Major William Sutherland commanded the 200 men remaining in the garrison.

Lee, well informed of the strength of the position by partisan scouts, planned to take the place with the bayonet somewhat after the fashion of Wayne at Stony Point, but the available assault strength would be only some 400 men, divided into three columns.

As planned, the right column would consist of 100 men of Woodford's Virginia brigade; the central force, two Maryland companies; and the left, to be led by Lee in person, 100 of Muhlenberg's Virginians and a troop of Lee's dismounted dragoons. The various elements left their cantonments about half past ten on the morning of August 18, rendezvousing at the New Bridge across the Hackensack River, fourteen miles from Paulus Hook.

It was four o'clock in the afternoon before they moved over the bridge and east on the Bergen road. Then they ran into difficulties. Their guide misled them into wooded country, a silly squabble over relative seniority arose between Major Jonathan Clark of the Virginians and Lee, causing about half of the Old Dominion soldiers to quit the expedition. But Clark—perhaps reluctantly—remained.

Nevertheless, Lee pushed on, reaching the marshland behind the Hook at four in the morning, with a rising tide threatening to make the ditch impassable. The defection of the Virginians necessitated revamping the assault into two columns. The right consisted of part of the remaining Virginians under Clark, the left was composed of a detachment of Virginians and the dragoons, under Captain Robert Forsyth of Lee's corps. The Marylanders were held out as reserve. As at Stony Point, detachments of axemen and suicide squads headed both columns.

Wading for two long miles through the marshland up to their breasts, the assaulters finally splashed through the ditch, arousing the British sentinels. Ignoring a sprinkle of musketry, the axemen tore at the *abatis,* and both columns surged through, with Clark's remaining Virginians in the lead.

Their impetus carried them over the central redoubt, and most of the dismayed garrison surrendered after a short struggle. Not a shot was fired by the Americans. Sutherland, the British commander, with some 50 Hessians, enclosed in a blockhouse, refused to yield. But by this time 50 British soldiers had been bayoneted, and the remaining 158 taken prisoner. Two Americans had been killed; three wounded.

Already alarm guns were arousing the British in New York. Lee felt his major objective had been gained. Delay might result in the attackers being trapped in the narrow area between the Hudson and the Hackensack. There was no time to attend further to Sutherland and his diehards in the blockhouse, nor to spike the guns. A plan to burn the barracks was discarded when Lee learned that there were women, children and sick soldiers inside. So, herding his prisoners before him, Lee made for Douwe's Ferry across the Hackensack below New Bridge, where he had arranged for boats. At New Bridge, too, a covering party of 300 men from Stirling's division was supposed to await them.

Leaving a detachment of the least fatigued men as a rear guard on the Bergen Heights, Lee's troops gained Douwe's Ferry, only to find no boats. The officer responsible—one of Lee's own command— had taken them back to Newark after waiting far beyond the appointed time for rendezvous. The command, with no ammunition (their powder had been wet in the marsh-wading), had trudged some 30 miles, fought and won a victory and was now stranded fourteen miles from the only other available crossing of the Hackensack, at New Bridge.

Dividing his force into three columns—each with part of the prisoners—Lee urged his tired men across country and along the Bergen road. An express went galloping to Stirling at New Bridge, urging him to meet them. At this time 50 of the defecting Virginians of the morning rejoined. Their ammunition was dry and Lee distributed them as rear guards to each of the columns. Then a detachment of Stirling's troops came hastening down from New Bridge.

It was high time, for as they reached Liberty Pole (now Englewood) the New Jersey Tories of the Paulus Hook garrison, returning from their foraging raid, struck the right flank. The rear guards with their dry ammunition, and a detachment of Lee's own dragoons, stood their ground sturdily and the Tories sheered off. By one o'clock that afternoon the entire command was safe across the New Bridge, including their bag of disgusted prisoners.

Once again the country rang with plaudits for a gallant and daring success. From the Congress came a vote of thanks and a medal for Light Horse Harry; to his troops a purse of $15,000 (Continental money, alas!). And once again Britain's Clinton, in New York, pondered the task ahead.

Even in the south, where Clinton hoped to gain the ultimate decision, disaster threatened the royal cause as d'Estaing and Lincoln besieged Savannah. So Clinton abandoned Newport and concentrated all of his forces in and around New York, in order to have sufficient troops to hold that base, and at the same time to send a strong expeditionary force to re-establish the situation in the south.

The arrival of the Newport garrison in New York brought British strength there up to 28,000 men, since during the summer Clinton had received reinforcements from England, including a composite brigade of the Foot Guards—the Grenadiers, Coldstreams and Scots. The army included 14,000 British regulars, more than 10,000 Hessians, and some 4,000 Provincials (Tory). But the new arrivals from England had brought a contagious fever with them, and nearly 6,000 men were in the hospital. Nonetheless, Clinton believed he had enough men to renew the campaign in the south. On December 26, 1779, he sailed from New York, taking with him Cornwallis and more than 8,500 of his best troops. Hessian General Knyphausen was left to command in New York.

28

★ ★ ★ ★ ★ ★

Conquest and Civil War
in the South

CLINTON'S EXPEDITIONARY FORCE FROM NEW YORK was convoyed by five ships of the line and nine frigates under Admiral Marriat Arbuthnot. The ships were buffeted by winter storms of exceptional severity, and were scattered all over the western Atlantic. One, in fact, was driven all the way across the ocean, to make port in Ireland. Another, loaded with cannon, was sunk; two other small vessels were lost, and practically all of the army's horses died during the voyage. Not until the end of January did the first ships begin to straggle into the rendezvous at the mouth of the Savannah River. Finally, with most of the vessels assembled, on February 10 Clinton sailed northwards, and next day began to land his troops on Johns Island, 30 miles south of Charleston.

Nothing had been done to improve the neglected defenses of Charleston since the hasty work done during Prevost's raid the previous April. Fort Moultrie (formerly Fort Sullivan) on Sullivan's Island, and Fort Johnson, opposite on James Island, were in ruins. Lincoln, assisted by Governor Rutledge and the citizens of the city, immediately began intensive efforts to improve the works. Fortunately for the defenders, Clinton advanced very slowly after his landing. Not until March 7 did the first British troops reach the Ashley River, across from Charleston. It was the 29th before Clinton pushed his first troops across the river north of the city. Thus, Lincoln's soldiers, and the 600 slaves furnished by Governor Rutledge, had plenty of time to strengthen the earthworks across the isthmus north of the city, to construct a stone redoubt in the center of the line, to build a series of small forts along the entire waterfront, and to repair and rearm Forts Moultrie and Johnson.

Meanwhile both sides were receiving substantial reinforcements. In mid-March General Patterson arrived with 1,500 British troops from Savannah, and a month later Lord Rawdon and 2,500 men from New York joined the British army, giving Clinton a total force ashore of about 10,000 men. Admiral Arbuthnot had about 5,000 seamen in his fleet, just off Charleston bar.

Washington had sent all of the Virginia and North Carolina Continentals from his army to join Lincoln. Most of these arrived in March and early April, giving Lincoln 2,650 Continentals, 380 Pulaski Dragoons (now commanded by Colonel Charles Armand), and 2,500 militia. About 500 of these, including all of the cavalry, were stationed under General Isaac Huger about 30 miles north of Charleston at Moncks Corner, near the headwaters of the Cooper River, in order to keep open a line of communications to the north. The remainder held Charleston and the two forts at the harbor mouth.

A small American flotilla of six frigates and three sloops of war, commanded by Commodore Whipple, was pulled back up the Cooper River. The guns were removed from five of these vessels, and they were sunk to form an obstacle between the town and Shute's Folly Island. The remainder of the warships would help keep open the Cooper River line of communications to the north.

Lincoln has been criticized for allowing himself to be cooped up in Charleston with practically the entire American mobile force available for operations in the South. It seems quite clear, however, that when he pulled back into the city, Lincoln felt that he had an adequate line of retreat up the Cooper River, and that in the direst of necessities he could move his troops directly eastward into the swampy lowlands and islands beyond the Cooper River, and thence to the mainland to the north. He was under great pressure from state and civic authorities to hold the city. He persuaded Governor Rutledge and part of his Council to leave in early April, in order to continue the administration of the state outside of the beleaguered city.

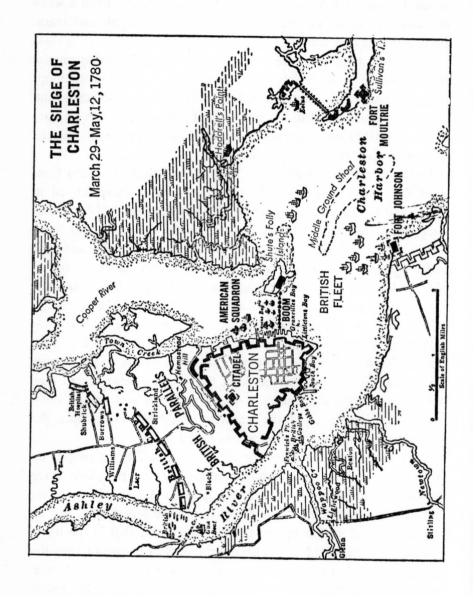

THE SIEGE OF CHARLESTON

March 29–May 12, 1780

Lieutenant Governor Christopher Gadsden and the remainder of the Governor's Council stayed in Charleston, however.

On April 8 the British fleet boldly entered the harbor, sailing past the two forts in a violent but relatively harmless exchange of fire. Two days later Clinton and Arbuthnot called upon the garrison to surrender. Lincoln refused. On April 13 the British siege artillery opened up on the defenders with shell and red-hot shot, causing much damage in the town.

Meanwhile, Clinton had sent a force of mixed infantry and cavalry to block Lincoln's Cooper River line of communications. This force was commanded by Lieutenant Colonel Banastre Tarleton, and included the 550 Tories, mixed cavalry and mounted infantry, of his British Legion, and the 100 men of Major Patrick Ferguson's American Volunteer Rifle Corps. At 3:00 A.M., Tarleton's troops launched a vigorous and successful surprise attack against Huger's 500 men at Biggins Bridge, near Moncks Corners. About 100 Americans were captured, and most of the remainder lost their horses. Tarleton was then joined by two British infantry regiments, and he proceeded to occupy the area east of the Cooper River, northeast of Charleston, completely blocking Lincoln's escape route.

At a council of war on April 20 Lincoln and his generals came to the conclusion that only an immediate evacuation of the city could save the army. Lincoln apparently believed that it would still be possible to get away to the east through the swamps, south of the region now occupied by Tarleton.

Lieutenant Governor Gadsden and the members of the Governor's Council attending this council of war violently protested against this plan to abandon them. One of the civilians went so far as to threaten that the citizens of Charleston would cut up the army's boats and open the gates to the British if the troops attempted to leave. In the face of this threat, Lincoln weakly gave in, and agreed to stay on, thus sealing the doom of his army.

On the 21st the American general opened negotiations with Clinton, proposing the evacuation of Charleston by his troops and his little flotilla with the honors of war, and without limitation on their further activities. Clinton naturally refused, and intensified his pressure against the city. An American sortie on April 24 sustained as many losses as it inflicted, but did little damage. Fort Moultrie was captured on

May 6, and British troops now stretched along the entire east bank of the Cooper River. By this time Admiral Arbuthnot had provided Clinton with 4,000 seamen to man the siege artillery, thus permitting Clinton to complete the difficult investment.

By May 8 the British siege lines had reached to within musket range of the American defenses, and Clinton prepared to assault. First he demanded the city's surrender. In reply, Lincoln agreed to surrender his Continentals as prisoners of war, but insisted that the militia not be held as such. He also demanded full honors for his troops, to march out with colors uncased,* his drums beating a British march, in accordance with traditional practice. Clinton and Arbuthnot were willing to go so far as to permit the garrison to march out with partial honors, but insisted that the American colors must be cased, and that they could not play either a British or an American march.

Lincoln again refused the British terms, and at 8:00 P.M. on May 9, hostilities resumed. The American cannon opened fire against the British, leading to a furious artillery duel that lasted through the night. The resulting bombardment caused severe damage to the city. The terrorized townspeople quickly shed their erstwhile bellicosity. They petitioned Lincoln to surrender, and so the American general accepted the British terms.

On May 12, the Continentals marched out, their colors cased, the drums beating a Turkish march. When the British saw how few regular troops had been holding the three-mile perimeter of Charleston, they were outspoken in their praise of the Americans' gallant defense. But gallant or not, the capitulation of Charleston was the most serious defeat the Americans had yet suffered during the war. In addition to 2,500 Continentals, some 2,000 militia surrendered; the British captured substantial stores and great quantities of weapons. American casualties during the siege amounted to almost 100 killed, and 150 wounded (about 90 percent amongst the Continentals). The British lost 76 killed and 189 wounded.

On May 18, after the consolidation of captured Charleston and the surrounding territory, Clinton sent three columns into the interior to pacify the entire State of South Carolina. Two of these were small, and went to the northwest, one to seize the post at Ninety-Six and the

---

* Colors, or regimental flags, are "uncased" if they are flying freely from their staffs; they are "cased" when wrapped tightly around the staff and covered with a wrapping.

other to occupy the region east of Augusta. The third column of 2,500 men, under Cornwallis, advanced northward towards Camden. Cornwallis sent Tarleton's cavalry raiding ahead of him.

Late in May, as the British were approaching Camden, Cornwallis and Tarleton learned that Colonel Abraham Buford with a force of approximately 350 Virginia Continentals, and a handful of cavalry under Colonel William Washington, was withdrawing toward North Carolina. Buford, on his way to join Lincoln, was at Lenud's Crossing, on the Santee River, when Charleston fell. He had fallen back to Camden, and now, upon the approach of Cornwallis' column, was continuing his retreat.

Tarleton, with 270 of his green-coated dragoons and mounted infantry, immediately pursued. Tarleton caught up with Buford in the region known as the Waxhaws, just east of the Catawba River, in the fertile, pleasant rolling country south of the border between North Carolina and South Carolina. Representing his strength as being 700 men, Tarleton demanded Buford's surrender. The American ignored the demand, and was continuing northward when Tarleton overwhelmed his rear guard. Buford hastily formed the rest of his force in the open, and then mistakenly ordered them to hold their fire until the charging dragoons were only ten yards away. The one American volley was too late to slow the momentum of the Tory horsemen, who broke through the thin Continental line. Buford attempted to rally his men, but finding himself assailed on all sides, surrendered.

Tarleton's dragoons, on the pretext that some of the Americans had fired after the surrender, gave no quarter. In an orgy of ruthless butchery, all save a handful of the Americans were cut down, 113 being killed outright, another 203 being very badly wounded and captured. At least half of these died during the following days and weeks. Tarleton, apparently pleased with the results, admitted the loss of five killed and twelve wounded. Returning from his victory at the Waxhaws, he terrorized Camden, which was occupied by Cornwallis on May 31.

Word of this "Massacre of the Waxhaws" spread like wildfire amongst the patriots of North and South Carolina. While it unquestionably inspired considerable dread of Tarleton and of the green-coated Tory troopers of his British Legion, it also stimulated enmity, and widespread determination for revenge.

His three columns having easily seized their objectives, Clinton was now confident that South Carolina was conquered, and that North Carolina would soon be occupied as well. On June 4 he issued a decree in which he outlawed anyone not taking "an active part in settling and securing His Majesty's Government" in the Carolinas, and voiding the paroles of any patriots who had been captured and released on parole. Then, leaving Cornwallis with a total of 8,000 troops, equally divided between British regulars and well-trained Tory volunteers, on June 5 Clinton sailed back to New York with the remainder of his army.

Cornwallis, equally satisfied that South Carolina had been pacified, returned from Camden by slow stages to Charleston, leaving behind Colonel (Lord) Francis Rawdon with a force of approximately 1,000 British troops. In Charleston Cornwallis intended to complete his arrangements for the early occupation of North Carolina, and the subsequent invasion of Virginia.

But Cornwallis had not yet reached Charleston when the supposedly pacified State of South Carolina erupted into a bloody ferment of revolt and civil war. The officers and militia who had been paroled at Charleston interpreted Clinton's last proclamation as voiding their paroles unless they pledged allegiance to King George. Furthermore, some, like Andrew Pickens, had found that their estates had been plundered by British or Hessian or Tory raiders, in violation of the terms of their surrender. On top of this, universal disgust inspired by Tarleton's Waxhaws Massacre kindled new fury among the patriots, and a determination to ignore legal niceties in their opposition to an apparently inhuman foe. Clashes between patriots and Tories erupted throughout the state, while guerrilla bands began to harass the British fortified posts, and to raid lines of communications between these posts and Charleston.

This was a true civil war, in every respect. Communities were split by faction and strife. Families were divided—fathers fought against their sons, brothers fought brothers. And as always with civil wars, the rising of tempers and spilling of blood led to violent outrages and atrocities on both sides.

Amongst the many patriot officers who gathered small bands of partisans to carry the war to the Tories and to the British, four men were outstanding: Colonels Thomas Sumter, Andrew Pickens, Francis

Marion and James Williams. During the remainder of 1780, and much of the following year, these men were constantly active, striking unexpectedly where they believed the British were vulnerable, inflicting as much damage as they could, and then as suddenly disappearing into the forests and swamps of the Carolina lowlands, or up into the wild hill region. They constantly frustrated every effort of the British and Tories to bring them to bay. Though their forces and fortunes fluctuated, they were always formidable, and they remained thorns in the side of the British lion to the end of the war. Sumter's area of operations was generally in the northern part of the state, in the Broad River region; Marion operated from the swamps of the Pee Dee, in the east; Pickens and Williams were active in the west.

Loyalist sentiment was still strong in the Carolinas, but though bitter, ruthless and bloody clashes were frequent between the patriot guerrillas and Tory partisans, strangely no Loyalist leaders emerged comparable to the four outstanding patriots. For leadership, therefore, the Tories turned primarily to two English regular army officers. One of these was Banastre Tarleton, whose green-uniformed British Legion combined the training and discipline of regular British troops with a ferocity found only in bitter fratricidal war. Perhaps even more effective than Tarleton as a partisan leader was Major Patrick Ferguson, a few years older, less flamboyant, but a dedicated, highly competent professional soldier intensely loyal to his King and country. It was perhaps fortunate for the Revolutionary cause that British military authorities had refused to adopt Ferguson's revolutionary, quick-firing, breech-loading rifle. But they did recognize his unique effectiveness as a leader of Tory partisan riflemen. Cornwallis sent him to the western part of South Carolina, where by late summer he had recruited nearly 4,000 Loyalists to his American Volunteer Rifle Corps.

The civil war which broke out in South Carolina quickly spread northward. Encouraged by the approach of British troops from the south, North Carolina Loyalists erupted in sporadic and premature violence. In mid-June, Tory Lieutenant Colonel John Moore had collected approximately 1,300 Tories at Ramsour's Mill, 35 miles northwest of Charlotte between the Catawba and Little Catawba rivers. Two separate forces of North Carolina patriot militia mobilized to deal with this threat. One of these, consisting of 800 men, under General Griffith Rutherford, was located near Charlotte. The other, some 400 men under Colonel Francis Locke, assembled at Mountain Creek, near Ramsour's Mill. On June 20, Locke made a successful surprise attack against Moore's camp at Ramsour's Mill, in a peculiar action in which the captains of each of the American militia companies operated entirely independently of the others, and with scant regard to instructions from Locke. Despite this lack of coordination, however, the surprise of the attack, combined with luck and the fierce determination of the Americans, threw the Tories into confusion. After each side had lost about 150 killed and wounded, the Tories were hopelessly dispersed, and fled the field.

In South Carolina, meanwhile, Sumter, already known as "the Gamecock," had become emboldened by a number of minor successes in June, and had attracted several hundred men to his standard. On July 12 part of his partisan group surprised and wiped out a detachment of Tarleton's Legion, about 100 strong, at Williamson's Plantation between the head of Fishing Creek and the Broad River.

By the end of July Sumter felt strong enough to attack British fortified posts. His first effort, against the British and Tory garrison of the post at Rocky Mount—30 miles northwest of Camden on the west bank of the Catawba—was not successful, since the garrison had been warned of his approach. Six days later, at Hanging Rock, twelve miles to the east, Sumter and William Davie of North Carolina, with a combined force of about 600 men, drove a garrison of 500 men from their earthworks in a very hard-fought battle, in which all participants, on both sides, were Americans. Collecting considerable booty, Sumter and Davis dashed away before British reinforcements could arrive.

Marion and Pickens, meanwhile, were being active farther south, causing much alarm to British garrisons and to Loyalist sympathizers in the region west and north of Charleston. Marion, less spectacular than Sumter, combined equal boldness with greater caution, and was probably the most effective American partisan of the war. On August 6, Cornwallis reported to Clinton and to the British government that "the whole country between Pee Dee and Santee [is in] an absolute state of rebellion."

29

★   ★   ★   ★   ★   ★

Stalemate and Treason
in the North

WHILE THE WAR WAS INTENSIFYING in the south, in late 1779 and
the early months of 1780, a stalemate continued to pervade the north.
Much as he deplored this, and anxious though he was to bring about
decisive action, Washington knew that there was little he could do to
rectify the situation so long as the British continued to exercise their
control of the sea. All hope for the return of d'Estaing having failed
by November, 1779, Washington went into winter quarters, with
Morristown again the principal concentration area, and the remainder
of his troops in observation nearer to New York. Counting militiamen,
his paper strength had been 27,000, but actual effectives were probably less than 15,000.

That same month Washington suffered a serious loss when lingering
illness forced John Sullivan to tender his resignation. Despite his
tactlessness, and sometimes bull-headed stubbornness, Sullivan had
been consistently reliable as a fighting, competent general capable of
exercising independent command as well as leading a division in
battle. Washington was well aware of the unfairness of the charges
blaming Sullivan for the defeats at Long Island and the Brandywine,
and among his subordinates, seems to have considered Sullivan second
in overall ability only to Greene. But though Sullivan was lost to
Washington as a field subordinate, he returned to his seat in the Con-

tinental Congress, where he consistently and vigorously supported Washington, greatly easing the Commander-in-Chief's difficult dealings with that often recalcitrant body.

For another miserable winter the Continental army—at first under canvas, and then in log cantonments—shivered through exceptionally severe weather, again short of food, fuel and clothing. Washington's early appeals going unheeded, he divided the state of New Jersey into eleven districts, assigning to each arbitrary allotments for the contributions of grain and cattle to be expected; he sent troops to collect the allotted supplies. The procedure was simple, soldierly and effective. Local magistrates were applied to, the requisitioning officers having been told to "delicately let them know you are instructed, in case they do not take up the business immediately, to begin to impress the Articles called for. . . . This you will do with as much tenderness as possible to the Inhabitants."

New Jersey folk came through, as Washington reported to the Congress, with "the earliest and most cheerful attention." So the army began to eat again. There was never sufficient, for the purchasing value of Continental currency had dropped almost to zero. However, the number of mouths to be filled also diminished as a result of enlistment expirations and the inevitable desertions.

Along the west bank of the Hudson, and in the Westchester County belt of no-man's land between the British outposts and Washington's cordon blockade, the usual sporadic clashes occurred during the winter. The principal one of these affairs was a successful British attack on an American outpost detachment at Mount Pleasant, near White Plains on February 2. The grenadier and light infantry companies of the newly arrived Guards Brigade, 100 Hessians, and a horse troop of Colonel James De Lancey's Tory regiment—some 450 men in all—made a night assault on a nine-company garrison of Connecticut and Massachusetts line troops of equal strength. American losses were fourteen killed, 37 wounded and 76 taken prisoner; the British lost only five killed and eighteen wounded.

With the beginning of summer things were still bad. Civilian and soldier alike suffered from currency depreciation—the one because he knew that payments for requisitions would be worthless paper, the other because his pay—if and when he drew it—had no purchasing power. Two regiments of the Connecticut line paraded in open mutiny May 25, but were finally persuaded by their officers to disperse.

Clinton, back from the south, learned of the disaffection in the dwindling Continental forces around New York, now less than 10,000 effectives. In mid-June he sent a 5,000-man task force under Hessian General Knyphausen over to Elizabeth from Staten Island. After some looting, and the slaughter of a few civilians, Knyphausen was met near Springfield on June 23 by Nathanael Greene, with 1,000 Continentals and a horde of untrained New Jersey militia. After some sharp skirmishing, later dignified in history as the Battle of Springfield, Knyphausen was checked, and withdrew.

Raids and forays continued in the lower Hudson Valley during the remainder of the summer, with no important consequences to either side. Clinton adhered to his basically defensive strategy in the north, and Washington lacked the strength to attempt any serious effort against strongly fortified New York.

On July 10 a French armada arrived at Newport. It was an expeditionary force of more than 5,000 troops, commanded by General Jean Baptiste D. de Vimeur, Comte de Rochambeau, escorted by a fleet of eight ships of the line and several smaller warships under Admiral the Chevalier d'Anzac de Ternay. Another, larger, French fleet under Admiral François J. P. de Grasse, with several thousand additional troops to reinforce Rochambeau, was due to follow shortly.

Washington was overjoyed. The arrival of the French army, combined with his own, would permit an attack against New York. Even without de Grasse, de Ternay's fleet was slightly stronger than that of British Admiral Arbuthnot, and thus should be able to support the land operations by blockading New York harbor. Washington at once sent Lafayette to Rochambeau, to arrange plans for the projected operations. Washington's memorandum to Rochambeau, dated July 15, expressed most forcefully the principle upon which he expected to operate, and reiterated his strong views on the importance of sea power to war:

"In any operation, and under all circumstances, a decisive naval superiority is to be considered as a fundamental principle, and the basis upon which every hope for success must ultimately depend."

Washington's enthusiasm was short-lived. Two days after the French began to disembark at Newport, British Admiral Thomas Graves arrived at Sandy Hook with a squadron including six ships of the line, thus re-establishing British naval superiority off the northeastern coast of the United States. Graves and Arbuthnot sailed promptly to blockade Newport. Then, in August, came word that de Grasse's fleet had been blockaded by the British in Brest.

On September 20 Washington met with Rochambeau and de Ternay at Hartford, Conn. The meeting was highly successful in enabling the American and French leaders to take each other's measure; both sides seem to have been equally pleased. The amiable and efficient Rochambeau, 54 years old, immediately won the confidence and respect of Washington. But the French general made clear that, even though his government had instructed him to place himself under the orders of the American Commander-in-Chief, his instructions also specified that the French fleet and army were to act in concert. Thus, until additional French naval forces arrived—now extremely doubtful in 1780—he felt duty-bound to remain in support of de Ternay's blockaded fleet at Newport.

And so the war in the north continued to drift in stalemate, disturbed by only one major, tragic, incident, which would leave one gallant British officer literally dangling from a noose, and one American officer—with a hitherto enviable record of gallantry—metaphorically drowned for eternity in a sea of infamy. It is not a pleasant story, but it must be told.

On September 23, 1780, a horseman in civilian clothing, bound south, was halted just above Tarrytown on the east Hudson bank by three American "skinners": irregulars prowling the no-man's land between the British and American lines. Forty-eight hours later Major General Benedict Arnold—hero of Quebec, Lake Champlain, and Saratoga—had fled his command at West Point. On board a British warship, Arnold, bared to the world as a Judas, was sailing down the Hudson to claim from British General Clinton his thirty pieces of silver, while at Washington's headquarters at Tappan young, handsome and gallant Major John André, Clinton's adjutant general, lay awaiting court-martial as a spy.

The story of the treason of Benedict Arnold is that of a conscienceless egotist inflamed to avenge a long chain of slights and affronts—

some of them fancied, many real.* The influence of a Tory bride of half his years cannot be discounted as an additional factor, but Arnold had apparently decided to betray his country even prior to his marriage to pretty Peggy Shippen, belle of Philadelphia.

He had been in cautious, coded correspondence with Clinton, via Major André, ever since the receipt in May, 1779, of a letter from Tory Colonel Beverly Robinson, high in Clinton's confidence. Robinson urged Arnold, as the "strong man" of the independence movement, to reconcile colonies and King.

The time was ripe; Arnold had never forgotten his shabby treatment by the Congress during the early years of the war. Now he was in the midst of another rumpus: charges brought before the Congress by certain Philadelphians for his high-handed actions in that city as military governor. So, even while clamoring for clearance of the charges against him—some of them trumped up, but a few with some validity—Arnold's dickering with Clinton continued. When Washington, April 16, 1780, reluctantly but firmly approved a court-martial verdict in the Philadelphia case and publicly reprimanded Arnold for misuse of government transportation and illegal issuance of a travel permit to a Tory woman, the balance was tipped.

Arnold bluntly informed Clinton that for the sum of £20,000 and the commission of a major general in the British Army, he would deliver up West Point, the new American citadel on the Hudson. He then wangled a transfer from his post in Philadelphia to West Point. Thus on August 3, Washington entrusted the command of the fortress to the man whose soldierly qualities he so admired. Benedict Arnold, he deemed, would be the individual best fitted to complete and to control the vital fortification. There Arnold received Clinton's reply: his terms had been accepted in principle. Settlement of details remained.

On September 21 André, in full uniform, was slipped ashore below Haverstraw from HM sloop *Vulture*, the British station ship on the Hudson. He and Arnold conferred on details of the proposed surrender and clinched the bargain—£20,000 and a major generalcy for success, all expenses and a brigadier generalcy if the plan failed.

---

* For another instance of treason—never clearly proven—see the case of Silas Deane, discussed in Appendix VII.

But before André could be put aboard the *Vulture* again, Fate intervened. An eager young American outpost commander at Teller's Point opened fire without orders on the British ship. Her skipper, unwilling to risk her safety against what he believed might be a heavy American battery, slipped his cable and sailed downstream to Dobbs Ferry.

Left thus in the lurch, André—against his better judgment—was persuaded to don civilian clothing and to work his way back overland on the east shore, with a guide and a safe conduct pass provided by Arnold. The guide left him just above Tarrytown; André continued to make his way south alone. Three militia irregulars held up the lone horseman, discovered in his stockings a batch of incriminating papers given him by Arnold, and turned him over to the outpost commander at North Castle.

Forty-eight hours later Arnold, at breakfast with his wife and three officers of Washington's personal staff (the commander-in-chief was due to arrive shortly, on return from his visit with the French at Hartford) received a report from his outpost commander, relating the arrest of one "John Anderson," carrying Arnold's safe-conduct but also carrying top-secret reports on West Point. "Anderson" was being held by Washington's own chief of secret service—Major Benjamin Tallmage—but his papers were being transmitted to Washington.

Poker-faced Arnold, excusing himself, left the table, rushed down to his ever-ready six-oared barge, and fifteen minutes later was splashing downstream, his pistol trained on the oarsmen. Behind him rose a hue and cry as the missing pieces in the mosaic fell in place, but by noon he was safe on board the *Vulture*.

André, who had frankly admitted his identity, went before a high-ranking court-martial of thirteen general officers which included Generals Greene, Lafayette, Knox, von Steuben and St. Clair. The court's directive, on Washington's order, was to report what penalty should be imposed on "Major André who came within our lines in the night on an interview with Major General Arnold in an assumed character and was taken within our lines in a disguise with the enclosed papers concealed upon his person."

Regretfully—since André, soul of honor, made no attempt to quibble—the court found him to be a spy and recommended a spy's fate. Washington approved. The execution was set for September 30.

Privately, Washington probably hoped that Clinton would surrender Arnold in exchange for his gallant but unwise adjutant general.

Clinton's appeal for reconsideration delayed the execution but was of no avail, particularly since with it came an arrogant letter from Arnold threatening "torrents of blood" in consequence.

So André, clad in full regimentals now, for his uniforms had been sent up with his soldier servant, swung from a gibbet at Tappan on October 2, 1780, mourned by both friend and enemy.

Perhaps, from some far-off Valhalla, the soul of Captain Nathan Hale observed. Hale's executioners had not been so sympathetic.

30 ★ ★ ★ ★ ★

Partisans and Regulars— Glory and Disgrace

IN APRIL OF 1780, six months before the discovery of Arnold's treachery, events in the South had prompted Washington to still further weaken the strength of his dwindling army. Hoping that reinforcements could reach Charleston in time to help Lincoln hold that city, Washington rushed off a division of Maryland and Delaware Continentals. The commander of this division was Major General Baron Jean de Kalb. Since this was his chosen name, we shall respect it.

De Kalb was a German soldier of fortune, born of Bavarian peasants in 1721, as plain Johann Kalb. A giant in height and strength, he had no right either to the title of baron, or to the aristocratic prefix "de" which he had adopted because of his ambition to gain advancement in the snobbish French army. By 1743 he had risen from the ranks to the grade of lieutenant, and fought in France's European wars for the next twenty years, retiring as lieutenant colonel in 1763. From 1767 to 1769 de Kalb, at the request of the wily Duc de Choiseul, far-sighted French foreign minister, had traveled—as we have already noted—through the American colonies to survey colonial public opinion, to assess the likelihood of revolt, and the chances of success in the event of such a revolt. Then, when the Revolution did come, he had returned to America with the Marquis de Lafayette in 1777, carrying with him Silas Deane's promise of a commission as a major general. He had arrived at a time when Washington and the Congress were tired of foreigners, but had succeeded in obtaining his major general's commission because of his close association with Lafayette. A capable, competent officer, de Kalb was at first contemptuous of the Americans, and critical of Washington. On the other hand, he was horrified by Conway's intrigues, and soon proved himself to be as energetic, honest, and intelligent as he was strong, vigorous and abstemious. By the spring of 1780 he had won Washington's respect as an able, loyal soldier. In return, de Kalb's former critical attitude toward Washington had changed to admiration and devotion.

De Kalb's small division consisted of two brigades, each between 600 and 700 strong. The 1st Maryland Brigade, of four regiments, was commanded by Brigadier General William Smallwood. The 2nd Brigade, three Maryland and one Delaware regiments, was under Brigadier General Mordecai Gist. These were probably the very best troops in Washington's army.

De Kalb and his men were in southern Virginia when they learned of the fall of Charleston. They continued slowly southward, de Kalb unsure what action he should take, reaching Hillsboro on June 22. To his surprise and annoyance, de Kalb found himself unable to get supplies from the civil authorities in North Carolina, and discovered that the groups of militia wandering around the state had neither interest nor desire in joining him, and thus subordinating themselves to the command of a foreign general. Accordingly, living off the country, and suffering from lack of adequate supplies as well as from the heat, de Kalb's division marched on to the Deep River, where he was joined by the remnants of Armand's (formerly Pulaski's) Legion, now consisting of about 60 cavalrymen and 60 mounted infantrymen.

De Kalb now halted briefly, to obtain more information about the country to the south, before continuing a cautious advance towards Camden. He soon discovered that the direct road from Ramsey's Mill, on the Deep River, to Camden traversed an inhospitable country, mostly swamp or sandy, infertile pine barrens. The few inhabited regions along this road were populated by predominantly Tory Scots. Although the route was 50 miles longer, de Kalb determined to move west to Salisbury, then south through Charlotte to Camden, in order to take advantage of fertile farming country, where supplies and provisions would be plentiful, and where people were predominantly patriots.

In mid-July, just as he was about to move off towards Salisbury, de Kalb learned to his relief that a new commander had been appointed in the Southern Department. This was to be General Horatio Gates, the hero of Saratoga. De Kalb waited for his arrival.

Gates, despite the suspicion which had been created by his peculiar activities during the Conway Cabal, was still a Congressional favorite. Thus, though Congress knew that Washington believed that Nathanael Greene was the man for the job in the South, Gates was appointed. Since he was to report directly to Congress, Gates was in effect independent of Washington, and a co-equal department commander. He was at this time in semi-retirement on his estate in Virginia. Upon receiving the invitation he immediately accepted, and started off for the South, after taking leave of his friend and neighbor, Charles Lee. "Take care," was Lee's sardonic warning, "lest your Northern laurels turn to Southern willows."

Gates joined de Kalb on the Deep River on July 25. The next day he issued orders for an immediate march on Camden. Despite de Kalb's recommendations, he decided to take the shorter but more difficult direct route. When other officers joined de Kalb in urging Gates to reconsider, he made it clear to them that he was a man of prompt and energetic determination, who intended by his vigor and direct action to reverse the dangerous trend of affairs in the Southern states.

Carrying only one day of rations, the little army started south on July 27. As his officers had expected, food was short, and the alternately swampy and sandy road was extremely arduous under South Carolina's summer sun. The troops were frequently close to mutiny, but were kept in line by their officers. Little food was available save for small quantities of green corn and green peaches. The combination of such provender with the kind of water they were able to obtain in this area created severe gastric troubles for most of the men. Nonetheless the march continued, and on August 3, after crossing the Pee Dee River, the little army began to be joined by numerous militia contingents.

On August 11, Gates reached Lynch's Creek, to find Lord Rawdon with about 1,000 British and Tory troops on high ground holding the opposite bank. De Kalb recommended that his division make a night march up the creek, to turn the British left flank, and to get around to Camden before Rawdon could withdraw. But Gates, suddenly substituting indecision for vigor, could not make up his mind. Finally, on the 13th, he began a slow daytime movement to his right, permitting Rawdon to fall back in plenty of time to protect his line of communications to Camden. Late on the 13th the American army reached Rugeley's Mill, about fifteen miles north of Camden. Here on the 14th Gates was joined by Brigadier General Edward Stevens, and 700 Virginia militia. This brought Gates' total strength to about 4,500 men, though only about three-fourths of these were fit for duty.

On the 14th, also, Gates received a request from Sumter for assistance in attacking a British supply train moving slowly north from Charleston to Camden. Since Gates also had word that reinforcements under Cornwallis were moving up to join Rawdon at Camden, it would seem that the last thing in the world for him to do would be to weaken his command on the eve of a battle. If he were to attack immediately, defeating Rawdon at Camden, he would then either be able to defeat Cornwallis in turn, or else drive him back to Charleston. In either event, he would be able to seize the slow-moving wagon train at his leisure. Gates' proper action, therefore, would have been to order Sumter to join him in an immediate attack upon Rawdon at Camden.

Instead, Gates sent off 100 Maryland Continentals, 300 North Carolina militia, and two guns in compliance with Sumter's request. He then spent the remainder of the 14th, and all day of the 15th, at Rugeley's Mills, permitting Cornwallis to arrive to join Rawdon at Camden.

Late on the afternoon of the 15th Gates gave orders for a night march to Camden, for the purpose of attacking the British the next morning. In issuing his orders, Gates referred to a total strength of 7,000 troops. When his efficient adjutant general, Colonel Otho Williams, pointed out to him that the returns showed only 3,052 fit for duty—1,000 Continentals, 120 men of Armand's Legion, and the remainder militia—Gates replied with a soldierly epigram: "Sir, there are enough for our purpose!" These were words fit to stand beside John Paul Jones' immortal: "I have not yet begun to fight"—if only Gates had been a Jones.

Gates turned aside de Kalb's suggestion that the militia were not adequately trained for night operations. Armand objected to the order of march, which placed his cavalry and mounted infantry in the van, suggesting that a force of horsemen cannot approach an enemy in the darkness unheard. Though he did not mention it, Armand was probably also worried by the fact that most of his men were British deserters, thus causing doubts as to the ardor with which they would fight in an exposed position in which they were needlessly placed in jeopardy. Gates refused to reconsider, so Armand's men led the march.

Fortunately provisions were plentiful at Rugeley's Mill. That night the troops were fed an ample quantity of food, but evidently only half-cooked. It was a common practice in those days to issue rum to the troops before an arduous march or an expected action. Having no rum available, Gates hit upon the idea of issuing a gill of molasses to each man. As it turned out, the molasses, on top of such a meal, proved to be a most effective physic. The result was that the men were breaking ranks all night during the march, and their intestinal disorders added to the exhaustion which could normally be expected from a march on a hot, sultry summer night in South Carolina.

By coincidence, Cornwallis had also decided upon a night approach march, with a view to a surprise dawn attack against the Americans the next morning. The British set out from Camden at 10:00 P.M., the same hour that the Americans left Rugeley's Mills. There was no moon, but the stars shone brightly through the heavy, breathless heat of the night.

At 2:00 A.M. Tarleton's British Legion and Armand's American Legion ran into each other on the road, opening fire simultaneously. With typical vigor and determination, Tarleton charged, driving back Armand, and the leading Continental units behind him. But after a brief recoil, the Continentals stood fast and repulsed the Tory dragoons. There were a few minutes of blind firing between the two deploying lines in the dark, then both stopped.

Gates immediately called an emergency council of war. De Kalb recommended a withdrawal, but Stevens said: "We must fight! It is now too late to retreat! We can do nothing else." Gates, agreeing, ordered his officers to return to their units to prepare for battle in the morning.

The armies were in an open, sparsely wooded pine forest. The ground, firm for a few hundred yards on each side of the main road, then became swampy in both directions. Thus the flanks of each army were protected. The Americans were on slightly higher ground; the British had a creek to their backs.

In accordance with Gates' orders, his army deployed and then tried to gain a little rest in the two or three hours remaining before dawn. This was impossible, however, because of desultory fire from British pickets.

On the right of the American first line, under the immediate command of de Kalb, was Gist's Maryland-Delaware brigade, about 600 strong. In the center were some 1,200 North Carolina militia. On the left flank were Steven's 700 Virginia militia. To the left and rear of the Virginians, at the edge of the swamp, was Armand's Legion.

In a second line, a few hundred yards behind the front, was Smallwood's 1st Maryland Brigade, probably less than 500 strong. Between the two lines Gates took his post, accompanied by able Otho Williams.

Cornwallis' army consisted of about 2,300 men, of whom over 1,500 were regulars. The remainder were Tories about equally divided between fairly well-trained militia and Tarleton's professional British Legion. Cornwallis put his Tory infantry on the left of his line, under the command of Lord Rawdon. On the right were about 1,000 regulars, commanded by Lieutenant Colonel James Webster. In reserve were two battalions of the 71st Highland Regiment, and about 150 of Tarleton's dragoons.

At dawn the British began to advance, while the artillery of both sides opened fire. There was no wind, and gunsmoke hung close to the ground, adding to the slight morning haze. The British approached in parallel march columns until about 200 yards from the American line, then they began to deploy, with the light infantry on the extreme British right, echeloned slightly forward. Seeing this, Williams immediately suggested to Gates that Stevens' Virginia militia should attack the light infantry while they were still deploying. When Gates agreed, Williams galloped forward to transmit the order to Stevens. Stevens commanded his men to attack, but the inexperienced Virginians were less than eager to comply. Williams personally tried to lead a few men forward, but without much success.

The British, meanwhile, had completed their deployment. Cornwallis seeing the confusion on the left of the American line, ordered

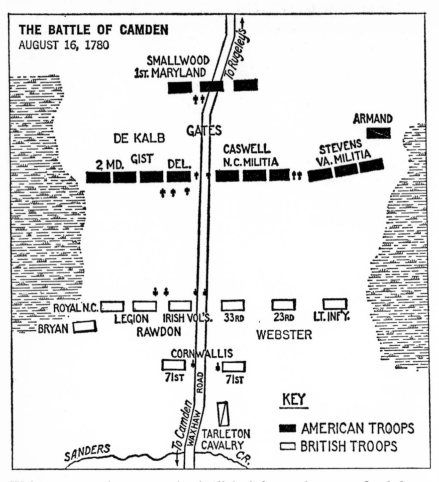

THE BATTLE OF CAMDEN
AUGUST 16, 1780

Webster to attack at once. As the light infantry, bayonets fixed, bore down upon them, Stevens' Virginians began to waver. At about 50 yards the British halted, fired a volley, and then charged. This was too much for the Virginians. A few men fired generally southward, but most simply dropped their loaded muskets and ran.

The panic spread to the North Carolina units on their right. Suddenly the entire left flank and the center of the American army melted away, since Armand's Legion was swept back by the combined weight of manpower and weight of panic, as the Virginians ran blindly through their ranks. Gates seems to have waved his sword and to have attempted to rally the panic-stricken troops. Most historians report that Gates was then "swept off the field" by the fleeing men. Smallwood's brigade was also thrown into considerable disorder, as the militiamen broke through their line. Smallwood, too, seems to have been "swept off the field," but his regiments rallied and quickly reformed under the command of their officers.

Colonel Williams, who somehow seems to have avoided being "swept off the field," now tried to find Smallwood, to suggest that he move his brigade up on the left of Gist's troops, who were at that moment throwing back a Tory attack. De Kalb, apparently sensing that something had gone wrong on the left, also sent back an order to Smallwood to move up. Thereupon Williams personally assumed command of the brigade and ordered it forward.

But it was too late. Webster's regulars had advanced to where the Virginians and North Carolinians had stood, and were now preparing to attack the left flank of Gist's brigade. Williams' advance with Smallwood's brigade caused the British again to shift front to the north, but they now occupied a position between the two American brigades, and repulsed Williams' efforts to join de Kalb and Gist. At this point Cornwallis seems to have ordered his reserve into the fight, and Tarleton's cavalry swept through the center, to take Smallwood's brigade on the right flank. This, combined with repeated charges by the reinforced British regulars, soon broke the already shaken Marylanders. Despite the efforts of Williams and the other officers, they fell apart under the terrific pressure from a force at least twice their numbers. They, too, began to flee, though many were cut down by Tarleton's troopers.

Meanwhile, Gist's brigade, under the inspirational leadership of de Kalb, was fighting one of the most glorious actions of the war. Not only had they repulsed the first Tory charge, but de Kalb had advanced, and in repeated attacks had driven the Tories back behind their starting position. At this point, Webster's victorious troops swung against his left flank. The giant French general, exposing himself courageously, reorganized his troops to face in two directions, then ordered still another bayonet charge. The uneven battle continued for an undetermined period of time, somewhere between fifteen minutes and half an hour.

When his horse was shot from under him, de Kalb got up, bleeding from numerous wounds; waving his sword he forced his way into the forefront of the fight on foot. Here for a few minutes took place what was probably the most violent hand-to-hand bayonet clash of the entire war. The result was a foregone conclusion, of course, with the Continentals now hemmed in on two sides by forces outnumbering them nearly four-to-one. Tarleton's dragoons, smashing into their rear, ended the battle. Gallant de Kalb sank down, mortally stricken by eleven wounds. British officers found him as Tory soldiers were tearing off his coat and decorations as souvenirs. One was actually starting to rip off his shirt. Cornwallis immediately had the giant hero taken back to camp, and given the best of medical care, but he died a few hours later.

British casualties were reported as 79 killed and 245 wounded. As in so many other instances, these figures must be somewhat suspect, if the mutually corroborating eyewitness reports of the fierce battle are to be accepted. American losses are not known. Estimates of dead have run as high as 900 or 1,000, but 600 is probably about right. The British apparently captured approximately 1,000 men, of whom more than half were wounded. Tarleton pursued until his horses were exhausted, killing and wounding fleeing American troops, and capturing considerable booty.

Gates himself arrived at Charlotte, 60 miles away, that night. His pace was hardly slower the next two days, since he arrived at Hillsboro, 180 miles from the battlefield, early on the 18th. In commenting on this, Alexander Hamilton wrote, "One hundred and eighty miles in three days and a half. It does admirable credit to the activity of a man at his time of life." Rarely has a general thus cravenly abandoned his army after an unsuccessful battle.

Cornwallis did not move after the routed Americans for three weeks. This delay can probably be excused by the fact that he first had to check upon the status of his embattled outposts around South Carolina before he could be sure an advance was advisable. Tarleton gave him a considerable assist in stabilizing the difficult partisan situation by inflicting a crushing defeat on Sumter. The American guerrilla leader had captured the British wagon train on August 15, taking 150 prisoners as well. While resting at Fishing Creek on the 18th, however, Sumter's security was atrocious, and his 700 troops (including the 400 Gates had given him) were surprised by Tarleton, who had only 160 of his British Legion. Tarleton killed 150 patriots, captured 300, recovered the British wagon train and released the 150 prisoners. In the process, Tarleton lost only sixteen killed and wounded.

Two days later, however, "Swamp Fox" Marion gained partial revenge by a successful dawn attack on a British-Tory column escorting prisoners from Camden to Charleston. Some 160 American captives were released, and fled to Marion's swamp refuge.

On September 8, Cornwallis began a slow advance up the east bank of the Wateree and Catawba rivers towards the Waxhaws. At the same time, Tarleton, with his Legion and a few other units, marched up the west bank. Further inland, and protecting the left flank of the British advance, Major Ferguson with 100 Tory Rangers (regulars) and about 1,100 of his Tory militia riflemen, moved northeastward along the foothills into the upper Catawba Valley.

While Cornwallis and Tarleton were resting for a few days in the Waxhaws, Tarleton's camp was surprised at dawn of September 21 by Colonel William Davie and a force of 200 mounted North Carolina militia, who routed Tarleton's troops. (Tarleton, sick at the time, was not in the camp.) When he heard the firing on the opposite bank of the river, Cornwallis rushed reinforcements to the assistance of the British Legion. They arrived too late to save the greencoated troopers from an ignominious defeat; Davie and his hard-riding men were already on their way back to Charlotte.

On September 25 Cornwallis moved north from the Waxhaws, Tarleton, again fit for duty, leading his Legion in the advance. To the surprise of the British, they found the intrepid Davie firmly holding Charlotte with about 300 men. Tarleton's first attacks were repulsed, and not until the main body of Cornwallis' army came up and began a full-scale attack did Davie withdraw.

Meanwhile Ferguson, to the northwest, had stirred up a hornet's nest. Roused by this threat to their homes, the mountaineer militiamen of North Carolina were assembling for battle. Included amongst them were several hundred who had journeyed eastward from regions beyond the mountains, to help in the defense of their native state. By early October more than 1,200 militiamen, mostly North Carolinians, but also including some Virginians and South Carolinians, had assembled in the vicinity of Rocky Mount, northwest of Ferguson's post at Gilbert Town. With reports of other militiamen flocking to the area, Ferguson decided to withdraw closer to Cornwallis' main army.

The principal militia leaders present were Colonels Isaac Shelby, Charles McDowell, John Sevier, William Campbell, and Benjamin

Cleveland. Since they could not agree upon a commander, on October 2 they decided to send a request to Daniel Morgan—known to be with Gates in the eastern part of the state—to take command. Meanwhile the five colonels elected Campbell to act as their "Officer of the Day," to carry out plans which they collectively adopted. The one thing upon which they could agree was to push closely after Ferguson. As they arrived at the Cowpens on October 6, they were joined by Colonel James Williams, the South Carolina partisan, with another 400 men. Then, fearing that Ferguson would escape, the six colonels selected their best mounted men—some 900—to hasten in a forced march after the retreating Tories.

Late on the 6th, warned by his scouts that the Americans were close behind, Ferguson selected a defensive position on Kings Mountain, a flat-topped eminence just south of the South Carolina-North Carolina border. Though the slopes of the hill were wooded, its long, oval summit was cleared. Here Ferguson camped, and organized a perimeter defense. Being short of provisions, he sent out about 200 men to forage. This left him a few more than 1,000 men to hold his lines at the top of the hill. He also sent a message to Cornwallis, reporting the rising of the Carolina patriots and requesting reinforcements: "Three or four hundred good soldiers," Ferguson wrote, "part dragoons, would finish the business." His closing words, however, revealed his alarm: "Something must be done soon."

October 7 was a miserable, misty, drizzly day. The Americans did not allow this to deter them, and reached the base of Kings Mountain shortly before noon. Discovering the British position, they dismounted and encircled the hill. Warned of their approach, Ferguson ordered his men to their posts at the edge of the open hilltop. In a more or less coordinated advance, the American sharpshooters worked their way up the wooded slopes, taking advantage of the cover afforded by the trees, and avoiding the fire of Ferguson's men.

By the time the American ring had reached to within 100 yards from the top, a fire fight was raging all around the hill. The Tories, more exposed on the open crest, were getting much the worst of it. After an hour, Tory losses were so heavy that the Americans were able to resume their advance up the slope. As they approached the top, Ferguson's men drove them down with bayonet charges. But as one attacking contingent was repulsed, another would advance, forcing

Ferguson to shift his reserve from one spot to another, while continuing to take heavy casualties from the concealed sharpshooters in the trees. Finally, as the Americans were closing in, Ferguson himself—the one British participant in the battle—was shot from his horse and killed.

At this point the remaining Tories lost heart and surrendered. But with the Americans scattered as they were around the circle, it was difficult to order a coordinated cease-fire. Furthermore, many of the militiamen had had friends or relatives killed by Tories in other

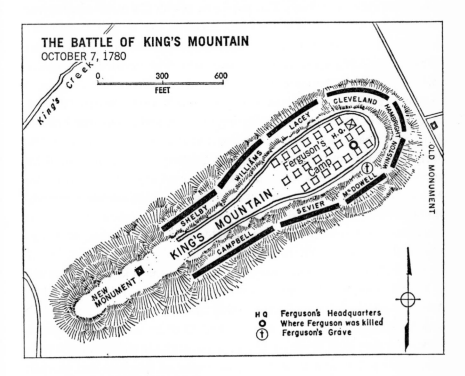

THE BATTLE OF KING'S MOUNTAIN
OCTOBER 7, 1780

H Q   Ferguson's Headquarters
O   Where Ferguson was killed
†   Ferguson's Grave

actions of the guerrilla war, and even those who had heard of nothing but the Waxhaws Massacre were reluctant to stop their firing. Finally, however, with the Tories huddled in one corner of the clearing, the patriot rifles were silent. The Tories lost 157 killed, and 163 severely wounded, in addition to many other slightly wounded amongst the 698 prisoners. Not one man of Ferguson's force escaped, save for the 200 men who were out on the foraging party. The Americans lost 28 killed and 62 wounded. Gallant Colonel Williams of South Carolina was among the American dead.

Most of the militia then dispersed and went back to their homes. One contingent took the prisoners to Gates' headquarters at Hillsboro, but many of the Tories were killed en route for real or fancied crimes, following summary trials—or no trials at all.

On October 6, Cornwallis had received Ferguson's message reporting the advance of the mountaineer militiamen. Early on the 7th he sent Tarleton to Ferguson's assistance. But before reaching Kings Mountain, Tarleton learned of the disaster, and reported back to Cornwallis. Shaken by the news, Cornwallis hesitated a few days at Charlotte, then withdrew. The partisans of the Carolinas, heartened by the victory at Kings Mountain, harassed the British incessantly throughout a miserable rainy, muddy, march. On the 29th Cornwallis stopped his army at Winnsboro, where he decided to wait for reinforcements he had ordered up from the south.

These reinforcements, however, were not easily to be spared from other posts in South Carolina. During October and November Francis Marion increased his activity between the Pee Dee and Santee rivers, stirring up further revolt against the English, and cutting off their supply trains. Tarleton was sent southeast by Cornwallis to deal with Marion's threat. The Swamp Fox, however, had little trouble eluding the Tories, and continued his depredations in hit-and-run raids.

Following Marion's example, Sumter also renewed his activities. Cornwallis sent a small British force under the command of Major Wemyss after Sumter. On November 9, the Gamecock, having learned a lesson from his disaster at Fishing Creek, was fully alert when Wemyss attempted a surprise attack at Fish Dam Ford. The British and Tories were ambushed, Wemyss and 25 of his men were captured.

Sumter then moved with 420 men towards the British fort at Ninety-Six, causing Tarleton to abandon his chase of Marion, and to dash to its relief. In the face of this threat, Sumter withdrew northward, to take up a position at Blackstock's Plantation. Tarleton, chasing vigorously after him, attacked on November 20, to suffer a disastrous repulse in which he lost about 100 men killed and wounded. The Americans had only three killed, and four wounded, of whom one was captured. After this setback, Tarleton rejoined Cornwallis at Winnsboro.

Clinton, meanwhile, had sent General Alexander Leslie, with 3,000 men, to Portsmouth, Virginia, for the purpose of raiding in the Old

Dominion. Leslie was placed under the overall authority of Cornwallis. In the light of his troubles in the Carolinas, Cornwallis now ordered Leslie to embark immediately for South Carolina, leaving only a detachment to garrison Norfolk. After the arrival of Leslie, Cornwallis intended to resume his offensive into North Carolina.

★ 31 ★ ★ ★ ★ ★

"Old Morgan Was Never Beaten"

IN THE FALL OF 1780, able Nathanael Greene became involved in controversy with the Continental Congress in defending himself against criticisms of his performance of duties as Quartermaster General. Although he had revitalized the administrative services of the army since he took over the office, early in 1778, there were a number of disgruntled men in the army and in the Congress who were anxious to find fault with a man who had so loyally and vehemently defended the Commander-in-Chief during the difficult days of the Conway Cabal. Furthermore, Greene's unbroken record of success was alone enough to cause some critics to search for an opportunity to make trouble. Thus, despite the great advance in logistical efficiency, every administrative failure was magnified and exaggerated in reports to Congress, and to Washington. Enemies and critics were particularly enthusiastic in following up rumors that, as Quartermaster General, Greene had awarded contracts to a private commercial enterprise in which he had a financial interest.

Finally, the indignant and disgusted Greene submitted his resignation as Quartermaster General, and requested Washington to return him to a line command as a major general. Reluctantly Washington approved, and at his recommendation on September 30, Congress replaced Greene as Quartermaster General by Timothy Pickering.

On October 6, Washington assigned Greene to command at West Point, the military keystone of the Northern states. Greene had requested this assignment in order to have an opportunity to spend a few months in a garrison post with his family. But Washington knew that there was one other field command that was even more important than that of West Point. Recognizing that after Camden Congress would probably relieve Gates of his command in the South, Washington told Greene that the West Point command might only be "temporary."

As a matter of fact, though Washington did not yet know it, one day earlier Congress had in effect offered him its apologies for having selected Gates as the independent commander of the Southern Department. Now Congress was requesting Washington not only to appoint a court of inquiry into Gates' conduct at Camden, but also to assign a new Southern Department commander. In this way Congress was informing Washington that in fact as well as in title, he was again invested with full authority as Commander-in-Chief of all of the forces of the United States.

Washington acted at once. He had recommended Greene for the Southern command before Congress had selected Gates. In his estimation Greene was by far the most reliable, most resourceful, and most efficient of his subordinates. Greene was assigned, and was directed to report to Washington at once for instructions. Though reluctant to leave West Point, and the anticipated pleasures of a quiet winter in garrison with his wife, Greene accepted, but asked if he might be granted a brief leave. Washington replied:

"I wish circumstances could be made to correspond with your wishes . . . but your presence with your command as soon as possible is indispensable. . . . I hope to see you without delay.'

Greene was a soldier. Sending a letter to his wife to explain why he would not be there to meet her at West Point, he rode at once to Tappan to report to Washington and to receive his orders.

Washington knew that after the catastrophe at Camden there was practically no Continental Army left in the Southern states. New regular units were being raised in North Carolina and Virginia; there were the semi-permanent, local, militia partisan groups under such men as Pickens, Marion and Sumter; and of course there were always the temporary militia units, who would join the army to fight for a few days or weeks, and then return home. To assist Greene in building and organizing an army, therefore, Washington assigned von Steuben to the Southern Department. In addition, to provide Greene with an existing and reliable force for reconnaissance and screening operations, Washington ordered vigorous young Lieutenant Colonel Light Horse Harry Lee to join the Southern army with his Legion of 100 dragoons and 180 light infantrymen.

After a brief visit with Washington, Greene headed south, accompanied by Steuben. In Virginia Greene asked Governor Thomas Jefferson to assist in the provision of Continental and militia forces. He left Steuben in Virginia, to train and organize the newly-created units, and to forward supplies and reinforcements to the field forces in the Carolinas. He then spurred south to take his command.

After Cornwallis' withdrawal to Winnsboro, in October, Gates had moved the remnants of his army from Hillsboro to Charlotte. Greene arrived there on December 2, and the change of command took place in a polite, cordial atmosphere. Gates was pleased, and somewhat surprised, by the courtesy and respect paid to him by his successor.

The formalities ended, Horatio Gates rode northward on a lonely journey to his home in Virginia. He would later be recalled to active duty by Washington, but never again would he command troops in battle. It should be noted, incidentally, that upon Greene's recommendations, Washington never held the proposed court of inquiry about Gates' conduct at Camden. With perhaps more generosity than the circumstances merited, Greene suggested that Gates' most serious dereliction had been in his personal precipitous flight from the Camden battlefield to Hillsboro, and that it would help neither the army nor the country to add further to the ignominy and disgrace already heaped on the unfortunate general.

Greene found that the paper strength of his army was 2,450 men —of whom 950 were Continentals. Actually present and fit for duty, however, were less than 1,500, about half Continentals, all terribly short of clothing, equipment, ammunition and food. But to somewhat offset this discouraging state of affairs, Greene found in his command at Charlotte one unexpected tower of strength: newly-promoted Brigadier General Daniel Morgan. Greene had known and admired Morgan for more than five years, had served with him frequently, and was well acquainted with his record.

Morgan's first military service had come in 1755, at age nineteen, with the Virginia militia in Braddock's disastrous expedition against Fort Duquesne. In subsequent years this large-boned, long-limbed, untutored backwoodsman displayed the qualities of leadership, incisive judgment, intelligence and aggressiveness which were to win him fame. A self-made man, he had become a landowner and a person of some wealth and consequence in the northern Blue Ridge country of Virginia, near the fringe of the frontier. Without formal schooling, Morgan had taught himself to read and write, and by 1775 his thirst for knowledge had led him to an appreciation of classical literature.

Morgan's humble origins, and the deliberate folksiness which he affected with his soldiers, have led some historians to assume that he was an uncouth hillbilly, barely able to read and write. How far this is from the truth is best revealed by reading his after-action report of the events of late December, 1780, and early January, 1781.

As a leader in his community, it had been natural for Morgan to recruit one of the "six companies of expert rifflemen" voted by the Continental Congress on June 14, 1775. Though his company had further to go than any of the other five, it was the first to report to Washington at Cambridge, Massachusetts, for the siege of Boston. His leadership qualities were so quickly evidenced that he was chosen to command the three rifle companies that marched with Benedict Arnold to Quebec. As we have seen, he played an outstanding and heroic part in that ill-fated expedition.

A prisoner for several months following the Quebec disaster, Major Morgan was exchanged in late 1776, after contemptuously refusing the offer of a British commission as a colonel. Rejoining Washington, he received a colonelcy in the Continental Army, and was appointed to command a select regiment of riflemen. His next great opportunity came in 1777, when Washington ordered him to rush northward with his rifle corps to help stop Burgoyne's invasion of northern New York. Morgan's contribution to the two American victories near Saratoga was second only to Arnold's. He was of course a supporter of Arnold in his controversy with Gates during that campaign, and like Arnold, his outstanding part in the battles was ignored in Gates' report to the Congress.

Partly because of this, partly because he had no friends in the Congress to push his name and to sound his praises, in the following years Morgan received from Congress even more shabby treatment than did Arnold. It is interesting to note, however, in this comparison, that though Daniel Morgan was embittered by Congress' refusal to grant him the promotion that George Washington had recommended, his bitterness never led to even a momentary thought of treason. His health had been shattered by the rigors of the Quebec campaign; he suffered severely from arthritis and other complaints. On the basis of ill health, therefore, when Congress failed to promote him in 1779, he resigned and returned to his Virginia home. Washington, apparently unaware of the true extent of Morgan's ill health, was for a time resentful of the fact that Morgan apparently had allowed personal bitterness to cause him to leave the army.

The following year, when Gates was appointed to command in the South, he seems to have requested that Morgan be recalled to active duty under his command. In light of the previous acrimony between these two men, it is not clear whether this was simply because Gates was belatedly admitting Morgan's sterling military qualities, or whether there had been some reconciliation between them during their months of retirement in Virginia. Nevertheless, though Congress "ordered" Morgan back to active duty in June, 1780, it still refused to promote him. He simply ignored the order.

The disaster of Camden, however, was another matter. All thoughts of personal honor, glory, and recognition were forgotten when Morgan heaved his aching joints onto a horse and rode rapidly down to Charlotte to offer his services to Gates. Upon renewed appeal from Washington and Gates, Congress had on October 13 finally appointed Daniel Morgan as a brigadier general, just in time for him to become Nathanael Greene's right hand man.

Although Charlotte was in an area that was strongly patriot in sentiment, Greene discovered that local good will had been greatly alienated by uncontrolled foraging and plundering by the troops. He felt, therefore, that his first steps must be to reorganize the army's supply system, and to permit it to get a fresh start in fresh surroundings. At the same time, however, he could not forget his enemy. Although the frontier militia victory of Kings Mountain had ended the first tentative British attempts to conquer North Carolina, Cornwallis still had nearly 2,000 men at Winnsboro, and British garrisons were scattered through numerous posts dominating the countryside of South Carolina. The partisans of Pickens, Marion, and Sumter were causing Cornwallis many headaches, but they were not seriously interfering with effective British control of the area. Greene apparently recognized that Cornwallis was only awaiting the arrival of reinforcements before he moved north to occupy North Carolina.

With all of these considerations in mind, Greene made the daring, unorthodox decision of dividing his small army into two portions. Evidently he thought that a division of his forces would enable his troops to forage for food more easily, and would at the same time permit him to worry Cornwallis by seeming to threaten two or more of the main British posts in South Carolina. The larger portion of the American army—about 1,000 men in a division commanded by General Isaac Huger, but under Greene's own direct supervision—would move from Charlotte to a more pleasant environment at Cheraw, South Carolina. Morgan would take the remainder—the best light troops of the army—across the Broad River into western South Carolina, to form a rallying point for the militia of the region, and at the same time to threaten the important British fortified post at Ninety-Six.

Though subsequent historians have gone out of their way in efforts to explain why this division of his army—in the face of a far superior foe—was a brilliantly unorthodox stroke of strategic genius, the truth is that this was the most serious military blunder which Greene ever made, and that it brought him dangerously close to catastrophe at the outset of his campaign.* That he was able subsequently, with a magnificent assist from Daniel Morgan, to rectify this error is, on the other hand, a real tribute to Greene's generalship.

Greene and Huger left for Cheraw on December 19. The following day Morgan started southwest, towards the Catawba River, with a force consisting of 320 Maryland and Delaware Continentals, about 200 Virginia "semi-professional" veteran militia riflemen, and 80 Continental dragoons commanded by Colonel William Washington. Fortunately the Continentals were survivors of de Kalb's division, which had fought so heroically at Camden; their commander, Lieutenant Colonel John E. Howard, was a first-rate officer.

---

* See Appendix V for a discussion of this controversial topic, and of the standard historical analyses of it.

After crossing the Catawba, Morgan was joined by several small militia contingents. By Christmas Day, when he took up a position of observation on the Pacolet River, a tributary of the Broad River, his little army had grown to nearly 1,000 men. Here he waited, in accordance with Greene's instructions, who now seems to have decided that the 140-mile gap between the two American contingents was as far as the division of forces should go.

While waiting beside the Pacolet, Morgan on December 28 sent Washington with his dragoons and 200 mounted militia to harass Tory partisans ravaging some Patriot communities in western South Carolina. Washington caught the Tories by surprise next day, near Ninety-Six, killing or wounding 150, and capturing 40 more, without suffering any losses. By coincidence, at this same time Greene had sent the newly-arrived Lee's Legion off from Cheraw to join Marion in a raid against the British post at Georgetown.

These daring American strokes, and the apparent impudence of Greene's division of forces, led Cornwallis to decide on an early punitive response. He had already intended to resume his invasion of North Carolina as soon as General Leslie arrived from Virginia. Meanwhile, thinking that Washington's raid might presage an American attempt against Ninety-Six, Cornwallis decided to detach a portion of his army under Tarleton to protect that post, and to deal with Morgan. Leslie and 1,500 men were expected in mid-January, when Cornwallis intended to advance rapidly northward, to throw his army between the two American forces, so as to cut off Greene's retirement from Cheraw, and also to block the retreat of any of Morgan's force that should survive its encounter with Tarleton.

Morgan, sensing Cornwallis' estimates and plan, became increasingly concerned about the gap between his command and Greene's. He wrote to his commander, recommending that both of their forces withdraw from their exposed positions. Greene, agreeing with the necessity for vigilance and caution, told Morgan to continue to threaten British posts west of the Broad River as long as possible, but to retreat at once if endangered by any British moves.

On January 1 Tarleton, with more than one-third of Cornwallis' army, left Winnsboro and headed westward across the Congaree River toward Ninety-Six. Shortly after his arrival there he received a message from Cornwallis ordering him "to push [Morgan] to the utmost. . . .

No time is to be lost." Tarleton replied that he understood that his orders required him either to "destroy Morgan's corps or push it before me over the Broad River toward Kings Mountain." When Cornwallis responded that this was exactly what he wanted, Tarleton left Ninety-Six on January 14, advancing vigorously northward over the Enoree and Tiger rivers on the 15th.

The exact strength of Tarleton's force has never been determined, but a fairly close approximation is possible. His own British Legion, a highly disciplined force of Tory volunteers and American deserters, was the principal unit: some 200 dragoons and a like number of mounted infantry. In addition he had a battalion each of the 7th Foot and the 71st Highlanders, both first-rate British regular infantry. These included about 300 men each. He also had the 17th Light Dragoons, British regular cavalry, probably about 100 strong. His Royal Artillery contingent, with its two 3-pounders, was no more than twenty men. Tarleton's total strength, therefore, was probably about 1,120 men. Intelligence reports which Morgan received from spies and from South Carolina partisans had led him to report to Greene his own estimate that Tarleton's force was between 1,100 and 1,200 men. Pretty good intelligence!

Learning of Tarleton's move on the 15th, Morgan planned to block the most likely crossing of the Pacolet River. But early next day Tarleton crossed the stream six miles further down. Morgan hastily withdrew north of Thicketty Creek, another tributary of the Broad River. That evening he camped in the sparsely wooded region within the great bend of the Broad River, just south of the North Carolina-South Carolina border. This area was known locally as "Hannah's Cowpens," or simply "The Cowpens," because here the local inhabitants rounded up their cattle before sending them east or south to market.

Morgan was making the best possible use of his regular and irregular cavalrymen, and keeping close tabs on Tarleton's movements. Thus he learned, soon after dark on the 16th, that the British had bedded down for the night at his old camp on the Pacolet River, a scant eight miles away. Morgan prepared for battle.

As with Tarleton, the exact strength of Morgan's little army cannot be documented. There is no doubt, however, that it was substantially larger than the 800 or 900 men that have been attributed to it in two recent popular histories.* In addition to his own 600 Continentals and Virginia riflemen, he had been joined by something like 500 militiamen. The principal units of these were some 140 ordinary North Carolina militia, nearly 200 North Carolina and Georgia riflemen in a unit under Major Charles McDowell, and thirty to forty Georgia and South Carolina militia horsemen under Lieutenant Colonel James McCall. On the 16th Morgan was joined north of Thicketty Creek by Colonel Andrew Pickens with about 100 of his reliable South Carolina militia partisans. Thus Morgan's total strength must have been very near to 1,100 men that night of 16-17 January.

Morgan's first actions, as they should have been, were to assure the security of his command against surprise attack. Additional mounted scouts were sent out to keep tabs on Tarleton. A line of patrols was established south of Thicketty Creek and about a mile in front of the position Morgan had selected for battle. After making sure that all men were properly equipped with weapons and ammunition, the baggage was sent northward across the Broad River soon after dark. Morgan then called his senior officers together and issued his orders for the following morning's battle.

Those historians who like to think of Morgan as a backwoodsman hillbilly, or as a simple leader of partisan warfare, have criticized him for the lack of military knowledge which permitted him to select a battlefield with an unfordable river in his rear. Others have suggested that the choice was perhaps "unorthodox" but "masterly." Though masterly, and perhaps unusual, it was certainly neither unorthodox, unmilitary, nor irregular.

In recent years military analysts have noted the striking resemblance of Morgan's dispositions to those of Hannibal in one of the renowned battles of ancient history: his victory over the Romans at Cannae in 216 B.C. Whether Morgan was acquainted with this historical precedent or not, is of no significance. His own soldierly experience was sufficiently rich, and his native military genius sufficiently well-developed, for him to conceive the same idea as that of the great Carthaginian, when faced with a comparable dilemma. Like Hannibal, Morgan had a heterogeneous, largely undependable force with

---

* (1) Roberts, Kenneth, *The Battle of Cowpens.* New York, Doubleday, 1958. (2) Davis, Burke, *The Cowpens-Guilford Courthouse Campaign.* Philadelphia, Lippincott, 1962.

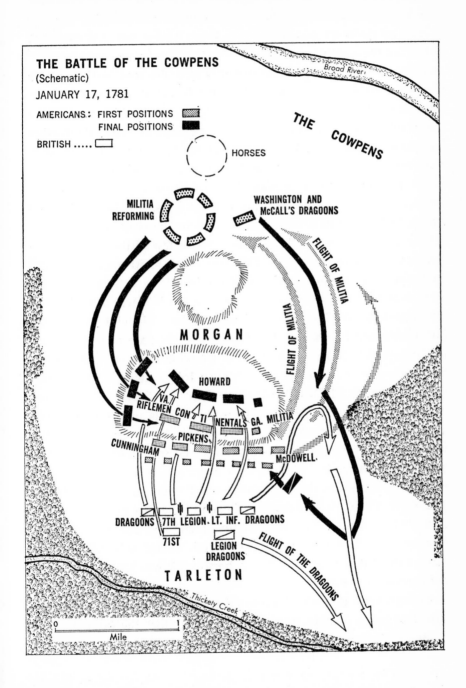

THE BATTLE OF THE COWPENS
(Schematic)
JANUARY 17, 1781

AMERICANS: FIRST POSITIONS
          FINAL POSITIONS
BRITISH .....

Broad River

THE COWPENS

HORSES

MILITIA REFORMING

WASHINGTON AND McCALL'S DRAGOONS

FLIGHT OF MILITIA

FLIGHT OF MILITIA

MORGAN

HOWARD

VA. RIFLEMEN   CON TI NENTALS GA. MILITIA

CUNNINGHAM   PICKENS

McDOWELL

DRAGOONS 7TH LEGION. LT. INF. DRAGOONS

71ST

LEGION DRAGOONS

FLIGHT OF THE DRAGOONS

TARLETON

Thickety Creek

0   1
          Mile

which he had to fight the finest regular soldiers in the world of his day. Like the Carthaginian general, Morgan decided deliberately to place himself in the bend of a river, thereby to obtain artificial means of bolstering the fighting capabilities of his least reliable troops.

The battlefield Morgan selected was near the southern edge of a wide clearing that extended south of the Broad River some three or four miles.* Here there was a gentle but commanding hill, overlooking the wooded banks of Thicketty Creek, perhaps another mile further south. Other woods flanked the central hill feature to east and west, but about half a mile away, and thus well beyond musket or rifle range, and providing no opportunity for a surprise envelopment.

The little army was drawn up in three lines. The Maryland and Delaware Continentals were just forward of the crest, with the Virginia riflemen on their right, and evidently a few of the most reliable Georgia militia on their left. This line of 500-550 men was under the immediate command of capable John Howard. Approximately 200 yards further forward, on the slope of the hill, was a line of 300 North and South Carolina militiamen under Colonel Pickens. Still further forward by another 150 yards, near the base of the hill, was a thin line of 150 Georgia and North Carolina militiamen, all expert riflemen and sharpshooters, under Majors John Cunningham of Georgia and Charles McDowell of North Carolina. McCall's horsemen, with a few mounted volunteers from other militia units—some 50 in all—were issued sabres and transformed thereby into cavalrymen, to join Colonel Washington's 80 dragoons. These mounted men were held in reserve under Washington's command behind another hill, about half a mile to the north of Howard's main line of resistance. The horses of the dismounted militiamen of the first two lines (practically all Southern militiamen were mounted) had also been thoughtfully collected in a sparse clump of woods behind this hill. Morgan made sure that the location of the horse park was known to all the militiamen.

Morgan knew that his militia could not and would not stand against British regulars. Rather than trying to fool either the militiamen or himself with the thought that they could form part of a substantial

---

* The exact site is undetermined. Descriptions in the accounts of Morgan, Tarleton and others could fit several possible locations. This description of the terrain, and of the battle, is based upon these accounts, which are generally corroborative.

battle line, he told the men in the first two lines that they merely had to wait until the enemy closed to within 50 yards of their position, fire three volleys, and then withdraw. He hoped that possibly some of the sharpshooters might fall back to Pickens' line, and that these might fire as many as four or five rounds. But sooner or later, he knew that they would break and run in the face of Tarleton's regulars. If they knew what was expected of them, and if this were not to be too much, he thought that they would try to meet expectations.

As to the militia withdrawal, he did not expect any kind of an orderly retirement. He was pretty sure that the men would run. Because of the nature of the ground, they could most easily run below the left flank of Howard's Continentals, back to the sheltered area where their horses were. He knew the psychology of untrained fighting men well enough to know that they would flee along the easiest route. One thing which he did not mention to his militiamen—but which was very much on his mind, as revealed by his later reports—was the fact that whether on foot or on horse, the militiamen could not run very far. Behind them was the unfordable Broad River.

During the early evening, Morgan, despite pain from his aching, rheumatic joints, limped around from campfire to campfire, joking with his men, impressing upon them his own apparently untroubled and confident attitude, shrewdly encouraging them to be prepared to do their utmost on the following morning. Time after time he repeated: "Just hold up your heads, boys, three fires and you are free." Then he would add: "When you return to your homes, how the old folks will bless you, and the girls kiss you, for your gallant conduct!"

Morgan and his officers did not let the soldiers forget the real and fancied atrocities on the record of Tarleton's green-coated Legionnaires. The men were eager for revenge. Inspired by Morgan's good spirits, and encouraging words, they felt sure that they would be successful.

Tarleton broke camp soon after midnight. Shortly after 4:00 A.M., Morgan's scouts reported the movement of the British column. Morgan seems not to have had time to sleep at all that night and now he roused his men with a deep-throated shout: "Boys, get up! Benny [Tarleton] is coming!" Then he again hobbled from one unit to another, checking their dispositions, making suggestions here, dropping a word of praise there, mixing rough jokes with fervent patriotic and religious inspiration. When he was satisfied, he mounted his horse and made one further circuit of all three lines, then went forward to check on his pickets. Satisfied that his patrols were doing their work, and that everyone was ready for action, he ordered his men to sit down and relax, so as to conserve their energy and their spirits until the battle was joined. "Ease your joints," he shouted, as he trotted in front of his troops, "Ease your joints!"

A chilly dawn was breaking when scattered shots to the front told that the patrols had sighted Tarleton's approaching troops. Soon the pickets had fallen back to their units, and Morgan had his men on their feet again.

Young Tarleton, having marched his men eight miles in the darkness of the morning, pushed rapidly ahead until he came in sight of the American position. While his infantry was deploying, he sent his English and Tory dragoons ahead to probe the American position. As the green-coated and red-coated cavalrymen galloped forward towards the skirmishers, they were met by an unexpected volley from the American sharpshooters. At least fifteen saddles were emptied, and many other men and horses wounded. The cavalrymen pulled their mounts up on their haunches, wheeled, and galloped back out of range. They had learned as much about the American position as they wanted to.

As his cavalry returned, Tarleton assigned them to their battle positions. The British dragoons were to form on each flank of the deploying line of infantry. This was made up of three contingents: the 7th Foot on the left, the infantry of Tarleton's Legion in the center, and the light companies of the 7th and 71st Foot on the right. The two artillery pieces were placed in the intervals to the left and right of the Legion infantry. Tarleton kept his own dragoons and the Highlanders in reserve. Without hesitation, and while the line was still being organized, impetuous Tarleton ordered an advance. It was 8:00 A.M., about one hour after daybreak.

All this time the American soldiers had been observing the precise British movements with admiration and awe. Stamping their feet on the ground to keep warm, they kept blowing their misty breaths on their hands, being particularly careful to keep trigger fingers warm and supple. Morgan, placing himself behind his line of skirmishers, kept shouting, "Don't fire! Don't fire!" Apparently as he trotted up and down the line he repeated Israel Putnam's famous words: "Don't fire until you see the whites of their eyes!"

Then, as Tarleton's troops approached with measured tread, a fierce shout rose from the British line. Morgan is reported to have cried, loud enough to be heard by Pickens' line and the skirmishing sharpshooters as well: "They give us the British halloo, boys. Give them the Indian halloo, by God!" Wild, enthusiastic shouts and cheers rose from a thousand American throats, and the sharpshooters took aim.

They did their duty, those skirmishers. At least two volleys, and possibly three, took heavy execution of the advancing British lines, but as the twinkling bayonets came close, the militiamen remembered what Morgan had said. Some of them scampered back to Pickens' line, some of them started running around the base of the hill towards their horses. Morgan himself trotted calmly back up the hill to join Pickens.

Moving at a quickstep, the British continued their steady advance up the long slope, to be met by another volley from Pickens' men. "Look for the epaulets," shouted Morgan. "Pick off the epaulets!" Holding their line and dressing as they advanced, the British muskets replied. Then, at the run, they dashed ahead up the hill with bayonets at the ready. Pickens' men, too, fired their two or three rounds and then started to run. As Morgan expected, most of them ran to the left rear, though a few found it quicker and easier to go around below the right flank of the Continentals. As the militiamen began to flee, the British dragoons galloped forward to cut them down.

Just as the red-coated dragoons were beginning to slash with their sabers at the stragglers of the throng of running militiamen, they were unexpectedly met by the charging line of Colonel Washington's regular and militia dragoons. Under the flashing saber blows of the close-ranked American cavalry, the surprised and scattered British horsemen found themselves at a disadvantage. Sheering away, they galloped to the south, pursued by Washington and his men, while the American militiamen continued to scamper in the opposite direction, without further interference.

But as they approached the horse park, the fleeing American militia found that their general was already ahead of them, waving his sword and barring the route to their horses. Joined by Pickens, stouthearted Morgan soon convinced the milling mob of men that they had escaped from the English cavalry, and that they were safe from pursuit.

"Form, form, my brave fellows!" Morgan cried, "Give them one more fire, and the day is ours. Old Morgan was never beaten!"

These words, combined with the vigorous efforts of Pickens and the other militia officers, soon brought some calm and semblance of order into the mob of refugees. Slowly, they were becoming soldiers again. Seeing that this part of his plan was going as it should, Morgan clapped his spurs into his horse's sides, and galloped back to the top of the hill, where the sound of musketry and the louder bark of the two British artillery pieces were waxing in intensity. He arrived at the crest, to find, to his dismay, that Howard, the Continentals and the Virginia riflemen were falling back rapidly. Indignantly he shouted at Howard, "What is this retreat?"

"A change of position to save my right flank," the Continental colonel replied calmly. Not satisfied, Morgan demanded: "Are you beaten?"

"Do men who march like that look as though they were beaten?" was the response. To the general's practiced eye, Howard's proud words were confirmed by the cool and unhurried manner in which the Continentals were moving to the rear, one squad behind each of the four columns firing effectively as skirmishers to slow down the continuing British advance.

"Right!" Morgan is said to have replied. "I'll choose you a second position. When you reach it, face about and fire!"

What had happened was that the British first line had been halted below the crest of the hill by the effective fire of Howard's Continentals and his Virginia riflemen. Since they were unable to advance, even with the assistance of their guns, Tarleton had sent Fraser's 71st Highlanders to extend his left flank, to try to envelop Howard's right. In the face of this threat, Howard had ordered the right flank riflemen and Continentals to fall back slightly and then to wheel to the right. The order was misunderstood. The right wing fell back, and the remainder of the line began to waver. Howard thereupon decided simply to shift his entire line a short distance to the rear, as he had informed Morgan.

Tarleton, seeing this withdrawal, decided the battle was won. He ordered his men to charge, and prepared to commit his reserve cavalry.

At this moment, in a simultaneous combination of events that was partly good luck and partly good planning, Morgan saw that Pickens and his militiamen were advancing up the draw between the hill and the woods to the right of the Continentals, just as a galloper spurred up to the general with a message from Colonel Washington. The cavalry colonel, re-forming his horsemen several hundred yards to the east, after having pursued the British dragoons for nearly a mile, saw that the onrushing British line had lost cohesiveness and order. His brief oral message was: "They're coming on like a mob. Give them one fire, and I'll charge them."

Morgan ordered Howard to halt. With precision the regulars immediately faced about, as did the disciplined Virginia riflemen, and began to pour a destructive fire into their pursuers. The British line, surprised and confused, came to a sudden halt. Only Fraser's Highlanders, on the extreme left, tried to continue their advance, but they too were soon halted by the accurate and effective fire. At this point Howard gave the order: "Give them the bayonet!"

The Continentals swept forward, at the very moment Pickens' militiamen began to swarm against the left flank and rear of the Highlanders. It could not have been more than a few seconds later that Washington's cavalrymen came slashing against the right rear of the British light infantry and the Tory Legionnaires.

Seeing what was happening on the crest of the hill, Tarleton's remaining cavalry Legionnaires refused his desperate order for a climactic charge. They could see that the entire line of British infantry was suddenly broken and running, as the American bayonetmen swept down the hill. Despite the shouts and curses of their young lieutenant colonel, the Tory horsemen saw no reason for dashing forward to what seemed to be certain death or capture. Except for a handful that stayed with Tarleton, the others turned and galloped off the field. After one brief clash with Washington's dragoons, Tarleton turned and followed his fleeing horsemen.

Save for Tarleton and the remnants of his British and Tory dragoons, the entire British force was captured or killed. First to surrender had been the Legion, the light infantry, and the 7th Foot. Less than five minutes later, surrounded by Continentals and militia, the Highlanders also threw down their arms and asked for quarter. Only the intrepid cannoneers of the two British artillery pieces refused to surrender. Fighting vainly to defend their guns, all were either killed or seriously wounded.

Washington's cavalry and McCall's mounted infantry now spurred after the fleeing British dragoons. Tarleton was able to rally a few of his men—perhaps 50 in number—for one last desperate saber fight against the straggling column of pursuing American horsemen. For a few seconds the English and American colonels were engaged in a personal saber duel, in the middle of a violent melée. But as the remainder of the American dragoons came up, the British again fled. Tarleton, swinging his horse around, galloped away. This ended the Battle of the Cowpens. It was not yet 10:00 A.M.

The British had lost 110 men killed, and more than 800 prisoners, of whom 229 were wounded. The Americans also captured both of Tarleton's cannon, more than 800 muskets, 100 horses, Tarleton's entire baggage train of 35 wagons, including a substantial supply of British ammunition and—as Morgan later reported to Gates—"all their music." Escaping with Tarleton were approximately 300 men, British and Tory dragoons. Morgan's losses were twelve killed and 61 wounded.

Fortune had smiled on Daniel Morgan on this, his last battle. But her smile was hardly more than recognition by that fickle Dame of one of the most exceptional demonstrations of simple, brilliant planning and superb tactical leadership in all of the long history of warfare. The Cowpens was a small battle, but it was a significant one. The effect on patriot morale in the north as well as in the south was comparable to the results of Trenton-Princeton and of Saratoga. Considered simply as a military operation, it was probably the closest approach to tactical perfection ever seen on the American continent —a complete double envelopment, the dream of every professional soldier.

★ 32 ★ ★ ★ ★ ★

The Race Is Not to the Swift

THERE IS NO BETTER PROOF of the professional competence of Daniel Morgan than his actions immediately after his great victory at the Cowpens. Realizing that Tarleton and his fugitives would quickly get word of the disaster back to Cornwallis, he also recognized that the British general could not afford to let such a crushing defeat go unavenged. Accordingly, Morgan did not even pause to count the dead and wounded. Within an hour of the last shot, he had his little army hustling northward, with the able-bodied prisoners and the booty herded in its midst, to cross the Little Catawba River before Cornwallis could cut him off. Behind him Morgan left a detachment under doughty Andrew Pickens, with a three-fold mission: to protect the rear, bury the dead, and collect and care for the more seriously wounded among the British prisoners. These unfortunates were gathered into tents, with a caretaking detachment of American surgeons under flag of truce: also under flag, Morgan sent a message to Winnsboro to inform Cornwallis of this humane action.

Morgan's evaluation of Cornwallis' reaction had been sound. Before dawn on January 19 the British army—over 3,000 men, now that Leslie had joined—was on the move. Fortunately for Morgan, slowed down as he was by his cumbersome train of booty and of prisoners, Cornwallis first headed northwest towards the battlefield, thinking that Morgan would remain there for at least 24 hours. Seeing, the next day, that he had misjudged Morgan's perceptiveness, the British general turned northeast towards the crossing of the Little Catawba at Ramsour's Mill. He reached there early on January 25, to find out that Morgan had crossed late on the 23rd.

On the 23rd, also, Greene received Morgan's hastily written, but remarkably well prepared report of his victory, scribbled while his army was preparing to march off the battlefield. After leading a brief celebration by his troops at Cheraw, Greene issued orders for an immediate retirement. He too saw that the British reaction would be as Morgan expected. In fact, even while he was preparing to retire northward from Cheraw, Greene received word that Cornwallis was on the march. Displaying that remarkable foresight and planning capability which had won Washington's high regard, Greene sent a message back to his quartermaster general and engineers to collect all available boats along the lower Dan River, against the possibility that it might be necessary for the army to retreat as far as southern Virginia. These actions were also significant as evidence that Greene was belatedly aware of the dangers resulting from his division of forces the month before.

Once his little force was on the move from Cheraw, and headed toward Salisbury as a tentative point for rendezvous with Morgan, Greene entrusted the command to General Huger. With a small cavalry detachment, he rode across country, through an area heavily infested with Loyalists, to join Morgan. This dangerous ride has been criticized as an act of foolhardy rashness on Greene's part. Since Greene had never before or after done anything which one could call either foolhardy or rash, it is more likely that he risked the danger because he knew that Morgan's illnesses were becoming so acute that he was finding it increasingly difficult to sit his horse. Greene's purpose in joining Morgan, therefore, was to relieve his brilliant second-in-command of the increasingly onerous burdens of herding his victorious little army away from Cornwallis' pursuit. He joined Morgan at the Catawba on January 30.

Back at Ramsour's Mill, on the Little Catawba, Cornwallis saw that Morgan had escaped him, and learned also that Huger's division was marching north. Eager to avenge the disaster of the Cowpens, and anxious to recover the 600 able-bodied prisoners with Morgan's column, Cornwallis continued the pursuit, forming his entire army into a column of light infantry. Except for a few wagons carrying ammunition, and the barest minimum necessities of food and surgical supplies, his entire wagon train was destroyed, including all heavy baggage, most of the provisions, and—to the horror of his troops—several hogsheads of rum. As an example to his men, Cornwallis personally set fire to his own belongings. These arrangements took all day on January 26. Early on the 27th, the British, stripped for the fastest possible movement, crossed the Little Catawba, two days behind Morgan, now approaching Beattie's Ford on the Catawba.

Despite heavy rains, which turned the roads into rivers of thick, oozing mud, the fast-moving British almost caught up with Morgan, whose little army completed its crossing of the north fork of the Catawba on the 28th. That evening the British van reached the river, to find that the rains had raised it to flood stage, and that the Americans had moved all the boats to the opposite shore. Morgan had planned to rest his troops for one more day, but the unexpectedly rapid approach of Cornwallis caused Greene and Morgan to continue the retreat on the 30th, pushing their tired men and horses to the limit of endurance.

For two days the frustrated British fumed by the banks of the river, while Tarleton's cavalrymen reconnoitered north and south, seeking other crossings. On the 31st, as the river began to subside, Cornwallis prepared to make a surprise crossing at Cowan's Ford at dawn the following day.

To cover the slow retreat of Morgan's army, Greene had ordered North Carolina militia General William Davidson to deploy his 800 men to cover all nearby fords of the Catawba. The British crossing at Cowan's Ford, led by Cornwallis himself, caught the militia sentinels on the far bank by surprise. After wading chest-high through the bitterly cold water, the British troops overwhelmed the militia outposts. Davidson, rushing to the scene with reinforcements, was killed, and his entire command was dispersed. Greene, waiting nearby to lead the militia as a rear guard behind Morgan, was almost captured by Tarleton's men, as he galloped northward to rejoin the column, thirty miles ahead.

The next two weeks saw one of the most hair-raising retreats and pursuits in military history. Greene and Morgan, determined to abandon neither booty nor prisoners, could move at a speed only half that of Cornwallis' troops. Greene had shown remarkable foresight in having his engineer, Colonel Thaddeus Kosciuszko, prepare wheeled carriages on which improvised pontoon boats could be hauled with the army. This, and his orders to have other boats collected at the crossing points, meant that the march was interrupted only briefly at each river. Also, his skill in employing his own light troops for delaying actions slowed down the British advance. In this he was also assisted by the continuing rains, and the high water which interfered with the British crossings over the Yadkin and Deep Rivers, as they already had over the Catawba. Cornwallis was delayed for at least a day or two on each of these rivers, and had the additional handicap of being forced to march over roads already churned up by the retreating Americans.

The two separated detachments of Greene's army joined at Guilford on February 6. Greene briefly considered standing to fight at Guilford Courthouse. At this time, however, his total strength was only about 2,000 men, of whom 1,400 were Continentals. Cornwallis had nearly 3,000, almost all British regulars. Greene understood that a battle under these conditions would almost certainly be suicidal.

At Guilford Courthouse, also, Morgan had to give up his painful efforts to continue active field operations. Aching from rheumatism inflamed by the cold and rainy weather, as well as by the arduous exertions of the past several weeks, and suffering from other ailments, the tough Virginia general was no longer able to sit astride his horse. Reluctantly, Greene ordered him into a litter and back to his home in Virginia.

By this time Greene's immediate operational plan was fully formulated. Seeing that Cornwallis, living off the country, without any wagon train of provisions or supplies, was rapidly marching away from his magazines and fortified posts in South Carolina, Greene was now deliberately trying to entice the enemy into further pursuit. He hoped that Cornwallis might permit himself to become as isolated from support and assistance as Burgoyne had been in northern New York. Greene therefore decided to continue his retreat across the Dan into Virginia. If Cornwallis were to be so foolhardy as to attempt to cross that river, then the American army would turn and fight.

Greene, heading for the lower Dan River, where his boats had been collected, encouraged Cornwallis to think the only line of retreat open to the Americans was by the fords of the upper Dan. Creating a light corps of some 700 infantrymen, he put it under command of

Otho Williams, with the triple mission of covering the main army's withdrawal, of delaying and harassing the British advance, and at the same time decoying the enemy towards the upper fords.

For the next four days, while Greene's main body was marching directly to the northward, during foul weather in which almost incessant rain was mixed with snow, Williams performed his missions superbly. At the same time Cornwallis, with a vigor, skill, determination and energy that were truly remarkable, pressed on behind. Skirmishing was frequent, but the British simply refused to be delayed.

Spreading his light corps across a broad front, Williams was successful in deceiving Cornwallis as to the true direction of the American retreat. Finally, on February 13, he made a sudden shift to the northeast, in accordance with Greene's orders, to rejoin the main army at the Dan. That day Lee's Legion, westernmost unit of Williams' command, was almost cut off in a sharp skirmish, and barely escaped a vigorous British pursuit. In sixteen hours, from midnight on February 13 until dusk on the 14th, Williams' men marched 40 miles. Yet for all their speed, the British van was still in sight of Williams' rear guard as the American light corps arrived at the Dan crossings, to find the boats that Greene had waiting for them there. By midnight the last American soldier was across the river, as the exhausted and frustrated British reached the southern, boatless, bank of the Dan River.

Cornwallis, bitterly disappointed, was now in an extremely dangerous situation. By destroying his wagon train he had come close to bagging Greene's army. But having failed in this, the entire British army, without supplies or baggage, was now more than 300 miles by road from its nearest important supply base at Camden, in South Carolina, or about 250 miles by road from the British-held seaport of Wilmington, in North Carolina. The army was exhausted, and had suffered severe losses from exertion and desertion. It was in an area where the population was hostile; there was no possibility of living off the nearby countryside.

Much as he hated to admit failure, and thus to provide encouragement to the Revolutionary cause, Cornwallis knew that he must retreat immediately. Falling back to Hillsboro on February 17, where foraging was better, and where there were some friendly Loyalists, the British general put the best possible face on his withdrawal by issuing a proclamation announcing the reconquest of North Carolina for the Crown.

Greene now saw that he could draw Cornwallis no further away from his base in South Carolina. To keep the British general occupied, and to prevent him from consolidating his position in northern North Carolina, on the 18th Greene sent Pickens' partisans and Lee's Legion back across the Dan. Two days later Lee and Pickens surprised a group of 400 Tories, marching to join Cornwallis. The Tories, mistaking the green coats of Lee's men for those of Tarleton's legion, were unprepared when the Americans suddenly opened fire, killing 90 and wounding 250 in a so-called "massacre."

On the 20th, also, Greene sent Williams' light corps back across the Dan, then three days later recrossed with the rest of his army, now somewhat augmented by Virginia militia, and by a few Continental reinforcements sent by Steuben.

With the American light troops closing around Hillsboro, and harassing his foraging parties, on February 26 Cornwallis reluctantly decided that he would have to retreat further. For the next two weeks the two armies maneuvered in the region northeast of Guilford, with Cornwallis vainly attempting to entice Greene into a battle. By March 13 Cornwallis had fallen back to New Garden, still waiting for an opportunity to pit his British regulars against the Americans, so as to retrieve the situation. By this time his army had shrunk to a strength of barely 2,200 men. The local Tories, terrorized by Pickens' and Lee's "massacre," were giving him little help.

On March 14, Greene arrived at Guilford Courthouse, where five weeks earlier he had briefly contemplated battle. He now had 4,300 men, of whom 1,600 were Continental infantry, and 160 were regular cavalry. He believed the time had come to fight. He therefore moved into a position which he had tentatively selected during the retreat northward.

Guilford Courthouse was located beside the main north-south road running through central North Carolina. The courthouse itself was in the northwest corner of the junction where a road from the west, on the crest of a long east-west ridge, met the main road. Opposite the courthouse to the east was a large clearing; most of the remainder of the ridge was wooded. Below the courthouse, to the south, the main road gradually ascended the slope of the ridge through a relatively shallow, almost dish-shaped, draw or valley. It was in this thinly wooded valley that Greene had selected his battle position, astride the main road. The woods were open enough to permit fair visibility for two or three hundred yards; they were dense enough to provide considerable concealment and cover for skirmishers.

Although the geography was considerably different, Greene followed Morgan's example at the Cowpens in the disposition of his troops in their positions. In addition he was unquestionably greatly influenced by a letter which he had received from Morgan just a few days earlier, in which the ailing warrior had included a number of helpful tactical suggestions. "If they [the militia] fight, you will beat Cornwallis. If not, he will beat you and perhaps cut your regulars to pieces." Morgan suggested that Greene pull out of the ranks of the militia a "number of old soldiers" and form them with the Continentals, to strengthen the main line. As to the remainder of the militia, "put [them] in the center," Morgan suggested, "with some picked troops in their rear to shoot down the first man that runs." On the flanks of the militia should be riflemen, under "enterprising officers," where the range and accuracy of the rifle could be exploited to the maximum in enfilade fire. Having outlined his basic philosophy of obtaining the maximum possible use of the militia, Morgan concluded: "If anything will succeed a disposition of this kind will."

Morgan's advice was obviously very much in Greene's mind as he put his troops in position. Part way up the valley, the road passed through a broad clearing, with a picket fence fringing it. Behind this fence, and on the edge of another nearby clearing just to the east, Greene placed his least reliable militiamen, the North Carolinians. On the right of this line, in the woods, but in sight of the clearing, and echeloned forward for enfilade fire, was Colonel Charles Lynch's corps of 200 Virginia riflemen. Further to the right was Captain Robert Kirkwood's élite Delaware company of Continental light infantry, with Washington's 80-odd light horsemen, slightly further to the rear in the woods, on the extreme right of the American first line. The left flank was organized in similar fashion, by another corps of 200 Virginia riflemen under Colonel Richard Campbell, and the infantry of Lee's Legion, with Lee's cavalry echeloned slightly to the left rear.

About 300 yards farther back, barely in sight of the front line

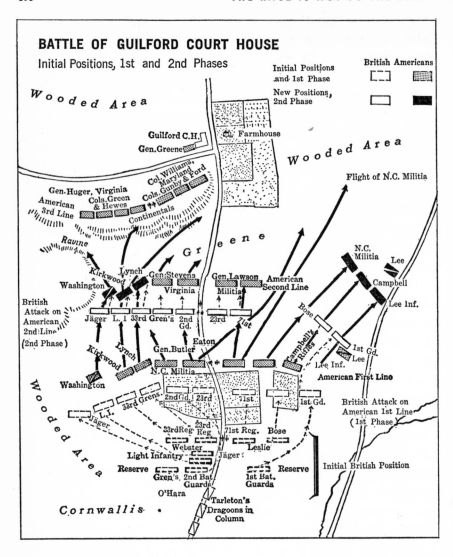

BATTLE OF GUILFORD COURT HOUSE
Initial Positions, 1st and 2nd Phases

through the scattered trees, was the second line. This was made up of Virginia militia, under the command of Brigadier General Stevens, whose brigade was in position west of the road, that of General Robert Lawson being to the east. Another 500 yards farther back, and displaced to the right in such a fashion as to be completely west of the main road, was the third and main line of the American army. Greene had placed it in this unusual location to the right rear in order to take advantage of a steep slope partly overlooking the main road as it approached the courthouse. Here Greene had his two brigades of Continentals: Colonel Williams with the 1st and 5th Maryland regiments on the left, and General Huger with the 4th and 5th Virginia regiments on the right. Greene had only four guns; two of these he placed on the road in the center of the North Carolina militia of the first line; the other two were between the Virginia and Maryland brigades in the third line.

When he put his troops in position late on the 14th, and in inspecting their positions again early on the 15th, Greene repeated to the militia the very words which Morgan had used at the Cowpens: "Three rounds, my boys, and then you may fall back."

As Greene had expected, his movement into a battle position was a deliberate challenge which Cornwallis, twelve miles to the south, could not ignore. The British general roused his men before dawn on the 15th. Without breakfast—due partly to the shortage of food, and partly to Cornwallis' impatience—they marched towards Guilford Courthouse. Screening the advance was Tarleton's cavalry. These dragoons soon ran into Lee's Legion, to whom Greene had assigned the mission of delaying and harassing the British advance. About noon Lee's men fell back to their assigned positions on the left. The Americans on the slope now had a grandstand view of the British column advancing steadily into the sloping valley.

As the British van approached the southern end of the clearing in front of the first American line, the first two American guns opened fire. Cornwallis pushed three of his own cannon forward to engage the American artillery, while he deployed his army. On the right he placed Leslie's brigade, which consisted of von Böse's Hessian regiment furthest east, the remaining battalion of the 71st Highlanders next to the road, and the 1st battalion of the Guards in support immediately behind them. On the left was Lieutenant Colonel Webster's brigade, with the 23rd Foot (Royal Welsh Fusiliers) beside the road, the 33rd regiment on the west, and the Hessian jägers and the army's light infantry just behind them. Behind Webster's brigade, west of the road, was a small reserve under the command of Lieutenant Colonel Charles O'Hara, consisting of the 2nd battalion of the Guards and the army's grenadier companies. Also in reserve, along the road, were Tarleton's dragoons. It was shortly after 1:30 when the British army—probably less than 2,000 strong—was deployed for battle. They had still had nothing to eat since the previous evening.

Though their clothes were a bit ragged, sometimes spotted, and the scarlet, green and blue coats were faded, the British cross-belts and gaiters were pipe-clayed pure white. All items of decorative metal —buttons, belt buckels, and breastplates—were brightly polished and glinted in the thin sun of this cool but cloudless spring day. Most important of all, their firearms were burnished and oiled, and the long, fixed bayonets at their tips twinkled menacingly. In the eyes of the American militiamen, this sight of serried ranks of men advancing in precise even step, through the open forest, and into the clearing, keeping cadence to the beat of the drummers behind the front lines —colorful, bright, forbidding—was both beautiful, awe-inspiring and fearful. But they remembered the words of their general, they crouched behind their fence and leveled their rifles or muskets at the advancing line of scarlet, white, blue and twinkling steel.

To the British and German regulars, superficially imperturbable, regimented to a common appearance, cadence and demeanor, there was something almost equally awe-inspiring in the line of muzzles facing them over the top of the fence to their front. One ragged volley rang out. The two American cannon briefly shifted their fire from the British artillery to the lines of infantry, then limbered up, and galloped off, up the road.

English, Scottish, Welsh and Hessian soldiers were beginning to fall. One British officer, without authority, ordered a halt to fire a volley in return. Without command, somewhat to the dismay of their officers, the entire advancing line came to a halt. For a few terrible seconds the two lines gazed at each other, each aware of the potentialities posed by the other. Colonel Webster galloped forward in front of the Royal Welsh Fusiliers, and rising in his stirrups, pointing his sword forward, shouted: "Come on, my brave fusiliers!"

The English colonel's words were a command to both sides. Some of the North Carolinians remembered their orders, and stayed to fire a third volley. Most, however, seeing that grim line of bayonets dashing up towards them, did what militia has usually done under similar circumstances. They ran. At a few scattered spots along the fence there were brief struggles as some of the braver Americans tried to dispute the British advance. Then they too ran.

The center of the first American line thus completely disappeared. On the flanks, however, extending beyond the British wings, the

Virginia riflemen and Continental troops kept up a steady enfilade fire. For the first time the British officers realized that they had taken most of their losses from these flank American units. Almost simultaneously, and as if in response to a common order, Webster's and Leslie's flank battalions made half wheels towards their tormentors. At the same time O'Hara, sideslipping slightly to the left, moved into the gap between the 33rd and 23rd Foot.

The fighting was now all in the woods. As the 33rd approached them, still maintaining alignment, but with the individual British soldiers taking advantage of the protection of the trees, Lynch's riflemen, and Kirkwood's light infantry fell back slowly according to plan to take up a new position on the right flank of Stevens' line of Virginia militia. On the British right, however, a more impetuous advance by the Hessians and Highlanders pushed Campbell's riflemen and Lee's Legion, with some remnants of the North Carolina militia, to the northeastward, away from the remainder of the American army, and onto high ground on the eastern rim of the battlefield valley.

Leslie, leaving the Hessians to continue the pressure against this isolated American force, swung northward again with the 71st Foot and the Guards. While firing continued on the east between the Hessians and the isolated American left wing, the British units advanced steadily through the woods towards the second line. They were now fighting effectively as skirmishing light infantry, yet at the same time maintaining near-perfect alignment in their advance.

For several minutes the Virginians held their positions valiantly and determinedly, keeping up heavy fire from their positions behind the trees. About two-thirds of the British line was now to the west of the road, under Webster and O'Hara. Stimulated by these two brave and impetuous officers, they began to roll back Stevens' right flank, first parallel to the road, and then back across it, at right angles to Lawson's brigade. Washington and Kirkwood, alarmed, attempted to counterattack in an envelopment of the British left flank. Webster immediately wheeled the British 33rd Foot to the left again, repulsed the counterattack, and then drove Kirkwood and Washington back up the ridge towards the American third line.

By this time Stevens' right flank, thrown back completely at right angles to its original front, cracked apart. Having thus completely swept away the right flank of the American second line, Webster, catching sight of the Continentals to his left front, now continued an impetuous advance up the steep slope towards the waiting American regulars, heading toward the middle of the line, where Kirkwood had fallen back to a position around the two artillery pieces. Webster now had under his immediate command only the 33rd Foot, the light infantry and the Hessian jägers; O'Hara and Leslie were still being held up by the amazingly determined stand of Lawson's Virginia brigade. As Webster's troops struggled up the slope, cheering loudly, they were met by a converging volley from the entire American third line, causing fearful destruction in their ranks, and bringing their charge to a complete halt. Upon individual impulse, but simultaneously, Gunby's Virginia regiment and Kirkwood's tiny corps of light infantry immediately counterattacked with the bayonet, driving back the British left flank in considerable disorder to their left rear, across a ravine, where they were completely out of touch with the remainder of the British army.

At this point, a George Washington, a Daniel Morgan, or a Benedict Arnold would have counterattacked with his entire command. The British had been stopped completely on the American left, and had been thrown into serious confusion on their right. Had Greene seized this moment, in the way Morgan did at the Cowpens, a complete victory would have been almost certain. Tarleton and other British officers were convinced that the battle was already lost.

Greene, however, was not that kind of a general. Early in the campaign, in a letter to Morgan, he had expressed the philosophy which would guide him constantly in the following months: "It is not our business to risk too much." In the back of his mind, evidently, was the fear that failure of an impetuous charge might result in the entire destruction of his army, and with it, the Revolutionary cause in the South. Some military analysts have praised this caution as being the wiser and surer way to eventual victory. On the other hand, the failure of a general to recognize the propitious moment to bring a quick, certain, and successful conclusion to a campaign is risking the graver dangers of the unpredictable fortunes of war. As a result, Greene gave to the British more chances to retrieve the battle and the campaign; they almost did both.

The moment passed, and with it the remainder of the American second line began to crumble. In the fight against the Virginians,

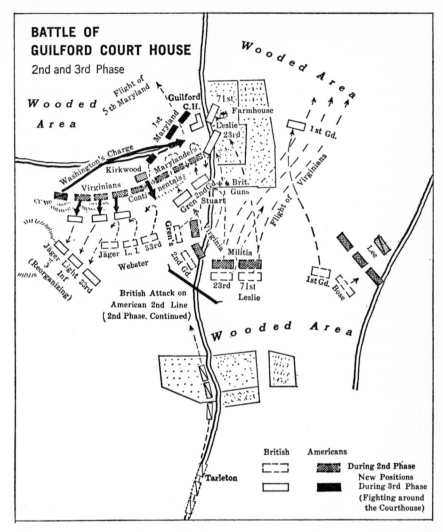

BATTLE OF
GUILFORD COURT HOUSE
2nd and 3rd Phase

O'Hara was wounded and his place was taken by Lieutenant Colonel Duncan Stuart, who led the British center up the road towards the courthouse and the left flank of the American third line. Leslie was now pushing the crumbling left wing of the Virginians to the northeastward, through the clearing on the crest east of the courthouse.

As Stuart came up within range of Williams' brigade, he halted the 2nd battalion of the Guards and the grenadier companies, realigned them, and then after one volley charged northwestward up the slope against the Maryland left flank. Leslie, seeing that he was now east of the main fight, sent the 1st battalion of the Guards chasing the

Virginia militia to the northeast, while he wheeled the 71st and 23rd to the left to follow Stuart. At the same time, Webster had also rallied and re-formed the British left wing, and was moving back up the slope against the Virginia Continental brigade.

The extreme left flank unit of the Continental line was the 5th Maryland Regiment, newly organized and here gaining its first real baptism of fire. In the face of the grim assault of the Guards and the grenadiers, these Marylanders suddenly broke and ran. Stuart pursued them up to the crest and past the courthouse. Colonel Washington, who had fallen back into reserve behind the third line, seeing what was happening on the left, galloped down the ridge road behind the American third line against the unsuspecting Guards and grenadiers. Though few in numbers, the American cavalrymen literally rode through and over the Britishers, completely halting their pursuit. Stuart was killed, and the wounded O'Hara resumed command of his shaken redcoats, now falling back as rapidly and in as much confusion as the 5th Marylanders had been in the other direction.

Meanwhile Gunby, commanding the 1st Maryland, had been wounded and was replaced by Howard (of Cowpens fame). At Otho Williams' orders, Howard had wheeled to the left, and now counterattacked against the shaken Guards and grenadiers. The amazingly resilient Kirkwood joined in this charge with his Delaware company. The British center was now on the point of complete dissolution. At this moment, however, Leslie with the Royal Welsh Fusiliers and the Highlanders came up just in time to prevent a rout. The grenadiers and the Guards fell back, while the Fusiliers and the 71st engaged in a prolonged fire fight with the Marylanders and the Delaware light infantry around the courthouse and the road junction.

The British troops, who had not eaten in over eighteen hours, had now been in an uphill battle for more than two hours. Exhausted, dispirited by the fierce resistance of the American regulars, the British center began to fall back. To Cornwallis it was obvious that the next few minutes would be critical. Webster had again been repulsed from the right flank of the American third line. O'Hara's troops were only slowly rallying. Leslie was now on the verge of defeat. Bringing up his three artillery pieces to the southwest edge of the clearing opposite the courthouse, Cornwallis ordered them to fire grape into the melée on the crest. O'Hara was horrified, since he knew that this would

mean indiscriminate losses to British as well as to Americans. But
Cornwallis, probably as considerate and compassionate a general as the
English army produced in the latter part of the 18th Century, con-
cluded that this was his one chance of halting the American attack.
If a few Englishmen were also killed or wounded by the artillery fire,
this was an unfortunate but unavoidable concomitant.

The result was what Cornwallis expected. With this intensive fire
of grape enfilading the right front of his new line, Williams ordered
Howard and Kirkwood to withdraw slightly behind the crest to re-form.
Leslie was given a reprieve, and fell back to the edge of the clearing,
near O'Hara, to re-form his battalions. Webster was reorganizing and
preparing for a fourth attack on the American main line. Cornwallis,
galloping between his scattered and shattered units, demanded one
more effort.

It was now nearly 4:00 P.M. Greene could see Webster returning
once more to a persistent attack against the right flank of his one
remaining line, while the remainder of the British were reorganizing
to the east of the road. Fearful that he might not be able to stop another coordinated British counterattack, he ordered his Continentals
to withdraw all along the line. The Virginians had some difficulty in
disengaging from the still-persistent Webster, but in one final volley,
in which the brave British colonel was mortally wounded, they halted
his last attack, and then fell back. The American artillery horses having
all been killed in the confused struggle around the courthouse, Greene
had to abandon his guns. Tarleton now came up to make one per-
functory effort at pursuit, but was quickly repulsed by the well-
directed fire of the slowly withdrawing Continentals. Tarleton then
turned to the east to assist the Hessians in driving Lee and the Virginia riflemen of the American left flank off the field. The Battle of
Guilford Courthouse had come to its bloody close.

The British admitted a loss of 93 killed and 439 wounded (more
than 50 of these latter died during the night). Losses amongst officers
were particularly heavy. Greene reported 78 killed and 183 wounded.
Both sides later claimed, with good reason, that the losses suffered
by their opponents were considerably greater than the figures that they
admitted. Whatever the actual figures, there is no question that the
British suffered at least twice as many casualties as the Americans,
and that Cornwallis lost at least 25 percent of his entire army.

It was an extremely tough battle, hard-fought on both sides, with many deserving of praise, and few of censure. The British regulars —attacking against odds of two-to-one, re-forming time after time despite heavy punishment, fighting on empty stomachs—were superb. Equally praiseworthy were the personal performances of the senior British commanders: Cornwallis, Leslie, Webster, O'Hara, and Stuart.

On the American side the North Carolina militia had performed less well than expected, the Virginia militia somewhat better than hoped for. The 5th Marylanders had proven themselves shockingly green; but the remainder of the Continentals had fought as staunchly as their British and Hessian counterparts. Among the American commanders, Lee, Washington, Williams, Howard and Kirkwood performed with their usual valor and reliability.

Greene probably obtained the maximum possible performance from his militia and regular troops, and from his fine subordinates. He had exposed himself with typical gallantry during the struggle on the courthouse ridge. But by fighting an essentially defensive battle, in which each of his three lines fought separate, uncoordinated engagements, he had failed to take the maximum advantage of what he had been able to obtain from his men. He permitted the much smaller British force to defeat his army in detail by bringing superior numbers of splendid professional soldiers against his own forces, militia and regular, at the points of contact. Had he coordinated the activities of his three lines, had he attempted a full-scale counterattack at any time after his North Carolina militia fled the field, it seems doubtful if the outnumbered British would have been able to continue the battle.

On the other hand, Greene's troops had proven—to themselves, to their general, and to the enemy—that under the right circumstances, they could stand up to the best of the British, and give as good as they received. And Greene, whose objective had been limited and defensive, had achieved what he set out to do. Though he had abandoned the battlefield, and had lost four artillery pieces, he had so seriously punished Cornwallis' army that the British general was in an even more desperate plight after the battle than he had been before. Greene's army, on the other hand, was intact, relatively cheerful, and ready to fight again.

33 ★ ★ ★ ★ ★

How to be Victorious without Winning Battles

No ONE WAS MORE AWARE OF THE DISASTROUS CONSEQUENCES of his hollow victory at Guilford Courthouse than was Cornwallis himself. He did not have to wait for Charles James Fox to say that "another such victory would destroy the British army." For the day and a half following the battle, while his surgeons were caring for the wounded —with equal solicitude for American and British*—and while his famished soldiers buried the dead as they waited for the slow and pitifully small supply train to come up, Cornwallis pondered his problem. During those hours his troops subsisted on the few scraps that they were able to obtain by scouring the immediate countryside. With his effective strength now well below 1,500 men, Cornwallis dared not send foraging parties any distance from his main body.

On March 18, leaving 70 wounded under a flag of truce to be cared for by the Americans, Cornwallis began moving to the southeastward, hoping that in the heavily Loyalist center around Cross Creek he would be able to find enough provisions for his army, permitting him to rest and rebuild its offensive strength. He informed young Lord Rawdon, now the senior British officer in South Carolina, of this movement, and directed him to maintain control over the principal regions of that strife-torn state.

---

* Greene sent some of his own surgeons back under a flag of truce to assist in caring for the wounded.

On arrival at Cross Creek, however, Cornwallis saw that his hopes of establishing a base there had been vain. The inhabitants, though still Loyalist in sentiment, had suffered much in the struggles with their patriot neighbors, and their resources were simply inadequate to take care of Cornwallis' army. So he continued his withdrawal to Wilmington, arriving there on April 7 with about 1,400 men fit for duty.

Greene had slowly followed Cornwallis as far as Cross Creek, with Lee's Legion, Campbell's riflemen, and Colonel Washington's dragoons harassing the British march. He reached Ramsey's Mill on March 29, only one day after Cornwallis had left that place. Here the Virginia militia decided that it was time to go home. The North Carolinians were also leaving. Greene briefly rested his army while he evaluated the new situation in the Carolinas.

Cornwallis' retreat to Wilmington had automatically restored most of North Carolina to effective patriot control. Greene knew that once Cornwallis reached a seaport such as Wilmington, the Americans could do him little more serious damage so long as Britain retained control of the sea. If the British army stayed there, it could not interfere with any future American operations in the interior. If such activities were to entice Cornwallis to return inland, so much the better. Meanwhile the American could be doing something to make the position of the British in South Carolina more uncomfortable, and possibly to recover important parts of that state for the Revolutionary cause.

At that time the main British concentrations in South Carolina were in the fortified towns of Charleston, Georgetown, Camden, Ninety-Six and Augusta. Other important garrisons were in Fort Watson, Fort Motte, Fort Granby and Orangeburg. Smaller detachments held additional scattered fortifications around the state. The total British force in South Carolina was about 8,000 men, of whom at least two-thirds were Loyalists. But Greene was well aware of the fact that the requirements of holding the fortified posts limited Rawdon's mobile field force strength to less than 1,500 men. These were concentrated under Rawdon's personal command at Camden.

Greene himself had a hard core of about 1,500 Continental regular troops. From experience, he knew that he could count on shifting strength amongst the militia contingents with the army, ranging from

1,000 to 3,000 men. More important than these militia units of questionable reliability, however, were the local militia partisans, experienced, semi-professional soldiers, commanded by men like Marion, Pickens and Sumter. Together with his own Continental and militia army, Greene felt sure that he could make use of these local partisans to harass the British, to capture a number of their posts, possibly to defeat Rawdon in battle, and perhaps even entice Cornwallis back into a disastrous renewal of field operations in the central Carolinas. His first objective was to drive the British from their positions along the Santee and Congaree rivers.

On April 6, therefore, Greene moved south on Camden. Lee's Legion went ahead, to cooperate with Marion against Rawdon's line of communications between Camden and Charleston. Greene had requested Pickens to step up his operations against the British fortifications at Ninety-Six and Augusta. He invited Sumter to join his main army near Camden. In this way, asking the partisans to operate in their own localities, he hoped to obtain the maximum possible effort and benefit from their activities. To cover his rear, in the event Cornwallis decided to pursue from Wilmington, Greene requested the North Carolina militia under General Jethro Sumner to take the field and to consolidate patriot control of their own home state.

Greene's strategy was immediately evident to Cornwallis. The British general knew that the logistic requirements of his army would prevent him moving overland behind Greene with any hope of interfering with operations in central South Carolina. Distance and scarcity of supplies would have made any such effort foolhardy. He briefly considered shipping his army by sea to Charleston, to renew the campaign in the Carolinas. He was deterred from this move both by shortage of shipping, and by the realization that this would simply re-establish the same situation which had led to the disastrous Cowpens-Guilford Courthouse campaign.

Because of the success of the partisans, Cornwallis believed that the only British hope in South Carolina was to hold on to the fortified posts, while winning a decisive victory elsewhere. The experience of the past month had proven to him that North Carolina was not the place. Virginia, where British Major General William Phillips and the new British Brigadier General Benedict Arnold were now operating, seemed the most likely region in which a British field victory could be obtained. Furthermore, a move to Virginia might draw Greene north after him, permitting Cornwallis, with Phillips and Arnold, to operate against Greene and Steuben on interior lines. So on April 24 Cornwallis led his army, 1,435 strong, on a long overland march northward towards Virginia; out of the Carolina campaigns, and to an unforeseen rendezvous with destiny and an old nemesis.

Ten days earlier the combined forces of Lighthorse Harry Lee and Swamp Fox Marion invested Fort Watson, midway between Camden and Charleston. Without artillery, and lacking entrenching tools or other engineer equipment, the lightly-equipped American troops were baffled by the stout stockade, held by a garrison of 120 men, two-thirds of whom were British. The Americans also knew that a flying column of approximately 500 regular British troops, under Colonel John Watson, was at that very moment trying to flush Marion out of his swamp hideout along the banks of the Pee Dee River. Colonel Hezekiah Maham, one of Marion's subordinates, now offered a suggestion based on his readings in ancient history: an 18th Century adaptation of the siege tower of antiquity. During the night of April 22-23, Lee's and Marion's men erected a stout log tower about 100 yards from the stockade, and overlooking its ramparts. At dawn, riflemen opened fire from the top of "Maham's Tower," while two parties of troops attacked the fort from different directions. As the defenders attempted to move to meet these new threats, they were picked off by the riflemen in the tower. Seeing that further resistance was hopeless, the British garrison surrendered.

Meanwhile, on April 19, after a fast march from Ramsey's Mill, Greene's army had taken up a position on Hobkirk's Hill, overlooking Camden. He now had about 1,400 men, including 1,100 Continentals. He waited in vain for Sumter to arrive, as requested. But the proud Gamecock, as independent as the fighting bird which inspired his nickname, had no intention of subordinating himself to anyone, and refused to come, much to Greene's disappointment.

At the same time Greene was cautiously observing his new foe: Lord Rawdon. The young British commander—only 26 years old— had a well-deserved reputation as an energetic, capable leader. His rapid rise in the British army had begun when, as a lieutenant, he had distinguished himself at Bunker Hill.

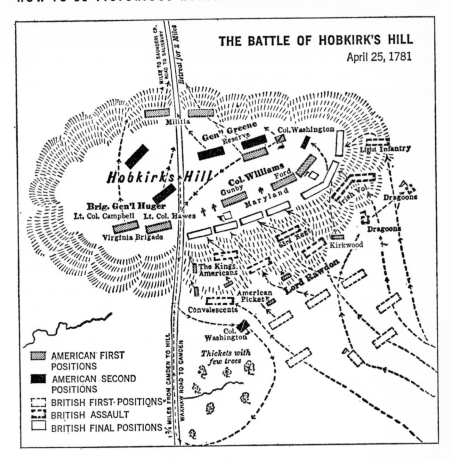

THE BATTLE OF HOBKIRK'S HILL
April 25, 1781

On April 25, while Greene's troops were drawing rations, Rawdon, approaching unexpectedly from the southeast with 900 men, suddenly struck the American outposts below Hobkirk's Hill. The pickets were thrown back in confusion, but the indomitable Kirkwood led his light infantry immediately to the base of the hill to conduct a delaying action while Greene formed his army on the crest. Williams' Maryland brigade was on the left, Huger's Virginia brigade on the right, as at Guilford Courthouse. Colonel Washington's 87 dragoons and a small contingent of North Carolina militia, 250 strong, were in reserve, to the left rear. Between the two Continental brigades Greene placed his three guns. Having accomplished his delaying mission, Kirkwood fell back to the left flank of the American main line.

About half of Rawdon's men were British regulars, the remainder

Loyalist regulars plus a few South Carolina Tory militia. As he advanced on a narrow front, Rawdon discerned that his efforts at surprise had failed, and that the American line now considerably overlapped his. With snap and precision the units in the British rear swung left and right into the line, extending the British front beyond that of the Americans, just as Greene's artillery began to open fire with grapeshot. While the British were still in the process of deploying, Greene's Continentals charged down the hill. At the same time, Washington made a wide encirclement to the right, planning to attack the British rear.

The sudden extension of the British line permitted Rawdon's men to bring all muskets and rifles to bear upon the advancing Americans. Colonel Gunby, commanding the 1st Maryland Regiment in the left center of the line, on his own initiative decided to halt briefly to fire a volley in return, before continuing the charge. The unexpected command, combined with the galling British fire, briefly threw this veteran regiment into some confusion. At the same time Gunby's abrupt halt caused the units to his right and left to hesitate, fearing to create a serious gap in the American line.

Rawdon immediately seized this opportunity to order a charge, devoting particular attention to the 1st Maryland. For some unaccountable reason these veteran troops, who had comported themselves so well in the battles and marches of the previous year, broke and ran. In vain did Gunby and Williams try to rally them. The 5th Maryland, which had broken at Guilford Courthouse, now took to their heels again. Panic spread to the right flank, where men of the 4th Virginia began to break ranks, and to run back up the hill. Only the 5th Virginia, one company of the 1st Maryland and Kirkwood's Delaware Light Infantry were unbroken.

Greene, dismayed by this unexpected collapse of his attack, ordered the 5th Virginia to cover the withdrawal. The remaining company of Maryland Continentals tried to protect the withdrawal of the three guns, but after a gallant defense were overrun by Rawdon's dragoons.

At this moment Colonel Washington's dragoons belatedly came up to the confused battlefield. Washington had been fighting his own private war in the British left rear, where he had captured 200 British supply and headquarters personnel. Rawdon himself had been surrounded, and nearly captured, before the British reserves drove off the American dragoons. Washington had salvaged 50 prisoners and was returning to the battlefield when he suddenly realized what was occurring there. Charging up from the southwest, he drove the British cavalry away from the American guns. Hitching the horses of some of his dragoons to the guns, he then withdrew, still holding determinedly to his 50 prisoners.

By this time Greene, Williams, and Huger had rallied their men, and a new American line had been formed near the crest of the hill. Rawdon now decided that he had accomplished enough, and withdrew while Washington and Kirkwood, holding the British dragoons at bay, rescued all of the American wounded on the battlefield. As Rawdon returned to Camden, Greene fell back to Sander's Creek, near the site of Gates' defeat eight months earlier. American casualties were 19 killed, 115 wounded and 136 missing. Rawdon lost 38 killed and 220 wounded and missing.

Had Greene stayed on the battlefield, as it seems he could easily have done, he might have been able to claim either a victory or a draw at Hobkirk's Hill. He had been so shocked by the inexplicable panic of his best troops, however, that he was unwilling to risk continued fighting that day, and decided to give his men a rest. On the 27th he fell back further to Rugeley's Mill, to recuperate. It was at this time that he wrote a philosophic letter to the French Ambassador to the United States, Chevalier de la Luzerne, in which he said: "We fight, get beat, rise, fight again."

Provender was scarce in the region around Camden, and on May 3 Greene marched southwestward to cross the Wateree, seeking food, and at the same time threatening Rawdon's line of communications, already severely jeopardized by the loss of Fort Watson. On May 7, Rawdon was joined by Colonel Watson, and made a brief but abortive effort to bring Greene to battle. The British commander now saw that he was in a dangerously exposed situation. His supply situation was even worse than that of the Americans. Also, he was having trouble, verging on mutiny in some instances, with American deserters who had enlisted in his volunteer units. Greene had hanged five such men who had been among the prisoners taken at the Battle of Hobkirk's Hill. The remaining American deserters had no interest in fighting and taking the risk of receiving a similar fate. All of these factors led Rawdon to conclude that he must abandon central South Carolina.

On May 10, therefore, Rawdon evacuated Camden, after burning everything of value. He left his badly wounded behind, to be cared for by the Americans. He also sent orders to the garrisons of Ninety-Six and Fort Granby (modern Columbia) to abandon their posts, and to come back to help him hold a consolidated area south and west of the Santee. These messages were intercepted, however, by the Americans, so that the garrisons remained in these two outlying British posts.

At this time Fort Motte, on the south bank of the Congaree River, near its junction with the Wateree, was being invested by Lee and Marion. Greene immediately pushed after Rawdon, to prevent him from interfering with this siege. On the 12th, however, the garrison of 175 men had surrendered after having been subjected to another ancient siege technique—use of flaming arrows as incendiaries, which set fire to the roofs of the buildings around which the Fort Motte stockade had been constructed.

Greene arrived at Fort Motte on the 13th, the day after its surrender. He learned that Sumter had captured Orangeburg on the 11th. He immediately sent Marion to attack the British post at Georgetown, while Lee was sent up the Congaree River against Fort Granby. Lee seized Granby on the 15th. The garrison of 352 men, mostly Tory, had given up easily to Lee's considerably smaller force, when the American colonel had wisely offered them the opportunity to withdraw without interference.

Marion harassed Rawdon's retreat, until the British finally halted at Monck's Corner. The partisan leader then moved against Georgetown, which was abandoned by the British on the 29th, as he approached. The garrison withdrew to Charleston.

Meanwhile Greene ordered Lee to join Pickens, who was operating against Augusta. After a siege of ten days, marked by extremely hard fighting and a vigorous defense by the 330 Tory militia and 300 Creek Indians of the garrison, Augusta surrendered on June 6. Save for the small section of territory between Charleston and Monck's Corner, where Rawdon had halted his retreat, the only important British post remaining in South Carolina now was Ninety-Six, toward which Greene was marching.

Ninety-Six was so called because it was a way station from Charleston to the old frontier posts, ninety-six miles farther west. The little village had been strongly fortified with a stockade, a ditch, and *abatis*. There were two strong outworks connected to the main stockade. The garrison consisted of 350 Tory regulars, and 200 experienced South Carolina Tory militia, commanded by Lieutenant Colonel John H. Cruger, an extremely able Loyalist officer.

When Greene reached Ninety-Six on May 21, his own strength had fallen to less than 1,000 Continentals, plus a handful of militia. Despite this weakness, Greene immediately began regular siege approaches, directed by his chief engineer, Colonel Thaddeus Kosciuszko. But though the Americans pressed the siege vigorously, Cruger and his men reacted with equal vigor and determination, despite the intense summer heat. Repeated Tory sorties greatly impeded American progress. Efforts to use the siege techniques which had worked so well at Forts Watson and Motte were unsuccessful. When a Maham Tower was built to overlook part of his defenses, Cruger merely bolstered the ramparts and heightened the walls with sandbags. The incendiary arrows were foiled by the simple expedient of tearing off the roofs of all the houses in Ninety-Six. At that time of the year, the only serious consequence of this was the removal of protection from the fierce sun.

With the arrival of Lee on June 8, closely followed by Pickens, Greene intensified his operations. Lee directed the siege approaches from the west, while Kosciuszko continued those on the east. Lee's parallel approaches soon made it impossible for the British to make regular use of their one water source, and by June 15 the garrison's situation had become desperate.

About this time, however, Greene received bad news from Sumter. British reinforcements had arrived at Charleston on June 3, and on the 7th Rawdon had started north with 2,000 good troops to relieve Ninety-Six. Greene asked Sumter to delay Rawdon's advance as much as possible, and ordered Pickens and Washington to undertake delaying actions on the road to Ninety-Six. He asked Marion to help, as well.

Rawdon, however, avoided American interception, partly because Sumter, ever the prima donna, refused to obey Greene's instructions. Despite the heat, Rawdon continued his approach to Ninety-Six by forced marches. On June 17, a messenger sneaked through the American lines to bring word to the garrison that Rawdon was only three or four days' march away. Learning of this, Greene decided that his

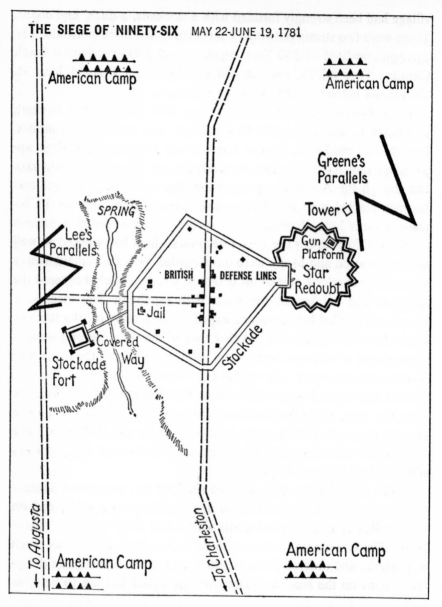

THE SIEGE OF NINETY-SIX MAY 22-JUNE 19, 1781

only recourse was to try an assault. This was undertaken at noon on the 18th. Lee's attack broke its way into the outer fort protecting the British water supply, but determined Tory defense stopped all of the other assaults. The Americans lost 57 killed, 70 wounded, and 20 missing, while the British had 27 killed and 58 wounded.

Though he had now completely captured the British water supply, it was obvious to Greene that Cruger was determined to hold on for another two or three days, until Rawdon could arrive. Reluctantly, therefore, on June 20 Greene raised the siege, and retreated slowly northward towards Charlotte. Rawdon arrived the next day, and briefly considered pursuing the Americans. His men were exhausted, however, and he recalled what had happened to Cornwallis in his efforts to pursue Greene into North Carolina. He also knew that Ninety-Six, despite its brilliant and gallant defense by Cruger and his men, was no longer tenable. Accordingly, he destroyed the fortifications, and early in July marched slowly back towards Charleston. Greene, immediately stopping his retreat, turned around to harass the British retirement.

By this time midsummer heat was causing great trouble to both armies. Greene decided to withdraw for a period of rest and recuperation into the High Hills of Santee, a region just east of the confluence of the Wateree and Congaree rivers. Here the rolling hills were above the malarial plains, the local population was friendly, the air was pure, the water clear, and supplies plentiful. The army stayed there for six weeks, regaining strength and stamina, while Greene mixed intensive drill with pleasant relaxation.

Rawdon, now seriously ill, returned to England, leaving Lieutenant Colonel Alexander Stewart in command of the small section of South Carolina still remaining under British control. Stewart, who had about 2,000 men and three guns, took up a position on the Santee River, near the site of former Fort Watson, only sixteen miles south of Greene's outposts. Although nearly half of Stewart's command were Tories, these were regulars with training, equipment and leadership comparable to the best British regiments.

By August 22 Greene was ready to resume the campaign. His army had been revitalized by its stay in the High Hills, and had been augmented. He now had 1,250 Continental infantry, 300 regular cavalry, and militia contingents totalling 900 more men, including Marion's and Pickens' experienced partisan commands.

The summer rains had flooded the Santee Valley, as well as the lower Congaree and Wateree rivers. In order to approach Stewart's position on the south side of the Santee, therefore Greene had to take a roundabout route. Marching north to Camden, he crossed the Wateree, then turned south across the Congaree, towards Orangeburg.

On the night of September 7, moving cautiously to effect surprise, he bivouacked seven miles northwest of Eutaw Springs.

The British camp was in a clearing southwest of sturdily-built brick Eutaw House near the south bank of Eutaw Creek, and south of the east-west Santee River road to Charleston. West of the clearing, the area was fairly heavily wooded, with the timber becoming extremely thick and tangled toward the Santee River and Eutaw Creek, northwest of the walled garden of Eutaw House.

Greene broke camp before dawn next morning to attack. Warned by deserters shortly after daybreak, Stewart, although he did not believe the Americans were approaching, sent out a mixed cavalry and infantry reconnaissance detachment under Major John Coffin. This force ran into Greene's advance not more than a mile from the British camp and was thrown back. A large British foraging party, unarmed, was also surprised and captured by the Americans.

Stewart hurriedly formed for battle. His line consisted of the 3rd Foot (the Buffs) on the right, Cruger's Tories from Ninety-Six astride the main road in the center, with the 63rd and 64th Foot holding the left. Protecting the right flank, near the banks of Eutaw Creek, the regular light infantry and grenadier companies were posted, under Major John Marjoribanks. Stewart's left flank, which was in the air, was covered by the cavalry—some 50 dragoons under Major Coffin— and a mixed detachment of 150 infantry apparently drawn from several other units. Stewart expected to use this force not only as a flank guard but also as a reserve. To cover his preparations, Stewart sent a detachment of Loyalists and one gun westward along the road to delay the American advance.

It was about 9:00 A.M. when this delaying force opened up on the advancing Americans. While Lee engaged them, with the assistance of two artillery pieces rushed forward to him, Greene deployed his troops in the woods, in accordance with his previously prepared plan. Because of the woods, both sides had pushed their cannon rather close to each other, and this initial part of the meeting engagement was, in the words of Otho Williams, "bloody and obstinate."

Following the pattern of the dispositions at the Cowpens, and at Guilford Courthouse, Greene placed his militia in a line in front of the Continentals. The center of the first line consisted of his least reliable militia units, those from North Carolina, under the command of French volunteer Colonel the Marquis de Malmédy. These were flanked to the right by Marion's South Carolina partisans, and on the left by those of Pickens. On the right of the second line was a newly-raised North Carolina Continental brigade under General Jethro Sumner. In the center, the Virginia Continentals were commanded by Lieutenant Colonel Richard Campbell; Williams' reliable Maryland brigade was on the left. Protecting the right flank of the army was Lee's Legion, while on the left was a mixed force of South Carolina infantry and cavalry under Colonels John Henderson and Wade Hampton. In reserve were Greene's old reliables: Washington's dragoons and Kirkwood's Delaware Continental light infantry.

It was probably not much after 9:30 when Greene was ready to resume his advance. Because of the denseness of the woods, the American line was able to approach to within less than 50 yards of the British before the fire of Stewart's troops forced them to halt. After several minutes of relatively harmless exchange of fire, Stewart ordered his left to charge. This bayonet attack soon had the North Carolinians and South Carolinians of the American center and right fleeing back through the woods towards the Continentals immediately behind them. Greene immediately ordered Sumner's North Carolina militia to move up into this gap, and then ordered a general advance. The British fell back in the face of this pressure, and so Stewart brought up his small contingent of reserve infantry, and counterattacked. The North Carolina Continentals were now in their turn forced to give ground.

At this point Greene ordered his Maryland and Virginia Continentals to charge, while Lee was to envelop the British left flank. This coordinated converging attack threw the British back in confusion, leaving intact only Marjoribanks' grenadiers and light infantry on the extreme right, and Coffin's small detachment of cavalry on the extreme left. Greene now ordered Colonel Washington to attack Marjoribanks with his cavalry and Kirkwood's Continentals. Washington, thinking that he could disperse the British by a simple cavalry charge, dashed off before Kirkwood came up, only to be repulsed by a combination of destructive fire from the British regulars, and the denseness of the forest thicket where they had emplaced themselves. The American cavalry suffered heavy losses; Washington was wounded and captured, and his surviving dragoons forced to withdraw. Kirkwood,

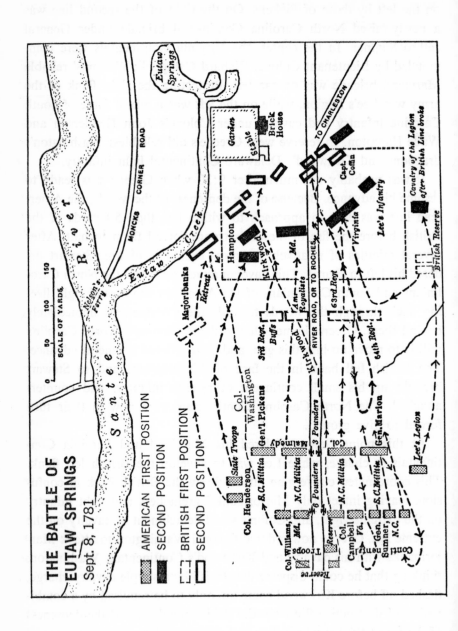

THE BATTLE OF
EUTAW SPRINGS
Sept. 8, 1781

AMERICAN FIRST POSITION
SECOND POSITION

BRITISH FIRST POSITION
SECOND POSITION

arriving soon afterward, charged with the bayonet and drove the British grenadiers and light infantry back to the palisaded garden to the northwest of Eutaw House. Here Marjoribanks' men, with their right flank protected by the creek, and their left by the garden, halted and repulsed Kirkwood's pursuit.

Meanwhile most of the British had fled through their camp, and past Eutaw House. Stewart threw a small detachment into the house, and a few more troops along the palisaded garden wall, in a last effort to save his army from complete destruction. With the remainder of his officers, he then attempted to rally his troops, still fleeing to the east.

By this time the Americans had captured 300 British soldiers and two of their guns. The battle was virtually won. Probably not more than 500 British troops were left in any kind of organized formation in and around Eutaw House and its gardens. The exultant Maryland and Virginia Continentals, sweeping after the fleeing foe, suddenly found themselves in the midst of the British camp. The temptation to loot, particularly amongst the tents of the British officers, became too strong.

Suddenly the victorious Americans became a mob of rioting pillagers, soon joined by most of the other militia and Continentals. At this particular moment, probably the only American units still retaining any cohesion were Kirkwood's Delaware light infantry near the creek, and Lee's Legion, which was attempting to force its way into Eutaw House, while the British defenders were still trying to organize it for defense. Greene, who was with Lee, was apparently completely unaware of what was happening to his right rear in the British camp. He seems to have assumed that his Continental brigades were still chasing Stewart's defeated men down the road.

Major Marjoribanks, commanding the grenadiers and light infantry, was apparently the first English officer to see what had happened to the American army. Counterattacking from the garden, he drove Lee away from the house, and captured the two artillery pieces which Greene had brought up to batter down the door. Meanwhile, further east, Stewart had rallied his men and was bringing them back to establish a new line behind the brick house.

Greene, now realizing what had happened to his army, ordered Kirkwood and Lee to fall back, and with the assistance of his brigadiers, began to reorganize and rally the mob looting the British camp. At this point Coffin's cavalry and Marjoribanks' grenadiers and light infantry counterattacked into the camp, suddenly awakening the American troops to their peril. Finally responding to Greene's frantic appeals, the men re-formed, and withdrew slowly to the woods west of the clearing where they had started the battle four hours earlier.

By unexpressed mutual agreement, the battle now ended. Both sides were too shaken, and too exhausted, to be able to undertake any further vigorous action that day. Greene fell back a few miles in the woods, where he completed the reorganization and rallying of his troops.

In this extremely hard-fought and bitterly-contested battle the Americans lost 139 killed, 375 wounded, and eight missing. British casualties were 85 killed, 351 wounded, and 430 missing (though Stewart only admitted a total loss of 525 casualties, including 247 missing).

Though the Americans claimed that Eutaw Springs was a drawn battle, it ended with the British clinging precariously to a portion of the field, and with the Americans withdrawing to lick their wounds. But Stewart had lost more than 40 percent of his army, and did not dare risk another battle. Early next morning he withdrew to Charleston, leaving 70 wounded to be cared for by the Americans. Once again, Greene had lost a battle, but had forced his opponent to retreat.

The Battle of Eutaw Springs for all practical purposes ended Greene's campaign in the Carolinas. Sending Lee and Marion to pursue Stewart, he took the rest of his army back for a brief rest and further recuperation in the High Hills of Santee. He then returned to blockade Charleston, now the only foothold retained by the British in South Carolina.

In a ten months' active campaign Greene had engaged the British in four major battles (one a siege) and had been repulsed or driven from the field in each one. It is a tribute, however, to his sound, cautious strategy, that after each of these battles, the British were forced to retire and to give up ground. Greene's Carolina campaign is the only known instance in military history where a general has won an extremely active and hard-fought campaign, without having been able to gain a single tactical victory.

34 ★ ★ ★ ★ ★

Maneuvers in Virginia
and in the North

ALTHOUGH THE PHYSICAL SUFFERINGS were perhaps not so bad as those the army had endured at Valley Forge, Washington and most of his men considered that the winter of 1780-81 was the worst they had experienced in the six and a half long, dreary years of the war. The troops were still painfully and desperately short of clothing and equipment. As in each of the five previous winters, the shortage of shoes was marked by bloodstains on the packed snow trails in and around the army's camps. Centered in the Hudson Highlands, these camps extended in a rough arc from Morristown through West Point, thence across the Hudson to southwestern Connecticut.

In previous winters the hardships had seemed at least tolerable because the soldiers could see that they were performing a useful service in defending their young country from reconquest by the British Crown. But to the bitter, half-naked men who huddled over fires in their huts that winter, there was little prospect that the stalemate of 1779 and 1780 would change in the following year. To many of them, who had enlisted for "three years or the war," it seemed that they were being wrongfully held beyond the terms of their enlistment when the three-year period had ended. On top of this, the men were particularly bitter about the depreciated value of the Continental money in which they were paid. "Not worth a Continental" had become synonymous with "less than worthless."

This seething discontent suddenly erupted on January 2, 1781, in the mutiny of six Pennsylvania regiments of Wayne's command at Morristown. Moving out of the camp in strict military formation, under the command of their sergeants, the soldiers headed towards Philadelphia to lay their grievances before Congress. Officers vainly attempted to re-establish control; two were killed and a number seriously injured in the attempt. Wayne, who had been away from the camp at the time the mutiny began, galloped to the head of the column and ordered his men to halt. Respectfully, but firmly, his men seized and disarmed him, then continued on towards the Delaware. A hastily-assembled committee of Congress met the disaffected troops at Princeton, and listened to their grievances. The congressmen then assured the troops that they would look into these matters, and make every possible effort to improve the affairs which had prompted the mutiny. As to the interpretation of the enlistment term, the congressmen also agreed to grant discharges to all who insisted that their enlistment terms had given them the option of three years or the war.

Having thus accomplished their purpose, strangely enough most of the mutineers promptly re-enlisted. Not only did they return to their camp, and to the bonds of discipline, but they arrested two secret agents that the British had sent amongst them to try to induce them to desert in a body to join the British service. The spies were speedily tried, convicted and hanged. The troops refused any special reward from Congress for this display of loyalty, insisting that they were merely doing their duty.

Inspired by the example of the Pennsylvania brigade, on January 20 three New Jersey regiments mutinied at Pompton and Suffern. Lest the infection of mutiny should spread further, Washington took prompt and firm action. Major General Robert Howe of North Carolina was sent with a strong force of New England troops to take the mutineers into custody. The ringleaders were tried, and two were hanged.

These mutinies finally convinced Congress that firm measures must be taken to place the nation's finances on a firmer foundation. On February 20 Congress appointed Robert Morris as Superintendent of Finance. When the Revolution started, this Liverpool-born merchant had headed a prosperous Philadelphia mercantile house. An ardent —though conservative—Whig member of the Continental Congress until 1778, he had played a major role in sustaining the financial affairs of Congress during the first three years of the war, and his money-raising activities, in which he risked his own credit, had helped Washington to save his army during the grim winter of 1776-77. Returning to his neglected business affairs in 1778, he still performed occasional banking functions for Congress—resulting in later unfounded allegations of improper manipulation of government funds.

Washington was highly pleased to learn of Morris' new appointment, rightly believing that this would make his own task easier. In his new position, Morris became a virtual financial dictator. He was also agent of marine, and thus was for all practical purposes the first head of the small American Navy Department. In his patriotic performance of his new duties Morris greatly strengthened public credit —which had become almost worthless—utilizing not only requisitions on the states, and foreign loans, but also his own pocketbook and credit.

But though the appointment of Morris as Superintendent of Finance relieved Washington of one of his great administrative and financial worries, the Commander-in-Chief was terribly depressed by the frustrating strategical situation existing throughout the nation. Despite Morgan's victory at the Cowpens, Washington was at that time fearful that Greene's retreat and hair-breadth escape across North Carolina might mean the loss of the three southernmost states, and pose a terrible threat to his own native state, Virginia. The continuing blockade of the French fleet (now under Commodore Sochet Destouches) and the French army in Newport by Admiral Arbuthnot's fleet seemed to rule out any possibility of a successful combined operation against Clinton's powerful defenses on Manhattan and the other islands around New York Bay. On top of this, British troops, commanded by the hated turncoat Benedict Arnold, were marching at will through eastern Virginia.

The Old Dominion was pervaded with apathy. This was due in part, perhaps, to the fact that, save for the terrorizing devastation of Mathew's raid, the war had bypassed the state. Governor Jefferson had been at least partly to blame, having failed to display himself, or to arouse in his fellow-Virginians, the fervor which he had expressed so magnificently in the text of the Declaration of Independence. We have already seen how Virginia's apathy had resulted in lack of adequate support to Clark in the West, even though the state had sufficient manpower to protect itself, as well as to carry on an aggressive war beyond the Alleghanies. Washington had warned Jefferson that the war was likely to spread to Virginia, but Jefferson and the Virginians seem to have ignored these warnings completely.

Encouraged by the success of the Collier-Mathew expedition of early 1779, late that year Clinton sent General Alexander Leslie with more than 2,000 men to Portsmouth to establish a base for more extensive raids into the interior of the state. But, to Clinton's annoyance, early in 1780 Leslie was ordered by Cornwallis to join him in South Carolina, leaving garrisons in Norfolk and in Portsmouth. So, on December 20, though claiming he could "ill spare it," Clinton sent a force of 1,600 troops under Arnold from New York to Virginia. Arnold's mission was to destroy military stores, to prevent reinforcements from being sent to Greene, and to rally Tories to the royal cause. Still having less than complete confidence in the American traitor, Clinton directed Arnold to consult with reliable Colonels John Simcoe and Thomas Dundas on all major matters.

Despite a storm which forced ships with 400 of his men to turn back, Arnold arrived at Hampton Roads on December 30. Shifting his troops to small boats, he moved up the James River, pushing aside some minor opposition from militia on the shore. He landed on January 4 at Westover, 25 miles from Richmond, which he seized the next day without opposition.

After devastating Richmond, Arnold marched back overland to Portsmouth, avoiding von Steuben's attempted ambush. He spent the remaining weeks of the winter quietly at Portsmouth. Washington, anxious to capture the traitor, and to mete out to him the punishment he deserved, decided to send Lafayette with three regiments of light infantry—1,200 men—to Virginia. He asked Destouches and Rochambeau if there was any way in which the French could cooperate in a combined operation against Arnold in Virginia.

At this very time a stroke of good luck gave the French an unexpected opportunity to cooperate. On January 22 a severe storm drove the British blockading squadron away from Newport, and so severely damaged several of the British ships as to give Destouches a slight superiority in effective strength over Arbuthnot. He immediately sent a small squadron of one ship and two frigates to Chesapeake Bay for the purpose of destroying the small naval force supporting Arnold.

Washington was disappointed that the French did not send a larger naval force, or a detachment of troops, since he feared that the British frigates in Hampton Roads would avoid the larger French vessels by moving up the shallow rivers. This in fact is what they did. Unable to accomplish anything, the French ships returned to Newport.

In response to Washington's repeated pleas for assistance, on March 8 Destouches sailed from Newport with his entire force of eight ships of the line and three frigates, carrying 1,200 troops. Two days later Arbuthnot, repairing storm damage in Gardiners Bay, across Long Island Sound from New London, learned of the departure of the French, and immediately sailed south after them. The English ships were slightly faster and, having more favorable winds, passed the French en route, neither fleet sighting the other.

The opposing squadrons met off the Chesapeake Capes on March 16 in comparatively equal strength—eight ships of the line each— with the weight of metal in British favor, since Arbuthnot had one 90-gun ship in his array, while one of Destouches' vessels was really only a heavy frigate. Dirty weather prevented the British from using their lower deck batteries, while the French—to leeward—had no difficulty in opening their windward gun ports.

Attempting to close, the three foremost British ships were severely injured aloft, but crippled the two leading French vessels. Destouches, signalling these to tack out of the action, succeeded in severely pounding the three already-disabled Britishers as he passed them with the remainder of his force. He then put out to sea again, to return to Newport, leaving Arbuthnot free to limp into the bay. The result of this action assured Arnold of a continued free line of communications by sea to New York, and denied Lafayette the expected cooperation of a division of French troops.

On March 26 British Major General William Phillips arrived at Portsmouth with 2,600 troops, superseding Arnold in command of British forces in Virginia. Clinton was still firmly opposed to undertaking any major operations in the interior of the state, but he wished to maintain sufficient force on the coast to discourage active Virginia participation in the war, and to permit raiding expeditions into the interior from a secure base at Portsmouth.

In conformity with Clinton's concept of operations in Virginia, in the latter part of April Phillips sent Arnold and a force of 2,500 men

from Portsmouth by boat to City Point, whence he marched overland
to Petersburg, easily driving off 1,000 militia under Virginia General
Peter Muhlenberg. Destroying substantial stores of military supplies
which had been collected in that town, Arnold marched northward
to Osborne's, on the James River, 15 miles below Richmond. Here
the Virginia militia had collected a small naval squadron of four
ships, five brigs, and ten smaller vessels, all laden with tobacco and
other supplies, apparently intended for French or Dutch ports in the
West Indies. Attacking the American vessels with vigorous artillery
fire from the river bank, Arnold destroyed the entire squadron.

Soon after this, learning of the approach of Cornwallis from North
Carolina, Phillips and Arnold marched to meet him at Petersburg.
Arriving there on May 10, Phillips suddenly became ill, and died of
a fever, leaving Arnold again in command of British forces in Virginia. On May 20 Cornwallis arrived, and Arnold was again super-
seded. Cornwallis had brought with him some 1,400 men. A few
days later 1,500 more reinforcements from Clinton reached Portsmouth, bringing the total strength of British army forces in Virginia,
including the Portsmouth garrison, to nearly 8,000. At the same
time, Clinton sent Cornwallis a letter expressing disapproval of his
march from the Carolinas to Virginia.

Lafayette, meanwhile, had moved to Richmond on April 29. His
total strength, including about 1,800 militia, was now 3,000 men.
An additional 550 newly-raised Continental troops were at that time
being trained by Steuben at Point of Fork, where the Rivanna River
meets the James.

Washington, alarmed by the devastating raids of Arnold and Phillips, and apprehending how seriously Lafayette was outnumbered,
decided to rush further reinforcements to Virginia. Early in the spring
he had sent Wayne's brigade to Pennsylvania, to recruit to full strength,
and to be re-equipped before continuing southward to join Greene in
the Carolinas. Washington now ordered Wayne to hasten immediately
to Virginia, where he was to serve under Lafayette temporarily, before
continuing on to join Greene. On May 20 Wayne started south from
York with approximately 1,000 men.

On May 24, Cornwallis moved northeast from Petersburg to cross
the James River, then headed towards Lafayette at Richmond. On

May 28, Lafayette retired hastily northward to avoid being cut off. He moved to Ely's Ford on the Rapidan, on June 4, to wait for Wayne.

Cornwallis followed as far as the North Anna River, where he halted on June 1. Remembering the results of his pursuit of Greene to the Dan, he had no intention of allowing himself to be lured any farther from his base. The next day he sent Tarleton raiding west toward Charlottesville and at the same time sent Simcoe and his Rangers against Steuben at Point of Fork.

Tarleton's Legion, 250 men strong, reached Charlottesville, where the Virginia legislature was in session, on June 4. Seven legislators were seized, and Governor Jefferson barely escaped capture by fleeing to the mountains to the west. Meanwhile Simcoe with 500 men had reached Point of Fork, which was hastily abandoned by Steuben, who did not believe that his raw troops were yet ready to face the British. Tarleton and Simcoe met at Point of Fork, and on June 7 joined Cornwallis, who had meanwhile marched to nearby Elk Hill. There the British remained for eight days.

On June 10, Wayne's Pennsylvania brigade joined Lafayette south of the Rapidan River. Lafayette, emboldened by this reinforcement, immediately moved south to threaten Cornwallis.

On June 15, Cornwallis decided to fall back towards Richmond, less because of his concern of the threat posed by Lafayette than in hopes of receiving orders and reinforcements from Clinton which would permit him to undertake a coordinated campaign of conquest of Virginia. After a brief halt in Richmond, Cornwallis continued on to Williamsburg which he reached on June 25. Lafayette followed the British into the Peninsula to a position just west of the confluence of the Mattaponi and the Pamunkey rivers at West Point. On June 26 the Americans had a small engagement with Simcoe's Rangers and a force of Hessian jägers on a foraging raid along the lower Chickahominy.

Early in July Cornwallis received the expected message from Clinton, but found it extremely disappointing. Clinton, repeating his desire to avoid entanglement in major operations in Virginia, informed him that New York was now threatened by a proposed Franco-American attack, and ordered Cornwallis immediately to send him 3,000 troops by sea. In order to understand why Clinton had sent this message, it will be necessary to turn our attention once more to operations in the north.

During the spring of 1781 Washington had come to the conclusion that it still might be possible for his army, in combination with that of Rochambeau, to assault successfully the British defenses of New York, despite continuing British command of the sea off the coast of the United States. On May 21 through the 24th he had held another cordial conference with Rochambeau at Wethersfield, Connecticut.

Rochambeau informed Washington that the Comte de Grasse, with a large fleet, had finally been able to break through the British blockade of Brest, and was at that very time probably operating against the British in the West Indies. Rochambeau apparently gave some hint that de Grasse might later move to the east coast of the United States, where he could then join forces with the French squadron still at Newport, now under the command of the Comte de Barras.

Apparently feeling that the arrival of de Grasse in the Western Hemisphere permitted him enough freedom of action to leave still-blockaded Newport, Rochambeau indicated to Washington his willingness to operate against the British elsewhere. He made clear, however, his preference for operations in Virginia, rather than against strongly fortified New York. Washington responded that so long as the English maintained control of the sea, a campaign in Virginia would not be able to accomplish much. Furthermore, the climate of his native state in midsummer would be extremely difficult for French and Northern troops. Under the circumstances he could see little to be gained by a long overland march of the French from Newport to Virginia, and of his own troops from New York. He implied, however, that he might look at the situation differently if de Grasse's fleet were to gain control of the waters off Virginia. Rochambeau accordingly agreed to take part in the proposed operations against New York, and promised to move his army overland from Newport to New York.

Early in June the British captured a letter from Washington to Lafayette, in which the Commander-in-Chief informed the Marquis that he was preparing an attack on New York. A few weeks later

Clinton learned that Rochambeau was marching to join Washington. Clinton, convinced that his defenses in New York would soon be assaulted by the combined American and French forces, then sent his message to Cornwallis, ordering him to send 3,000 troops back to New York.

As a matter of fact, exciting information from Rochambeau on June 13 had caused Washington to begin considering the possibility of operations either in Virginia, or against Charleston, rather than the proposed attack on Manhattan Island. Just before he left Newport, Rochambeau had received word from de Grasse that he would sail north from the West Indies to the American coast some time in July or August. Immediately the French general reported the news to Washington. He also replied to de Grasse, suggesting either New York or the Chesapeake Bay area for operations, but privately indicating his preference for the latter.

Until he had more definite information about the arrival of the French fleet, Washington was determined to press ahead with the preliminaries of an attack against New York. He planned a surprise advance to overwhelm and capture British outposts north of the Harlem River for July 2. Despite his efforts at secrecy, however, the British got wind of the plan. Because of this, and because of inadequate coordination between some of the American columns, all of the British outposts were successfully withdrawn across the Harlem River, save for a strong bridgehead at King's Bridge.

The arrival of Rochambeau's army, just following this failure, gave Washington a combined allied force of only slightly more than 10,500 men: 4,800 French and nearly 5,800 Continentals. Because of the apathy in the north, there were no militia. A few hundred additional Continentals, under Stirling, were at Saratoga, watching the invasion route from Canada.

On July 22-23, a joint American-French demonstration in front of King's Bridge gave Washington and Rochambeau an opportunity for a careful and thorough reconnaissance of the British defenses along the Harlem River. It was obvious to both generals that these were formidable. Since Clinton now had at least half again as many troops on Manhattan and Staten islands as there were in the entire allied force, Washington began to think still more seriously of operations in Virginia, if de Grasse and the French fleet could wrest control of the nearby seas from the British. He wrote to Lafayette, telling him to report every move of Cornwallis' army.

Meanwhile, on Virginia's Peninsula, on July 4 Cornwallis had started for Portsmouth to carry out his orders to send 3,000 troops to New York. At the same time he sent a letter to Clinton in which he stated his conviction that with his strength so seriously reduced there was little more that could be accomplished in Virginia, and that it might be better to withdraw all British forces completely from that state, than simply to adopt a defensive posture. He decided, however, to try to take advantage of a possible opportunity of striking a decisive blow against Lafayette.

Sending false information by pretended deserters, Cornwallis led Lafayette to believe that he would complete his crossing of the James, at Jamestown Ford, on July 5 and 6. In fact, however, he merely sent a small portion of his army across the river, holding the remainder in ambush in forests between Green Springs and the ford. Late on the 6th Wayne, whose brigade preceded the American army, pushed vigorously against Tarleton, commanding the British rear guard. Believing that most of the British army was on the other side of the river, Wayne saw an opportunity to defeat, and perhaps capture Tarleton and the few British units still remaining north of the river. Tarleton, in accordance with Cornwallis' instructions, withdrew slowly, leading the Americans back towards the waiting British army. Lafayette, who later claimed that he had some suspicion of the British plan, did not follow Wayne closely, though he did send him a few hundred reinforcements.

Wayne unexpectedly found himself attacked by Cornwallis' entire army. Although surprised, Wayne made a hasty estimate of the situation, and saw that he was about to be enveloped on both flanks. He feared, however, that if he gave an immediate order to retreat, his shaken troops might be routed and completely overwhelmed by the pursuing British. Thus, to Cornwallis' astonishment, Wayne ordered a bayonet counterattack against the British left, while spreading out his few riflemen and light infantry to delay the advance of the British right. The American charge was halted by heavy British fire, but the result was what Wayne had intended. The British left was stopped temporarily while the British right was slowed down by the skirmishers.

After a fire fight of less than 15 minutes, Wayne withdrew his troops slowly and in good order. He had suffered 145 casualties, and had lost two guns, while the British had had only 75 killed and wounded. On the other hand, his unexpected counterattack had so delayed the British that darkness had begun to fall. As a result Cornwallis did not pursue, and Wayne's entire command withdrew without further loss. Some people, unaware of the background, assumed that Wayne had deliberately taken on Cornwallis' army with his own brigade, and thus received further apparent confirmation that he was indeed "Mad" Anthony.

Cornwallis now continued across the James to Suffolk. Sending the 3,000 troops to Portsmouth, to prepare to embark for New York, at the same time he unleashed Tarleton on a raid to the west. Tarleton rode as far as Bedford County and the foothills of the Blue Ridge near Lynchburg, ravaging the countryside as he went. In fifteen days he moved more than four hundred miles, avoiding a militia effort—led by Daniel Morgan, painfully and briefly in the field again—to intercept him near Petersburg.

Meanwhile, on July 8, Cornwallis had received new orders from Clinton, telling him to send the 3,000 men to make a diversion at Philadelphia instead of to New York. Four days later he received another message from Clinton, ordering him to rush the men to New York at once. This second change was the result of the arrival of Rochambeau's army at White Plains. The embarkation of the troops for New York was almost complete when, on July 20, Cornwallis received still another message from Clinton, telling him that he need not send the troops to New York at all, if he still believed them necessary in Virginia. In this same message Clinton ordered Cornwallis to occupy a strong position on the Peninsula at Old Point Comfort, and also to occupy Yorktown if possible.

Cornwallis decided to avail himself of the option left him by Clinton, and to keep all of his troops. Following a reconnaissance, Cornwallis decided that Old Point Comfort was less defensible by land and by sea than was Yorktown. Accordingly, he moved his troops and the entire garrison of Portsmouth by water to Yorktown, arriving on August 4. He immediately sent a portion of his command to Gloucester, on a point on the opposite bank of the York River from Yorktown.

Lafayette, meanwhile, had been in camp at Malvern Hill, waiting for Cornwallis to make the next move. When he heard that Cornwallis had sailed from Portsmouth, he started to march north, on the assumption that the British army was heading for Baltimore. Learning a few days later that Cornwallis had landed at Yorktown, Lafayette marched down the Pamunkey River to take up a position of observation at West Point on August 13. He immediately wrote to Washington, informing him that "Cornwallis had established himself at Yorktown, where he had deep water on three sides of him, and a narrow neck in front." While at West Point, Lafayette was joined by von Steuben with 1,000 men. This brought his army to 4,500 men, of whom 1,860 were veteran Continentals, 425 new Continentals trained by Steuben, and about 2,200 Virginia militia.

A few miles away, at Yorktown, Cornwallis had more than 7,000 British regulars. This force, he knew, was far too small to carry out the aggressive campaign which he believed would recover Virginia, and with it the remaining colonies, for the Crown. It was, at the same time, unnecessarily large for the strategy preferred by Clinton, and was poorly located for the war of raid and harassment visualized by the British commander-in-chief.

This situation was the natural result of the clash of personalities and views of the two English generals. Clinton, who possessed the greater strategical and analytical talents, lacked the vigor and decisiveness of Cornwallis. Clinton's fatal vacillation was strikingly revealed in his series of orders to Cornwallis about the 3,000 reinforcements. While the two generals exchanged increasingly sharp letters, the impasse which their dispute had created was about to be exploited by the combined efforts of stronger and better men: an American general and a French admiral.

★ 35 ★ ★ ★ ★ ★

Sea Power Shapes the End—1780-81

DURING THIS PERIOD THE DESTINY of the new United States was shaped by momentous events overseas, and on the high seas, where the tall ships of England wrestled with those of France and Spain. The little Continental navy, slowly being blotted out by British naval pressure along the Atlantic seaboard, played only a minor part in this great struggle. Nor were the stinging raids on Britain's commerce and military transport by the 440-odd American privateers then afloat more than extremely annoying flea bites.

More significant in early 1780 was the action of Catherine II of Russia. On February 24, in conjunction with Sweden and Denmark, she promulgated the so-called "Armed Neutrality Agreement," clashing violently with England's claim of the right to search and seize any goods carried in neutral bottoms. Catherine's move was, of course, not predicated upon any desire to assist the United States, but was for the protection of Russian interests.

The Agreement, later subscribed to by the Netherlands, Prussia, Portugal and Austria, contended in substance that neutral vessels could engage in the coasting trade of belligerents; that property of belligerents carried in neutral bottoms was safe from seizure; that no articles save arms, equipment and munitions of war were contraband; and that blockade, to be binding, must include an adequate naval force stationed in close proximity to the ports blockaded.

Most important to the United States was Holland's subscription to the Armed Neutrality Agreement on December 16. Four days later England, which already had been in serious disagreement with the Netherlands on the subject of trade with the rebellious colonies, declared war. Although this superficially added to the burden of the Royal Navy, in substance it merely put Holland's colonies and commerce at the mercy of British ships of war, while England's geographical position effectually blocked the Dutch fleet from joining the other Allies. The net result, as Britain intended, was to throttle the vital American war munitions traffic with the Dutch West Indies.

But the overextended Royal Navy was still unable to take any effective counteraction against the Spanish land and naval forces operating along the Gulf coast of West Florida, under Don Bernardo de Galvez. The Americans reaped an unexpected—and unintended— bonus from these entirely selfish operations of their Spanish quasi-ally. The Cherokees and English had finally persuaded the Creeks to join in the war against the southern patriots, and had been planning fresh depredations against the Carolina and Georgia frontiers. The Spanish operations against the British fortified posts in West Florida, however, diverted to the west and south almost all of the attention of the Florida English and their Indian allies. Galvez, nevertheless, continued his successful advance, captured Mobile in 1780, then besieged English General John Campbell in Pensacola. Campbell was forced to surrender in May, 1781, thus ending the British hold on West Florida.

Meanwhile, of a number of individual clashes between American and English ships at sea in 1780, two are worthy of mention. Captain James Nicholson in the US frigate *Trumbull,* 28, slipping out of Boston harbor in late May, dodged the blockade only to fall in with the British privateer *Watt,* 34, on June 1. The *Watt,* larger and more heavily gunned than the usual privateer, was a worthy opponent. The vessels fought a drawn action for two and a half hours before they broke off the fight by mutual consent. Nicholson put in to Philadelphia to refit.

On June 7, the Massachusetts frigate *Protector,* 26, Captain Williams, engaged in a sanguinary combat with another big British privateer, the *Admiral Duff,* 32. The *Duff,* battered by the superior gunnery of the Massachusetts ship, finally sank with her flags still flying; only 55 of her complement were saved by the American ship.

By this time French and British fleets had already engaged in the West Indies. British Admiral Sir George Rodney, with 22 ships of the line, had arrived to take command of British naval forces there in late March, after successfully convoying supplies and reinforcements to Gibraltar. En route Rodney on January 11 had defeated a smaller Spanish squadron off Cape St. Vincent, in the so-called "Moonlight Battle."

In late April Rodney fought three indecisive actions, between Dominica and Martinique, with a French fleet of approximately equal strength under Admiral Duc Urbain de Guichen. Then a Spanish squadron of twelve additional ships of the line reinforced de Guichen and Rodney retired to Santa Lucia. But an epidemic at Martinique so weakened the Allies that they made no attempt to engage him.

De Guichen himself, with fifteen of his ships, returned to France in August, much to the chagrin of Washington, who had hoped the French admiral would sail northward to break the blockade of Newport. Instead, it was Rodney who, hurrying up from the West Indies with half of his fleet, arrived in New York on September 12, to ensure British command of the sea off the northern United States, thus foiling Washington's plans for 1780.

In early December, Rodney, satisfied with the preponderance of British naval strength in the Newport-New York sector, returned to the West Indies. There, at the year's end, he received Admiralty instructions to move against the Dutch West Indies.

On February 3, 1781, Rodney, who had been joined by Rear Admiral Samuel Hood and a reinforcing squadron, hit St. Eustatius. The little island—only some eight square miles in area—by this time had become a teeming center of contraband trade; the shores of its open roadstead, Orangeburg, lined with miles of crowded warehouses. Unaware of the outbreak of war between England and the Netherlands, St. Eustatius' tiny garrison could not offer even token resistance. Some £3,000,000 worth of booty fell into Rodney's hands, together with a number of blockade runners loading for the United States. This was a body blow to the cause of American independence.

But the cloud of gloom had a silver lining. For avaricious Rodney became so preoccupied with securing his immense prize money booty —he would send home 24 shiploads—that he took no proper steps to intercept a French fleet known to be on the way from Brest to Martinique. So it was that Admiral de Grasse, with twenty ships of

the line, convoying troops and munitions, instead of having to fight
Rodney at a disadvantage in the Windward Passage, safely made Fort
Royal, Martinique; the first step toward a greater end. To add to the
irony of the situation, most of Rodney's booty-laden transports were
captured on the way home to England by French and American privateers. Rodney shortly afterwards went home, leaving Hood in
command.

Meanwhile, across the Atlantic, an English naval attempt to capture the Dutch possession of the Cape of Good Hope was thwarted
in the Cape Verde Islands. Commodore George Johnstone, with five
ships of the line (though three were only 50-gun vessels), some smaller
craft, and 35 troop-laden transports, had been sent on a secret mission against the Cape. Johnstone stopped to water at Porto Praya,
where he was surprised on April 16 by French Admiral Pierre André
de Suffern with five of the line. Suffern, who had left Brest March 22
in company with de Grasse, was also under orders to proceed to the
Cape of Good Hope, to protect it against English attack.

Audacious and impulsive, Suffern came bowling into the harbor
and, disregarding Portuguese neutrality, fell on Johnstone's squadron,
battering it so badly that the British expedition was called off. Had it
not been for the timidity of his captains Suffern would have captured
Johnstone's entire force. As it was, Suffern's victory was won at great
odds—only two of his vessels being engaged. The Frenchman then
continued on to India, where he would soon make a name as one
of the great naval commanders of the age.

In the midst of these fleet actions between England and France,
wrestling for command of the seas, we must interject the one notable
American naval exploit of 1781: the cruise of USS *Alliance,* 36,
indestructible queen of the little Continental navy. With portly, Irish-
born John Barry in command, this fine frigate sailed out of Boston
February 11, manned by a crew scratched up from the sweepings of
the waterfront, and bound for France on a diplomatic ferrying mission. She carried young Colonel John Laurens, Washington's capable
aide. Despite an abortive mutiny of his recalcitrant sailors, hard-bitten
Captain Barry, with his crew literally flogged into obedience, captured
two British privateers on the way to France, but was so short-handed
he had to let two other prizes go. On the return trip Barry on May 29
fell in with the British sloops of war *Atalanta,* 16, and *Trepassey,* 14,

off Cape Sable. With the wind falling to a flat calm, the English vessels got out sweeps (long oars), worked their way up behind the motionless frigate, and stationed themselves off her quarters where none of her guns could be brought to bear, then systematically pounded the American ship. Considerable damage was done, and Barry himself was severely wounded before a puffy breeze enabled him to get under way. Barry then proceeded to pummel his adversaries into surrender and the *Alliance* returned safely to Boston with her prizes.

Not so fortunate was the *Trumbull,* out of Philadelphia again on August 8, on another cruise. She fell in with two captured American ships in British service—the *Iris* (ex-*Hancock*), 32, and the *General Monk* (ex-*George Washington*), 20, and struck to them after a battering engagement. The loss of the *Trumbull,* last of the original thirteen frigates built by the Continental Congress, left the *Alliance* as the only remaining major American warship afloat.

Only one fleet action occurred between England and the Netherlands. On August 5, 1781, Sir Hyde Parker's squadron convoying a homeward-bound English merchant convoy from the Baltic, encountered—off the Dogger Bank in the North Sea—Rear Admiral Johann Arnold Zoutman's squadron escorting a Dutch merchant convoy outbound from the Texel to the Baltic. The opponents were of equal strength—seven ships of the line each—but Parker's pugnaciousness prevailed and the Dutch returned to port, with 550 casualties. Parker lost 450 killed and wounded.

Meanwhile the struggles of the European titans in the West Indies continued. De Grasse undertook a series of skillful operations, which included taking Tobago from the British on June 2, the while evading conflict with Hood's main force. In late July the French admiral put into Cap François (Cap Haytien), Haiti, for a rendezvous with destiny.

The conference of Washington and Rochambeau at Wethersfield on May 21-24 had resulted in the dispatch of a fast French frigate to the West Indies to carry messages to de Grasse, urging immediate cooperation in a move against either New York or the Chesapeake. These missives were waiting for de Grasse when he entered Cap François on July 26. Accepting the proposals, he dispatched a reply immediately.

★ 36 ★ ★ ★ ★ ★

The World Turned Upside Down

B<small>Y</small> THE END OF J<small>ULY</small>, 1781, W<small>ASHINGTON</small> had concluded that Clinton's defenses and garrison on Manhattan Island were too strong to crack that summer. He had already quietly begun preparations for a quick march southward with a combined Franco-American army. He had also written Lafayette to keep a close watch on Cornwallis, and to report any British moves at once. On August 12, Washington's tentative decision to operate in Virginia, should de Grasse and the French fleet arrive, was confirmed by the arrival at New York of 2,400 Hessian reinforcements, raising Clinton's total strength to something between 15,000 and 17,000 men.

Two days later Washington and Rochambeau received an electrifying letter from de Grasse. The French fleet would leave the West Indies for the Chesapeake on August 13—one day before the message was received—carrying with it 3,500 troops from Haiti. De Grasse would be available for combined operations against the British until October 15, when other commitments, and the arrival of the hurricane season, would force him to leave.

Washington's reaction was immediate and decisive. For a period of at least six weeks, he could count on British seapower being neutralized by the French fleet. New York was too strong for attack, even if blockaded by de Grasse. But on the Peninsula of Virginia lay Cornwallis, vulnerable to combined land and sea attack.

Washington warned Lafayette to prevent Cornwallis from escaping to North Carolina. He also sent Duportail to the entrance of Chesapeake Bay with a message for de Grasse, saying that he and Rochambeau would soon meet the French admiral there. Some 3,000 troops would be left north of New York, under the command of General Heath. But with the remaining 2,000, and all of Rochambeau's French troops, he would immediately march southward to join Lafayette and the French troops of de Grasse, to defeat and to capture Cornwallis. For success, time was of the essence.

The one great danger in this plan was that Clinton would sense what was happening. In that case, he might attack the small Franco-American army on the road through New Jersey, or else concentrate overwhelming force against Heath's contingent north of New York. Clinton could even move to Virginia himself, either by land or sea; but Washington's knowledge of Clinton's nature caused him to believe that the cautious and vacillating British general would not attempt this. The critical period would be during the first few days of the march, while the allies were still within striking distance of Manhattan and Staten islands.

Accordingly Washington undertook a number of elaborate deceptive measures to keep the British from discerning his intentions. As the Franco-American army crossed the Hudson River at Dobbs Ferry, the British were encouraged to believe this was preliminary to an attack upon New York or Staten Island. The collection of all available boats close to Staten Island, on the Jersey shores of New York Bay, furthered that deception, as did the establishment of supply depots at Elizabeth and New Brunswick. Finally, the concentration of the troops in camps near the Kill Van Kull heightened the threat to Staten Island. The actual march towards the Delaware from these camps in eastern New Jersey began on August 25. Not until September 2 was Clinton first cognizant of Washington's and Rochambeau's move towards Virginia.

Some of the Northern Continentals were unhappy to be marching south, and demanded pay that was in arrears. Washington asked Morris for the money to make this payment; Morris, in turn, borrowed it from Rochambeau's war chest.

On September 5, while riding south past Chester, Pennsylvania, Washington received word that the French fleet, 28 ships of the line, accompanied by the promised 3,500 troops, had arrived at the entrance to Chesapeake Bay on August 26, and was anchored at Lynn-haven Bay, just inside Cape Henry. Never had Washington's staff seen their commander so joyful and enthusiastic. After informing Rochambeau of this news, he hastened southward.

Only one concern remained in Washington's mind. On August 27 a British fleet of fourteen ships and frigates under Admiral Hood had reached New York, to join that of Admiral Thomas Graves—who had relieved Arbuthnot. The combined fleet, now consisting of nineteen ships of the line, had then sailed from New York on August 31. Washington knew that Admiral de Barras, with the remainder of Rochambeau's army, and quantities of siege artillery and important supplies, had just sailed from Newport towards Chesapeake Bay. It would be a disaster if this squadron—eight ships of the line, four frigates and eighteen transports—were to be met at sea by the larger English fleet under Graves. It would be a catastrophe if Graves were then able to defeat de Grasse, or to drive his fleet from the Chesapeake. Thus, his joy tempered with concern, Washington and his staff continued to ride down the dusty roads through Delaware, into Maryland, anxiously awaiting news of events at sea.

Those events had been dramatic. Admiral Hood, who had recently relieved Rodney in command of the British West Indies fleet, had sailed north as soon as he had learned of de Grasse's departure from Haiti. He had put into Chesapeake Bay three days before de Grasse's arrival, to find it empty. Leaving two frigates to report if the French fleet later arrived, Hood had sailed north on August 24, joining Graves, as we know, on the 27th. Graves, as senior officer, took command.

As Washington had feared, Graves and Hood had sailed out to try to intercept de Barras on his way from Newport to the Chesapeake. Failing in this, they turned southward to seek de Grasse. Graves incorrectly believed that the Frenchman had only twelve ships of the line. De Grasse's arrival at Chesapeake Bay was unknown to him because the French had captured the two British picket frigates.

De Grasse had at once sent four ships and some frigates to block the James and York rivers, and to cooperate directly with Lafayette's troops on shore. He landed 3,000 French regular troops under General the Marquis de Saint-Simon, and in response to Washington's request, sent a few smaller vessels up the Chesapeake to assist Washington and Rochambeau to come down by water from Elkton and Baltimore.

Early on September 5, about 2,000 French seamen were sent ashore to collect wood and water for the fleet. Soon after this a French patrol frigate at the entrance to Chesapeake Bay reported the approach of a large fleet. Without waiting to get his men back on board ship, de Grasse immediately made sail, and by noon the French fleet was beginning to round Cape Henry.

If the French were surprised by the approach of the British, the British were astounded both by the presence of the French fleet, and by the number of ships now sailing out to meet them. Graves had the weather gauge, and had he pressed in vigorously while the French fleet—in some haste and confusion—was trying to get out to sea, he could possibly have forced de Grasse ashore on Cape Henry. However, rendered hesitant and over-cautious by surprise, Graves maneuvered so as to head eastward in a line parallel to and windward of the French fleet straggling out to meet him.

Because of the haste with which they had sailed, the French fleet was divided into three groups of eight ships each, somewhat separated, and echeloned to the right rear, away from the British. By signal flag Graves ordered his rearmost ships to close in against the straggling French vessels bringing up the rear of de Grasse's line. The orders were misunderstood, however, and so only the first eight French ships, and some eight or nine of the British, were actively engaged in the running fight which ensued for the next two hours. In this, although the English had the advantage of the wind, superior French gunnery and a heavier weight of metal inflicted considerable damage on the British ships, while the French did not suffer so severely. Thus, as de Grasse pulled away at dusk, in order to correct his line, the leading British ships were unable to keep close contact, and the remainder were unable to catch up. During the night lights were kept blazing on both fleets, which continued to sail in parallel column, just out of range of one another, until morning.

During the following two days and nights the two cautious admirals maneuvered generally to the southward, while carpenters and riggers were busy repairing damage. By the 8th they were off the coast of northern North Carolina. That day a heavy wind arose, causing serious

leaks in HMS *Terrible,* which had been badly battered in the battle
on the 5th. Graves ordered the vessel abandoned and blown up, thus
increasing the French advantage to six ships. During the maneuvering
on the 8th and 9th the two fleets worked their way back northward,
with de Grasse maintaining the initiative and keeping himself between the English fleet and the entrance to Chesapeake Bay. Graves,
unable to get an opportunity to engage part of the numerically superior French fleet, avoided de Grasse's effort to bring him back to
battle.

On the 9th, de Grasse sighted a number of sails to the north.
Though unfavorable winds prevented him from checking on the
identity of this strange squadron, he presumed it was de Barras, and
so made sure to keep between it and the British fleet. It was indeed
the French Newport squadron and, protected by de Grasse, de Barras
continued safely into Chesapeake Bay with his convoy of transports.

During the night of September 9-10, the British fleet disappeared.
Graves had set course for New York to repair damage. De Grasse
returned to his anchorage, arriving early on the 11th, where he captured two British frigates trying to destroy the buoys which he had
left there.

Tactically the Battle of the Capes had ended with a slight advantage in favor of the French, who were able to claim credit for
the loss of the *Terrible,* as well as the two captured frigates. Strategically, it was the most important battle of the war. It confirmed
to the French, and to their American allies, command of the sea off
Chesapeake Bay. Cornwallis was thus completely isolated.

Meanwhile, on September 6 Washington had reached Head of Elk,
just as the leading units of his column arrived at that northernmost
point of navigation on Chesapeake Bay. They had marched 200 miles
in 15 days. Here, following orders Washington had issued three weeks
before, all available local fishing boats on the bay had been gathered.
These, however, were only sufficient to carry about 2,000 men, who
were embarked. The rest of the army would march on towards Baltimore and Annapolis, where they would be picked up by French ships.

The head of Rochambeau's column began to reach Head of Elk on
September 8, and Washington informed Rochambeau of the arrange-
ments he had made. Then he spurred on by horse to Baltimore, with
Rochambeau following more slowly. Another long day's ride brought

Washington to Mount Vernon by evening of the 9th, the first time that he had seen his home in six years and four months. He stayed there for two days, briefly entertaining Rochambeau and the senior officers of the French army.

Early on September 12, Washington continued on towards Fredericksburg, Richmond, and Williamsburg, arriving midafternoon of the 14th. Greeted enthusiastically by Lafayette, the General received the salute of his own troops and those of Saint-Simon. Next day Washington's great anxiety about the situation at sea was relieved, when he received a message informing him of de Grasse's victory over Graves, and of the arrival of Barras.

Two days later Washington visited the French fleet at the Capes, on a ship thoughtfully provided by the French admiral. He spent most of the 18th with de Grasse on his magnificent flagship, the *Ville de Paris,* 120, the largest and finest warship in the world in her day. Around him in the anchorage lay 31 other French ships of the line—guaranteeing the control of the seas for which Washington had been dreaming for more than six years.

Washington found de Grasse to be as courteous and cooperative an ally as Rochambeau. A vigorous, enthusiastic man, the tall French admiral informed the American that, despite his early intention to leave by October 15, he had now determined to stay on until the end of October, if this should be necessary. He also agreed to provide a contingent of marines and sailors for land operations, but only for a short period of time.

Arriving back at his headquarters at Williamsburg on September 22, after four days' delay by adverse winds, Washington learned that another English naval squadron had arrived in New York, under the command of Admiral Digby, to reinforce Graves and Hood. De Grasse had heard the same news at about the same time, and sent a message which Washington and Rochambeau received the next day, telling of his intention to sail to New York, to fight the British, rather than waiting passively for the reinforced enemy fleet to come down to fight him at their own convenience. He told the generals that he would leave two ships and four frigates for the blockade, and would sail northward with thirty-four ships of the line.

Washington and Rochambeau, after a brief conference, sent separate protests to de Grasse, pointing out the paramount importance of blockading the entrance of the bay against the possibility of relief for Cornwallis. In view of the gravity and importance of the message, Washington sent Lafayette as his personal messenger. To the infinite relief of the American and French generals, on September 25 de Grasse agreed to remain at his anchorage at the mouth of the Chesapeake Bay.

Washington now completed his preparations for the investment of Yorktown. He had about 9,500 effective American troops, including 3,200 militia. Since Washington was Allied Commander-in-Chief, Lincoln exercised direct command of the American forces. Lafayette, von Steuben and James Clinton were the division commanders. Rochambeau's army, including the contingent of Saint-Simon, consisted of more than 7,500 men. With a detachment of marines later provided by de Grasse, the entire allied force was slightly more than 18,000 strong.

Since early September Cornwallis and his army of 7,800 had busily prepared the defense of Yorktown, or York, as it was then known. The town was on a bluff on the northern shore of the Peninsula, overlooking the broad, tidal York River. Here Gloucester Point poked deeply southward from the north bank, reducing the river from an average width of two miles to approximately half a mile. In the narrow roadstead between Gloucester and Yorktown were two British frigates, three large transports, and several smaller vessels. These were manned by a naval force of nearly 1,000 men.

Yorktown itself was well protected by geography. Just to the west and southwest of the town was marshy Yorktown Creek, flowing through a ravine which was a veritable moat. On the south were the headwaters of Wormeley Creek, which flowed in an easterly direction into the York River about two miles below the town. Between the marshy headwaters of Yorktown Creek and Wormeley Creek lay a flat plain, less than half a mile in width, known as the "Pigeon Quarter." This was the only easy overland approach to Yorktown. The Pigeon Quarter was within the extreme range of British guns in the so-called "hornwork," a redoubt projecting from the very southern tip of the extensive line of fortifications surrounding Yorktown itself. In addition to this inner line of defenses, four redoubts had been built in the Pigeon Quarter, to make the overland approach more difficult. One other large redoubt, known as the "Star," or

"Fusiliers" Redoubt, was just west of Yorktown Creek, on a low bluff overlooking the York River.

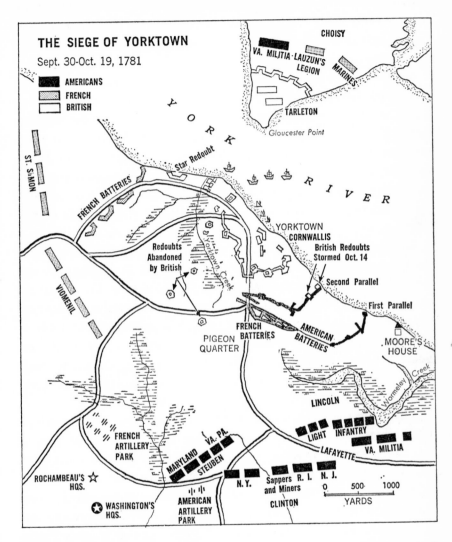

THE SIEGE OF YORKTOWN
Sept. 30-Oct. 19, 1781

AMERICANS
FRENCH
BRITISH

CHOISY

VA. MILITIA-LAUZUN'S LEGION

MARINES

TARLETON

Gloucester Point

ST. SIMON

YORK

Star Redoubt

FRENCH BATTERIES

RIVER

YORKTOWN
CORNWALLIS

British Redoubts
Stormed Oct. 14

Redoubts
Abandoned
by British

Second Parallel

VIOMENIL

First Parallel

FRENCH
BATTERIES

AMERICAN
BATTERIES

MOORE'S
HOUSE

PIGEON
QUARTER

Wormeley Creek

LINCOLN

LIGHT INFANTRY

FRENCH
ARTILLERY
PARK

VA. PA.

LAFAYETTE

VA. MILITIA

ROCHAMBEAU'S ☆
HQS.

MARYLAND

STEUBEN

N. Y.

Sappers
and Miners

R. I.

N. J.

0   500   1000

WASHINGTON'S
HQS.

AMERICAN
ARTILLERY
PARK

CLINTON

YARDS

Cornwallis had also fortified Gloucester Point, to assure control of both sides of the York River, and of the roadstead between the two towns. In command of Gloucester was Lieutenant Colonel Dundas, with some 700 men, including Tarleton's Legion. Early in the siege Dundas was recalled to Yorktown, leaving Tarleton in command at Gloucester.

On September 28 the American and French armies marched from

Williamsburg to invest the line formed by Yorktown Creek, the Pigeon Quarter redoubts, and Wormeley Creek. In accordance with the customs of the age, the American Army, being in its own home country, held the right of the line; the French, as allies, were on the left. British covering parties and patrols skirmished briefly with the approaching allied columns, then withdrew behind the redoubts.

Because of the length of the blockading lines, Washington could not afford to send a large force to the opposite side of the river to blockade Gloucester. Some 1,500 Virginia militia, under General Weedon, were already observing the Gloucester position, but were unable to interfere seriously with Tarleton's foraging expeditions. At Washington's request, Rochambeau sent the Duc de Lauzun's cavalry legion, some 600 strong, to join Weedon, while de Grasse sent 800 marines. These two French contingents and the Virginia militia were placed under the overall command of the Marquis de Choisy.

On September 29 Cornwallis received a message from Clinton telling him that naval reinforcements had arrived from England, and that a relief expedition was being prepared to come to his assistance. On the basis of this heartening information, Cornwallis decided to conserve his strength by consolidating his troops in the inner defenses of Yorktown, instead of trying to hold the fortifications in the Pigeon Quarter. Thus, on September 30, the allies disovered that these redoubts had been abandoned. They promptly moved in and converted the forts to their own use.

During the remaining week the allies completed their preparations for a close investment and regular siege approaches to Yorktown. One of the most serious problems was to get the heavy French siege guns—and a few that Knox had brought from New York—to the Pigeon Quarter from the landing place at Jamestown. Horses and oxen were scarce, but Quartermaster General Timothy Pickering collected teams from all over the Peninsula, and gradually the batteries began to build up in the Pigeon Quarter, some 700 yards from the British hornwork. Washington did not permit his guns to respond to intermittent British harassing fire, wishing to be sure to gain the physical and psychological benefit of the impact of opening fire with massed batteries of heavy cannon. During these days all of the American and French soldiers were put to work constructing fascines and gabions for the approaching siege. Meanwhile on the opposite shore the Marquis de Choisy closed in on Gloucester, completing the investment on October 3, after a sharp skirmish between Lauzun's Legion and Tarleton's, which was out on a foraging expedition.

During the night of October 6-7, the bulk of the French and American army began to dig the first parallel,* eastward across the Pigeon Quarter, towards the river between Wormeley Creek and Yorktown. Because the only feasible approach to Yorktown was from the southeast, within the American sector, Washington and Rochambeau agreed that the approach trenches would be manned equally by the French and the Americans, with the Americans on the right. To divert British attention from this activity, Saint-Simon's troops, on the extreme left, staged a noisy demonstration against the Fusiliers Redoubt. Despite a persistent legend, it is doubtful if Washington ceremoniously wielded a pick to initiate the digging of the first parallel. It is not consistent with his character.

Equally apocryphal is the legend that Washington held the match which fired the first siege gun against Yorktown on October 9. Actually the firing was begun by the French "Grand Battery," on the left of the first parallel. This was followed soon after by an American battery, a few yards to the right.

Next day, red-hot shot, or "carcasses," † from Saint-Simon's guns, opposite the Fusiliers Redoubt, set fire to the British frigate *Charon*, 44, as well as to two British transports. These and one or two smaller vessels burned to the water line during the following night. By this time some fifty allied siege guns were keeping up an almost incessant hail of fire against the British defenses. The response of the British artillery steadily diminished, partly because of the effective allied fire, and partly because of shortage of ammunition. Casualties mounted steadily amongst the defending troops. A British attempt to land behind Choisy's lines at Gloucester was repulsed by French artillery from both sides of the river.

During the night of October 11-12, the allies began the second parallel, less than 300 yards from the British hornwork and the defending trenches east of Yorktown. Since the British still held two powerful redoubts near the riverbank, east of the inner line of defenses,

---

* For a discussion of 18th Century siegecraft, see Appendix IV.
† See Appendix I.

this second parallel could only extend about halfway from the head of Yorktown Creek to the York River. While the engineers and troops were doing their work that evening, the British were kept busy by an intensified bombardment from the growing allied siege batteries, now numbering almost 100 guns. Particular attention was devoted to the two outlying redoubts.

By October 14 Washington and Rochambeau were satisfied that the second parallel had progressed as far as it could until the two British redoubts were eliminated. Orders were issued that these should be assaulted during the following evening. The one closer to the river, known as Redoubt No. 10, was to be attacked by the Americans; the other, 100 yards further inland, known as Redoubt No. 9, was to be taken by the French. Shortly after dark 400 picked French troops, under Colonel de Deux-Ponts, attacked Redoubt No. 9, while an equal number of Americans, under Lieutenant Colonel Alexander Hamilton, charged Redoubt No. 10. These were bayonet assaults, after the pattern of Stony Point. In a spirited engagement, both of the assaulting forces carried their objectives, though the French had a more difficult time, since the artillery fire had not smashed the protecting *abatis* as thoroughly at Redoubt No. 9 as around Redoubt No. 10.

The two forts having been captured by 10:00 P.M., allied work details feverishly labored for the rest of the night to extend the second parallel northeastward to the river, to include both of these forts. To distract the British from this activity, Saint-Simon's troops again demonstrated against the Fusiliers Redoubt.

Next day, as the allied artillery fire waxed in intensity, Cornwallis wrote to Clinton that "the safety of the place is . . . so precarious that I cannot recommend that the fleet and army should run great risque in endeavoring to save us." He was determined, however, not to give up without at least one more effort.

Just before dawn on October 16 a picked British force of 350 men raided the second parallel, at the junction of the French and American sectors. The raiders were in the process of spiking the guns of American and French batteries in the second parallel, when they were struck by a vigorous French counterattack led by the alert Viscomte de Noailles, brother-in-law of Lafayette. The British were driven back, after they had succeeded in spiking seven guns. They had inflicted 17 casualties on the allies, and had lost 12 themselves. But when Washington inspected the position soon after daybreak, the exultant French and American cannoneers informed him that they had removed the British spikes and demonstrated to him that the guns were already back in action.

October 16 was another terrible day for the defenders of York-town. The allied artillery kept up an incessant hammering of the trenches, and of the remnants of the battered town. Cornwallis de-termined to make one last effort to escape from the trap. He planned to move his entire garrison across the river that night to Gloucester, whence he would break out through the besieging lines. He hoped then to march rapidly northward into Maryland and Pennsylvania, living off the countryside, outdistancing the more heavily encumbered allies. It was a desperate plan—but he was in a desperate situation. Just after dark a number of boats were loaded with troops and sent across the river to Gloucester. While they were crossing, the wind rose, and by the time they had reached the far bank had grown to gale intensity. A few of the boats tried to get back across the river, and were blown away into Chesapeake Bay. The effort was aban-doned. Early next morning, when the wind had abated, the allies could see the remaining boats, full of troops, returning from Glouces-ter to Yorktown.

It was the anniversary of Burgoyne's surrender at Saratoga. Shortly after 9:30 A.M. a British drummer stepped up on the parapet of the inner defenses, and began to beat his drum, the signal for a parley. The noise of the bombardment was such that the sound of the drum could not be heard; but watchful sentries in the allied trenches im-mediately saw the drummer, and in a few moments, the fire had stopped. At this point a British officer stepped out of the hornwork, waving a white handkerchief as a flag of truce. An American officer jumped from the trenches, ran to meet him, and after tying his own handkerchief around the eyes of the Britisher, led him back to Wash-ington's headquarters. The British officer delivered a note to the allied Commander-in-Chief. Washington read:

"Sir, I propose a cessation of hostilities for twenty-four hours, and that two officers may be appointed by each side, to meet at Mr. Moore's

house, to settle terms for the surrender of the posts at York and
Gloucester.

> "I have the honor to be &c
> "Cornwallis"

Washington immediately sat down to write a reply:

"My Lord: I have had the Honor of receiving Your Lordship's Letter
of this date.

"An Ardent Desire to spare the further Effusion of Blood, will readily
incline me to listen to such Terms for the Surrender of your Posts and
Garrisons of York and Gloucester, as are admissible.

"I wish previously to the Meeting of Commissioners, that your Lordship's proposals in writing may be sent to the American Lines: for which
Purpose, a suspension of Hosilities during two Hours from the Delivery
of this Letter will be granted. I have the honor, etc.

> "Washington"

Disappointed that Washington would permit him only two hours
to indicate the terms that he expected, Cornwallis nevertheless responded within the time limit. He requested, among other things, that
the garrison be granted the honors of war, and that the surrendered
prisoners be permitted to return to England or to Germany on parole
not to serve against France or America during the remainder of
the war.

From this reply, though some of its terms were inadmissible, it
was clear to Washington that Cornwallis was serious in his intent to
surrender. He therefore agreed to continue the suspension of hostilities
during the night, promising to reply early the following morning.

Washington's response of the 18th refused the proposed condition
"of sending the British and German troops to the parts of Europe to
which they respectively belong." He grimly added that "the same
Honors will be granted to the Surrendering Army as were granted
to the Garrison of Charles Town."

In other words, the honors of war would be limited; the British
would have to march out with their colors cased, and their bands
would not be permitted to play either an American or a French
march. He acquiesced generally to the other conditions requested by
Cornwallis, the details to be worked out by commissions from each
side. Once more he gave Cornwallis only two hours in which to agree,
or to suffer a renewal of hostilities and of the bombardment. Mean-

while the troops lined the trenches on both sides. A serenade by British bagpipes was returned by a French band concert.

Again Cornwallis responded within the limited time, accepting the general terms established by Washington, requesting one or two minor additional points, and agreeing to name two officers to act as his commissioners "to digest the articles of capitulation."

During the remainder of that day the four commissioners negotiated surrender terms at the Moore House, behind the allied lines. Lieutenant Colonel Thomas Dundas, and Major Alexander Ross represented Cornwallis; Lieutenant Colonel John Laurens (recently returned from a trip to France), and the Viscomte de Noailles spoke for Washington and Rochambeau. The British were aghast at not being allowed the full honors of war, but received a firm, unequivocal reply from Laurens, who had been in the surrendering garrison at Charleston. Late that night the allied commissioners presented to Washington the results of their deliberations.

Early the next morning—October 19—Washington ordered the articles of capitulation to be written up in final form, after making a few minor modifications. The papers were then sent to Lord Cornwallis with word that Washington "expected to have them signed at 11 o'clock and that the garrison would march out at 2 o'clock." Shortly after 11 the papers were returned, signed by Cornwallis and by Captain Thomas Symonds, the senior naval officer present in Yorktown. Washington, Rochambeau, and the Comte de Barras (de Grasse, being ill, could not be present) then signed the papers themselves in the trenches opposite the surrendered city.

The French and American troops then formed up along the main road to Yorktown leading across the Pigeon Quarter and past the allied trenches. At precisely 2:00 P.M. the British and Hessian troops came marching out. Their cased colors contrasted somberly with the fluttering French and American colors lining the road ahead of them.

It is not clear from the record whether each separate band and drum corps played the same march, or whether these were different. It is a treasured tradition that the British and Hessian bands played an old English tune appropriately entitled "The World Turned Upside Down," but this cannot be definitely ascertained. Whatever march or marches were played, it was as obvious to the defeated troops as to the victorious allies lining the road, that this ceremony was in fact evidence of "The World Turned Upside Down." A British army was surrendering a seaport to the French and Americans because Britain no longer exercised command of the sea. More significant, most of those present realized that this surrender meant that Great Britain had lost her last chance to reimpose royal authority on her rebellious American colonies.

Leading the British troops was Brigadier General Charles O'Hara, Cornwallis' second-in-command. One French account implies that O'Hara was about to deliver his sword to Rochambeau when the French general and his aides indicated that he should surrender to Washington, the allied Commander-in-Chief. This legend, also, is doubtful, because the same account indicates that O'Hara rendered his sword in the surrender ceremony, while other eyewitness reports do not mention this—an omission that can have no chauvinistic implications.

Whatever may have been the preliminaries, O'Hara reported to Washington, and may have offered to surrender his sword, apologizing for the absence of Cornwallis, who pleaded illness. Washington courteously referred O'Hara, as Cornwallis' second-in-command, to General Lincoln, who was his second-in-command. If O'Hara did give his sword to Lincoln, that general immediately returned it to him. It was an appropriate coincidence that the surrender of the British at Yorktown was thus received by the officer who had surrendered to them at Charleston.

Lincoln then informed O'Hara where the British troops were to lay down their arms, in a Pigeon Quarter field surrounded by French hussars. As the surrendering column marched past it was obvious that a number of the British soldiers were under the influence of liquor, but that the Hessians were as soberly soldierly as ever. Evidently, until Lincoln protested, a number of British soldiers threw their weapons down vigorously in hopes of breaking the locks.

Washington did not stay to witness this final act in the ceremonies. He returned to his headquarters, after issuing an invitation to O'Hara and the other senior British officers to dine with him that evening.

The British force which surrendered at Yorktown consisted of 7,247 soldiers and 840 seamen. During the siege the British had lost 156 killed, 326 wounded, and 70 missing. Reported American casualties during the siege had been 23 Continentals killed and 65 wounded; it has been estimated that there were about 30 additional militiamen lost. French losses were 60 killed and 193 wounded.

Ironically, on the very day that Cornwallis surrendered, Clinton set sail from New York for Chesapeake Bay with an army of 7,000 troops, convoyed by Admiral Graves' fleet of 27 ships of the line and 8 frigates. Arriving off Chesapeake Bay on the 24th, Clinton learned of Cornwallis' surrender. Seeing that he was too late, he did not risk an engagement with the numerically superior French fleet, but returned to New York.

37 ★ ★ ★ ★ ★

Slowly Falls the Curtain

THE AMERICAN VICTORY AT YORKTOWN convinced the British Government and people that they could not beat their erstwhile colonies into submission by force of arms. King George at first refused to accept the inevitable, but the English people were tired. The English economy was suffering; the resources of the nation were strained to the utmost by a war which had spread the world over.

On March 4, 1782, Parliament took the first step. It adopted a resolution virtually calling for the ending of the war and the recognition of the independence of the "revolted colonies." The North ministry fell sixteen days later; a new ministry, headed by Lord Rockingham and including such friends of the colonies as Edmund Burke and Charles James Fox began wrestling with the task of how best to make peace. To this end, conversations with American commissioners began in Paris, on April 12. On May 9, Sir Guy Carleton arrived in New York to succeed Clinton in command of British forces in North America, and set about concentrating all his troops in New York.

The war, however, was far from being ended.* In the United States more than a year of desultory combat and bitter privations faced the ragged Continental Army. On the high seas the remnants of the Continental Navy and a lusty host of privateers dared the continuing blockade of the coast by more than 70 English warships.

Around the globe from the West Indies to the Bay of Bengal and along the littoral of India, England's soldiers and sailors would con-

---

* For a summary of military operations after Yorktown, see Appendix VIII.

tinue waging desperate war with America's ally, France, and quasi-allies Spain, and the Netherlands. In the United States, Greene's tatterdemalion troops slowly swept Georgia and the Carolinas clean of redcoats, while back in the old Hudson River stamping grounds, penning Carleton in New York, Washington and his Yorktown victors spent more than a year of discontent. The Congress, it seemed, was all too willing to forget the officers and men who had so loyally served it to bring freedom.

This was a grim and bitter period, in which Washington was required to exercise to the utmost his painfully-acquired skill in holding together an army plagued by injustices—particularly when the homesick men knew that peace would come when the commissioners in Paris concluded their debates. Yet he found time to write, at Alexander Hamilton's request, his immortal "Sentiments Upon a Peace Establishment," which still stands today in principle as a blueprint for American national defense.

All the while, the poison engendered by Congressional indifference —which left them unpaid, and which threatened their very security in the future—was coursing through the veins of the Continental Army, to reach even into the officer corps. Their grievances flamed with the infamous "Newburgh Addresses," March 12-15, 1783, only to be quelled by Washington's last great display of military leadership, in which he recalled to the officers the virtues of patriotism and the essential subserviency of the military to the civil power under all circumstances.

The "Newburgh Addresses" were the darkness before the dawn. For on April 19, from the steps of the New Windsor "Temple," the great meeting hall of the Continental Army near Newburgh, the "cessation of hostilities between the United States and the King of Great Britain" was formally announced—eight years to the day from the fusillade on Lexington Green. The Revolutionary War had come to an end.

The peace negotiations had been conducted in a masterly fashion by the American peace commissioners in Paris: John Jay, Benjamin Franklin, John Adams, and Henry Laurens. On November 30 their lengthy conferences with Richard Oswald had resulted in the signature of preliminary articles of peace, to be effective upon the conclusion of England's lingering wars with France and Spain. French foreign minister Vergennes had been surprised by the extremely favorable terms obtained by the American commissioners, and was annoyed that they had not consulted him. Tactful Benjamin Franklin had mollified him, however, pointing out that America would not abrogate the Franco-American alliance, and had no intention of withdrawing from the war until England also signed peace with France and Spain. This took place on January 20, 1783, and Britain formally announced cessation of hostilities on February 4. Congress received the text of the Treaty of Paris on March 13, proclaimed cessation of the war on April 11, and ratified the treaty on April 15. The final treaty would not be signed at Paris, however, until September 3, to be ratified by Congress on January 14, 1784, with the anticlimactic exchange of ratifications eventually taking place on May 12.

The picture of the Revolutionary War, as woven on history's tapestry, is indeed a "many splendoured thing." It depicts the birth of a nation through force of arms. Across its surface runs the resiliency of men who could rebound from Bunker Hill, from Quebec, from Long Island, from the Brandywine, from Germantown, and from Camden to Trenton, Princeton, Bennington, Saratoga, Monmouth, Kings Mountain, the Cowpens, and Yorktown. The image of Valley Forge, with its red prints of shoeless, starving men, epitomizes eight dreadful winters which these men endured.

This is no series of disconnected incidents. Linking them is one golden thread: the unselfish genius of George Washington, who could transform stubborn freemen, who refused to submit to unjust law, into professional soldiers capable of meeting on equal terms the best that Europe could produce. His was the inspiration which guided these men to discard the primal instinct of self-preservation for that of the patriotic will to win. His was the iron will and military acumen which substituted victory for defeat, no matter how hopeless the situation.

It is no reflection on the fighting ability of these men, nor the genius of their leader, to point out that after 1779 England stood alone in a hostile world.

It was indeed fortunate for the Revolutionary cause that this conflict differed markedly, in two major respects, from the many wars which traced the desperate struggle for world mastery between England and France during the preceding century, and during the following four decades as well. It was invariable English strategy in these wars to subsidize European allies to keep France busily engaged in continental land war, while England devoted her own full energies to naval and colonial warfare. France, naturally principally concerned with the security of her land frontiers, and with the increase of her power and influence in Europe, was thus always at a disadvantage at sea and overseas—in all wars save this. England, unable from 1775 of 1783 to find a continental ally to keep France busy in Europe, was for the first and only time forced to engage in a maritime and overseas war with the undiverted resources of France—which were still formidable, despite the decay which was leading to the French Revolution.

By a coincidence, at the start of the war, years of political neglect had brought the English navy to a low ebb, while a resurgent French navy was led by a group of the most able sailors in the maritime history of France. As a result, England lost her formerly unquestioned command of the seas. France, and to a lesser degree Spain, were thus enabled to project their land and sea power to the American continent and to the West Indies, to give direct and indirect assistance to the Americans which was probably decisive in shaping the outcome of the Revolution. It was only incidental to this result that by the close of the conflict a supreme effort on the part of the Royal Navy would once more re-establish Britain's maritime supremacy, and cause the war to end in a deadlock—save only for the independence of the former Thirteen Colonies.

Envoi

OUT-BOUND FROM NEW YORK on April 26, 1783, a sad congregation set sail: some 7,000 Tories—men, women and children—the last of nearly 100,000 Loyalists who, fighting for King George and resisting independence for their homeland, were now leaving it forever. Their departure was preliminary to the exodus of the British troops.

On June 13, the disbandment of the Continental Army began; a hurried departure, with the penniless men merely streaming away with promissory notes and final settlement certificates in lieu of the "hard" money they so deserved and needed. They grumbled, but they went. The one jarring note was the mutiny of a group of Lancaster, Pennsylvania, recruits, who marched to Philadelphia to demand redress, so scaring the Congress that it decamped first to Princeton, and then to Annapolis. The mutineers, however, disbanded without violence before a detachment of the remaining troops, whose enlistments had not yet expired, could round them up.

During late November, the British forces around New York were concentrated within the city itself, while Washington, with the 700 Continental troops remaining—a regiment of infantry and a few companies of artillery—moved down to Harlem Heights. On the 25th, the last English troops left New York for their embarkation point on Staten Island, and General Knox entered the city with the Continentals. Behind them Washington and Governor Clinton, with their respective staffs, rode solemnly in. By December 4 the British flotilla of transports and warships cleared Sandy Hook, and that same day, at noon, Washington took leave of his officers in a touching ceremony at Fraunce's Tavern in Pearl Street. Then the Commander-in-Chief was rowed in his barge from the Battery to the Jersey shore, homeward bound. He stopped at Annapolis—where Congress was assembled—on the long ride south, after receiving ovations at Brunswick, Trenton and Philadelphia.

Here the finale of Washington's military career took place on December 23: his farewell to the Congress, concluding with words which still can stir all American hearts:

"Having finished the work assigned me, I retire from the great theater of action, and bidding an affectionate farewell to this august body under whose orders I have so long acted, I here offer my commission and take my leave of all the employments of public life."

By Christmas the Father of his Country was home at last, with Martha at Mount Vernon.

Appendix I: Army Weapons, Tactics, and Uniforms

Small Arms

THE STANDARD BRITISH INFANTRY HAND-ARM was the "Brown Bess" or "Tower" musket; so-called from the Tower of London inspection stamp it bore. This was a flint-lock, muzzle-loading smooth-bore, four feet nine inches long, weighing about eleven pounds. It threw a spherical lead ball of slightly over one ounce weight, .75″ in caliber, for a maximum range of 125 yards when fired horizontally from the shoulder of a standing man. In practice, a good marksman might have a 50 percent chance of hitting a standing man some 75 yards away. Actually—since British soldiers were taught not to aim, but merely to point the piece towards the target and, upon order, to pull the trigger in volley fire—little accuracy could be expected at ranges of over 50 yards. Seemingly to discourage any attempt at aiming, this piece had no rear sight. On the other hand, the three-quarter inch ball, if and when it hit a human target, could inflict a devastating wound.

Loading and firing this or any other musket was a most complicated process. The powder and ball were combined in a paper cartridge. The soldier had to bite off the powder end, sprinkle some of the powder into the flint-lock pan, then shove the remainder of the load into the muzzle and ram it home. He next put the weapon to his shoulder and pointing it, hoped that his pull on the trigger would bring down the hammer—which held a flint—upon the steel frizzen of the pan with sufficient force to produce a spark which would ignite the loose powder in the pan. Theoretically, this flame would flare through the touch-hole, igniting the powder charge in the piece, and thus produce the explosion which would send the bullet on its way. Success, in the end, was dependent upon the weather, since rain would dampen the priming and cause a misfire.

In theory, a well-drilled soldier might fire five rounds a minute under the best conditions. Actually, in combat he would be lucky indeed to get off three shots. All in all, the Tower musket with its complicated firing mechanism was, like most flint-lock muzzle-loaders of its ilk, a most unreliable firearm. Its principal function was to carry a twenty-one inch bayonet, which British regular soldiers were able to use to maximum advantage.

Except for the jägers, noted below, the German troops carried a musket similar to the British arm.

The Americans, perforce, were armed with a multiplicity of firearms, ranging from Tower muskets to fowling pieces. Rare indeed was the colonial household without a handarm of some sort. Many of these weapons were of local manufacture; gunsmithing was not an uncommon vocation in America. Few of these weapons were equipped with bayonets, or indeed could be fitted with them, if available. Militia regulations, recognizing this lack, called for the soldier to possess either a bayonet or a tomahawk. French and other European military firelocks obtained later during the war had much the same characteristics as the Tower musket. When cartridges were not available the soldier carried powder in a flask or horn, and balls in a pouch.

The basic distinction between British and Americans (Tory as well as patriot) lay in the use of the musket. For the colonists, particularly rural dwellers, had been ingrained in the use of firearms since childhood, both for defense and for hunting. Powder and lead were expensive; and in either Indian-fighting or in hunting, the first round from the slow-loading firelock was the vital one. Thus marksmanship was essential. As a result, on the American firing line, individual aimed fire was the rule; sharp contrast to the British Army formal, unaimed, volley fire. And, much to the rage of both British and Hessians, their officers—brave in gold lace, white crossbelts, glittering metal gorgets and other insignia of rank—were prime targets. Very effective, too, at close range, was the "buck and ball" load frequently used by American troops: two buckshot rammed in with the ball.

But some Americans carried a much more accurate firearm: the rifle. Practically unknown in New England, the rifle, with its grooved bore, causing the bullet to rotate, had become the principal firearm of the western frontier areas—the Pennsylvania mountains, Virginia's Blue Ridge and beyond, Tennessee, and the Carolinas. This so-called "Kentucky rifle" was an offspring of the European hunting rifle of Switzerland, Bavaria and the Rhineland. The European prototype was short and heavy, with caliber varying from .60″ to 1.00″. The lead bullet was tight-fitting, it had to be pounded down the muzzle and into the grooves by a small hammer or mallet. The jäger elements of the Hessian and Brunswick soldiery in the British service carried such pieces.

German and Swiss emigrants had early brought the rifle with them to America, and patient gunsmiths along the frontiers had evolved the Kentucky rifle—much longer-barrelled than the original, and of smaller caliber: about .50″. Instead of being hammered into the bore, the bullet was easy-fitting, wrapped in a greased cloth patch to fit snugly into the grooves. These American rifles were individual works of the gunsmith's art, and in the hands of trained marksmen were weapons of amazing accuracy; deadly at ranges of 200 yards or more, as the British found out early in the war. The Kentucky rifle's big drawback as a military weapon was that a bayonet could not be fitted to it. And, of course, in common with all other flint-locks, it was a creature dependent in last resort upon the weather.

Most Tory elements of the British forces in America were armed and equipped upon standard British lines. However, the Tories of the south—partisans and regulars alike—were as much marksmen and riflemen as the patriots of the same areas. And British Major Patrick Ferguson's partisan force was in some small measure armed with a workable breech-loading rifle of Ferguson's own invention; an innovation which in 1776 had been flatly turned down by the British War Office.

Cavalry of both sides were armed with the musket or a lighter musketoon (carbine), as well as the saber. Again, the British were equipped with standardized weapons; the Americans with such hodge-podge of muskets, pistols and sabers as could be amassed.

Horse-pistols were a part of the British dragoon equipment. All British and American officers carried pistols as private hand arms. British subaltern infantry officers also carried spontons—a type of light halbard used mainly for signaling commands. The sponton was occasionally seen also in the American ranks.

Ordnance

Field guns, cast of bronze, brass or iron, were of four general classifications—12-, 8-, 6- and 4-pounders—according to the weight of the solid iron balls they threw to ranges up to one mile. For use against troops in the open, at close range, grapeshot (clumps of iron balls in a metal frame), and canister (smaller lead balls in a container) were used. In both cases the projectiles flew apart shortly after leaving the muzzle of the piece, to sweep a wide but shallow area, in a manner similar to buckshot from rifle or musket. All cannon were smooth-bore muzzle-loaders.

In addition to the more common solid round shot, artillerymen were beginning to make increasing use of shell: hollow cannon balls, filled with gunpowder, and intended to explode in the ranks of the enemy. Shell was generally fired from howitzers—shorter and lighter than guns of corresponding calibers. Since the shell was detonated by a length of fuse presumably—but not always—ignited by the powder charge, shell fire was neither accurate nor dependable. The smaller howitzers were called "coehorns." The howitzer threw its projectile in a high, curved trajectory. Mortars, with even higher, shorter trajectories, were particularly applicable to dropping shells inside and behind enemy fortifications.

Siege ordnance consisted of heavier pieces, firing projectiles weighing up to 24 pounds and more. These weapons were used primarily to batter down fortifications, though they also fired shell for anti-personnel effect against the garrison, and incendiary shot against houses and wooden installations. The principal incendiary projectile was called a "carcass": an iron shell, packed with tar or other combustible material, with holes permitting the flames to blaze. It was during this war that red-hot shot came into general use as an incendiary—notably by the British against the Franco-Spanish fleet during the siege of Gibraltar. Coast defense guns were comparable to siege artillery and heavy naval ordnance.

Tactics

Eighteenth-century European armies were aggregations of battalions (the terms "regiment" and "battalion" were practically synonymous), gathered into larger units for convenience of command. These larger elements might be called brigades, divisions, corps or wings—the terms bearing little relationship to the standardized nomenclature of today. For battle, armies were drawn up in several lines, each of which was composed of battalions in line, each battalion being three files (men) deep. Insofar as the British Army was concerned, the French and Indian War—and Braddock's 1755 defeat in particular—had proven that such rigid formations were ineffective in the wilderness. From that time dated the British development of light infantry: regular soldiers trained to fight, if necessary, in open skirmishing order, and to make use of cover. However, the basic concept of infantry assault of the day, considering the power and limitation of the foot soldier's musket, was still the movement of a mass of men upon a given objective, the delivery of one or more volleys—fired at the last possible moment and at the shortest possible range—and then a final rush with the bayonet.

British infantry regiments of the period were in fact single-battalion units; normally commanded by a major. The battalion consisted of ten small companies—each from 20 to 40 men strong. Eight of these were "battalion" or "line" companies. One additional company—composed of the largest and strongest men—was the "grenadier" company (so-called originally because big men were picked to throw clumsy hand grenades). The other company was made up of the most agile men in the regiment; this was the "light infantry" company. These two elements—commonly referred to as "flank" companies because at ceremonies the grenadiers took the right of the regimental line, the light infantry the left—were the élite of the regiment. In campaign the "flank" companies were usually detached from their respective units and formed into provisional battalions—grenadiers and light infantry. It should be noted that the grenadiers who in theory constituted the reserve—the power punch—were entirely distinct from and bore no relation to the Grenadier Guards Regiment, which, with the Coldstreams and the Scots composed the Royal Foot Guards. Composite Guards brigades served in America and they, too, were divided into "line" and "flank." The German contingents serving in America followed the general pattern, but the line infantry, grenadier and jäger (light infantry) elements appear to have been usually separate units.

It was quite natural that colonial and Continental infantry tactical formations should follow, in general, the British type of organization. However, except for Wayne's short-lived light infantry corps—selected from picked elements of all the Continental regiments—and a few other exceptions, demarkation between "flank" and "battalion" units in a regiment did not exist. In fact, all the Continental infantry fell into the light infantry class.

The ranger was another type of foot soldier found in both the opposing forces. He, like the light infantry, was another product of necessity dating from the French and Indian War, when Roberts' Rangers—combining woodcraft, knowledge of Indian-fighting, marksmanship and discipline—were incorporated into the British forces. As a matter of fact, all the original rifle units of the Continental Army could be lumped into the ranger class, while on the British side were also a number of Tory ranger units—most celebrated, perhaps, being Butler's Rangers (who, however, were not riflemen).

Neither side had many cavalry units in the Revolution; those which did exist were almost invariably dragoons—that is, they were armed, equipped and trained to fight on foot as well as to employ the shock action of most European cavalry of the period. Only two regular British cavalry units served in America—the 16th and 17th Light Dragoons. The one small unit of German cavalry—Brunswick dragoons—came over without horses and except for a few who served around Burgoyne's headquarters, were never mounted. In addition to the few Continental dragoon units, many Southern militia formations were mounted, but their animals served as means of transportation and not as shock weapons; they were mounted infantry, pure and simple.

The "legion," so-called, was usually composed of both dragoons and light infantry, sometimes with a few pieces of artillery added. This was a hybrid unit found in both the Continental Army and in the British Loyalist (Tory) formations. Tarleton's Legion was perhaps the best known in the British service, Pulaski's and Lee's in the Continental Army.

Army Uniforms

The British wore a blouse or coatee of scarlet; the facings differing in the various corps. Tory troops wore either a red or a green coatee; again with a multiplicity of facings. Brunswick and Hessian line infantry and grenadiers in general wore blue; the jägers green—the traditional huntsman's color.

On the American side, the first attempt at Continental uniform dress was that of the riflemen—a brown hunting shirt and overalls—although some of the militia already had distinctive uniforms, notably the blue and buff of Virginia, immortalized as General Washington's uniform. However, in general the American troops were clad in whatever they could find to cover—sometimes unsuccessfully—their nakedness. Occasional shipments of uniforms from France —both blue, brown, and occasionally green—were welcome equipment. A few individual units were clothed with some care, as for instance Baylor's 3rd Continental Dragoons—"Lady Washington's Horse"—whose white with blue facings was seen around the Commander-in-Chief's headquarters in 1777 and 1778. Colonel Moses Hazen's 2nd Canadian Regiment—"Congress' Own" (recruited in Canada)—wore brown, faced with red. And, so far as possible, the four artillery regiments were clad in dark blue or black coatees faced with red, and white drill overalls.

Appendix II: Naval Weapons, Tactics, and Uniforms

Naval Tactics and Terminology

NAVAL COMBAT OF THE PERIOD was a combination of rigid, battering hammer-and-tongs procedure, tempered by the niceties of the art of seamanship—ship-handling. Application of firepower, expressed in weight of metal thrown, was dependent upon the ability of the sailor to maneuver his practically rigid line of broadside guns so that they could bear on his target. In other words, steering the vessel was of necessity a component factor of naval gunnery. This, in sailing vessels—dependent upon wind and weather for steerage way and maneuver—required high technical skill and experience.

In last result, naval combat was a slugging-match, ship against ship, side by side, and sometimes lashed there, until one gave up. In single-ship actions—between two opposing vessels—the *coup de grâce* was often the boarding party: sailors from one vessel pouring across the bulwarks of the other, to engage on the deck in hand-to-hand combat with cutlass, musket and boarding pike.

In squadron or fleet actions the accepted formation was that of "line ahead"; the ships, in single file, engaging those of the enemy, who was in the same formation, thus producing a succession of single-ship actions. Rodney, in the Battle of the Saints, broke with tradition by sailing into and breaking up the enemy formation, and concentrating superior fire on portions of the then disordered French fleet.

To obtain the best advantage of the prevailing wind, opposing ships and fleets commonly jockeyed for the "weather-gauge." This meant putting themselves between the wind and the enemy; advantageous because they could then either close for battle or avoid combat. The ship or ships on the leeward side, while they could avoid battle, would be forced to "beat" against the wind, and approach in zig-zag fashion—called "tacking"—were they desirous to give battle.

A further advantage obtained through holding the weather-gauge was that the ship to windward could put herself more easily across the path of the other vessel and sweep her from stem to stern. The vessel so "raked" could not make an effective reply since her broadside guns could not be brought to bear. In fleet actions, however, this "crossing of the T" was rare. When achieved, it resulted in concentrating the fire of many ships against the few of the enemy van.

A sailing ship, with the wind astern pushing her, might change direction by "wearing." Working against the wind, a vessel with the wind blowing from the right (starboard) hand was on the "starboard tack." Conversely, she would be on the "port tack" when the wind came from the left front. To change so that the wind would come from the opposite direction was to "tack," but the actual movement into the wind was "luffing." If, in so doing, the ship was so slowed up that she lost steerage way and hung motionless, she had "missed stays," and was helpless until her yards had been braced (turned) to catch the wind and start her moving again. In such case she might for a time be "making stern way" (moving backward). A change of direction taking a vessel away from combat was termed "hauling off" or "hauling out." A ship's forward movement could be halted or slowed by shifting the yards so that the wind was pushing against the sails. This was called "backing" the sails.

An anchored vessel swings on her cable to rest head up to the wind or tide. Short of getting under way—weighing (hoisting) the anchor or slipping the cable free, and setting sail, the anchored sailing ship was of course unable to change her position without mechanical leverage. This could be obtained by fastening a line to the anchor chain or cable and passing this line to the vessel's stern. By heaving on this line, the ship could be gradually hauled around until she faced in the opposite direction. The line was called a "spring line," and common parlance for this arrangement was to "put a spring" on the cable.

On meeting an unidentified vessel, it was an accepted part of naval deception to fly the flag of a neutral nation or that of the enemy until within cannon range. But before engaging in combat it was a point of naval honor to "break out" (hoist) authentic national colors. "Striking" (hauling down) the colors signaled surrender.

A becalmed vessel might in emergency be towed by the ship's rowing boats, or moved by "kedging." A kedge (light anchor) with cable attached was carried by small boat a distance from the ship and dropped. The crew then pulled the vessel up to the kedge by heaving in on the cable. The process could be repeated as needful.

Warships of the day fell into three formal classes. The ship of the line, as her name signified, was a vessel large enough and carrying sufficient armament to slug it out in the line of battle. Ships of the line carried from 64 to 110 guns in three tiers. Frigates—faster and lighter and built for commerce destruction, escort and patrol—came next; vessels carrying from 24 to 44 guns on two gun decks. Larger frigates—50 guns—were few; these were compromises, they were sometimes used in the line of battle, and considered as small ships of the line. Sloops of war carried from 16 to 24 guns. All these vessels, except sloops of war, were square-rigged three-masters. The sloop, whose name bore no relation to her rig, might be ship—(three masts; square-rigged), brig (two masts; square-rigged)—or brigantine (two masts; square-rigged on foremast only) rigged. Smaller craft were usually known by the name of their rig (usually sloop, schooner, or ketch).

The above is a tremendously over-simplified summary of a most complicated subject. It is hoped, however, that it will give the unnautical reader some orientation on the technique of the naval combats narrated here.

Naval Ordnance

Naval ordnance consisted of 9-, 12-, 18-, and 24-pounder cannon. However, light craft, and in particular the American privateers, were usually armed with much lighter guns: 4- and 6-pounders. By 1779 another piece of ordnance, the carronade, had been added in the Royal Navy. This was a shorter, lighter—and cheaper—gun, throwing 32- or 42-pound projectiles for relatively short distances. At close range, the smashing effect of the carronade in single-ship combat, where the vessels lay broadside to broadside, was terrific. Many of the British ships in the Battle of the Saints, the First of June and the Moonlight Battle were armed with carronades. The big drawback of the carronade was its short range. A capable commander, whose vessel was armed with guns of smaller caliber but longer range, could beat a carronade-armed ship to pieces before its smashing broadside came within range of him.

Naval ammunition, in addition to solid iron balls, also included not only grape and canister, but also bar- and chain-shot—projectiles linked together—which raised hob with canvas, rigging and spars. After its introduction by the British at the siege of Gibraltar, red-hot shot was also used against other ships and against land targets.

Naval Uniforms

While uniform regulations had been established for Royal Navy officers by this time, no specific regulations governed the enlisted men. By long custom, the British tar wore a blue jacket, white canvas trousers, and a tarpaulin hat. A black silk kerchief might be worn about the sailor's head, or as a neck-cloth, to protect his jacket from the greasy pig-tail into which his hair had been twisted. Officers' uniforms, despite regulations, appear to have been matters of personal taste, with gold lace, epaulettes of fantasy, and embroidered waistcoats topping off a basic blue coatee, white knee-breeches and cocked hat. American uniforms, while perhaps plainer, followed more or less the same pattern.

Appendix III: Utilization
of American Manpower*

MORE THAN 395,000 MEN PASSED THROUGH THE RANKS of our armies during the eight years of war. The distribution and sources of procurement were:

Continental Army:

Massachusetts	67,907
Connecticut	31,939
Virginia	26,678
Pennsylvania	25,678
New York	17,781
Maryland	13,912
New Hampshire	12,497
New Jersey	10,726
North Carolina	7,263
South Carolina	6,417
Rhode Island	5,908
Georgia	2,679
Delaware	2,386
Total	231,771

Militia:

Conjectural estimate	164,087
Grand total	395,858

These are imposing figures for a nation whose population at the end of the war was less than 3,000,000 (of whom about 500,000 were Negro slaves). Yet the greatest number of troops that Congress was able to raise during any one year (1776) was 89,600 men—42,700 of them militia. The Americans were

* Data noted herein are abstracted from Report of the Secretary of War, May 10, 1790, as published in *American State Papers—Military Affairs*, vol. 1, pp. 14-19. The Secretary, General Henry Knox, compiled his report from existing incomplete strength returns and conjectural estimates.

never able to concentrate at any one time a force exceeding 20,000 men. And, as we know, Washington's principal preoccupation during the war was to keep any field strength at all in being—the nadir being the Trenton-Princeton campaign (1776), when his effective strength was less than 4,000.

It is interesting to note that early in 1776, when total British strength in America was slightly over 20,000, there was a total of 89,600 men mobilized in patriot forces. Of these, Washington was able to assemble only about 20,000 to defend New York. Five years later, in 1781, British strength (including Hessians and Loyalists) had grown to 42,000, while the patriots could muster only 29,340, and Washington had barely 6,000 in his army blockading New York. This fluctuation, and the discrepancies, require some explanation.

The fact was, as we have noted, that from the beginning to the end of the Revolutionary War, Congress expressed the dread of the American people for standing armies, by a short-sighted, extravagant, haphazard procurement policy, relying upon short-term volunteer enlistments.

Despite Washington's continued warnings and pleas that all enlistments should be for the duration of the war, the Congress long resisted any service period for more than one year, and only grudgingly assented to a later "three year or the duration" term. Meanwhile, as patriotic volunteers were not forthcoming in sufficient numbers to meet the continuous, crying need, a pernicious system of bounties was instituted, its promises waxing in an inflationary spiral with the depreciation of the Continental currency. Beginning in 1776 with $20 and 100 acres of land, these bonuses grew to offers of clothing, of more land, and of $200 in currency.

The Congress annually specified the proportional quotas of Continental troops to be raised in each state. These quotas were never fully achieved, since the appeals competed with the magnetic lure of prize money offered by privateering, the recruiting clamor for the little Continental Navy, and—most attractive of all perhaps, for this offered a minimum of hardship service with a maximum of safety and inaction—the efforts of each individual state to fill its own militia ranks. State bounties vied with the Congressional offers.

So critical was the recruiting situation in 1778 that Congress, on Washington's recommendation, threatened a draft, upon which the states began to drag their areas for the dregs to fill the Continental ranks. Many deserters from Burgoyne's prisoner army were coaxed up—poor bargains, these, for the majority, it seemed, deserted again as fast as they arrived.

In further effort, the states now began offering additional bounties of their own for enlistments or re-enlistment in their Continental troop quotas. By 1778, for instance, New Jersey was offering an additional $250; and Virginia $750, a suit of clothes, and an additional 100 acres of land. The result of these offers, of course, was to put a premium on desertion. Thousands of men—their number will never be known—became "repeaters," enlisting, deserting and re-enlisting to obtain further bounties.

The net result of this policy—or lack of policy—when the normal attrition of war and disease were added, was to produce a continuous ebb and flow in the Continental ranks. Old soldiers—their enlistments expiring (frequently at the most inopportune time) were leaving; recruits were joining. Discipline and training were disrupted. Serious gaps were filled in emergency by hurried calls upon untrained and untried militia brought into service for periods ranging from 60 days to six months; further compounding the difficulties of command and troop-leading.

The fact is that the overall number of men enlisted during the war, more than 395,000, as shown above, bears no relation to the number who actually served. For instance in the hard core of Continentals who fought through the war there were many who themselves were legitimate "repeaters"; they had, perforce, passed through several enlistment terms.

These men—who served honestly and patriotically despite appalling hardships; who were never adequately paid, fed or clothed; who patiently and faithfully fought and died at George Washington's behest—were magnificent.

It has been estimated that total American casualties in the war included 4,435 men killed in action, and 6,188 wounded. There is no record either of the casualties inflicted by disease, or of civilian lives lost in the war.

Appendix IV: Fortifications and Siegecraft

THE REVOLUTIONARY WAR, like European conflicts of the period, was largely one of posts and positions—the seizure or defense of strategically important locations. Thus the fortifications and siegecraft techniques of the war were based primarily upon those developed in the seventeenth century by French master-engineer Sebastian de Vauban. His methodology dominated all military engineer-craft. Naturally, obvious modifications were made in adapting these patterns to the less highly developed coastal regions of America, and to the inland wilderness, but the basic pattern remained the same.

Essential to the fortified position was a wall, or rampart. This could be constructed of logs, as was the case in the simple blockhouse or log stockade. More often, however, the rampart was simply an earthen wall, composed of a trench and the packed-down earth thrown up as a parapet in front of a trench. The earthen counterpart of the blockhouse was the simple redoubt, an enclosure, surrounded by trench and parapet. If time permitted, the redoubt was improved by excavating the interior of the enclosure, building up the outer wall or rampart, and installing gun emplacements. Frequently logs or fascines (bundles of brushwood tied tightly together) were used as the base of these earthen ramparts, or to provide exterior firmness and strength as a wall facing. These same methods were employed for the construction of more extensive forts, or lines of fortifications.

Whenever possible an exterior ditch—a moat of sorts—was dug to heighten the walls, and to impose an additional barrier to attackers. Beyond the ditch, and frequently in it, *abatis* (felled trees with sharpened branches) or *chevaux de frise* (frameworks set with sharpened stakes) provided formidable obstacles, comparable to modern barbed wire.

Straight walls permitted attackers to take advantage of "dead space," directly under the wall, or at the corners, where defensive fire could not reach unless the defenders dangerously exposed themselves. To counter this, rudimentary towers called bastions projected beyond the line of the main wall, particularly at the corners. Defenders could fire from embrasures in these projecting, triangularly-shaped bastions, to rake the length of the adjoining wall without unduly exposing themselves.

The Vauban system of siegecraft provided for the systematic approach of the attackers and their artillery to a fortification, by means of entrenchments. The ultimate objective was to permit the attacking siege artillery to blast a breach in the defensive wall and in the covering obstacles, through which an infantry column could make an assault. Sometimes a successful assault could be made under the cover of fire from the approach trenches without waiting for the siege artillery to breach the walls. In such case the attackers would have to be prepared to cut their way through the defending obstacles, and to climb the wall, under the cover of artillery and small arms fire from the approach trenches. Fascines were usually used to fill up ditches before such an assault.

The method of approach was almost invariable. A "First Parallel" was dug some 600-700 yards from the fortifications. As the name implies, this trench was parallel to the line of defenses, to prevent the defenders from enfilading— firing down the length of the trench. The distance was fixed because it was close to the maximum effective range of defending and attacking artillery of the age. When the parallel was dug, additional earthworks were thrown up in

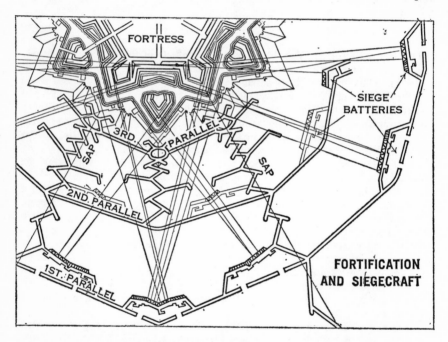

front of it as protection for siege artillery emplacements. To expedite this construction, fascines were used as the basis of these earthworks. Under the cover of fire from these guns, the attacking engineers began to dig "saps," or approach trenches, toward the fort. (Thus the origin of the word "sapper" for engineer.) These were dug at an angle, and zig-zagged back and forth, again to prevent the defenders from getting an opportunity for enfilade fire. The sappers were protected from the defending fire by shelters, called gabions: wicker baskets filled with earth, and frequently put on wheels so they could be pushed in front of the sap.

When the approaches had reached to within about 300 yards from the de- fenses, a "Second Parallel" was dug, and new artillery emplacements pre- pared. From these positions the siege guns could begin an intensified bom- bardment, to drive the defenders from the ramparts, to silence their artillery, and to begin to batter a breach in the wall. The defenders would, if possible, sortie in limited counterattacks to prevent the completion of the second parallel, and to try to destroy, or to "spike" the attacking guns. (Guns were "spiked" by driving spikes, or nails, or bayonets down their touch-holes, thus rendering them useless until the spike could be removed.) The attackers had to be ready for such sorties, and strong forces of infantry were maintained constantly in the parallels, to protect the guns and cannoneers.

If the defenders persisted, and if the attackers did not believe they could assault successfully from the second parallel, approach saps were again pushed forward—this time in the face of musket and rifle fire from the defenders—to within a few yards of the ditch in front of the walls. Here a "Third Parallel" was constructed. While attacking infantry prevented the defenders from manning the walls, the breaching batteries were emplaced to batter the wall at point-blank range. The assault then followed, if the garrison did not first surrender.

Appendix V: The Historians and the Generalship of George Washington

Few Americans accept the legend of George Washington and the cherry tree. Yet most of us, including normally reputable historians and military analysts, seem still to think of Washington in terms which that legend represents. He is visualized as a man of awesomely noble rectitude, somewhat colorless in personal characteristics, tremendously impressive physically; a man of great courage and determination, but lacking real military genius. His ultimate victory is attributed to the fact that by personifying the nobility of the Revolutionary cause, and by his steadfast and unwavering devotion to that cause, he became the locus around which the patriots rallied, year after year, despite the many defeats he suffered at British hands, until French military assistance and British war-weariness finally forced King George to abandon the struggle.

There is, of course, some basis to this stereotype. There can be no doubt of the nobility of character of this austere man. He was defeated by the British on several occasions, and the ultimate victory was primarily due to his determination and steadfastness in the face of defeat and discouragement, plus the tremendous assistance rendered by the French. What is wrong with the stereotype, however, is its failure to recognize that defeat would have been inevitable if Washington had not been both a brilliant strategist and an extremely competent, charismatic battlefield leader. He did not ride to victory on the fighting and administrative capabilities of better soldiers—as has been suggested by admirers of such men as Greene, Steuben, Lafayette, Wayne, Morgan, de Grasse and Rochambeau—and even Benedict Arnold. He was not saved from disaster by ineptitude or lack of determination on the part of such opponents as the Howe brothers, Clinton, Cornwallis or Burgoyne. Washington both shaped and exploited the successes of his most able subordinates. The top British leadership in the Revolution was relatively competent in terms of eighteenth-century warfare; if these men made more mistakes than Washington, and if he was able to take advantage of their mistakes, this should redound to his military credit, rather than providing a mere excuse for victory.

It is our opinion—substantiated, we believe, by the facts presented in our text—that Washington was by far the most able military leader, strategically and tactically, on either side in the Revolution. He started the war in 1775 as an inexperienced commander, well aware of his own deficiencies. By 1781 he had developed a competence worthy of favorable comparison beside

Alexander at the Granicus, Caesar at the Rubicon, Hannibal at the Alps, Genghis Khan at the Great Wall, Frederick the Great at Prague, or Napoleon at Montenotte. In other words, if he had been called upon to fight further after Yorktown, it is our contention that Washington would have merited inclusion in the very limited ranks of the great captains of history.

To substantiate this view, we offer brief analyses of historical commentary on three campaigns of the Revolution, to demonstrate how, consciously or unconsciously, most historians have accepted the stereotype of Washington's military limitations, and have thus contributed to its perpetuation.

Washington and the Howe Brothers at Long Island

American and British historians are almost unanimous in condemning Washington, General Howe and Admiral Howe for their respective actions, or inactions, immediately after the Battle of Long Island. Washington's movement of additional troops from Manhattan to Brooklyn, after the defeat, is castigated as foolhardy, it being argued that this was merely sending additional troops to join those already in a trap beyond an unfordable river, vulnerable to penetration by the Royal Navy. Those whose criticisms have been relatively lenient, excuse this as evidence of Washington's inexperience, and also find some mitigation in the masterly manner in which he withdrew his troops across the East River once he had comprehended the magnitude of his error.

More deserving of censure in the eyes of most historians, however, was the failure of the Howes to take advantage of the opportunity granted them by Washington. Sir William, they argue, should have pressed an immediate attack against Brooklyn while the Americans were still shaken by their defeat, and before Washington could complete his evacuation. Most believe that Lord Richard's failure to send his fleet up the East River was perhaps less culpable, since his ships were frustrated by continuing adverse winds. Nevertheless, the combined failure of the Howes to spring the trap that would have caught Washington and half his army seems to be explicable to most historians either as evidence of their utter incompetence, or of their near-treasonable Whig sympathy for the colonists. From this line of reasoning, of course, it is inferred that Washington was saved from the consequences of his own military failures by inexplicable British lethargy.

Christopher Ward is particularly critical of Washington and of General Howe, though he makes much of the unfavorable winds in defense of Admiral Howe (*The War of the Revolution*, New York: Macmillan, 1952, p. 229 ff.). He quotes copiously from Trevelyan and Fortescue to support his contentions. This, too, is the brief assessment of Matthew F. Steele in *American Campaigns* (Washington: Government Printing Office, 1901, pp. 29 and 36-37), and the carefully documented opinion of Douglas S. Freeman in *George Washington* (New York: Scribner, 1948-1954, v. IV, p. 164 ff.). The same criticisms are expressed in several other books, including J. F. C. Fuller's *Decisive Battles of the USA* (New York: Beechhurst, 1953, p. 17). It is interesting to note that Oliver L. Spaulding's assessment (*The United States Army in War and Peace*, New York: Putnam, 1937, pp. 62-63) is largely in agreement with us that Washington's communications across the East River were secure. It should be noted, furthermore, that Spaulding makes no attempt to minimize Washington's errors or inexperience.

It should be recalled that not more than about 3,500 American troops had been engaged around Gowanus and along the Long Island Heights during the forenoon of August 27. Admittedly this was a mistake, and Washington should not have permitted Putnam to allow a portion of his force to be thus easily defeated under the very eyes of some additional 7,000 or 8,000 American troops manning the Brooklyn fortifications. On the other hand, the mistake having been made, these fresh troops were available to hold these defenses, in addition to the 2,000-odd survivors of the morning battle. Weapons and ammunition were plentiful. Though not quite finished, these fortifications were formidable, particularly in comparison with the hasty redoubt thrown up on Breed's Hill a little more than a year before. There must be a very serious doubt whether the British, despite the momentum of their morning's victory, could possibly have been successful in an immediate assault upon the Brooklyn lines under the circumstances. On the contrary, it is quite possible that the Americans, fighting under conditions in which they excelled, would have inflicted upon the British army a bloody and complete defeat. Thus, an objective assessment of the situation that faced General Howe on the afternoon of August 27 must support his decision not to attack.

What, then, of the criticism that Washington compounded his earlier, unquestioned mistakes by rashly bringing more of his men into a trap where they were not only in danger of being overwhelmed by the superior British army to their front, but were even more seriously threatened by a likely movement of the British fleet up the East River? The fact is that he believed that the batteries and obstacles blocking the entrance to the East River from New York Bay were impenetrable to the British fleet. Although he did receive some assistance from a combination of a northeaster rainstorm, followed by dense fog, this basic fact is not altered. British armies and fleets in this and other wars had not been deterred by adverse weather. The failure of the Howe brothers to attack, either jointly or individually, is further evidence that they agreed with Washington's estimate of the security of his East River crossings.

Washington had probably been wrong in trying to defend New York, in permitting himself to be lured into battle on Long Island, and in not exercising firmer control of the engagement. These were neither the first nor the last of Washington's mistakes. But it is not possible to find another instance in which Washington could seriously be accused of foolhardiness. He had shown before, and would show again, his willingness to gamble boldly, but this was another matter. The circumstances being as he viewed them, and feeling reasonably secure that the British fleet could not cut him off from Manhattan, his movement of more troops to Long Island cannot be severely criticized.

As for General Howe, he was a man who had shown in the past, and who would show again, considerable deliberation and slowness. He was, nevertheless, a fairly competent and rather typical eighteenth-century general. His plan of attack for the morning of August 27, and the manner in which this was carried out, would have been creditable to any general in history. He was unduly cautious in his subsequent movements, perhaps, but neither cowardly, stupid, nor incompetent. He and his subordinates were, however, understandably cautious in approaching fortifications defended by American colonists, particularly when fresh reinforcements were appearing in those fortifications. The slaughter of Bunker Hill was still too fresh in the minds of men like Howe and Clinton. In addition Clinton had the experience of the Battle of Sullivan's Island to remind him of the fortitude which raw colonists could show when protected by any kind of fortification.

As to Admiral Howe, he had demonstrated his hopes that the rebellious colonies could be persuaded to rejoin the mother country with a minimum of bloodshed. His abortive efforts to negotiate with Washington and with congressional representatives, however, had proven to him that this would not be possible until the rebels had suffered a severe military defeat. Lord Howe, like his brother, was to prove his patriotic devotion to his country's welfare in future combat, as he had in the past. He has a reputation in British history as an extremely able and gallant admiral. It is therefore as difficult to impute to him, as to his brother, either treason or imbecility in those critical days between the 27th and 30th of August, 1776.

It is perhaps recognition of the ability, reputation and loyalty of Lord Howe, and realization, too, of the offensive tradition of the Royal Navy, that many historians have excused his failure to sail up the East River during those days because of unfavorable winds. It should be remembered, however, that British naval officers of that day never hesitated to tow their vessels, or to kedge them, in order to get within range of an enemy. Under the circumstances that existed near Brooklyn, when General Howe's army could have provided support to Admiral Howe's navy, and vice versa, it is truly incredible that neither of these men would have attempted to attack—if they had felt an attack had any possibility of success.

Even if Sir Peter Parker had not been present to remind him of his humiliating experience at Charleston harbor, it would have been evident to Lord Howe that his ships would have had a most difficult time in forcing their passageway into the East River, either through the main channel, or up Buttermilk Channel, in the face of crossfire from batteries on the Brooklyn shore, in New York, and on Governors Island. Adding to that, the difficulties they would have encountered in trying to maneuver past the obstacles which Washington had thoughtfully placed in the East River and in Buttermilk Channel, indicate that to undertake such an operation under crossfire would have been suicidal.

Analysis of the actions of General Washington, Sir William Howe, and Lord Richard Howe, indicates that all three recognized clearly the ability of the Americans to deny to the British fleet access into the narrow channel of the East River. Realization of this prompted Sir William, during the night of August 28-29, to commence deliberate siege approaches to the Brooklyn defenses. This, combined with the ever-present threat of naval gunfire support to such a siege approach, finally caused Washington to realize what he should have known even before the start of the campaign: ultimately New York was indefensible against superior British land power, supported by unchallenged control of the sea. Eventually and inevitably, as the British leaders also realized, this combined superiority of military force would overcome the American defenses, at which time the division of Washington's army between Manhattan and Long Island would become fatal. Accordingly he evacuated Long Island.

Washington and the 1777 Campaign

Unquestionably nothing has contributed so much to the false stereotype of Washington's generalship as the inevitable contrast when Gates was winning decisive victories at Saratoga in 1777, while Washington was being defeated by Howe in the Philadelphia Campaign. A representative assessment is that of respected historians Henry Steele Commager and Richard B. Morris (*The Spirit of 'Seventy-Six,* Indianapolis: Bobbs-Merrill, 1958, p. 607): "The Pennsylvania campaign revealed, on the one hand, Washington's inadequacies as a battle commander and, on the other, his inspired qualities of courage, candor, and dedication to the cause in the face of overwhelming discouragement." These writers did note—as most others have not—that Washington "weakened himself by sending substantial troops to Gates," but they suggest that this was a mistake, and that Washington should have taken his entire army north, early in the summer, to "crush Burgoyne, and then swung south to meet Howe."

Admittedly Washington made tactical mistakes in the Brandywine-Germantown campaign—so did Howe; but Howe had professional officers and soldiers to rectify his errors. It is interesting to note, however, that Washington never repeated these tactical errors, and that his future tactics were as sound and professional as was his truly superb strategy. His problem had been to defend the coastal heartland of America from simultaneous invasions, from two directions, by an enemy superior in numbers and quality. Washington had the advantage of interior lines, but this was not very useful to him because of the great distances involved, and the difficulties of movement. It would have been utterly impossible for him to have shifted to northern New York and then back to New Jersey to fight in turn both Burgoyne and Howe (even if Congress would have allowed it—which it would not). This would have permitted Howe to capture Philadelphia, central New Jersey, and the strategic Hudson Highlands without a fight. Howe would then have carried out the plan he had made for such an eventuality, moving north to concentrate with Burgoyne against Washington somewhere between Albany and Crown Point, where the entire American army would have been crushed—not Burgoyne.

What Washington did do was to make the maximum possible use of his interior lines, and to take advantage of every strategic error made by Howe and Burgoyne. There was never any possibility that he could do more than fight a defensive campaign against Howe. He recognized that so long as the British retained control of the seas no permanent or decisive results could come from one or two battles won or lost in the coastal regions of the lower Hudson or lower Delaware, so long as an American army in being were maintained in those regions.

Burgoyne's army, however, had moved beyond the reach of British sea-power and its coastal bases, and offered an exceptional opportunity. The record shows that Burgoyne was defeated by, and surrendered to, an army commanded by General Gates. The careful historian notes that much of this army had been sent north by Washington—at the expense of his own—and that the able leadership of Benedict Arnold, and the effective fire of Morgan's riflemen, smashed the British at Freeman's Farm and Bemis Heights. The military analyst must unquestionably award to Washington's strategy the credit for these victories at Saratoga, which were to lead directly and inevitably—if somewhat slowly—to the final victory at Yorktown.

A Comparison with Greene

The same historians who are unanimous in condemning Washington's splitting of his army between Long Island and Manhattan Island in August, 1776, are almost equally vehement in their praise of Greene's division of his forces by some 140 miles in December, 1780, just before the Battle of the Cowpens. Is the distinction valid, or is this another evidence of the stereotype?

There is much in Greene's Carolina campaign to baffle historians and military analysts. Not least is the fact that this amazingly successful campaign was won despite the fact that Greene was defeated or repulsed in every one of his four major engagements. And so it is perhaps not unnatural for the historians, aware of the end results of the campaign, to praise this as the first of a number of unorthodox moves which were nevertheless successful. Because of success, critical comment has been negligible, and the authorities have searched for reasons to show why this apparent violation of sound military doctrine was really brilliant strategy.

Christopher Ward (*op. cit.*, pp. 750-751) recognizes that Greene must certainly have realized that by dividing his army in the face of a superior enemy, he was violating accepted military practice. He suggests that Greene, having decided to move his army from Charlotte to Cheraw, more distant from Winnsboro, was afraid that this might be interpreted as a retreat. To send Morgan's detachment to threaten western South Carolina would then be considered an offsetting aggressive move. Ward also asserts that the division of force was necessary to permit the army to subsist properly on the countryside.

Neither of these reasons has validity. Before he left Charlotte, Greene had revitalized his army's commissary system. At Cheraw he would have had no trouble in finding adequate supplies for the 600-1,000 men that Morgan had under his command in the Cowpens operation. And although Cheraw was possibly ten miles further from Winnsboro than Charlotte, as the crow flies, it was an advance from North Carolina to South Carolina, which placed Greene in a position to threaten the British line of communications back toward Charleston. No one—least of all Cornwallis—could possibly have considered such a move to be a retreat.

There could perhaps be more justification to Steele's suggestion that Greene made the division of forces for diversionary and raiding purposes, in order to avoid battle and to carry on partisan operations (*op. cit.*, p. 47). The argument fails, however, since Greene's slow and deliberate moves, combined with the record of his councils of war, and his message to Morgan before the Battle of the Cowpens, all show that such were not his intentions.

Among others who search for reasons to explain and to justify the division of forces are Scheer and Rankin (*Rebels and Redcoats,* Cleveland: World, 1957, pp. 425-26); Burke Davis (*The Cowpens-Guilford Courthouse Campaign,* Philadelphia: Lippincott, 1962, pp. 60-61), Kenneth Roberts (*The Battle of Cowpens,* New York: Doubleday, 1958, p. 48), and Sydney G. Fisher (*The Struggle for American Independence,* Philadelphia, 1908, v. II, p. 377). Spaulding (*op. cit.*) does not comment—unusual for this forthright, scholarly giant among American historians. Apparently baffled by the results of Greene's decision, he prefers to let the facts speak for themselves.

Most other commentators—less wisely, it seems to us—have permitted their bafflement to lead them to an uncritical endorsement of Greene's division of forces simply because, in Ward's words: "the proof of its validity was that it worked."

Impartial analysis of the situations facing both Greene and Cornwallis in December, 1780, and of the subsequent actions of both generals, leads us to the conclusion that Greene's decision to separate his small army into two contingents, 140 miles apart, was a most serious—almost disastrous—mistake. Cornwallis made only a slightly less serious blunder in failing to take advantage of the opportunity offered to him by the American general. Cornwallis could have interposed his army between the two divided portions of Greene's army—and almost did, despite his failure to take adequate action in time. An objective evaluation of the subsequent heroic actions which Greene had to take to avoid the consequences of his blunder, shows that he must have realized the danger to which he had exposed himself and his small command. The margin of his escape was an extremely slender one. Had it not been for the prompt and shrewd movements of Daniel Morgan immediately after the Battle of the Cowpens, and for the equally prompt and sagacious preparations which the efficient Greene then undertook to facilitate his retreat, a catastrophe would have ensued. But though the retreat was masterly, this cannot absolve Greene from blame for the mistake which made the retreat necessary.

We are most emphatic in our opinion that Greene, for all of his unquestioned competence and ability, is in no way to be compared with Washington as a general. Greene was an exceptionally efficient administrator. He was a wise, usually cautious, strategist, whose conduct of the Carolina Campaign deserves our respect and admiration—after he rescued his army from the incipient disaster which he invited by mistakenly dividing his forces. The high caliber of his overall leadership was demonstrated time and again by his ability to hold his little army together, and to keep it an efficient fighting force, despite defeat, discouragement and appalling shortages of rations, clothing and weapons. His tactical weaknesses are discussed in the text in connection with the Battle of Guilford Courthouse. These weaknesses, however, were not failures. Perhaps aware of his own limitations as a battlefield leader, Greene preferred to avoid all possibility of risk. Though this involved him in greater risk, over a longer period of time, we cannot be more critical than this of a man who deliberately set his sights on limited objectives, and then, persevering under conditions of great adversity, systematically achieved these in his own somewhat pedestrian fashion.

Appendix VI: David Bushnell's Submarine

THE WORLD'S FIRST OPERATIONAL SUBMARINE, the *Turtle,* was the invention of Captain David Bushnell of Connecticut. Completed in the spring or early summer of 1776, the little, wooden, barrel-like craft was large enough for one man to operate, either from a standing or sitting position. Propulsion was provided by paddles, formed like the arms of a windmill, which were turned by a crank. The operator turned this with one hand, while steering with the other. The rate of speed "by vigorous turning of the crank," was "about three miles an hour in still water." During movement the upper portion of the craft protruded a few inches above the surface of the water, where air holes permitted air for the operator to breathe. It was because of this arrangement that the submarine could be used only in the very calmest weather. When approaching an enemy vessel, these air holes could be closed, and by an ingenious ballast arrangement the submarine would go below the surface and then be steered by means of several small portholes in the upper portion of the submarine. The period of complete submersion had to be relatively short, of course, since the only oxygen available was that already collected in the interior of the craft. Bushnell had provided a sharp iron screw projecting from the top of the submarine, which could be cranked into the bottom of an enemy vessel. A charge of explosive was attached to this screw, and when detached from the submarine a time clock automatically gave the operator approximately 20 minutes in which to depart from the vicinity of the target vessel.

In August, with Washington's approval, Bushnell prepared to attack the British fleet in New York Bay, near the Narrows between Staten Island and Long Island. He was for several weeks frustrated by adverse meteorological conditions.

During the first week of September, while waiting for a suitably calm, moonlit night, Bushnell became ill. He had foreseen this possibility, however, and had trained a Sergeant Ezra Lee to operate the machine. Weather conditions finally permitting, Lee took the submarine down the upper Bay towards the anchored British ships. Selecting one of these (probably HMS *Asia,* though some reports have suggested that it was Lord Howe's flagship, HMS *Eagle*), Lee submerged and commenced his attack. He was frustrated in his efforts, however, by copper sheathing on the bottom of the ship, which the submarine's screw would not penetrate. With his oxygen supply getting low, Lee withdrew from the British vessel and surfaced. He briefly contemplated attacking another vessel, but decided against this since the sun was now rising. He therefore began paddling back up the Bay. As he passed Governors Island he was pursued by a British barge. Fearing capture, Lee released his explosive charge in order to make sure that he would not be blown up when the British attempted to investigate the mechanism. His pursuers decided that this was merely some "Yankee trick," and so turned back to Governors Island. A few minutes later the magazine exploded at the mouth of the East River.

Before Bushnell or Lee could make another attempt to use their submarine, Washington's troops abandoned New York. The *Turtle* was destroyed, and Bushnell did not build another.

Appendix VII: The Strange Case of Silas Deane

SILAS DEANE, THE FORMER CONGRESSIONAL AGENT, and one of the diplomatic commissioners who negotiated the vital treaty with France in February,
1778, was then subjected to wild accusations by his fellow commissioner,
Arthur Lee, who charged Deane with improper use of the funds entrusted to
him by Congress for procurement of foreign supplies and weapons. Though
Deane's honesty and patriotism were defended eloquently by the third commissioner—Benjamin Franklin, who was also subjected to wild, false accusations by Lee—Deane was recalled to the United States and forced to defend
himself against the charges. He did so successfully, and returned to France
in 1780.

Apparently embittered by the lack of confidence which Congress had
demonstrated, Deane entered into secret and possibly treasonable communications with British agent Paul Wentworth. Possibly he believed that the cause
of independence was hopeless, and that the best course for America was peace
with England without independence. Some letters to this effect, allegedly
written by him, were intercepted and published in New York in 1781. The
facts are obscure, and the case has never been proven conclusively one way
or another. But animosity against Deane, caused by the publication of these
letters, caused him to remain in England after the war. He died there in
1789, just as he was about to return to the country which he helped to make
free, and which he undoubtedly loved. His claim for reimbursement of funds
due him was finally approved by Congress in 1842, and $37,000 was voted
to Deane's heirs.

Appendix VIII: Summary of Operations Following Yorktown

Franco-British

FRANCE'S NAVAL SUPREMACY in the Atlantic was short-lived. De Grasse, hurrying back to Martinique after Yorktown, expected to be joined by de Guichen with additional warships and troops. But de Guichen was defeated and his armada dispersed by British Admiral Richard Kempenfelt, with a force inferior in strength, off Ushant on December 12, 1781.

De Grasse, with 29 sail of the line, after jockeying with Hood's (Rodney was still absent in England) 22 vessels in the West Indies, delayed coming to conclusions until too late. Rodney returned with 12 additional ships of the line. He met de Grasse with his combined force on April 12, 1782, off the Saints, an island group lying between Guadeloupe and Dominica. In the greatest fleet action in 80 years Rodney broke through the French line, splitting it into three disorganized segments, and shivered it in disastrous defeat. In a day-long conflict seven French ships were captured, including de Grasse's flagship, the great 120-gun *Ville de Paris*, with the admiral on board. Revolutionary new developments in English naval gunnery played a major part in the outcome.

England's morale, boosted by Rodney's victory, was soon shaken by disaster at home. Kempenfelt's flagship *Royal George*, 100, careened in Portsmouth harbor for emergency repairs, on August 29 plummeted to the bottom with all on board when her rotten frame timbers gave way. Kempenfelt, his crew of 750 men and at least 200 visitors—mainly women and children—were all lost.

In the Mediterranean, Gibraltar's stout resistance to repeated Franco-Spanish assaults gladdened English hearts. The Duc de Crillon's final bid, September 8-13, was repulsed. On October 11, 1782, Admiral Lord Howe with a formidable fleet, escorting fifty supply ships plus the entire East Indies trading fleet, entered the Gut of Gibraltar. These reinforcements of men, supplies and ammunition rendered British possession of Gibraltar secure until the end of the war.

In the Indian Ocean, however, France's brilliant Admiral Suffern, without benefit of bases or reinforcement, was threatening British hegemony in India. Four times Suffern outfought Sir Edward Hughes' squadron: south of Madras, February 17, 1782; near Trincomalee, April 12; off Cuddalore, July 6; and again off Trincomalee, September 3. Capture of the port of Trincomalee crowned Suffern's outstanding naval campaign. These brilliant naval successes, however, were completely negated by the land victories in India of General Sir Eyre Coote, over French land forces and those of their ally, Hyder Ali of Mysore.

Americans at Sea

Compared to the great Franco-British fleet actions of 1782, the exploits of the American-flag vessels seem insignificant indeed, unless we appreciate the scope of the privateering operations. By the conclusion of the war the Congress had issued letters of marque to no fewer than 1,697 vessels, ranging from full-rigged ships to tiny sloops. The privateers captured 3,178 British vessels—merchantmen, privateers and at least one Royal Navy ship. The value of the more notable prizes captured—more than 600 British merchantmen and transports—amounted to over $18 million.

Two of the exploits of the more than 400 privateers still operating in 1782 are notable. In the spring of 1782 Captain Joshua Barney's Pennsylvania ship *Hyder Ally*, 16, fought and captured HM sloop of war *General Monk*, 20, and the Tory privateer *Fair American*, 16, in the Delaware River mouth and brought them safely up to Philadelphia. Barney, like Thomas Truxton of New York, whose privateering career was uniformly successful, would in later years shine in the U.S. Navy.

Most privateering was lone-wolf operation, but in 1782 four Massachusetts skippers consorted in a raid remarkable both for its precision and success, against Lunenburg, Nova Scotia, a prosperous fortified Tory refugee port. Captain George W. Babcock in the schooner *Hero*, 9; Noah Stoddard in the schooner *Scammel*, 16; Herbert Woodbury in the brigantine *Hope*, 6; and John Tibbets in the cutter *Swallow*, 5, on July 1 put a 90-man landing party ashore two miles south of the town. The four vessels then maneuvered just out of range of the British guns until the landing party stormed the defenses. Overwhelming the small garrison and spiking the guns, the Americans extorted a ransom of £1,000 from the terrified townfolk and sailed away with a goodly quantity of supplies and munitions.

As for the Continental Navy, it had captured in all 196 enemy ships, but by the war's end there remained of it only one frigate, USS *Alliance,* and a handful of smaller craft. The peripatetic *Alliance,* still under command of hard-fisted John Barry, continued to shuttle back and forth across the North Atlantic on diplomatic missions. It remained for her to win the last naval action of the war.

On March 10, 1783, on the way north from Havana, Barry handily fought off and silenced HMS *Sybil*, 32, which, with two other British warships, had attacked him. Barry, who was carrying a large quantity of specie for Congressional use, brought his cargo home safely.

Americans on Land

Up in the north, while the dramatic finale at Yorktown was still in the making, two significant events had occurred. The first was Benedict Arnold's final appearance on the stage of war.

Clinton had recalled him from Virginia in June, 1781, and now Arnold proposed a scheme for invading Connecticut, in hope of diverting part of Washington's army back from the blockade of Yorktown. Clinton approved, and gave him 1,700 troops—British, Loyalist and German.

On September 6, Arnold made an amphibious landing at New London. The local defenses were manned by about 160 militia, who fought with surprising firmness and determination. Finally, after repulsing three attacks, the defenders were overwhelmed. When the American commander, Lieutenant Colonel William Ledyard, offered his sword to Lieutenant Colonel van Buskirk of the New Jersey Volunteers, the Tory officer ruthlessly slew Ledyard with the tendered sword, to start one of the worst atrocities of the war. The British, Tory and Hessian troops butchered the surrendered men without mercy, killing 85 and wounding 60 others—many of whom died later. The town was then completely destroyed. Groton, too, was put to the torch. Arnold then re-embarked, having conducted the last active engagement of the war in his own home state, and having at the same time compounded his crime of treason with that of murder.

The second event of importance was the eradication of the Tory-Indian plague in the Mohawk Valley. In October, 1781, some 800 of Butler's Rangers and Royal Greens, with 200 Indians, all under command of a Major Ross, made a surprise raid into the Oneida Lake area. They pushed east towards Johnstown. Pugnacious Colonel Marinus Willett, who had distinguished himself at Fort Stanwix and at Peekskill, commanded the state troops and militia in the area—many of whom were veterans by this time. He gathered a force of 400 whites and some 60 Oneida Indians, and on the 24th met the invaders near Johnstown, fighting them to a standstill, despite the flight of most of the American militia. Ross retreated, but Willett, in a forced march through heavy snow, caught up with him at Jerseyfield, on Canada Creek. In a desperate fight Captain Walter Butler (John's son), commanding the Rangers, was killed by an Oneida bullet, and the British Indians fled, carrying the rest of Ross' command with them. Willett's tenacious pursuit scattered them through the woods, never to reassemble.

In the south, the indomitable Greene, reinforced by detachments from Washington's army after Yorktown, continued his uphill task of uprooting remaining British occupation. Wayne, who had come down with the reinforcements, was sent on January 12, 1782, with a 600-man scratch force of Continentals and partisans to clear up Georgia. Sweeping all the way to Savannah, he blockaded it until the small British garrison evacuated the place by water on July 11.

Greene himself, with his main force, closed in on Charleston, where British Major General Alexander Leslie stood with some 3,000 men. Not until July was Greene able to get "materials for a check shirt, a pair of overalls and a coatee" for each of his own 3,000 men. In early December, Leslie, who had been unable to penetrate the strangulating blockade by Greene's half-naked fighting men, embarked his garrison on board British ships sent down from New York. On the 14th he departed, taking with him some 3,800 Tories and more than 5,000 of their slaves.

Nathanael Greene's mission was accomplished.

Bibliography of Works Consulted

Adams, Henry, *History of the United States.* 9 vols. New York: Scribners, 1891.

Albion, Robert G., *Forests and Sea Power.* Cambridge: Harvard University Press, 1926.

———, *Introduction to Military History.* New York: Appleton-Century-Crofts, 1929.

Alden, John R., *The American Revolution.* New York: Harper, 1954.

Allen, G. W., *Naval History of the Revolution.* 2 vols. Boston: Houghton Mifflin, 1913.

American Heritage (editors), *The American Heritage Book of the Revolution.* New York: American Heritage, 1958.

American State Papers—Military Affairs (vol. 1). 7 vols. Washington, D.C.: Gales & Seaton, 1832-1861.

Anburey, Thomas, *Travels Through the Interior Parts of America.* 2 vols. London, 1789.

Bakeless, John, *Turncoats, Traitors and Heroes.* Philadelphia: Lippincott, 1959.

Belcher, Henry, *The First American Civil War.* 4 vols. London, 1911.

Bill, Alfred H., *The Campaign of Princeton, 1776-1777.* Princeton: Princeton University Press, 1948.

Bemis, Samuel F., *Diplomacy of the American Revolution.* Indiana University Press, 1935.

Blumenthal, Walter Hart, *Women Camp Followers of the American Revolution.* Philadelphia: McManus, 1952.

Bolton, Charles Knowles, *The Private Soldier under Washington.* New York: Scribner, 1902.

Bowman, Allen, *Morale of the American Revolutionary Army.* Washington, D.C.: American Council of Public Affairs, 1943.

Burgoyne, John, *A State of the Expedition from Canada.* London, 1780.

Callahan, North, *Henry Knox: General Washington's General.* New York: Rinehart, 1958.

Carrington, Henry B., *Battles of the American Revolution.* New York: Barnes & Noble, 1876.

Chidsey, D. B., *The American Privateers.* New York: Dodd, Mead & Co., 1962.

Clinton, Henry, *The American Rebellion* (Abridgment of *Clinton Papers*). Edited by William B. Willcox. New Haven: Yale University Press, 1954.

Coburn, Frank W., *The Battle of April 19, 1775.* Lexington, Mass.: Privately printed, 1912.

Commager, Henry S., and Richard B. Morris, *The Spirit of 'Seventy-Six*. 2 vols. Indianapolis: Bobbs-Merrill, 1958.

Court Martial of General Arthur St. Clair. New York Historical Society: 1880.

Davis, Burke, *The Cowpens-Guilford Courthouse Campaign*. Philadelphia: Lippincott, 1962.

Digby, William, *The British Invasion from the North (with the Journal of William Digby)* (introduction and notes by James Phinney Baxter). Albany, 1887.

Dupuy, R. Ernest, *Governors Island, 1637-1937*. New York: Hq. 2nd Corps Area. 1937.

———, *Compact History of the U.S. Army*, New York: Hawthorn, 1956. 2nd edition, 1961.

———, *The Battle of Hubbardton*. Unpublished monograph prepared for State of Vermont Historic Sites Commission, 1960.

Dupuy, R. Ernest and Trevor N. Dupuy, *Military Heritage of America*. New York: McGraw-Hill, 1956.

———, *Brave Men and Great Captains*. New York: Harper, 1959.

Eelking, Max von, *Memoirs, and Letters and Journals of Major General Riedesel*. . . . (translation of William L. Stone). 2 vols. Albany: 1868.

Esposito, Vincent J. (ed.), *The West Point Atlas of American Wars*. New York: Praeger, 1959.

Farmer, J. S., *Regimental Records of the British Army*. London, 1901.

Fisher, Sydney G., *Story of the American Revolution*. Philadelphia: Lippincott, 1908.

Fonblanque, E. B. de, *Political and Military Episodes . . . Life and Correspondence of the Right Hon. J. Burgoyne*. London, 1876.

Force, Peter (ed.), *American Archives* (Fourth Series). 6 vols. Washington: Clarke & Force, 1837-1846.

Fortesque, Sir John W., *A History of the British Army*. 13 vols. London, 1899-1930.

Foster, Thompson, *Diary* (unpublished); excerpts in *Military Review*, April 1962, in Essame, Maj. Gen. H., "A Redcoat Surgeon's Account of 1776."

Fraser, Simon, "General Fraser's Account of Burgoyne's Campaign on Lake Champlain, Proceedings." Vermont Historical Society, 1898.

Freeman, Douglas S., *George Washington*. 6 vols. New York: Scribner, 1948-1954.

French, Allen, *General Gage's Informers*. Ann Arbor: University of Michigan, 1932.

Frost, Halloway H., *We Build a Navy*. Annapolis: U.S. Naval Institute, 1929.

Fuller, J. F. C., *Decisive Battles of the USA*. New York: Beechurst, 1953.

Ganoe, William A., *History of the United States Army*. New York: Appleton-Century-Crofts, 1942.

Gibbes, R. W., (ed.), *Documentary History of the American Revolution*. 3 vols. New York: Appleton, 1853-1857.

Gordon, William, *History of the American War*. 4 vols. London, 1788.

Greene, Francis Vinton, *General Greene*. New York: Appleton, 1893.

———, *The Revolutionary War and the Military Policy of the United States*. New York: Scribner, 1911.

Greene, George W., *Life of Maj. Gen. Nathanael Greene*. 3 vols. Cambridge, Mass.: Hurd & Houghton, 1871.

Hadden, James N., *Journal and Orderly Book*. . . . Albany, 1884.

Ketchum, Richard M., "The Decisive Day is Come," *American Heritage*, August 1962 (vol. XIII, No. 5).

Knox, Dudley A., *A History of the U.S. Navy*. New York: Putnam, 1936.

Laurence-Archer, J. H., *The British Army*. London: Bell, 1888.

Lengyel, Cornel, *I, Benedict Arnold*. New York: Doubleday, 1960.

Lewis, Michael, *The Navy of Britain*. London: Allen & Unwin, 1948.

Lincoln, Chas. Henry, *Naval Records of the American Revolution*. Washington, D.C.: Library of Congress, Gov't. Printing Office, 1906.

Lossing, Benson J., *The Pictorial Field Book of the American Revolution*. New York, 1851.

———, *History of the American Revolution*. New York, 1865.

———, *Life and Times of Philip Schuyler*. New York, 1873.

——, *The American Revolution and the War of 1812*. New York: New York Book Concern, 1875.

Mahan, Alfred T., *The Influence of Sea Power upon History*. Boston: Little, Brown, 1894.

——, *Major Operations of the Navies in the War of American Independence*. New York: Little, Brown, 1913.

Marcus, G. J., *The Formative Centuries (A Naval History of England)*. Boston: Little, Brown, 1961.

Montross, Lynn, *Reluctant Rebels, The*. New York: Harper, 1950.

Moore, Frank, *Diary of the American Revolution*. 2 vols. New York: Scribner, 1860.

Morgan, Edmund S., *The American Revolution: A Review of Changing Interpretations*. Washington, D.C.: American Historical Association, 1958.

Morison, Samuel E., *John Paul Jones*. Boston: Little, Brown, 1959.

Moultrie, William, *Memoirs of the American Revolution*. 2 vols. New York: Longworth, 1802.

Nickerson, Hoffman, *The Turning Point of the Revolution*. Boston: Houghton Mifflin, 1928.

Palmer, John M., *Washington, Lincoln, Wilson*. New York: Doubleday, 1930.

——, *General von Steuben*. New Haven: Yale, 1937.

——, *America in Arms*. New Haven: Yale University Press, 1941.

Paullin, Chas. O., *The Navy of the American Revolution*. Cleveland: Burroughs, 1908.

——, *Atlas of the Historical Geography of the U.S.* New York: Carnegie Foundation and American Geographic Society, 1932.

Pratt, Fletcher, *Compact History of the U.S. Navy*. New York: Hawthorn, 1957.

Roberts, Kenneth, *The March to Quebec*. New York: Doubleday, 1938.

——, *The Battle of Cowpens*. New York: Doubleday, 1958.

Scheer, George F., and Hugh F. Rankin, *Rebels and Redcoats*. Cleveland and New York: World Publishing Co., 1957.

Sheppard, E. W., *A Short History of the British Army*. London: Constable, 1950.

Spaulding, Oliver L., *The U.S. Army in War and Peace*. New York: Putnam, 1937.

Stedman, Charles, *The History . . . of the American War*. 2 vols. London, 1794.

Steele, Matthew F., *American Campaigns*. Washington: U.S. Government Printing Office, 1901.

Stone, William Leete, *Letters of Brunswick and Hessian Officers During the American Revolution*. Albany, 1891.

Thayer, Theodore, *Nathanael Greene, Strategist of the American Revolution*. New York: Twayne, 1960.

Upton, Emory, *The Military Policy of the United States*. Washington, D.C.: U.S. Government Printing Office, 1917.

Trevelyan, Sir George C., *The American Revolution*. 6 vols. London, 1909-1914.

U.S. Army, Office Chief of Military History, *The Army Lineage Book, Infantry*. Washington, D.C.: U.S. Government Printing Office, 1953.

U.S. Department of Commerce, *Historical Statistics of the United States*. Washington, D.C.: U.S. Government Printing Office, 1961.

Ward, Christopher, *The War of the Revolution*. 2 vols. New York: Macmillan, 1952.

Index

THE AUTHORS AND THEIR BOOK

COLONEL R. ERNEST DUPUY, UNITED STATES ARMY, RETIRED, *was born in New York City on March 24, 1887. He was graduated from the Augustinian Academy, Staten Island, New York, 1905; the Field Artillery School, 1924; and the Command and General Staff School, 1933. His army career spanned nearly half a century, beginning with enlisted service in the New York National Guard in 1909 and continuing until his retirement in 1946 as Acting Director of the War Department's Bureau of Public Relations. From 1909-17, he was reporter, ship news editor and feature editor for the New York Herald. He entered federal service in 1917 as a first lieutenant, and was a Field Artillery battery commander in World War I. He subsequently served in various posts until 1938, when he became public relations officer at the United States Military Academy at West Point, where he remained until 1941. He was chief of the news division, War Department, from 1941-43, and from 1943-45 was public relations officer, Supreme Headquarters A.E.F. in Europe. He was the officer who announced the invasion of Normandy to the world by radio on June 6, 1944, and was a member of the SHAEF official party at the German surrender ratification in Berlin, May, 1945. His first book,* With the Fifty-Seventh in France *(Our Army, 1929), now heads a long list which includes* If War Comes *(With George Fielding Eliot; Macmillan, 1937),* World in Arms *(Military Service, 1939),* Perish by the Sword *(Military Service, 1939),* Where They Have Trod *(Stokes, 1940),* Civilian Defense of the U.S. *(with Hodding Carter; Farrar & Rinehart, 1942),* To the Colors *(with T. N. Dupuy; Row-Peterson, 1942),* Lion in the Way *(Infantry Journal, 1948),* Men of West Point *(Sloane, 1952),* Military Heritage of America *(with T. N. Dupuy; McGraw-Hill, 1956),* The Compact History of the Civil War *(with T. N. Dupuy; Hawthorn, 1960). Married to the former Laura G. Nevitt, Colonel Dupuy is the father of Colonel Trevor N. Dupuy, U.S.A., Retired.*

COLONEL TREVOR N. DUPUY, UNITED STATES ARMY, RETIRED, *was born in Staten Island, New York, May 3, 1916. After studying for a year at St. Peter's College, he entered West Point in 1934. Upon graduation in 1938 he received his commission as second lieutenant* in the Army, serving in command and staff assignments in Field Artillery units from 1938 to 1943. He was then assigned to Burma as a liaison officer with Chinese artillery units, subsequently becoming the commander of a Chinese artillery group and acting division artillery commander of a British Artillery division. He became a staff officer in the War Department General Staff in 1945, was appointed military assistant to the Undersecretary of the Army in 1947, then served in the Plans, Policy and Operations Division of SHAPE in France from 1951 to 1952. As Professor of Military Science and Tactics at Harvard, 1952-56, he was an original faculty member of the Harvard Defense Studies Program. He directed the Ohio State University Military History Course in the summers of 1956 and 1957. His last military position was in the Office of the Army Chief of Staff, 1956-58. In June, 1957 he was elected President of the American Military Institute. At present he is President and Executive Director of the Historical Evaluation and Research Organization, a non-profit organization in Washington, D.C. He is the author of To the Colors *(with R. E. Dupuy; Row-Peterson, 1942)*, The French and Napoleonic Wars *(1955)*, Military Heritage of America *(with R. E. Dupuy; McGraw-Hill, 1956)*, Brave Men and Great Captains *(with R. E. Dupuy; Harper, 1959)*, First Book of Civil War Land Battles *(Watts; 1960)*, and The Compact History of the Civil War *(with R. E. Dupuy; Hawthorn, 1960)*.

THE COMPACT HISTORY OF THE REVOLUTIONARY WAR *(Hawthorn, 1963) was set in type by Pyramid Composition Company, New York, and printed and bound by The Book Press, New York. The title page illustration is by Gil Walker. The typeface is Times Roman, originally designed for the use of the London Times.*

A HAWTHORN BOOK

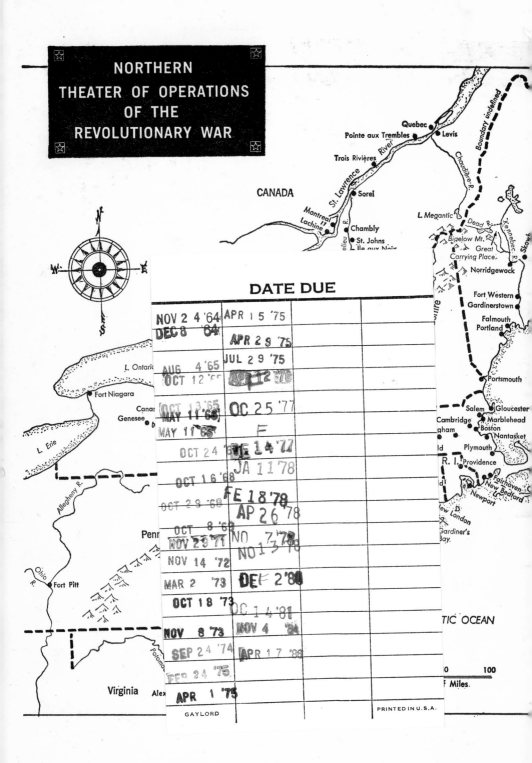